COGNITIVE COPING,
FAMILIES,
AND DISABILITY

COGNITIVE COPING, FAMILIES, AND DISABILITY

Edited by

Ann P. Turnbull
Co-Director
Beach Center on Families and
*   Disability*
Life Span Institute
University of Kansas
Lawrence, Kansas

Joan M. Patterson
Director of Research
Center for Children with Chronic
*   Illness and Disability*
University of Minnesota
Minneapolis, Minnesota

Shirley K. Behr
Chairman
Department of Occupational
*   Therapy*
St. Louis University Medical Center
St. Louis, Missouri

Douglas L. Murphy
Program Analyst
Social Work Research Unit
Colmery-O'Neil Veteran's
*   Administration Medical Center*
Topeka, Kansas

Janet G. Marquis
Research Statistician
Schiefelbusch Institute for Life Span
*   Studies*
University of Kansas
Lawrence, Kansas

and

Martha J. Blue-Banning
Research Assistant
Beach Center on Families and
*   Disability*
University of Kansas
Lawrence, Kansas

·P A U L·H·
BROOKES
PUBLISHING Co Baltimore • London • Toronto • Sydney

Paul H. Brookes Publishing Co.
P.O. Box 10624
Baltimore, Maryland 21285-0624

Copyright © 1993 by Paul H. Brookes Publishing Co., Inc.
All rights reserved.

Typeset by Brushwood Graphics, Inc., Baltimore, Maryland.
Manufactured in the United States of America by
The Maple Press Co., York, Pennsylvania.

Permission from Darrell Bolender to reprint the poem on page 62 is gratefully
acknowledged.

Library of Congress Cataloging-in-Publication Data
Cognitive coping, families and disability
    edited by Ann P. Turnbull . . . [et al.].
        p.   cm.
    Includes bibliographical references and index.
    ISBN 1-55766-114-6
    1. Developmentally disabled children—Family relationships—
Congresses.   2. Developmental disabilities—Psychological aspects—
Congresses.   3. Adjustment (Psychology)—Congresses.   4. Parents of
handicapped children—Congresses.   5. Developmentally disabled
children—Family relationships—Research—Congresses.   I. Turnbull,
Ann P., 1947–
RJ506.D47C63   1993   92-23348
618.92′85889—dc20   CIP

(British Library Cataloging-in-Publication data are available from the British
Library.)

Contents

CONTRIBUTORS

Aaron Antonovsky
Ben Gurion University of Negev
Department of the Sociology of Health
Faculty of Health Sciences
Beersheva
ISRAEL

Glenn Affleck
Department of Psychiatry
University of Connecticut Health Center
Farmington, CT 06032

Shirley K. Behr
Department of Occupational Therapy
Saint Louis University
St. Louis, MO 63104

Martha J. Blue-Banning
Beach Center on Families and Disability
3111 Haworth Hall
University of Kansas
Lawrence, KS 66045

Pauline Boss
Department of Family Social Science
University of Minnesota
St. Paul, MN 55108

Jonathon D. Brown
Department of Psychology
N1-25
University of Washington
Seattle, WA 98195

Beverly A. Bush
Department of Psychology
University of Maryland, Baltimore
    County
Baltimore, MD 21228

Corinne W. Garland
Child Development Resources
P.O. Box 299
Lightfoot, VA 23090

Laraine Masters Glidden
Division of Human Development
Saint Mary's College of Maryland
St. Mary's City, MD 20686

Tamar Heller
University Affiliated Programs in
    Developmental Disabilities
University of Illinois at Chicago
1640 West Roosevelt Rd.
Chicago, IL 60608

Michael J. Kiphart
Division of Human Development
Saint Mary's College of Maryland
St. Mary's City, MD 20686

Marty Wyngaarden Krauss
Florence Heller Graduate School
Brandeis University
P.O. Box 9110
Waltham, MA 02254-9110

Evelyn Lusthaus
Educational Psychology Department
Faculty of Education
McGill University
Montreal, Quebec
CANADA H3A 1Y2

Charles Lusthaus
Administration and Policy Studies
McGill University
Montreal, Quebec
CANADA H3A 1Y2

Janet G. Marquis
Research Associate
Computer Applications Unit
Schiefelbusch Institute for Life Span
    Studies
University of Kansas
Lawrence, Kansas 66045

Hamilton I. McCubbin
University of Wisconsin
School of Family Research and
  Consumer Service
1300 Linden Drive
Madison, WI 53706

Donald J. Meyer
Children's Hospital and Medical Center
Education Department
4800 Sand Point Way, N.D.
Seattle, WA 98105

Douglas L. Murphy
Social Work Research Unit
Colmery-O'Neil Veteran's
  Administration Medical Center
Topeka, KS 66622

Judy M. O'Halloran
3443 Hancock Bridge Pkwy.
North Ft. Myers, FL 33903

Joan M. Patterson
Center for Children and Youth with
  Chronic Illness and Disability
University of Minnesota
P.O. Box 721-UMHC
Harvard St. at East River Rd.
Minneapolis, MN 55455

Florene Stewart Poyadue
Parents Helping Parents
535 Race St., Suite 227
San Jose, CA 95126

Jane B. Schulz
Professor Emerita
Western Carolina University
Rt. 3, Box 466
Sylva, NC 28779

Marsha Mailick Seltzer
Waisman Center and School of Social
  Work
University of Wisconsin
1500 Highland Avenue
Madison, WI 53705

George H.S. Singer
Department of Clinical Genetics & Child
  Development
Dartmouth-Hitchcock Medical Center
1 Medical Center Drive
Lebanon, NH 03756-0001

C.R. Snyder
Department of Psychology
University of Kansas
Lawrence, KS 66045

Howard Tennen
Department of Psychiatry
University of Connecticut Health Center
Farmington, CT 06032

Anne I. Thompson
University of Wisconsin
School of Family Research and
  Consumer Service
1300 Linden Drive
Madison, WI 53706

Elizabeth A. Thompson
University of Wisconsin
School of Family Research and
  Consumer Service
1300 Linden Drive
Madison, WI 53706

Suzanne C. Thompson
Department of Psychology
Mason Hall
Pomona College
Claremont, CA 91711

Ann P. Turnbull
Beach Center on Families and Disability
Life Span Institute
3111 Haworth Hall
University of Kansas
Lawrence, KS 66045

H.R. Turnbull, III
Beach Center on Families and Disability
Bureau of Child Research
3111 Haworth Hall
University of Kansas
Lawrence, KS 66045

Janet Vohs
28 Littell Road
Brookline, MA 02146

Jennifer C. Willoughby
Division of Human Development
Saint Mary's College of Maryland
St. Mary's City, MD 20686

PREFACE

Cognitive Coping, Families, and Disability is a unique contribution to the professional literature. Its primary uniqueness is the merger of content on cognitive coping with a participatory research process for addressing that content.

Cognitive coping involves thinking about a particular situation in ways that enhance: 1) self-esteem, 2) a feeling of control, and 3) a sense of meaning. The particular situation addressed in this book is giving birth to and/or raising a child with a developmental disability over the entire life span. In the past, it was automatically assumed that the birth of such a child was a major tragedy that "victimizes" a family for decades. Cognitive coping theory allows us to view the adaptation of families of children with disabilities in a new light. For example, when families have reported finding positive benefit from having a family member with a disability, it has often been regarded by others as evidence of denial or rationalization. Cognitive coping theory suggests the alternative view that recognizing these positive benefits is a positive adaptation to stress. Thus, this book is unique because it is one of the first attempts in the developmental disability field to focus on cognitive coping theory and research as a means to creating and extending ways of enhancing family well-being.

The second unique aspect of this book is that it introduces a participatory process for planning a research agenda. This participatory research process involves the collaboration of family members, service providers, theorists, and researchers so that research is more likely to become a means rather than an end in terms of enhancing family well-being. Participatory research assumes that research is the enterprise of not only scientists, but also consumers of research including families and service providers. It seeks to combine scientific knowledge and experiential knowledge to enhance quality outcomes.

The impetus for this book was a participatory research conference in which families, service providers, researchers, and theorists collaborated for several days in sharing their perspectives. This conference was sponsored by the Beach Center on Families and Disability at the University of Kansas and the Center for Children with Chronic Illness and Disability at the University of Minnesota.

The book is divided into an Introduction and two sections: Individual Perspectives and The Participatory Process in Action. The Introduction provides a brief background on the initial application of cognitive coping for families who have a member with a developmental disability, as well as on the participatory research process. It provides the rationale used by the Beach Center on Families and Disability and the Center for Children with Chronic Illness and Disability for holding the conference and for compiling this volume.

Section I provides the individual perspectives of families (Chapters 1–4), service providers (Chapters 5–7), and researchers and theorists (Chapters 8–20). From each of these research stakeholders, essays are included that generally follow the same format—

background of issues, current personal and professional priorities, and future directions related to cognitive coping research that are likely to have the greatest pay-off for families. We encouraged chapter authors to "examine the forest rather than the trees" in looking for trends, themes, and significant implications. For example, rather than focusing on a single research study, typically his or her latest one with the most precise review of data, we encouraged researchers to take a broad view of their work—analyzing what they have learned or what they even have hunches about concerning cognitive coping and the future directions that they believe will have the highest pay-off for enhancing quality of life of families.

In Section II, Chapter 21 provides a synthesis of in-depth small group discussions that were incorporated into the conference agenda. The following question was presented to participants: "What are the methodological, sampling, and dissemination problems with family research and what are the potential solutions?" Participants were asked to identify the major issues or challenges as they relate to cognitive coping in individuals and in families, to identify potential strategies for addressing the issues and challenges, and to consider the implications of the strategies for research activities.

Also in Section II, the last chapter of the book provides a research agenda. Working in small groups, participants were asked to address the following questions: What is the research agenda for the next decade in cognitive coping? What are the next steps in research on cognitive coping in families who have a member with a disability? The research agenda is organized into the following four sections: Conceptual–Definitional Issues, Determinants and Influences on Individual Coping, Family Issues, and Difficulties of Research in Families and Coping. Within each section, research questions are posed for individual and family issues.

We see this research agenda as the heart of the conference outcome. Again, our major goal was to conceptualize a research agenda that holds promise for enhancing the cognitive coping success of families with a member with developmental disabilities.

We hope very much that you will find this book instructive and insightful in anticipating your next steps of contribution related to cognitive coping, family well-being, and/or participatory research.

ACKNOWLEDGMENTS

We gratefully appreciate the many individuals whose efforts and support made the conference and this volume possible. We specifically want to acknowledge the valued contributions of:

- The conference participants, who authored the chapters in this book and were responsible for the success of the conference
- Dorothy Johanning, who managed the conference logistics and assisted with coordinating and producing this manuscript
- Patrick Dilley, who assisted with editing the chapters
- Patricia Barber, who served on the conference planning committee
- David Eckert, Susan Tebb, and Nona Tollefson, who served as facilitators for the small group meetings
- David Jones, Ilene Lee, and Betsy Santelli, who served as recorders for the small group meetings
- Stephen Schroeder, who welcomed the conference participants on behalf of the University of Kansas in his capacity as director of the Schiefelbusch Institute for Life Span Studies
- Patrick Dilley, Richard Harrison, Brian Kresin, Harriet Shaffer, and Jane Wallace, who took charge of transportation needs
- Vicki Turbiville and Janet Williams, who served as conference notetakers

As representatives of the University of Kansas Beach Center on Families and Disability and the University of Minnesota Center for Children with Chronic Illness and Disability, we also want to highlight what a privilege it is for our two centers to collaborate in joint projects. Our funding agency, the National Institute on Disability and Rehabilitation Research (NIDRR), encourages collaborative activity among its rehabilitation research and training centers, and we appreciate their encouragement in this regard.

Our centers' first NIDRR project officer, Naomi Karp, was a major contributor to this effort. Naomi played a key initial role in sharing her vision of the potential contribution of family research in supporting and strengthening families and in obtaining resources to put our collective visions into action. We salute her role as an "advocrat" (advocate working in the bureaucracy) in helping us, in a significant way, conceptualize participatory research principles and activities.

It is always a pleasure to work with Paul H. Brookes Publishing Company. Melissa Behm, Vice President, helped us crystallize our ideas for shaping this volume and shared her vision for an ongoing series on family well-being and participatory research. We acknowledge her valuable conceptual and editorial leadership. We also gratefully appreciate the editorial/production assistance of Ben Furnish from the Beach Center and Roslyn Udris, Susan Gray, Sue Vaupel, and Ken Foye from Paul H. Brookes Publishing Company. They have been an invaluable and indispensable part of this team effort.

Last, but most important, we express our profound gratitude to the many families of persons with disabilities who have become partners in the research of our centers and formed a mutual commitment to, ultimately, make a positive difference in the quality of family life.

COGNITIVE COPING, FAMILIES, AND DISABILITY

introduction

Participatory Research on Cognitive Coping
From Concepts to Research Planning

Ann P. Turnbull and H.R. Turnbull, III

The main objective of this book is to merge substantive content on cognitive coping with a participatory process for planning a research agenda. In this chapter, we provide an overview of cognitive coping and participatory research as a foundation for the chapters that follow.

COGNITIVE COPING

Cognitive coping is defined as thinking about a particular situation in ways that enhance a sense of well-being. Although theory development and research on cognitive coping have been ongoing in the field of social psychology for a number of years, cognitive coping as a research focus is relatively new to the developmental disability field.

At the Beach Center on Families and Disability, Lawrence, Kansas, we and our colleagues were prompted to investigate, in a preliminary way, cognitive coping as a line of research starting about 6 years ago. Both as parents of a son with mental retardation and autism and as researchers, we had concerns about what appeared to be an unbalanced pathogenic focus in the professional literature. Our reviews of the literature indicated that children with developmental disabilities were almost always described as being a major burden to their families. We identified two types of pathogenic statements in the literature. The first is a pervasive negative generalization. An example of such a generalization is:

> In most families in which there is a defective member, pervasive guilt permeates the family and is expressed in its characteristic style. The birth of a retarded child, his presence in the home, and even the knowledge that such a child once lived at home, greatly exacerbates this existential guilt. (Martino & Newman, 1974, p. 168)

1

The second type of pathogenic emphasis is the explanation of unanticipated positive findings through a negative interpretation. An example of this is:

> Jacobs (1969) . . . found that most of the normal brothers and sisters of a group of retarded children were sympathetic, helpful, and understanding and did not seem to have been adversely affected by their mentally retarded siblings. It is quite possible, however, that these siblings were outwardly helpful and cooperative while manifesting adjustment problems in other ways. (Wasserman, 1983, p. 622)

As we were reading this literature, we had an opportunity to analyze letters to Congress written by parents, relatives, and individuals with disabilities for the purpose of commenting on the 1983 proposed regulations concerning the medical treatment of newborns with disabilities. (This legislation was being proposed to prevent the withholding of food, water, and appropriate treatment from newborns on the basis of disability alone.) We conducted a qualitative analysis of 174 letters to identify the reasons given for the almost unanimous support of the regulations (of the 174 letters reviewed, 173 expressed support for the regulations and one letter expressed neither support nor disapproval) by family members (H.R. Turnbull, Guess, & Turnbull, 1988). Of the eight categories identified that reflected reasons given by parents, relatives, and individuals with disabilities for supporting the regulations, one of the categories included was the positive contributions that persons with disabilities make to their families.

In further analyzing the letters regarding positive contribution statements (A.P. Turnbull, Blue-Banning, Behr, & Kerns, 1986), we identified six categories of contributions, describing the person with a disability as being: a source of happiness, a source of love, a source of learning life's lessons, a source of fulfillment, a source of pride, and a source of strength. The following quote illustrates the category of learning life's lessons:

> Our life and the lives of our family were changed forever on January 18, 1980. At about 6:00 P.M. our daughter Sarah was born. She weighed three pounds. Her diagnosis from the doctor was hopeless, 24 hours to live, deaf, blind, severely retarded.
>
> As I looked at her, fighting to live, held her in the palm of my hands, amazed that this little one was my daughter, hope became eternal for me.
>
> For the next 26 months she taught us more about love, courage, faith, and life than most of us can teach or learn in 100 years. (A.P. Turnbull et al., p. 132)

A second example represents a much later point in the life span. In the following quote, the mother of an adult son with a disability commented on what his presence has meant to her and her husband: "My son and only child is 34 years old and considered profoundly retarded. His presence has strengthened our family ties and he is a source of pride. Surely the lives of my husband and I would be barren indeed without him."

Our interest in cognitive coping was strongly spurred by reading these letters and by identifying the gap between what typically was written in the professional literature and what we found in these letters. Additionally, we recognized the strong similarity between the letters' passages and the other writings by parents describing their family experiences. We were keenly aware in our own family life that there was a mixture of positive and negative experiences associated with our son, as well as with our two children who do not have a disability. We were perplexed by the assumption that was operating in professional circles that children without disabilities were categorically "easy to raise" and children with disabilities were categorically "burdens." (We often identify with the statement of a mother of eight children, the youngest of whom has Down syndrome. She related to us that it was almost a relief to learn that her youngest child had Down syndrome because she simply "did not have the energy to go through another normal adolescence!")

We began to gather literature from other disciplines that would provide a theoretical framework for our initial hunches about the potentially positive interpretation of disability. We first turned to Victor Frankl (1963) and his theory of logotherapy and existential analysis:

> We who lived in concentration camps can remember the men who walked through the huts comforting others, giving away their last piece of bread. They may have been few in number, but they offer sufficient proof that everything can be taken from a man but one thing: The last of the human freedoms—to choose one's attitude in any given set of circumstances, to choose one's own way.
> And there were always choices to make. Every day, every hour, offered the opportunity to make a decision, a decision which determined whether you would or would not submit to those powers which threatened to rob you of your very self, your inner freedom; which determined whether or not you would become the plaything of circumstance, renouncing freedom and dignity to become molded into the form of the typical inmate . . . It becomes clear that the sort of person the prisoner became was a result of an inner decision, and not the result of camp influences alone. Fundamentally, therefore, any man can, even under such circumstances, decide what shall become of him—mentally and spiritually. (pp.104–105)

The parallels of this theoretical orientation were highly consistent with the writings of parents of children with disabilities (as contrasted to the professional literature). Clara Claiborne Park (1982), the mother of a child with autism, provided a disability example of the theory advanced by Frankl:

> I do not forget the pain—it aches in a particular way when I look at Jessy's friends. Some of them just her age, and I allow myself for a moment to think of all she cannot be. But we cannot sift experience and take only the part that does not hurt us . . . . Through it we have learned the lesson that no one studies willingly, the hard, slow lesson of Sophocles and Shakespeare— that one grows by suffering. And that too is Jessy's gift. I write now what 15 years past I would still not have thought possible to write: That if today I were given the choice, to accept experience with everything that it entails, or to refuse the bitter largesse, I would have to stretch out my hands—because out of it has come, for all of us, an unimagined life. And I will not change the last word of the story. It is still love. (p. 320)

From an analysis of Frankl's work, we searched the literature from other disciplines and found Taylor's article (1983) entitled "Adjustment to Threatening Events: A Theory of Cognitive Adaptation" to be very relevant to disability issues. Taylor proposed a theory of cognitive adaptation to explain the adjustment process that individuals use when they experience personally threatening events. She suggested that there are three adjustment themes: 1) searching for meaning of the event, 2) increasing self-esteem, and 3) establishing mastery over the event in particular and over one's life more broadly. Upon our first reading of her article, we were struck by the similarity of quotes that she used illustrating the reactions of women with cancer to threatening events to the reactions we had heard so often from families who have a member with a disability. It was almost as if we could substitute disability for cancer and have practically the same quoted passage.

In summary, our early work led us to believe that cognitive coping has the potential for enhancing the well-being of families. We were generally optimistic that we might be able to learn something about how families frame their situations in a way to increase their own success. Focusing on what could help families be successful seemed to be a far more productive type of inquiry than the pathogenic emphasis that we had found in the literature.

Given our focus on cognitive coping, we want to make a cautionary point: We do not want to convey that we see cognitive coping as the most important coping strategy or the only coping strategy appropriate for families. Rather, we see it as one of many different coping styles that may be useful to families in some situations and not to families in others. It does not replace more instrumental coping such as access to financial resources, professional services, and social support.

Given our interest in cognitive coping as a promising approach to research and family support, it was an obvious topic for our first participatory research conference, which served as the impetus for this book. There appeared to be ample evidence from the Beach Center's research, and from research in the fields of developmental disabilities, cognitive psychology, social psychology, sociology, and family studies, that cognitive coping has significant potential for making a positive difference in the lives of individuals and families. From our own search of identifying and beginning to understand this area from the contributions of diverse constituencies, it was also obvious that cognitive coping would be strengthened by a broad analysis. We sought to create an opportunity for this broad analysis by bringing together theorists and researchers from a variety of disciplines, families, and service providers to explicate key concepts and to discuss important research progress and future directions. This approach provides the basis of the participatory research model described in the next section.

PARTICIPATORY RESEARCH

Participatory research is a value that has evolved at the Beach Center on Families and Disability over the last 5 years. Participatory research involves theorists, researchers, service providers, and family members collaborating in the research process by together defining questions, designing and implementing methodologies, analyzing and interpreting data, disseminating findings, and using results (Whyte, 1991). Participatory research promotes the use of research as a means rather than an end; and, as applied to families who have members with developmental disabilities, it is aimed at making a positive difference in the overall quality of family life (Turnbull, Turnbull, & Senior staff, 1990).

There have been two major catalysts for our adoption of participatory research. First, we have had a growing concern with the nature of some family research. Second, this concern prompted us to host a Consensus Conference on Principles of Family Research (Turnbull & Turnbull, 1990) sponsored by the National Institute for Disability and Rehabilitation Research (NIDRR) and to produce a report. We now briefly review each of these background influences.

Concerns About the Nature of Family Research

Our move toward participatory research has been influenced by four major concerns about the nature of some family research: 1) incongruous roles of people involved in family research, including theorists, researchers, service providers, and families; 2) discontinuity of knowledge available from different disciplines related to family well-being; 3) power differentials between researchers, service providers, and families; and 4) family research's limited benefit to service providers and families.

Our first concern has been and continues to be the incongruous roles of the various research stakeholders. This concern has been manifested in a variety of ways:

- The lack of cooperation and the presence of communication gaps between family theorists and family researchers results in the bulk of family research being atheoretical in nature.
- There is a dearth of research instruments that are grounded in theory and available for use by family researchers.
- The gap in communication and lack of collaboration between researchers and service providers means that a great deal of family research has limited service utility.
- Researchers perceive that service providers are not sufficiently scholarly to appreciate the research literature and service providers perceive that researchers are not attuned to "reality."
- Families, for the most part, are unaware of the availability of family research.
- Families have 24-hour reality demands as caregivers, with the result that they sometimes perceive research as an "irrelevant" activity and feel that service providers "do not understand."
- Service providers are "disappointed" when parents do not fulfill the roles and responsibilities assigned to them through public policy (e.g., active

participation in conferences to develop individualized education programs [IEPs]), not realizing that many families do not have access to information that even tells them what an IEP is, much less how to participate actively in developing one according to state-of-the-art procedures.

Our concern derives as well from our joint roles as researchers and teachers in the field of developmental disabilities and as parents of a 24-year-old son with mental retardation and autism. On the one hand, when we enter the "research world" we have been struck by some researchers' lack of awareness of the strengths, needs, and preferences of families. On the other hand, when we enter the family world we have noted the frustration that some family members have for the research process and their assumption that, if one is in academia, then one cannot also be "part of the real world."

Our second major concern has been the discontinuity of family research contributions developed by different disciplines. Some examples of this discontinuity are:

- Each discipline tends to have its own journals and conferences and typically the members of one discipline do not have the resources and time to access and absorb the information from other disciplines.
- Family theories from different disciplines have been developed in isolation from each other so that there has not been an opportunity for cross-fertilization of theorists' concepts.
- The disability field has produced family research, often in isolation from root disciplines of social psychology, sociology, and family studies.
- Service providers who work with families on a daily basis have limited access to information on either family theory or research, perhaps because the professional schools where they received their training were not connected to the knowledge base of root disciplines.
- Because each discipline has its own communication networks, many families do not even know what the disciplines are, much less where to go to gain information.

Our third major concern about the nature of family research has been the power differential between researchers, service providers, and families. Some examples of this power differential include:

- Researchers receive a salary for their work, research assistants receive a salary for data collection, and families typically receive no reimbursement for providing data—implicitly suggesting that the families' time is less valuable and their role in the research process is less important than that of the research director or research assistant.
- Academic institutions typically reward theorists and researchers for publishing in scholarly journals—the more scholarly the better—and fail to

reward, and sometimes even punish, theorists and researchers for publishing in practitioner and family journals and newsletters.

- Research planning committees on family research convened by federal funding agencies consider themselves progressive if they include one parent (perhaps unintended tokenism)—it is typically unheard of to include equal numbers of researchers, service provides, and families.
- There is an assumption that the only worthwhile knowledge is that which has been quantified through statistical methods—knowledge gained from qualitative research, clinical experience of service providers, and personal experience of families lacks sufficient credibility.

Fourth and finally, we believe that family theory and research has generally provided limited benefits for service providers and families while, perhaps, producing greater benefits for theorists and researchers. True, many family researchers state that the purpose of their work is to help families, yet some practices belie that assertion:

- A substantial portion of family research focuses on attempts to document the pathology of families (mostly middle- and upper-middle–class white mothers) and has limited service or policy implications for enhancing the success of families.
- The majority of families are unaware of the major findings of family research.
- Research journals are typically unavailable to the vast majority of families.
- Publishers of research books typically market to college bookstores and do not market to retail outlets, so that families are unable to access information on family research from community or mall-based bookstores.
- Theorists and researchers are rewarded academically for generating theoretical and empirical knowledge, yet, by contrast, families tend to rely on practical and accessible information and the personal experience and insights of "veteran families" who have had similar experiences.

Although we are unaware of any survey of families' awareness of research findings and the application of those findings in their daily lives, anecdotal evidence suggests that the vast majority of families simply are unaware of family research results. Many family researchers who have published their findings in scholarly journals have received academic promotions and academic awards, but their work has not been translated for the benefit of families and service providers. Further, we do not assume that researchers are always the most appropriate translators. Disseminating research results that can be used to benefit families and service providers is a challenging task—perhaps a task for which few people, whether researchers, service providers, or families, are adequately prepared.

These concerns prompted the Beach Center and NIDRR to sponsor a conference on researcher–family relationships related to family research. The conference report documented these concerns and recommended guiding principles.

Consensus Conference on Principles of Family Research

The purpose of the Consensus Conference on Principles of Family Research, held in 1989, was to analyze the roles of researchers and families in the research process and to articulate principles to guide the process. There were 34 attendees at the conference: half were researchers and half were persons who had a family member with a disability (given fiscal constraints, the conference did not address issues associated with service providers and theorists).

Five questions formed the basis for large and small group discussions:

1. What processes should federal agencies, researchers, and families follow in formulating research questions and identifying research priorities?
2. What values and practices should guide procedures to obtain informed consent and to ensure that no harm comes to families participating in research?
3. What research sampling strategies will increase participation by all family members and underrepresented groups of families?
4. How can research methodologies become more respectful of families?
5. How can research results be disseminated to families more effectively?

Participants formed five small groups, one group for each question. After plenary sessions analyzing the nature of problems associated with family–researcher relationships, each small group met for 6 hours and prepared group reports. Then representatives from each group synthesized the groups' reports and developed a set of five principles. A final plenary session gave all participants an opportunity to analyze, comment upon, modify, and eventually adopt the principles.

The five principles, unanimously adopted by the participants, are:

1. Research is a means, not an end. Its goals are to develop information and to test strategies and interventions that themselves are designed to accomplish certain goals. Those goals are to:
   a. expand choices
   b. build strengths
   c. promote independence and productivity
   d. promote integration in school, work, recreation, residence, and other community environments
   e. expand relationships and friendships within family and community
   f. recognize and expand positive contributions
   g. identify challenges and enhance the capacity of all family members to meet them
   h. change systems to promote the foregoing purpose
   i. expand visions and possibilities

j.   improve the basic and theoretical understanding of families

k.   prevent and ameliorate the effects of disability

2. Research should be a collaborative endeavor based on mutual respect, trust, potential benefits, and acceptance of each party's responsibilities.

3. Research should be sensitive to cultural, socioeconomic, ethnic, lifestyle, and life-span pluralisms.

4. To achieve the foregoing purposes, research should allow for a combination of paradigms and methodologies.

5. Funding for family research should be expanded to achieve the stated principles.

The participatory theme obviously pervades the five principles, as illustrated below:

1. The First Principle reflects *Participation* in the purposes and mission of research.

2. The Second Principle reflects *Participation* in the roles that people carry out.

3. The Third Principle reflects *Participation* by families with diverse characteristics.

4. The Fourth Principle reflects *Participation* by researchers with diverse skills.

5. The Fifth Principle reflects *Participation* by funding agencies. (H.R. Turnbull, III et al., 1990, p. 50)

It is clear that this group advanced the notion that all the stakeholders who are affected by research should participate across a broad range of research activities.

In a sense, a pervading theme of participatory research is related to participatory democracy. Just as a democratic government exists by, of, and for the people, so should research exist by, of, and for the associated stakeholders. Thus, research on families of people with disabilities is associated with the public interest in two ways. First, it is a means to the end of promoting families' well-being, particularly aimed at promoting effective means for service providers to support and enhance the families' well-being. Second, the way it is conducted should also reflect fundamentally democratic principles and ensure the participation of people affected by it.

The conference participants recognized that there are roles for different kinds of family research, including basic research (e.g., in areas such as prevention), that may require many years of work before generating results and implications for service providers and families. The five principles do not require immediately useful results and implications.

A report of the conference findings, including explanations and justifications for each of the principles, is available from the Beach Center. The report has been distributed to family leaders, researchers, research and family organizations, and funding agencies. The principles served as the fundamental guide for the planning of the Conference on Cognitive Coping, discussed in the next section.

CONFERENCE ON COGNITIVE COPING

After the 1989 conference, our next task became obvious. As one of the consensus conference participants stated, "Words are cheap, almost as cheap as principles." We undertook to use the five principles to develop a research agenda for the 1990s that passes the litmus test of participation. The substantive topic we chose was cognitive coping. To accomplish this task, we sponsored a conference with the goal to formulate a research agenda on cognitive coping in families who have a member with a developmental disability.

In sponsoring the conference on Cognitive Coping in Families Who Have a Member With a Developmental Disability: Theoretical and Empirical Implications and Directions, the Beach Center secured the cosponsorship of the Center for Children with Chronic Illness and Disability at the University of Minnesota, Minneapolis. Researchers at that center, headed by Robert Blum and Joan Patterson, also conduct research on how families can be supported to cope in the most positive ways possible. Furthermore, both centers share a commitment to participatory research. The cognitive coping conference was held in Lawrence, Kansas, in June 1991. The conference's purposes were: 1) to synthesize theory, research, practice, and personal experience related to cognitive coping in individuals and in families; and 2) to conceptualize a research agenda aimed at supporting families to enhance cognitive coping.

Conference Participants

To accomplish the synthesis of theory, research, practice, and personal experience, the conference convened theorists, researchers, service providers, and families, thus giving roughly equal attention to each of the important dimensions of disciplinary and experiential knowledge. (There were more researchers than participants in the other three groups; the rationale was to include the range of family researchers in the disability field whose work has significant implications for effective use of cognitive coping.) We invited people with stellar credentials in family sociology, cognitive psychology, social psychology, family studies, and developmental disabilities.

We realized the importance of recognizing diversity in the "unit" of research analysis. Research on cognitive coping essentially has two foci: research on individuals and research on family units. Most of the former has been done in the disciplines of cognitive psychology, social psychology, and sociology. By contrast, the majority of the latter has been done in the fields of family studies and developmental disabilities. Thus, we included theorists and researchers with specialization in individual cognitive coping and those specializing in family cognitive coping. These were two groups who rarely have had the opportunity to reflect upon the accomplishments in each area and the contributions of one area to the other.

To have diversity among service providers, we invited those working in a hospital-based program, a parent-directed resource center, and an early intervention program. One of the service providers specialized in providing support to siblings; others addressed the needs of all family members. Similarly, we sought family members representing diverse life-span stages; we also ensured that various types of developmental disabilities were represented. A shortcoming is that the family members were all mothers. (The one invited father was unable to attend.)

Conference Orientation

The conference's overall orientation was not on pathology and dysfunctionality but on health and success in families who have members with developmental disabilities. At a theoretical level, Antonovsky best articulates this orientation by his salutogenic perspective (see chap. 8, this volume). As applied to this conference, the salutogenic perspective calls for theorists, researchers, families, and service providers to identify factors that contribute to families' successful functioning. This perspective assumes that families inevitably will be faced with stressors but have the potential for active adjustment. Accordingly, the role of service providers is to enhance family strengths rather than to focus solely on deficits. For families, the salutogenic perspective implies discovering and learning how best to use one's resources to meet the challenges of life.

Thus, we intended for the conference to stimulate research that ultimately would support families *to use cognitive coping to enhance their positive well-being.* We were actively looking for the state of current knowledge and for ways to extend that knowledge in the most promising direction.

Definitions

Because of the participants' different backgrounds, it was imperative to define three basic terms: coping, cognitive coping, and developmental disabilities.

The term *coping* refers to the things people do (acting or thinking) to increase a sense of well-being in their lives and to avoid being harmed by stressful demands.

The term *cognitive coping* means thinking about a particular situation in ways that enhance a sense of well-being. People use many different types of cognitive coping strategies, including:

- Making favorable comparisons of one's situation to others—for example, concluding that a child with a developmental disability is really less challenging in some ways than a "typical" teenager, such as with peer pressure to use drugs or driving under the influence of alcohol.
- Finding positive benefits from an event or choosing selectively to ignore negative aspects—for example, family members may concentrate on the positive contributions of the person with a developmental disability in being the catalyst for assertiveness, sensitivity, and family unity.

- Attributing a meaningful and self-enhancing cause of the event—for example, a family may decide that a person with a disability has a special purpose in life.
- Having a sense of control or influence over the event—for example, a family may perceive that they can shape educational or employment opportunities for their family member, thus reducing their feelings of helplessness and despair.
- Finding humor—for example, families may find something humorous about inappropriate behavior in public and transform the situation from one of embarrassment to one of light-heartedness.

The term *developmental disabilities* is defined by U.S. law to mean a condition that:

a. is attributable to mental or physical impairment or a combination of mental or physical impairments;
b. is manifested before the person attains age 22;
c. is likely to continue indefinitely;
d. results in substantial functional limitations in one or more of the following areas of major life activity:
   i)   self-care,
   ii) receptive and expressive language,
   iii) learning,
   iv) mobility,
   v)   self-direction,
   vi) capacity for independent living,
   vii) economic self-sufficiency; and
e. reflects the person's need for a combination and sequence of special, interdisciplinary, or generic care, treatment, or other services which are of lifelong duration, and are individually planned and coordinated. (Public Law 101-496, Developmental Disabilities and Bill of Rights Act of 1990, 42 U.S.C. § 6001 [5] [October 1990])

Tasks/Agenda

The criteria for inviting participants were their unique perspectives in: 1) generating theory related to cognitive coping in individuals and/or families, 2) conducting research encompassing some aspect of cognitive coping in individuals and/or families, 3) providing services to people with developmental disabilities and their families, or 4) having experience as a parent of a person with a developmental disability. Each participant prepared an essay in advance of the conference and presented highlights of it at the conference.

We asked all participants to focus their essays and presentations on a common set of questions. These questions essentially asked participants to identify major milestones or accomplishments related to cognitive coping within their area of interest over the last 5 years, to identify current issues that hold promise for enhancing cognitive coping success, and to project future directions related to their area of interest over the next 5 years that hold the most promise for enhancing cognitive coping success of families. In asking these questions, we purposefully encouraged participants to concentrate on themes, trends, and patterns of implications. We were particularly interested in participants' "examining the forest rather than the trees." Thus, we encouraged them to reflect on the past, present, and most promising future of cognitive coping. We felt that this "big picture" view would yield the basis for conceptualizing a research agenda on cognitive coping for the 1990s.

The conference agenda enabled participants to share highlights of their essays. We sought to create a conference climate in which participants were encouraged to analyze their ideas for meaningfulness and current and future contribution rather than needing to defend their most recent work. Further group discussions focused on generating responses to the following questions:

- What are the methodological problems with family research? What are the potential solutions?
- What are the sampling problems with family research? What are the potential solutions?
- What are the dissemination problems with family research? What are the potential solutions?
- What are the next steps in research on cognitive coping?
- What are the next steps in research on cognitive coping in families who have a member with a disability?

The participants' conference essays served as the foundation for Chapters 1 through 20. Chapter 21 discusses the problems and potential solutions associated with methodology, sampling, and dissemination. Chapter 22 presents the research agenda that resulted from the group discussions on the next steps in cognitive research for individuals and families.

ABOUT THE AUTHORS

Ann P. Turnbull, Ed.D.   As co-director of the Beach Center on Families and Disability, my major emphasis is on planning and coordinating research aimed at making a positive difference in the lives of families. My teaching role primarily focuses on doctoral preparation for students majoring in family studies and disability and also frequently working with family organizations and service providers in consultation and training. I have been profoundly influenced through my experience of being a parent of a 24-year-old son with mental retardation and autism. One of my major challenges has been and continues to be to establish and maintain credibility as a researcher, teacher, and family advocate.

H. Rutherford Turnbull, III, LL.B.   As a parent of a young man with mental retardation and autism, I have written and spoken often about how my son turned my life upside down, impelled me into a new career, and gave me professional insights I could not have gained otherwise. His gifts and their significance are part of my psychological journey, which some would call one of cognitive coping. As a lawyer I have been concerned with participatory democracy and its concomitant, participatory research, a major theme of this book and the Beach Center's research projects.

REFERENCES

Frankl, V.L. (1963). *Man's search for meaning*. Boston: Beacon Press.

Jacobs, J. (1969). *The search for help*. New York: Brunner/Mazel.

Martino, M.S., & Newman, M.B. (1974). Siblings of retarded children: A population at risk. *Child Psychiatry and Human Development, 4*(3), 168–177.

Park, C.C. (1982). *The siege: The first eight years of an autistic child*. Boston: Little, Brown.

Public Law 101-496, Developmental Disabilities Assistance and Bill of Rights Act of 1990. (October 1990). 42 U.S.C. §6001 (5).

Taylor, S.E. (1983). Adjustment to threatening events: A theory of cognitive adaptation. *American Psychologist, 38*, 1161–1173.

Turnbull, A.P., Blue-Banning, M., Behr, S., & Kerns, G. (1986). Family research and intervention: A value and ethical examination. In P.R. Dokecki & R.M. Zaner (Eds.), *Ethics of dealing with persons with severe handicaps: Toward a research agenda* (pp. 119–140). Baltimore: Paul H. Brookes Publishing Co.

Turnbull, H.R., Guess, D., & Turnbull, A.P. (1988, June). Vox populi and Baby Doe. *Mental Retardation, 26*(4), 261–272.

Turnbull, H.R., III, Turnbull, A.P., & Senior staff. (1990). *Report of Consensus Conference on Principles of Family Research*. Lawrence, KS: Beach Center on Families and Disability.

Wasserman, R. (1983). Identifying the counseling needs of siblings of mentally retarded children. *Personnel and Guidance Journal, 61*(10), 622–627.

Whyte, W.F. (Ed.). (1991). *Participatory action research*. Newbury Park, CA: Sage Publications.

SECTION I

INDIVIDUAL PERSPECTIVES

The authors of the chapters in this section were asked to address a common set of issues:

- Past and current professional work or personal experience related to the use of cognitive coping strategies
- Future directions for professional work or anticipated uses of cognitive coping in meeting new personal challenges
- Suggestions for future research

In this section, the family perspectives are presented first, then those of the service providers, concluding with the perspectives of the researchers and theorists.

FAMILY PERSPECTIVES

Each one of the families has a member with a disability. **Judy O'Halloran, Jane Schulz**, and **Evy** and **Charles Lusthaus** detail coping strategies that have been used extensively and successfully in their families. **Janet Vohs** challenges the meaning often assigned to disability by parents, professionals, and society-at-large. She suggests that changing the presuppositions with which one approaches the situation leads to a more empowering method of dealing with challenges.

SERVICE PROVIDER PERSPECTIVES

Each of the service providers is involved in a program that provides services to families that have a member with a disability. **Corinne Garland** works with families who have preschool children with special needs. She discusses the history of approaches to serving these families and the way early intervention services can be structured to support family coping skills. **Donald Meyer** is involved in programs that provide support to fathers, siblings, and grandparents of children with special needs. He discusses coping strategies often used by

15

these family members and points out the need for more support programs for adult siblings. **Florene Poyadue** works with Parents Helping Parents (PHP), a parent-directed family resource center for children with special needs. She describes the many programs offered by PHP and discusses an approach that looks at the transition from acceptance to appreciation.

RESEARCHER/THEORIST PERSPECTIVES

Aaron Antonovsky sets the stage for the other chapters in the book with his chapter on the benefits of taking a salutogenic, rather than pathological or pathogenic, perspective in the study of coping in individuals and families. A salutogenic orientation focuses on why people cope well, in spite of difficulties. In contrast, a pathogenic orientation focuses on why people fail to cope (Antonovsky, 1987). Taking a salutogenic approach to studying cognitive coping might lead to the investigation of different processes and outcomes than would taking a pathogenic approach. In addition, he explains the sense of coherence (SOC) construct as the core of his theory of successful coping. Next, **Jonathon Brown** traces the development of cognitive illusions, which involve "overly favorable views of the self, an exaggerated sense of one's ability to control environmental events, and a naive belief in the brightness of one's future (p. 131, this volume)," and explains how they facilitate coping. **Glenn Affleck** and **Howard Tennen**'s chapter describes and illustrates what they have learned from parents of infants with medically fragile conditions about their uses of cognitive adaptation strategies. In particular, they focus on the processes of construing meaning and searching for mastery and control in the midst of coping with major medical problems. The chapter by **Shirley Behr** and **Douglas Murphy** explains the background and findings of their research among parents of children and adults with disabilities. They examined the following four perceptions associated with three cognitive adaptation themes (search for meaning, attempt to gain mastery/control, enhancing self-esteem): 1) citing positive contributions of the family member with a disability, 2) attributing a cause for the disability, 3) believing that one has control over outcomes for the family member with a disability, and 4) making comparisons of oneself with others.

    Suzanne Thompson extracts themes from her work on how individuals use cognitive strategies to cope successfully with a variety of distressing events. She considers possible influences on one's use of such strategies and discusses the implications of past and current research for families dealing with misfortunes. One of the few teams studying later-life families, **Marty Krauss** and **Marsha Seltzer** discuss the varieties of coping strategies they observed in a large-scale study of mothers of adults with mental retardation. Their findings support the adaptational hypothesis that these mothers have "prevailed" in their later lives. The chapter by **Laraine Glidden, Michael Kiphart, Jennifer Wil-**

loughby, and **Beverly Bush** summarizes results of studies on adoptive and birth families and their adjustment to a new child in the family. They describe the role of specific cognitions and values as important determinants of adjustment in these families. **Tamar Heller** reports on studies that indicate that perceived self-efficacy—a mastery and control strategy—plays a major role in the mother's adaptation to the providing of care for a child with mental retardation.

Reflecting on his and other's work on using cognitive behavior therapy to help families manage stress, **George Singer** emphasizes the need for research and practice to place cognitive coping techniques in the larger perspective of coping, not neglecting the importance of active coping. He also addresses the role of meanings, especially socially shared meanings, in the coping process. **Joan Patterson** takes up the topic of meaning in her chapter, explaining levels of meaning, the relation between meaning and family schemas, and the role of individual and family meanings according to the Double ABCX and Family Adjustment and Adaptation Response (FAAR) theoretical models. The Double ABCX Model is a conceptual framework "used to describe the outcomes of family efforts to achieve a new level of balance after a family crisis" (McCubbin & Patterson, 1983b, p. 13). This model relates the stressful event (Factor A), the family's resources for dealing with crises (Factor B), and the family's perceptions of the event (Factor C) and their roles in the outcome for the family (Factor X) (McCubbin & Patterson, 1983a). In the FAAR Model, the components of the Double ABCX Model are reconceptualized as demands (stressors and strains), capabilities (resources and coping capabilities), and meanings (perceptions and definitions). The interplay among these components is described in the context of the family's experience of repeated cycles of adjustment, crisis, and adaptation (Patterson, 1988). **Hamilton McCubbin, Elizabeth Thompson, Anne Thompson,** and **Marilyn McCubbin** provide an account of the central role of family schema and family paradigms in guiding the family's adjustment and adaptation to stressful events. The Resiliency Model of Adjustment and Adaptation is explained in terms of changes in the family's paradigm. A family paradigm is defined as the family's shared expectations and beliefs that guide how it functions in such areas of family life as work, communication, spirituality and religion, recreation, and childrearing. Cognitive processes involved in changes in the paradigm are described. **Pauline Boss** examines the construct of boundary ambiguity as a hindrance to cognitive coping processes. Boundary ambiguity was introduced and initially defined almost 20 years ago (Boss, 1975); it is "a state when family members are uncertain in their *perception* of who is in or out of the family or who is performing what *roles and tasks* within the family system" (Boss, 1987, p. 709). **Boss** states that boundary ambiguity develops as a result of: 1) situations where facts are unavailable or unclear, and 2) situations where families ignore or deny information. Finally, **Rick Snyder** describes his theory of hope, underscores the importance of cognitive appraisals of one's goal-related capabilities, and explains the development of his scales to measure hope in adults and children.

REFERENCES

Antonovsky, A. (1987). The salutogenic perspective: Toward a new view of health and illness. *Advances, 4*(1), 47–55.

Boss, P.G. (1975). *Psychological father absence and presence: A theoretical formulation for an investigation into family systems interaction.* Unpublished doctoral dissertation, University of Wisconsin, Madison.

Boss, P. (1987). Family stress. In M.B. Sussman & S.K. Steinmetz (Eds.), *Handbook on marriage and the family* (pp. 685–723). New York: Plenum.

McCubbin, H.I., & Patterson, J.M. (1983a). Family stress and adaptation to crises: A Double ABCX Model of family behavior. In D. Olson & B. Miller (Eds.), *Family studies review yearbook* (pp. 87–106). Beverly Hills: Sage.

McCubbin, H.I., & Patterson, J.M. (1983b). Family transitions: Adaptation to stress. In C.R. Figley & H.I. McCubbin (Eds.), *Stress and the family: I. Coping with normative transitions* (pp. 5–25). New York: Brunner/Mazel.

Patterson, J.M. (1988). Families experiencing stress: I. The Family Adjustment and Adaptation Response model; II. Applying the FAAR Model to health-related issues for intervention and research. *Family Systems Medicine, 6*(2), 202–237.

chapter 1

Welcome to Our Family, Casey Patrick

Judy M. O'Halloran

For my husband Roger and me, having a child who is developmentally challenged has taken us on a tandem journey. We are partners in marriage, partners in parenting, and partners in the struggle to provide Casey with the best opportunities we can. So, references made in the first-person singular reflect, to a large degree, Roger's opinions as well.

Our two older sons are obviously not as involved with Casey's special needs as we are. When I asked Sean, 18, and Ryan, 14, how they "cognitively cope" with having a brother who is developmentally challenged, they looked at me as if I were nuts. After much probing, the bottom line was the same for both of them. Most of the time, they just think of Casey as a *normal* younger brother. (Of course, this may not be much of a compliment since younger brothers are frequently regarded as pests, brats, geeks, and, in general, a subspecies.)

We have been very open with the boys and have told them that we are doing everything we can now to develop Casey's independence so he will not be their responsibility in the future. In all probability, they may not focus on Casey's differences because they don't have to. They don't have to fight for educational, social, or vocational opportunities. They can believe, as Ryan puts it matter of factly, "He's just a little brother."

I could look for deep psychological reasons for their lack of input. But I think I'll just be happy with the probability that they are simply better adjusted than I.

INTRODUCTION

"Welcome to our family, Casey Patrick. We love you." The brightly colored banner greeted us as Roger and I drove up to the house on April 13, 1981, with our newborn son. Our older boys, Sean, 8, and Ryan, 4, had printed the message in huge letters and stretched the banner across the garage.

The next morning, Roger came home from work to drive me to the doctor's office so Casey could have a quick, routine phenylketonuria (PKU) test. Since Casey had been born in a hospital 40 miles from our hometown, we were anxious for our regular doctor to see him. We figured we'd be in and out like a flash.

But our long-time pediatrician and friend gave Casey a very thorough exam, during which he asked a lot of questions. I became amused. "Boy," I thought, "Irwin really has changed his newborn visits in the last 4 years. He must have attended some seminars that emphasized the psychological aspects of parenting."

I remember his asking, "How do you plan to raise Casey? Do you plan to do anything differently than you did with Sean and Ryan?" That seemed to be a strange question, but since we'd known each other a long time and since he seemed to be in this psychological mode, I didn't give it much thought.

"Gosh, Irwin, he's the third one. I'm an old hand at this. I'm sure I'll be a lot easier on him. Besides, Sean and Ryan are 180° apart in personality. Casey has to fit somewhere in between. So raising him will be a piece of cake."

A few minutes later, Irwin put Casey back in my arms. Then, with tears in his eyes, he said, "I strongly suspect Casey has Down syndrome."

CRASH! Our world fell apart. And with it crumbled all that confidence.

Over the years, our confidence has returned. Through trial and error, we've learned some principles that have helped us in parenting a child with a *difability*, a term I prefer to use because it reminds me to look at Casey's *diff*erent abilities rather than his *dis*, or lack of, abilities.

As it turns out, raising Casey has not been a piece of cake. But in this day and age, raising any child conscientiously is no easy task.

COGNITIVE COPING OVER THE LAST 5 YEARS

The toughest adjustment for us came, not surprisingly, right after Casey's birth. In the past 5 years, we have gone through the second most stressful experience: Casey's education. (In some respects, however, it seems the most stressful because the struggle appears endless.)

But the good thing about going through the second most stressful period is that we use coping skills learned during the first. We fine tune these skills, giving additional thought as to how we can adapt them to the present situation. Then we act. For us, then, cognitive coping is an attitude or way of looking at the present situation based on our experiences of what has provided good results in the past (our actions).

Consequently, the whole process is a tapestry of cognition and action. In this manner, we have found the following cognitive coping strategies to be most successful. We:

Love Casey for who he is
Look for the "just likes"
Lean on others

Line up goals on several levels
Live positively one day at a time
Let Casey demonstrate his potential
Learn as much as possible
Lead with confidence
Limit the limelight on Casey
Laugh much of the time

We Love Casey for Who He Is

All of us in the family love, accept, and respect Casey for who he is. We all loved Casey from the first moment he came into our lives. Roger and I were lucky that we were not told that Casey has Down syndrome until he was 3 days old. We had the opportunity to bond unconditionally, untethered by feelings of loss, anger, or despair. Once we learned Casey had Down syndrome, the love continued—but we were emotionally and intellectually tainted by society's stereotype of "retarded" children.

We have worked to undo that which society stresses and conditions us to believe—that bigger, stronger, and brighter is best. And so we accept Casey for who he is: a wonderful, worthwhile, important, integral part of our family. We respect his individuality and uniqueness. We are in awe of his tenacity and determination. And we're even beginning to regard that stubborn streak of his as evidence that he'll do just fine on his own in this world.

Roger and I have had to "work" at this concept more than Sean and Ryan, probably because they have not been conditioned by society's expectations for as long as we have. It was easier for them to see Casey for who he really is right from the very beginning.

We Look for the "Just Likes"

Actually, it has taken Roger and me quite a long time to look at Casey as a pretty normal kid. I think there are a couple of reasons for this. First, early intervention programs are wonderful; but, by design, they have us concentrate on our infant or young child's deficiencies. We worked so hard at overcoming Casey's differences that we overlooked the similarities.

Second, Casey is a pioneer of sorts in our county. As a result, there are many more conferences, questions, and uncertainties. If he were following in the footsteps of a dozen or so other children with difabilities, the teachers and administrators would feel more comfortable and we would not be constantly reminded of his differences.

Now, we make a point of frequently acknowledging Casey's similarities. We'll make comments such as, "Your haircut looks *just like* Adam's" or "Thanks, Case, you got ready for church all by yourself *just like* your brothers." Not only does this reinforce the multitude of similarities for us, but it is teaching Casey to do the same.

We Lean on Others

Roger and I have a terrific support system. It includes God, each other, family, friends (with and without children with developmental difabilities), support group members, and other parents and professionals whom we have met locally and nationally.

We have established a network that has been essential to our well-being. Its diversity makes coping very easy. As we progress from one stage to another, we have resources available and people anxious to share their experiences and give their advice.

Important, too, are those friends who help us to balance our lives. These friendships have been made on common grounds other than developmental difabilities and may include career, church, neighborhood, or the boys' schools. Therefore, our activities are many, varied, interesting, and meaningful.

God plays a very important role in our support system. Right from the beginning, Roger always had faith that God gave us Casey and has something wonderful planned for us. I wasn't nearly so gracious or accepting. In fact, I went through a spiritual desert for a year and a half where I questioned—even denied—God's existence. But my journey brought me to a belief that God is a vital and personal part of our relationship, and I try to remember to ask for guidance in everything I do.

We Line Up Goals on Several Levels

Life is just so much easier for Roger and me when we set goals for ourselves. Early in our marriage, we would individually write down 1-year, 5-year, and 10-year goals in the areas of family, finances, career, home, and recreation. Then we would compare our dream sheets.

With Casey, our goal setting has become more defined in the last 5 years. A good part of the first 5 were spent groping. We really couldn't set goals because we didn't have enough information, confidence, or wisdom.

We have defined goals in three areas. First, we have established somewhat vague long-term goals. That is, we hope Casey will be an independent, productive, happy adult with a meaningful job and a wide circle of friends. (Incidentally, that's nothing more and nothing less than we hope for Sean and Ryan.) But that's as far as the goal goes. We don't define or worry about any of the components—that is, just how much independence or exactly what kind of job.

Second, we set broad short-term goals. For instance, if we believe Casey has the right to work in a "regular" job in the "regular" workplace, then we believe he should be educated in the "regular" classroom with "regular" kids. Therefore, our broad short-term goal is that Casey be educated in the least restrictive, most integrated environment.

Third, we determine specific immediate goals. For instance, we stated on his individualized education program (IEP) that Casey would be in a regular second-grade classroom. His support resources included a part-time aide in the classroom, occupational therapy, and speech therapy. Naturally, we had even more specific and detailed educational goals that supported this placement.

Goal setting, then, gives us a clear (well, at least most of the time) direction in which to proceed.

We Live Positively One Day at a Time

I am, by nature, a pessimist. Roger is an optimist. Like the positive little boy who, in the old joke, shovels through the pile of manure muttering to himself, "I know there's a pony in here somewhere," Roger will always look for the bright side.

His positive attitude has rubbed off on me. I now gravitate toward individuals who act in a positive manner. I have also discovered that if I make a conscious effort to apply this attitude to all aspects of my life, it carries over very easily to parenting Casey.

It helps immensely not to worry about the distant future. Too many things can happen over which we have no control, so we just concentrate on the present. It sure makes life a lot easier and brighter.

We Let Casey Demonstrate His Potential

This philosophy ties in with accepting and respecting Casey. But it goes further. It also gives him the opportunity to be all that he can be.

At first, I would get depressed when I would compare Casey's life with his brothers. I would lament, "He'll never go to the same school, or play basketball, or date. He won't go off to college or have his own family." Finally I realized, "That's right, Judy. He won't. Because you don't believe he will. And if that's the message you give him, that's the message he'll live by."

So now Roger and I give Casey the opportunity to show us what he can do. We start him out in the most usual, most normal situations and then adjust according to his accomplishments.

We did not place him in a special Sunday school class. He goes to religion classes with the other children and made his First Holy Communion right alongside them.

He's on a regular beginning bowling team and is a member of a regular Cub Scout troop. And he's always been in regular classrooms.

Midway through second grade, Casey's schedule was adjusted so that he went out of the class for math in the special education room and reading in Chapter I. Why? Not because that's the county policy, but because he showed us that he would benefit from a remedial approach in these areas. I repeat, we did these things because Casey showed us what he needed.

It's easy to *assume* what's best for Casey. But we try to give him opportunities to show us what he can do and where he needs help. We think that's a valuable gift we can give him: the opportunity to be challenged to grow and do his best.

We Learn as Much as Possible

This has been one of the most successful ways for us to cope with erroneous perceptions, archaic policies, and limitations in general. We believe the more we know, the better decisions we can make.

In the last 5 years, we have had to deal with the public school system. "Downtown" can be very intimidating. Although the school administrators say otherwise, county policy has been to have the exceptional student fit the program, not the program fit the individual, though thankfully this is changing. The only way to challenge the system is to come into it armed with information, including a thorough knowledge of PL 94-142.

For that reason, Roger and I read, listen to tapes, and attend conventions—local, state, and national. We formed a support group. We attend workshops. We give workshops. He does legal research; I observe in classrooms. We have made contacts locally and across the nation. We keep current on school board decisions and exceptional-student education policies.

Obviously, this is very time consuming. But it has made all the difference in opening up opportunities for Casey.

We Lead with Confidence

Research leads to knowledge. Knowledge leads to confidence. Confidence leads to action.

Because we know what Casey's entitled to, we can assume a role of leadership when it comes to his placement. Our approach is one of being active members of Casey's educational team.

Once we settle on an appropriate placement, we never sit back and say, "Whew, that's over. Thank heavens we finally found a good school [or good class]." We look at the situation as being appropriate for Casey at this particular time with this particular set of circumstances.

Casey's principal, a woman we respect tremendously, once said to me after we were discussing some options, "Judy, I'll do what you want. You're the expert in this."

Years ago, I would have hung my head, shrugged my shoulders, and sheepishly insisted, "Oh, no. Oh, no." Instead, I smiled and replied,

> I better be. Casey is the only person I have to worry about at this school. I don't have to know about qualifications for free lunch programs; I don't have to know whom to call when the sewer lines back up into the bathroom; I don't even have to know how to use the intercom. I don't expect you to be an expert on 94-142 [the Individuals with Disabilities Education Act]. But his father and I better be.

It took Roger and me a long time to realize that we are actually experts in raising our child with special needs. Having acknowledged that fact to ourselves, we work in a cooperative team manner with Casey's other experts (physicians, educators, therapists, etc.) But we also take the lead when necessary, and do so with confidence—because we know we can make a difference. After all, no one knows Casey better than we do.

We Limit the Limelight on Casey

From a personal standpoint, the major reason I try to limit the limelight on Casey is to ease my guilt. I am acutely aware of the inordinate time and attention Casey requires. So now that he is older and does not need as much supervision, I make it a point to be involved in Sean and Ryan's various activities. (Of course, now that they are teen-agers, they'd just as soon I not be too involved in their lives!)

I have always told the boys, "More time does *not* mean more love." But when I can share my time a little more equitably, I think it helps.

Besides easing guilt, there are other benefits to spreading out our time and attention. Roger and I have more time to focus on each other. If we're too tired or too busy to spend time with each other—to go out for a cup of coffee, to take a walk, to go to a movie—then we, and Casey, are in really big trouble.

We have time as individuals and as a couple to pursue other interests, and we have time as individuals and as a couple to spend more time with friends, family, and recreational pursuits.

I figure if breaks were not vital to our well-being and productivity, employers would not give employees paid vacations. Taking time to be with friends and family and to have fun gives us the breaks we need in our daily lives to keep going.

But perhaps one of the most important reasons to limit the limelight on Casey is that it fosters his independence and gives him a better perspective of himself. Casey is an important part of our family, but he is not always the most important part. At times he is. But at one time or another, each one of us, for one reason or another, is the most important.

I believe that by realizing the family does not revolve around him, Casey will not expect the "real-world" classroom and the "real-world" workplace to revolve around him.

We Laugh Much of the Time

The way I look at it, it's better to crack up with laughter than to crack up with stress. And quite honestly, there have been times when a good laugh was the only thing that has gotten us through the demands of parenting a child with a difability.

Even in serious matters, it's important to keep things in perspective and look at the lighter side. For instance, one afternoon, after a hectic and stress-filled day, I picked up Casey from kindergarten. Four little kids came running up to me on the playground and chanted, "Casey said a bad word. Casey got in trouble."

His teacher did come up, and since the heralds had already announced his transgressions, she whispered that Casey had said "f---."

"Great," I joked. "I spend $25 a half hour on speech and the only word everyone can understand is the queen mother of no-no's."

It helps to be able to look at the world 23° off center. Thankfully, I was born with this gift. Roger wasn't born with this perspective, but he has acquired the knack. The boys, too, have terrific senses of humor. For example, one evening I was getting ready to put dinner on the table. Noticing that everyone was in the family room except Casey, I asked, "What happened to Casey?" Sean answered, "It has something to do with his chromosomes." I guess it's part heredity, part environment, and part survival skills.

ADVICE TO OTHER FAMILIES
TO ENHANCE COGNITIVE COPING

All of the skills just discussed are important to us. They shift in degree of importance depending upon what the circumstances are, what our goals are, and just where we happen to be in our lives.

Since hindsight is better than foresight (or "duringsight"), I would suggest to other parents that they not focus on their child's difability. Look at that child and see the endless similarities between him or her and the kid down the block. In addition, it's important to set high expectations, to know your child's rights, and to keep your child in the most normal surroundings possible.

But above all, I think that parents have to do what they feel is best for their families. They can listen to all sorts of advice, but they have to determine what is right for their own circumstances.

So if I could say only one thing, I would advise,

> Believe in the dignity of your child. Accept and celebrate his or her uniqueness. Then do whatever you feel is right so that you can look your child in the eyes 20 years from now and say, without hesitation and with sincerity, "I did the best I could."

THE NEXT 5 YEARS

So, how will we cope over the next 5 years? Well, for starters, we won't worry too much about it now. As I said, one of the coping strategies we follow is to try to live positively one day at a time. It really does help immensely not to worry about the distant future. Too many things can happen over which we have no control.

My next reaction is to proclaim that I won't know how I'm going to cope until I'm in the midst of the problem. But actually, I know that we will build on the coping strategies that have already proved successful for us. Once again, we will fine tune these skills for the specific situation.

For now, we have identified areas that we anticipate will cause us stress. They fall into three main categories: adolescence, Casey's education, and Casey's social life. Having identified them, we can form a foundation (by listening to "experienced" parents talk about their situations and solutions, for instance) upon which to build our specific coping strategies at a later date.

Thus far, the academic arena has produced the most stress for us, and we would expect that to hold true for the future. Even though integrated settings have opened up on a limited basis on the elementary level, at present the middle school level is not looking ahead to educate students with difabilities in the least restrictive environment. The thought of "taking on" a whole new group is depressing.

Casey's growing awareness of his developmental delays will bring a new aspect into our educational choices. His self-esteem has always been of the utmost importance to us. Up to this point, his delays have not been so significant as to cause problems with his self-concept, but we will need to monitor this area carefully.

Casey's social life and his entering adolescence are two areas that I anticipate will bring new stresses for us. With regard to the former, there are no children Casey's age (chronological or developmental) in our immediate neighborhood. Although we have "imported" classmates and friends in for play sessions after school and on weekends and Casey has visited their houses, his social skills need sharpening. Also, as Casey's friends without Down syndrome "outgrow" him, how will he feel? What will he do? What will we do?

I think this is where our "Learn as much as possible" coping strategy will come in. We will seek out suggestions from other parents, look for workshops on this topic at conventions, and otherwise learn how we can facilitate this area.

We spend the least amount of time contemplating Casey's entering puberty. Having already experienced the roller-coaster existence of adolescence with two teen-agers, we don't even want to think about what life has in store for us when Casey's testosterone kicks in. So, the way we cope with this area is to ignore it for now.

On the one hand, we don't worry too much about the future *too soon* because we know there is always pain and frustration involved. So why worry about it before it is necessary? On the other hand, we know that we have learned successful strategies in the past, and we have always come through. Therefore, we are confident that we will come up with successful strategies in the future.

We know that as time progresses, we will include Casey more in our general discussions and decision making. His input will be important and helpful to us.

Perhaps most important, Roger and I will bring to the cognitive coping process a different perspective than we used in past years: one with more depth and maturity. When Casey was first born, and for some time thereafter, we concentrated on how he was different and what we could do to help him.

We still try to help Casey in every way we can, but we realize now we're really not coping with Casey—we are coping with society, its misconceptions, its stereotypes, and its limitations.

FUTURE DIRECTIONS IN
RESEARCH FOR COGNITIVE COPING

As a parent, I feel that figuratively and literally the future direction in research needs to incorporate more vertical movement. There is a strong horizontal flow between researchers and between theorists. They read each others' papers. They quote each other. They borrow and learn from each other. There is great interaction in this wealth of knowledge and thought.

But for this knowledge to benefit families who have a member with a difability, the information must "get down to" us. Hence the vertical direction.

Cognitive coping in families could be facilitated if families were aware of findings in such areas as:

- Which situations and events are likely to cause stress. What is the *real* source of stress? Is the real source the child or is the *true* source society and its perception of people with difabilities?
- Proven, successful coping strategies.
- Methods to increase parental confidence.
- Extended studies with families who feel they are coping well. Studies that include families' reactions over a long period of time give more realistic strategies than the one-time "slice-of-life" results.

Families need reliable information. And we need it in ways that are easily accessible to us. Families will, I believe, enthusiastically and gratefully read material in books and in magazine and newspaper articles, listen to audiotapes and talk shows, and attend support groups and workshops.

But the information needs to be explained in language that the average parent can understand. This is not to say that parents are incapable of understanding academic jargon. Many can. We just shouldn't have to. Families who have a member with a difability are under enough stress and time constraints. It is far easier to digest information if it is presented to us through concrete examples and common experiences explained in lay terms.

Service providers can form a vital link between researchers and families. Service providers have more exposure to academic findings and should be able to relay the information in simple language.

Perhaps more parent–researcher collaboration would be a vehicle for achieving a good exchange of information. For instance, parents who write and speak on difability issues could work with researchers to achieve effective ways to disseminate the material.

But one thing is certain: The information is far too valuable not to reach and be used by the people it is intended to help.

CONCLUSION

In the past 10 years, our family has adjusted individually and as a unit to having a member with a developmental difability. We are positive. We communicate. We are happy. And we still proclaim—more strongly than ever— *"Welcome to our family, Casey Patrick. We love you."*

ABOUT THE AUTHOR

Judy M. O'Halloran   I have a B.S. in English education from Florida State University and I have experience in teaching and freelance writing, but I still consider myself "just a wife and mom"—the toughest, most challenging, and guilt-ridden career anyone could pursue. As a parent of a child who has Down syndrome, "just a mom" means I have become an organizer, advocate, and expert. Currently, I do motivational speaking and conduct workshops on parenting children with a *difability*—all the while hoping those neighbors within earshot of my house and yard don't come to any of the sessions.

chapter 2

Heroes in Disguise

Jane B. Schulz

The normal developmental changes that every family experiences require coping strategies, but families who have members with developmental disabilities face different and, in many cases, more challenging situations. While the term *cognitive coping* may be unfamiliar to our family, the process of restructuring stressful events in positive ways is not a new strategy.

COGNITIVE COPING DURING THE LAST 5 YEARS

The last 5 years may have been the most traumatic, challenging, and revealing years that our family has ever had. My husband Bill had a massive stroke 5 years ago and has been in a nursing home for a year; two of my sons have dissolved their marriages and one son had a business failure; my daughter's husband completed work for a doctorate, after which they moved and have had two children; I retired from Western Carolina University after 19 years of teaching; my oldest grandson has come to live with me; I have had elusive health problems that, not surprisingly, appear to be related to stress; and Billy, my son who has Down syndrome, had a change in his job status.

As I enumerate these changes, it appears that some events are negative, some are positive, and some fit both categories. The most obvious conclusion is that our family member who has a developmental disability contributed less stress to the family than did other members. In fact, during this time, when I was caring for my husband at home, Billy became my most valuable and practical support.

During the past decade, the problems associated with Billy's transition into adulthood, the difficulties in finding suitable housing and work for him, and the lack of resources to assist us with these problems created tremendous stress for our family. It was interesting and revealing to find that his problems were no longer our chief focus, and that his contributions far outweighed his demands. However, there is a more subtle problem concerning Billy than is apparent on the surface.

In family system theory, we frequently state that what happens to a person with a disability happens to the entire family. What we fail to mention is that what happens to the family also happens to the person with a disability. Explaining the changes that have taken place in the last 5 years and helping Billy to understand and deal with them has been difficult.

We find, therefore, that we have had to deal with the issues surrounding Billy's disability, the issues surrounding my husband's disability, and the interfacing of the personal changes taking place in the family. We have discussed the issues and our cognitive coping strategies within the family, and feel that our chief ways of coping have been family support, past experience with coping, and humor.

Family Support

Our family is not perfect, but it is a close, loving family. At any given time, I could call any or all of our four children and ask for help. They would come immediately without question. This knowledge is in itself a tremendous comfort. When my husband had a stroke, our family dynamics changed drastically. Now, instead of having help from my husband, we had two family members, each with a disability, to consider. The long hospitalization, 6 weeks in a rehabilitation center, and careful monitoring at home meant that I was stranded. I had no one to help with Billy's transportation (a tremendous problem in a semi-rural area) and was unable to be away from home for any extended period of time. My daughter came and stayed a week with her father so I could have a vacation; one son came and took care of the yard, planting flowers for my pleasure; another son visited his father frequently and helped with his personal care. It was at this time that Billy became my chief resource. Since he lives near us, I could call him whenever I needed help lifting his father or with other difficult tasks. I would phone him, asking if he could come. He always said, "Sure, Mom."

Our family is supportive of me and of each other. When I have problems with Billy, I talk with the other children, and frequently get good advice and practical suggestions. For example, I asked Billy's sister for suggestions to help him lose weight. She made out menus, shopping lists, and cards color-coded for each day to help him select the proper foods. Although he has not stuck with the plan, he does pull it out when he is motivated to lose weight.

Our family gatherings are always fun. Billy is very much a part of celebrations at birthdays and holidays and his brothers and sister are not only careful to include him, they enjoy him.

Past Experience with Coping

During the time that my husband was in the hospital, a friend called and talked with Mary, our daughter. I heard Mary say to the friend, "Mom's okay. She has a Ph.D. in coping."

I do find that strategies learned in the past have helped with more current problems. Due to state budget cuts, Billy's job at the university was affected and his hours were diminished by half. After my first panic reaction, I remembered the assertive approaches I had had to use in getting him educational services in the past. I contacted influential people I knew, and through one of them, Billy got a part-time job at the Burger King.

My husband's nursing home is in another county, which adds to my travel time in going to visit him. The nursing home in our community has no vacancies and his name has been on the waiting list for over a year. Just recently, I remembered that I needed to be more aggressive in this situation, and am now in the process of calling everyone I know who might have some influence and who could intervene for us. I am confident that a place will be available soon.

Another cognitive coping strategy that I have learned from past experience is that sometimes I just can't deal with another problem, and so I simply put the latest one on hold.

Humor

We are sometimes criticized for laughing at Billy. But he is funny, and in most cases he will join us, shaking with laughter.

On one occasion, several family members met at the Atlanta airport to welcome Mary home from Holland. My nephew, who has cerebral palsy and was in a wheelchair, also joined us. Mary had long flowing hair and was quite stunning. As we walked up a ramp, I noticed that people were staring and all at once, we realized what a picture we made: Johnny in his wheelchair, Mary with her tall good looks, Billy with his Down syndrome features, and me bringing up the rear. It was so funny that all of us convulsed with laughter.

A few years ago Billy and I were taking a trip to visit my son John in Georgia. As usual, I was trying to engage Billy in skills of observation, and asked him to look for Highway 53. After a while, he said, "We getting close, I see lots of 55s."

Some of the humor is derived from Billy's lack of understanding of certain terms and concepts. Recently, two of our friends invited Billy to go to supper and a movie with them. In planning for the meal, they asked, "Have you ever been to Fuddrucker's?" Billy instantly replied, "I can't say that word—my mom would kill me!" A few weeks ago, Billy and I went to see the movie "King Ralph." He especially wanted to see it because there is a scene related to Burger King, where he works. When this scene came onto the screen, I whispered to Billy, "There's your Burger King." His reply: "No, Mom, that's a different one."

After her marriage to Jos, who is Dutch, Mary proclaimed, "I speak three languages: English, Jos, and Billy." We derive a great deal of pleasure from some of Billy's language, and then find ourselves using it because it is so practical. At the end of a telephone conversation, he will say, "Well, me are nothing left to say" and hang up. One of our favorite, and most frequently used expressions, is "case instead," which means "just in case something else happens and instead of Plan 1." I even hear my friends use it, as in "I may not be home, but call me case instead." One day I was in the car while Billy went into the post office. He came out, and became engaged in a long conversation with a person I didn't know. When he got into the car, I asked who it was. He replied, "I no idea."

The ability to laugh at differences in ourselves and others has generalized to experiences at the rehabilitation center and nursing home where my husband Bill has been treated. One Sunday we went to visit him at the rehabilitation center and were told he was in the meeting room for church service. We didn't want to disturb the sermon, so we stood outside the door, listening, as our eyes roved among the people in wheelchairs. "Behold," said the very Southern minister, "our bones are dried up and our hope is lost; we are clean cut off." We raised our eyebrows at each other, questioning the appropriateness of his text for this particular audience, and waited through the lengthy description of the valley of dry bones. Directly addressing the assembly of patients, the minister yelled, "O dry bones, hear the word of the Lord!" With one accord, we mouthed to each other the words of the old spiritual, "Dem bones gonna rise again," let our arms fly into the air, and had such a hard time stifling our laughter we had to leave the hall.

We find humor in unexpected places. A photograph of Bill taken in front of a Christmas tree at the nursing home happens to contain a sign on the wall that reads: Month—December. Season—Monday.

Now that my visits to the nursing home have led to friendships with the other residents there, I find myself laughing a great deal with them. James, who has severe physical handicaps, was working for several minutes trying to get a slippery slice of canned peach from his bowl to his mouth. One slice after another of the elusive fruit plopped into his lap and slithered onto the floor. The silent tension in the room shattered as James's fifth attempt caused everyone present (including James) to laugh with gusto.

Frequently, Bill adds his touch of humor to situations in the nursing home. I'm always interested in the diagnosis of physical and psychological problems, and once asked Bill, "What's wrong with Frank?" He replied, "He's from Florida." It is the small ironies, the things that don't make sense, the repetition, and the unexpected that have turned many moments from gloom to humor.

CURRENT STRATEGIES

The cognitive coping strategies that we are currently using have evolved as we have grown. We have learned that as a family we have contributions to make that will help other people cope with their problems related to disabilities. As the one who is primarily involved with both family members who have disabilities, I have learned to take care of myself. And finally, but most important, we have all learned to appreciate Billy's unique personality and characteristics.

Helping Others Cope

Each member of our family is sought as a counselor. John, who is a landscaper, has hired people who have learning disabilities and other learning problems. Invariably, he becomes their confessor, counselor, and teacher. Tom, the artist and builder, has been active in his church and frequently finds himself in an advisory role. Mary has had similar experiences, and is always available to people who need a friend. We pay attention to people. I believe that this characteristic is a direct result of our listening to Billy, empathizing with him, and trying to help him unfold the mysteries of his life.

During the past few years, Billy and I have made a number of presentations to parents and teachers who find hope in his accomplishments and comfort in our relationship. This practice began when a former student of mine, who became principal of a school for children with developmental disabilities, asked me to speak to the parents of his students about "letting go" of their children. I suggested that Billy would be a good influence on them, and the principal immediately invited both of us to speak. I found myself in a quandary, because Billy does not verbalize well. It occurred to me that visual prompts would facilitate his communication and we put together a slide presentation, depicting aspects of his work, his family life, his church affiliation, and his living skills. Mary and Jos keep our slides up-to-date as Billy's situations change, and we have continued working together in this way. Billy meets with classes on campus, and several times has done presentations without me. Usually I address a specified topic and Billy concludes the presentation. (I'm too smart to follow an act like that!) The audiences that we feel are most receptive are parent groups, especially parents of children who have Down syndrome. Billy makes a real contribution here, as indicated by a letter from a little girl with Down syndrome, transcribed by her father: She stated that since her parents had met Billy, they were not so afraid of the future.

My class evaluations always include comments from students about the importance of my experiences as the parent of someone who has a developmental disability. The department head who hired me as a special education professor frequently declared, "Her best credentials are not on paper."

Overcoming Martyrdom

Realizing that no one likes a martyr, I have learned to take care of myself. This strategy requires a great deal of cognitive restructuring, since I have always tried to be the "super mom."

I take care of myself physically, exercising and eating wisely (most of the time). My walking is combined with social interaction with friends who walk and talk with me and who occasionally laugh and cry with me. The friendship and the exercise are equally important. As we walk and talk, I realize that my friends also have problems and accomplishments and that we can help each other with our difficulties and we can rejoice in our victories.

I am teaching part time, which supplements my income and allows me to do what I like to do best. Although I miss the collaboration with my peers, I also escape the pressures of full-time university commitment.

I have added "No, I don't want to do that" to my repertoire of responses. I choose community service organizations I want to be part of and belong to one club that has no central purpose at all, except socializing. I have a meaningful church membership and teach a Sunday School class for young people who have no disabilities.

I have accepted the fact that I can't do it all alone. Sometimes I ask my friends to help with Billy's transportation and have engaged a student to assist him in an exercise program. I acknowledged that I could no longer care for my husband at home and he agreed with me.

Mary said that my stress management program is evidenced by the articles on my bedside table: a clock with the alarm turned off, a Bible, a book of essays, a novel, and a roll of Tums.

Appreciating Billy's Personality and Characteristics

Billy is a lot of trouble. There are things about him that I don't admire—things I would like to change. And yet, I can't imagine my life without him. He greets me in the morning with "Happy Tuesday!" and "Mom, you look pretty today." He is so thoughtful of me. Once we were in the grocery store, and it started raining; he went to the car and brought my umbrella to me. One winter day I was leaving Mary's house in Tennessee when Billy called to tell me it was snowing in Sylva and he thought the roads would be dangerous. I waited until the next day to leave.

Billy is a social genius. He instinctively knows how to save a social situation. Many years ago, we knew a girl who also has Down syndrome. Her brother was killed in Vietnam and her family was, of course, devastated. In an effort to help, we had Carol come to our house for the day but found that we didn't know what to say to her about her brother's death. As we were sitting in silence, Billy got up, went to her, put his arm around her, and said, "Carol, I sorry 'bout your husbin." She immediately opened up to all of us and we were able to talk about what had happened.

Not long ago, we went to a new dentist who came in and, without a word, began to examine Billy. Billy put out his hand and said, "Hi, I'm Billy." The dentist stopped and chatted for a few minutes before continuing his work.

Recently Billy was spending the weekend with Tom in Asheville. Tom took him to a party at an impressive home, with people who were rather stilted. They all sat around looking at each other, not having a good time. Billy looked at the hostess and said, "I bet I can beat you arm wrestling." Everyone started arm wrestling and the party got moving.

As a family and as individuals, we are just beginning to understand who Billy is and how he has affected our lives. I have asked the people who know him best, his brothers and his sister, to describe the things about Billy that mean the most to them.

John wrote:

I have two brothers—Tom and Billy. I am 8 years older than Tom and 10 years older than Billy. Keep this in mind.

Tom and I first developed a special relationship when he was 17. Billy and I always had a special relationship. I often feel that I neglect Billy and I am prone to impose guilt feelings on myself for this reason. I live in another town far away and don't see Billy as often as I would like. Keep this in mind.

Periodically I will talk to Billy on the phone, mostly by accident. He is always glad to hear my voice. I will say, "What's happening, Billy?" He will answer, "Fine." Before the conversation is over, Billy will always get around to saying, "I have a wonderful brother."

"What's his name?" I ask.

"John."

When Tom and I are around Billy, he will often say, "I have a wonderful brother!" Tom and I jump on this, saying, "What's his name?" This turns into a wonderful game with Billy being very diplomatic. Billy will usually end up telling us a poem that he wrote himself:

> I have a brother name is John
> I have a brother name is Tom
> I love my brother name is John
> I love my brother name is Tom.

Then he laughs and hugs us.

I have one thing to say for Billy: I have a wonderful brother. Keep this in mind.

Tom wrote:

In my life, everything bears the seed of beauty and everyone wears the mantle of heroics. For the most part, I owe this vision to my brother Billy. Growing up in a family graced by his joy and directness has expanded my concept of what is the essence of potential: that is living life delicately balanced between the sanctity of each individual moment and the broader spectre of genetic predestination.

Billy says to me, "We have twin eyes." And I wish that was true if only for a moment. Then I could see the world as he does. Truly it must go way beyond what any of us could ever imagine. Billy asks questions that none of us will allow ourselves to. He is the Vasco de Gama of feelings. He sails around uncharted emotional territory when 2 years after my marriage has ended he asks me, in front of my daughter, "Tom, when you and Michelle get back together?" I know that I must tell the truth. I don't always know what to say. Sometimes he grabs my hand with his hand that is like a paw or a catcher's mitt and he says, "I love you" or "Don't worry—it will be all right" and I think, who is this guy?

I can never be so tired that I do not think of Billy forcing himself to climb a set of stairs to go to a concert. I can never be shy without seeing him turn to a stranger and saying in this voice so full of melody, "Hi, my name is Billy."

Billy has taught me that there exists a simpler path. When he is tired he sits down. When he is happy he says so. And when he doesn't want to do something, he is completely immovable—defying most natural laws of the universe. I often rationalize the complexity of my "normal" life by comparison: "Oh yes but he doesn't have kids to raise and tax bills due." But for every life situation that has ever arisen calling out to me, "Hey, Tom, deal with me with anxiety and fear" I picture Bill and his brick-like smooth-surfaced countenance and know there is another way.

I would never pretend that Billy has no problems. For if nothing else is mine to hold it is the knowledge of his humanity. Just below his surface ripple emotions as deep as the ocean. But I do fantasize that one day I will open up to the joy of living, the boundless offerings of love available, and the graceful navigation of stormy social seas just like my brother Billy.

For he is my hero.

Mary wrote:

Bill has four beautiful, admirable qualities which often stir my intentions toward self-improvement. They are all aspects of character which I think are seldom found among us in the genuine way they are combined in Billy.

The first is his truly generous spirit. He does Christmas the way it is meant to be done: He shops until he says, "My sister would love that" (and he's always right, because he pays close attention to those he loves). The cost of the gift, whether a little or a lot, is immaterial, and Billy would truly rather give than receive—he always digs under the tree for the gifts he's giving to distribute first.

The second quality Billy has is a deep concern for the feelings of other people. He has a kind nature, and I cannot remember ever hearing a malicious word leave his mouth. When anyone in the family travels, Billy calls to be sure we arrived safely. And when someone has a problem, is ill, or has died, Billy's sincere sympathy is heartwarming.

Billy's natural, abiding faith in God and love of church is the third quality I admire in him. He always *wants* to go, as opposed to our feelings often that we'd rather do something else but *ought* to go to church.

And the last, most wonderful and enviable trait Billy reveals is a contentment with his home, his work, his family. He accepts his retardation not with resignation, but with aplomb. He has a routine at home that looks so peaceful to me, and he'll smile and say to me with a happy sigh, "I *like* my life."

ANTICIPATION OF THE FUTURE

There are serious issues in the future. The family has scattered and started families of their own—families whose needs must come before mine and Billy's. There is the age-old question of who will care for him if something happens to me. We have planned the best we can; we have provided for Billy financially; he has skills that, with supervision, should enable him to continue his contented life. But who will supervise him? Who will provide his transportation? What if he loses his job? Who will be his aggressive, persistent advocate? I find myself thinking, as many parents of persons with disabilities have thought before me, that it would be easier if I outlive him. These are issues that we can't laugh about, or shrug off.

The next 5 years are unpredictable as far as my husband's condition is concerned. His health is gradually declining; we see people in the nursing home who are on support systems and know we don't want that for Bill. I wonder how Billy will react to this gradual change and to the possibility of the death of his father.

Since my grandchildren are spaced far apart, I see a particularly sad situation reoccurring. I am reminded of the time our oldest grandson asked Billy to read a story to him and exclaimed, "You are 18 years old and you can't read!" There are more explanations in the future as our younger grandsons become aware of Billy's difficulties with seemingly simple tasks. Hopefully they will also become aware of his strengths.

My greatest fear of the future is the one that all of us have: I don't know what to expect! And, in viewing my past, I'm glad.

FUTURE RESEARCH DIRECTIONS

In approaching the subject of future research directions on cognitive coping, I find that I have many questions based on our experiences with Billy—questions that have implications for research.

1. *Can cognitive coping strategies be taught to some families by investigating the strategies of others?* The inclusion of family members in discussions concerning cognitive coping skills is certainly a start in the right direction. In talking with other parents, it is clear that strategies differ with different family styles. Could knowledge about various aspects of individual family life enable researchers, service providers, and educators to match cognitive coping strategies to particular families?

2. *Can family members who have developmental disabilities learn to use cognitive coping strategies to solve their own problems?* We have seen Billy adapt to so many situations, without help, that I feel sure he could be taught to use more sophisticated strategies. For example, in singing rhymes, he is a beat behind the rest of us, catching the words without being able to read. There are so many things he doesn't understand. From my conversations with him, I would envision the following questions as candidates for cognitive coping: Why can't I drive a car? Why can't I get married (Mary is younger than I am)? He needs strategies to deal with being overweight, with prejudice, and with understanding the changes in the family.

3. *How can the professional level of those dealing with adults who have developmental disabilities be raised? Why can we not expect the same legal*

requirements, the same standards of quality, the same accountability, for adults *that we expect for our* children *who have disabilities?* Our experiences with agencies dealing with adults who have developmental disabilities have been frustrating and unsuccessful. When Billy began working at the library, where he has worked for 12 years, he was trained by a staff member from the sheltered workshop. At that time, he also worked at the workshop on a part-time basis. He began to be dissatisfied with his workshop experience, and wanted to quit. I told him that it was his decision, and asked why he wanted to leave there. He responded in a way that told the story: "I tired of playing bingo."

Our experience with group homes was equally frustrating. Billy's last placement was in substandard housing, with limited supervision. We removed him from the program when we found he had no heat during a severe cold spell. The agencies involved were angry with us for leaving the program.

These experiences occurred over a decade ago, and I realize that a number of positive changes have been made. However, as I visit programs for adults who have developmental disabilities, I am aware that we still do not have the same standards, the same salaries, and the same expectations that we have for school-age children.

4. *What help is there for families who choose to be their own case managers? How can such help be made available in sparsely populated areas?* As we have dealt with the problems of transition, work, and independent living, we have had to search for answers. For example, it was years before we realized that Billy qualified for Social Security, which pays more than Supplemental Security Income, and that he could have help with his rent through the Department of Housing and Urban Development. We stumbled across these resources, and could have benefited from assistance in discovering and implementing them earlier.

CONCLUSION

As a family, we believe that Billy has been a positive influence in our lives. From the day we discovered his developmental disability, we have been forced to analyze our problems and to seek immediate solutions. We have found that there are elements in our lives that we can't help, alter, or control. But we do believe that anything can be accomplished once understanding sets you free to deal directly with a situation.

ABOUT THE AUTHOR

Jane B. Schulz, Ed.D. My professional goals and achievements have closely paralleled the growth and development of my family. Because I returned to college when my youngest child started school, my education entailed a total family commitment. During this time I acquired a number of coping strategies that have served me well in later years. As a professor in special education at Western Carolina University, my chief teaching and consultation focuses have been in the areas of mainstreaming and professional–family collaboration. Since my retirement, I have continued to teach part-time and to be an advocate for persons with disabilities.

chapter 3

A "Normal" Life
for Hannah
Trying To Make It Possible

Evelyn Lusthaus and Charles Lusthaus

As parents of four children with very special needs, we have enjoyed preparing this chapter. It has been most interesting to actually think about the ways we have tried to cope with our family stresses and to put these ideas into words. The last few years have been extraordinarily challenging—even brutally difficult at times—and often, we haven't coped very well at all! So it has been enjoyable to think about how we DO cope. In this chapter, we try to articulate several of the ways we have thought about our children and our family's circumstances that have enabled us to move from crisis to family stability, health, and functioning.

Just a word about our family's make-up before we turn to our coping strategies. Our two oldest children, ages 18 and 15, are adopted by us: our son Peter when he was 5 years old, and our daughter Rebecca before she was 1 year old. They each had extremely traumatic experiences and a great deal of disruption in their backgrounds before joining our family, and they have faced many difficult challenges in their growth, development, and adjustment.

Our two youngest children, ages 13 and 10, are both girls. Our 13-year-old daughter Hannah is the focus of this chapter, because she was born with a developmental disability; and our 10-year-old daughter Sarah was born without any labels whatsoever, but she struggles to find her rightful place among siblings with very intense needs.

We have identified six approaches to living that we have used that have played a role in helping our family's well-being. These might be considered cognitive coping strategies. The first four strategies are those we have used throughout the years; the last two are newer to us, and are strategies we anticipate we will need more as we move into the future.

CURRENT STRATEGIES

Being "Normal"

On Saturday morning, May 25, 1991, our daughter Hannah stood on the pulpit of our synagogue and recited her Bat Mitzvah. She conducted herself with grace, dignity, and joy, and she did an absolutely splendid job in reciting her blessings and prayers. Everyone in the synagogue was touched with the sense of her gifts, her ability to have grown so beautifully, her capacity to persevere and work hard, her courage, and her success.

As we watched Hannah with great pride and joy, we thought back to the time when she was born. She had been extremely sick and weak, unable to suck or move, diagnosed as having Down syndrome, placed into intensive care, fed through a tube, thought to be profoundly mentally handicapped. The memory of those first days and weeks in the hospital will always be with us. Yet, although she was born with severe impairments, Hannah has grown slowly and painstakingly into a healthy, vibrant, loving child. Now, 13 years later, she was standing tall and proud, reciting her Bat Mitzvah, just like children of Jewish descent from generations past and for generations to come.

In having a Bat Mitzvah, Hannah did what is normal for girls her age in our Jewish culture, and her Bat Mitzvah symbolizes for us the most important strategy that we have used in adjusting to having a member with a developmental disability: that is, to think of her as "normal" and to give her the opportunity to live normally. She is a normal member of our family, she goes to normal school, she plays normal baseball, she likes normal hockey, and swims in a normal pool—she is just *normal*.

In our family, we have a normal, though hectic, lifestyle: We work, go on trips, have other kids, get tired, have fun, lose our temper, make friends, and just try to be normal. We try to keep a normal family, with a normal routine and a normal rhythm. We have normal good times and normal bad times, normal fun going out together, and normal arguments over bedtime! Hannah is not the center of our family; she's just a normal member.

By thinking of ourselves and our family and Hannah as normal, we do not mean to say that her developmental disability does not present difficulties or challenges—but we choose to think that it's normal for childrearing to present challenges. Just talk to any parents—they will tell you that parenting is a complex task!

Also, by thinking of ourselves and Hannah as normal, we do not mean to imply that we ignore the fact that Hannah has special needs. When Hannah goes to a regular class, for example, we expect her and the teacher to get extra help. When she needs support, or a tutor, or some assistance making friends, we try to get these needs met. So normal doesn't mean being the same. In fact, it's normal to be different.

In sum, the foremost strategy we have used in adjusting our family to having a child with a developmental disability is to think of her as a normal person, and to think of our particular situation as a part of normal living. We try to create the circumstances that enable her to be fully involved and included in every aspect of everyday life. Fundamentally, we believe that she is entitled to a normal life, and that her best chance for having a normal life in the future is to have a normal life in the present.

Getting Help

We also think that we (as a whole family) are entitled to a normal life, and we have learned that in order to achieve this, we have to ask for help.

In raising our children, we have needed help along the way from social workers and therapists, from friends and family. We have learned to say we don't know answers and that we can't do everything ourselves, and to ask for and get help.

From the very beginning of Hannah's life, we have needed support. The first help came from close friends, who stood by us when we were in a great deal of pain; and also from a nurse, who taught us how to feed and take care of our baby. As the years passed, we got help from early intervention specialists, teachers, and therapists. When it was time to get Hannah into school, we had help from a parents' group and from friends who encouraged us. When we have had problems in the family, we have had help from family therapists and individual counselors, and we still continue to have family and individual counseling.

Now, as Hannah graduates from sixth grade in a regular school, we are gratefully accepting help from some professionals within our school system who have advocated for her to be able to go on to regular high school. They are carrying out our dream for Hannah to attend a normal high school, a dream that has become their own dream.

Of course, not everyone's attempt to help has been helpful. Some advice from friends and professionals has been devastating and destructive. We have had family members and doctors who told us to institutionalize our daughter, school administrators who wouldn't accept her into their school, teachers who only saw her limitations and told us she didn't belong with other children, and therapists who blamed us for our difficulties and our children's problems.

In seeking help, we have learned the importance of the number "one"—the fact that one single helpful person in a situation is often all that is needed. When we were fighting to get Hannah into our local elementary school, there was no one in the system who would support us; literally everyone said it was impossible. After months of meeting with some school officials, and having them tell us that we were completely unrealistic to think our child could go to school with the other children on the block, we felt very discouraged and very angry. Evelyn stopped into the school one day and on her way out, a teacher approached her. "Are you the mother trying to get your daughter into school?" she asked. "Well," she said, "I can't wait to be your daughter's teacher. I hope I will see her next year." In those lonely first days of pressing for change, one person gave us the hope and encouragement to go on.

In all, during 15 years of childrearing, we have needed help in almost every aspect of raising our family, and we have become accustomed to asking for it and expecting it.

How is asking for help a cognitive strategy? Perhaps it lies in the way we have changed our thinking about our need for help: Rather than seeing this as a sign of weakness or incapacity, we now view it as a normal part of life. And so, again, we return to the concept of normal living. It's normal to give and receive help. In our case, we have asked for and received a lot; we also have given a lot. But in order for us to cope, we have had to learn to think that it is fine to ask and receive.

Remembering We Can Cope

In the midst of stress, when feeling discouraged and defeated, we talk over the progress that we have made, and remind each other that we have been through stressful times before, that we can and will cope. We bring to mind the difficult situations we have encountered, and remember the fact that we have faced them and managed to get through them.

We try to reframe our thinking from "Oh no, here we are again, won't we ever be done with crises!" to "Okay, we have been here before, what can we bring from our past experience to have this situation resolved as easily as possible?" Stress has been interwoven into the fabric of our family's functioning (or malfunctioning). Thus, when we face stressful situations, we remember the fact that we DO have skills to deal with the stress, so let's use them! This way of reframing the problem seems to help our family's well-being, for it reinforces our capacity to cope with our situation.

Recently, we faced a pile-up of stresses. Our 18-year-old son, Peter, who has a chronic illness, was extremely ill and was admitted to the hospital. We were terribly worried about him. At exactly the same time, our 15-year-old daughter, Rebecca, who had been away at a private school, had a crisis and was sent home by the school for the remainder of the school year. At exactly the same time, our 13-year-old daughter, Hannah, was rejected from the high school that we thought she would be attending. We had worked so hard to find an appropriate school. We had so much hope. And now we were told the teachers and staff didn't want her there!

The stress was pressing in on us. It was a terrible time, but we had been in these places many times before, and we knew we could manage—not easily—but we knew we could. We called on people to help us, and they did. We have learned that one of our greatest stress reducers is the knowledge that there are people and resources, including our own experience, to help us through the crisis times. We try to reframe the message of "We can't cope" to "We can cope."

Celebrating Our Child's Gifts

When we feel particular stress about Hannah and her struggles, we look back over the tremendous progress she has made, remembering the positive qualities she has brought to us and others, and this strengthens us.

We had a wonderful experience the evening before Hannah's Bat Mitzvah that brought home to us the joy and the gift that she has been to our family and to others. It is customary in our synagogue, that the evening before the Bat Mitzvah, the family of the Bar or Bat Mitzvah child attends the Friday night services. At the service that Friday evening, a family had brought their new-born baby for a baby-naming ceremony. The rabbi called the parents to the pul-pit with their baby, and with them were both sets of grandparents and even one set of great-grandparents. Everyone was enthralled to see this precious, healthy baby being named and blessed.

The mother spoke this prayer, a universal hope of parents for their children:

> Give us, O God, the wisdom, courage, and faith to raise our child to be a strong and compassionate and loving person. Bestow your blessing on our child. May she learn all that is good and beautiful and true to be a blessing to society and joy to our family.

As we heard this prayer, we were filled with joy—for we realized that, in her 13 years, Hannah had fulfilled this hope. She had grown into a person of compassion and love, and she contributed to her society, and she most certainly was a source of joy and pride to our whole family and the community. It was a moment of gratitude for us, as we realized that our daughter—whom society so often thinks of as a burden or a tragedy—had already, at age 13, fulfilled the hopes and dreams that all parents hold for their sons or daughters.

Letting Go of Fear

We are learning to have faith in our daughter's ability to adapt to life's hard-ships, to survive them, and to enjoy her life!

When a child is born with a serious developmental disability, it is normal, yes, inevitable, that parents will worry about the future. How will she survive? What will happen to her? How will she cope with the hardships of life in a complex, competitive world?

As the years pass, we are learning to reframe our fear of Hannah's future into a recognition that she is able to cope with her life and its hardships. Time and time again she has shown us that she is a person capable of living life with enjoyment, and that our fears are useless burdens to all of us! A few examples follow.

When Hannah was 4 years old, she wandered away from the house, and we were frantic looking for her. We worried that maybe she'd been hit by a car or fallen into a neighbor's pool. We searched the neighborhood well, and when we called the police for their help, we found that she was at the police station, happily typing away on their typewriter. Our panic was unfounded.

Several years later, when Hannah began second grade, Evelyn met with the teacher, and then came home and cried her heart out. The woman had nothing but terrible things to say about our daughter! We worried, how will Hannah ever survive this year? This teacher will destroy her self-confidence. But Hannah had an "alright" year, not unlike most of the children in the class;

she learned to adjust to a critical, fault-finding teacher, as did the other children. She showed us she's not so fragile; she showed us that our fears were unnecessary.

This year, in sixth grade, some classmates started calling her mentally retarded. Hannah was sad; she felt rejected and came home crying. We thought, "Okay, this is finally 'it'; it's too much for her!" But Hannah herself went to the principal at school to complain, learned to stay away from the kids who were giving her a hard time, found another group of kids to play with at recess time, and ended up enjoying her year at school thoroughly. She shows us time and time again that she can adapt—she recognizes and feels the pain at times, but she can and will carry on.

We are learning that our fears for her are not helpful in any way—in fact, they are a burden to her and to us. Of course, we do the best we can to plan for her future. But we want to change the way we think about her future. We want to learn to think in ways that enhance her well-being; in other words, we want to learn to think of her as a person with the capacity to adapt and to enjoy life.

Now, as she moves on to high school, we are choosing our way of thinking: Will we worry about her possible rejection and isolation, creating an additional stress for her? No. Instead, we are trying to have confidence in her and are trying to support her in taking her risks and living her life. She tells us, "Don't worry, be happy," and we are trying to learn.

Being Kind to Ourselves and Accepting Our Own Limits

As we continue to raise our children through their adolescence, we have begun to realize our own need to take time for rest and respite, to build in much-needed time for ourselves. We have tired ourselves out trying to nurture and raise our children and we need to take time to nurture ourselves as well. We're learning our energy is finite and our bodies and spirits have to be replenished. We're depleted. We have to "take in" now.

Fifteen years ago, we were young and energetic—we felt we wanted to change the world and we thought that we could! We were blind to our own limitations and our own needs! We embarked on a journey that was more difficult than we ever expected; now, we are more aware of what we can and cannot do. We are learning to accept ourselves and our own limitations.

As we continue to grow as a family, we are realizing that our family's health and well-being requires that we invest time and acceptance into ourselves and each other. We're learning to say to ourselves and to each other, "We're doing the best we can," and to let it rest at that.

NEXT 5 YEARS

This is the beginning of the next 5 years, as Hannah moves from elementary to high school, which spans a 5-year period from grades 7 to 12 in our home province of Quebec, Canada. What cognitive coping strategies do we anticipate will be important in adjusting to this period?

We will need to learn to think of our daughter as an adolescent, with her own tastes, preferences, dreams, and desires. She will want to live like the adolescents in her high school, "hanging out," dating, and driving! How realistic will this be? How will we have the wisdom to guide her lovingly through the turbulent period of teen-age years? We are grateful for the experiences we have already had with our other children, for the lessons we have already learned about parenting during this period (and we could never learn enough!). But what role will her disability play in her emerging concept of herself as a young woman living in this society? What will be the implications for her, of being a pioneer, of being a "handicapped" student integrated into a "normal" high school? We simply do not know the answers, and we would benefit from the reflections and experiences of others whose children have already made this passage.

We are concerned about the kind of coping strategies she will need to use to adjust to the inevitable challenges of her high school years. We have been impressed beyond measure with her capacity to adapt and adjust and to "make her way." Will the skills she has already developed be adequate for the next 5 years? How can she learn means of finding new skills when she needs them? Who will be her mentors? Who will be her advocates? How and when will she learn to advocate on her own behalf?

During all of Hannah's life, our own clear vision of her role in her family, school, and community has enabled us to advocate for her and cope with difficulty. We have had our eyes on our goals about her full inclusion! But now we must learn to shift, such that we are sensitive to *her* vision and *her* goals. What does *she* want for herself? What is important to *her*? How does *she* want to live? How do we listen well enough so that we can hear her ideas, and how does she learn to speak for herself? Perhaps these questions are no different from the ones asked for any child who is entering adolescence . . . .

RESEARCH DIRECTIONS

Research questions that seem interesting to us include the following:

How do people cope? What role does cognitive coping play in an individual's overall coping or adjustment process? What are the cognitive coping skills people use? How do people develop their cognitive coping skills? What are the family, personality, cultural, developmental, and other contextual factors that affect the extent to which people develop and use cognitive coping skills?

Can cognitive coping skills be taught? If so, under what circumstances? For example, are they best taught before, during, or after a crisis? By whom are they best taught? Are they best taught by professionals? Peers? Other family members or friends? What is the role of parent-to-parent support in developing cognitive coping skills in family members?

Focusing particularly on people labeled as having intellectual disabilities, how do they cope? Is the way they develop cognitive coping skills different from nonlabeled people? What skills do individuals labeled as having mental retardation use to cope, adjust, and advocate for themselves? How do they learn these skills? Can these skills be taught? By whom? For example, what is the role of self-advocacy groups, such as People First, in transmitting these skills to others? What is the role of family members, friends, professionals in the development of coping skills among people who are labeled?

CONCLUSION

In conclusion, it has been fascinating to reflect on our own family experience in light of the concept of cognitive coping. This is not a concept we have thought about previously in a conscious way.

In preparing this chapter, we have been struck once again by the recognition that our family is a complex system, as are all other families. We have our times of great joy and victory, as well as our moments of frustration and despair. We have periods when we are managing well the stress of living with children who have very special needs, and other periods when we are not coping well at all.

And yet, as we meet other families, families who don't have children with labels, we find that all families seem to go through these periods of strengths and difficulties. In seeing this, we are reinforced in our belief that our most potent strategy for enhancing the health and well-being of our family is to think of ourselves and our child with a developmental disability as "normal" and to lead a normal life. The cognitive strategies we have chosen have assisted us in meeting this goal. As we look to the future, we hope that our daughter Hannah and all of our family members will learn effective strategies that empower her to lead a normal life. We look forward to learning more from others on how the process of cognitive coping can contribute toward making this goal a reality.

ABOUT THE AUTHORS

Evelyn Lusthaus, Ph.D., and Charles Lusthaus, Ph.D.   We are both professors in the Faculty of Education at McGill University. Charles's interests lie in the management of educational organizations in Canada and in the developing world. I work in the field of special education, focusing on issues of educational reform and inclusive schooling. We have each worked extensively in family advocacy, community development, and community integration. Our work has been enriched by personal experiences with our children and by relationships with individuals who have disabilities and their families.

chapter 4

On Belonging
A Place To Stand, A Gift To Give

Janet Vohs

Before I begin, I would like to offer a few words on the definition of cognitive coping and the focus of this chapter.

On the definition of cognitive coping: I have adopted the definition of cognitive coping as presented by the editors of this book and have focused, therefore, specifically on ways of *thinking* that "enhance a sense of well-being." Using that definition, I would say that cognitive coping has been the empowerment strategy par excellence in my life. Interestingly, the very notion of coping is one to which I have given considerable thought. To me, that word has always connoted a sense of putting up with, or enduring, an undesirable situation. I personally decided many years ago that the possibility of a life gauged against a standard of coping as the highest value did not inspire me. So, while I accept the definition and the notion that our thinking about a situation is the ultimate avenue for empowerment, I find the choice of the word *coping* unfortunate. This thought is explored further in my chapter.

On my family: Jessica is my only child, and we have always lived together as a single parent and child. Although we usually have lived with a few housemates, some of whom we have come to consider family, we have lived alone for the past 6 years. Jessica's father and my parents and siblings live quite a distance away. Although they provide a valuable extended-family context, the actual contact is by telephone and annual visits. Therefore, for the purpose of this chapter, I have taken the liberty of focusing on myself and Jessica and the kind of thinking that has empowered us.

BACKGROUND

I sometimes think of my experience of being Jessica's mother as having my own personal guru—or maybe I should say cognitive coping coach—for the past 20 years. Our relationship, in which we have been both student and teacher to each other, has given me a distinct vantage point from which to consider the whole notion of cognitive coping. The coping strategies I have invented, learned, or discovered are, in themselves, of less interest and usefulness in many ways than the vantage point itself: It is that perspective for which I would like readers to have some appreciation before going on to specific strategies.

My decision to devote attention to what I think of as the background or underlying principles was fortified by a story about Tom Peters, the celebrated business management leader, teacher, and author of such books as *Passion for Excellence, Pursuit of Excellence,* and *Thriving on Chaos.* There was an investigation into why Peters's ideas, which had proven to be so successful in the companies with which he studied and worked closely, seemed to be having minimal long-term impact on the larger business world. The authors concluded that widespread adoption of Peters's ideas over time was hindered because managers were too eager to pick up these tips and lay them on top of entrenched management structures without adopting the underlying principles of which the tips were merely the most superficial expression.

For myself, I have always viewed tips, even the most benign, as a sort of tyranny imposed from the outside—another piece of advice, which, if I were *really* committed, or good, or cared at all, I would follow. But mostly they occurred for me as an imposition, another burden: "What, now I have to be funny, too!" Or, "Oh, no! Don't tell me I have to be good to myself! I'm all out of energy for taking care of anyone, even if it is me." Without an empowering set of background assumptions, tips might work for awhile, but seldom have the power to make any real difference. When I review my history with Jessica, what I have appreciated most along the way have been those thoughts that have had the power to alter me, the thinker—thoughts that have enabled me to generate my own tips and principles from the opportunity to see the world from a new vantage point. Before I go on to specific thinking strategies, I would like to share a couple of these major shifts in perspective because they do provide the background from which all the rest of my thinking derives its power.

Shift I: The Private World

When Jessica was diagnosed with cerebral palsy at age 1, I knew something bad, really terrible, had happened. I was very confused, upset, and scared. I personally did not have to make up the interpretation about the badness or wrongness of the situation. It was something everyone knew, a given: To be disabled or to have a child with a disability is a tragedy. Of course, by the time she was a year old, I was also *hopelessly* in love with her. And, from early in Jessica's infancy, I was committed to having a life of joy. This new information about Jessica did nothing to diminish my love or my commitment; it meant that now I would just have to be in love and committed in spite of this situation. It was as if the "in spite of" translated into a permanent little dark cloud or shadow under which I would have to live and with which I would have to cope.

I can still remember the moment—Jessica was around 2½—when I became aware of this little cloud and its attendant mood of sadness. Nothing extraordinary was going on, it was just a quiet afternoon. The immediate justification for the mood was, "Of course I am sad. This is a terrible situation. Jessica has cerebral palsy." Almost simultaneously came a question about what *exactly* was the matter. I asked myself if anyone was in pain or was suffering and instructed myself to observe what actually was happening. I looked at Jessica. I saw a beautiful toddler, happily playing, grinning, and cooing. It was a warm spring day. I checked myself out—I felt good, I had friends, we had food, shelter. We were comfortable. Neither of us was suffering at that moment.

Yet there was the sadness and it was connected to the fact that Jessica had cerebral palsy. Since no one up to that time had been able to give me a coherent description or definition of cerebral palsy and what this condition might really mean for Jessica, I did not have dire predictions of the future to deal with other than a generalized notion that she would be disabled. In looking a little deeper into the cause of the sadness, what I saw was that the disability meant something, and it was the meaning, not the actual disability, that caused me sadness. One of the meanings was that this was a situation that really should not be the way it was, that in and of itself it was wrong.

In the exercise of looking at what actually was going on and separating it from the interpretation I had about what it meant, amazingly the sadness dissolved. Was it possible that suffering was not an inevitable correlate of having a disability or a child with a disability? I did not really believe it, but I was willing to suspend my disbelief long enough to consider and entertain the possibility. At the time, *merely* asking the question, a simple unassuming act of cognition, cracked the solid wall of reality that I had previously accepted as the truth: Disability equals tragedy, a life of sadness and coping as best one can with this terrible reality.

When I reflect on what thoughts made the most difference to me in my own growth with Jessica, what stands out the most was the first occurrence of the notion that maybe the suffering was not necessary. What that thought allowed me to do was to begin to *observe* what was actually going on in the world rather than in my head. While there was not an instantaneous change of behaviors or beliefs, I began to cultivate the view that disability was a natural part of life, that there was nothing inherently wrong with having a disability.

As I was able to define disability as a legitimate part of ordinary life, I became freer to interact with Jessica and her disability separate from the impulse to try to make her better. Suffering over the fact of a disability eventually became totally inconsistent with the idea that Jessica was whole and complete. (Obviously this thinking opened up whole new problems, such as how to motivate myself to continue doing therapies and other exercises that seemed to reinforce the notion that something was wrong. The idea of goals as stemming from personal visions and values, as a delightful way of participating in life's unfolding, not rooted in the need to adapt to or right a wrong, was a whole other language I had not even begun to hear or invent for myself. More on this subject later.)

The point here is that suffering arose from a background assumption of what it meant to have a disability, namely that something was wrong and should not be the way it was. Learning simply to identify or notice these assumptions as assumptions is a way to pull the presuppositional rug out from under thoughts and interpretations that result in suffering, and is a major cognitive coping strategy. *It allows one to separate the world or whatever is happening from the interpretation or meaning ascribed to it.* It also opens the door to the possibility of inventing or choosing new descriptions and interpretations, ones that may be more personally empowering.

Shift II: Us and the World

The next assumptional axis shift had to do with our place in the larger society, beginning with my own immediate family. I pretty much felt that my acceptance of Jessica was a private matter, and that the world, although I expected it to be "nice," did not necessarily share my view. Therefore, I had two strategies (really two sides of the same strategy): I would try as much as possible to be around only people whom I felt confident shared my view of Jessica. And, I was determined *not* to be around folks who saw us as tragic. Unfortunately, that included my family, most professionals, and just about everyone else I knew. In a valuable piece of coaching, one of my friends offered the suggestion that the world—in particular, my family—would accept Jessica to the extent that I did. An interesting paradox, that a possible measure of my love and acceptance of Jessica could be the degree to which she was accepted by the world. (What made this piece of advice so "listenable" to me, by the way, was that I knew this person absolutely adored Jessica and me and she offered it more as a hint than as advice that I should follow.)

This possibility presented a challenge that I found a bit more daunting. For me, it was one thing to feel some power with regard to my own personal acceptance of Jessica, but quite another to begin asking others for a place in the world. When I asked myself what exactly was so scary, there seemed to be a lot more charge to this little black cloud than to the other one: I was afraid of the shame and embarrassment my family would feel and of their rejection. I did not have those feelings of shame and embarrassment myself (or so I thought), but I assumed and felt that they did.

My own personal history with my family had a crucial impact: As a 1½-year-old, I was hospitalized for 18 months for traction and surgery to correct dislocated hips. My parents were discouraged from visiting because, according to the nurses, the only time I was distraught was when they came. In order not to hurt me, they stopped visiting. By the time I came back home at age 3, there was my older brother; a new sister half my age whom I had never met (and who, my parents say, played a major role in teaching me to speak once I came home); a new baby due any day; a mother overwhelmed with the stresses of parenthood, and probably broken-hearted over what had happened to me; and a dad in the Air Force who had been transferred to another city. I was essentially going home to a new family that already had its fill of stresses. Once my belonging was broken by being gone for so long and by what I interpreted as a weak welcome home, I never felt as though I belonged. In fact, in my 3-year-old mind, I was convinced there was something *really wrong with me* that made me not "belongable." As I grew up, my outsider stance was reinforced by a family ethos that preached independence; in the family context, there was really nothing wrong with being "unbelongable" except that I was miserable.

In my young adulthood before Jessica, it was obvious to me that I should definitely limit my world to places where I was accepted and, therefore, belonged. Needless to say, I was pretty much of a loner. I would have rather lived isolated than face being rejected or having Jessica be rejected.

Viewing myself as Jessica's primary ambassador to the world, however, meant I had quite a job to do to love and accept myself and deal with my own issues of belonging. I had learned early on to "cope" by becoming deeply resigned to the fact of my own unworthiness. Being Jessica's ambassador meant reconstituting myself as a valued member of my own family, as a person who belonged in the world. One does not undertake lightly re-creating oneself, nor does one accomplish it without pain. It was the desire and commitment to create a place of belonging in the world for Jessica that made loving and caring for myself a project worth bothering about. I could no longer afford the outsider stance; I had had my fill of coping, and of the misery of not belonging. My commitment, inspired by my love for Jessica, was that we would be happy, dammit.

Although I did not know how to do this, I had heard and read a little about transactional analysis and the idea that we each have a child who is still part of us. I began immediately to take on the role of parenting myself and of telling my "child" self that I loved her, that she was beautiful, that, most of all, she belonged—all the things I wanted to make sure Jessica had as part of her self-image. In the process, I discovered that I longed to hear those words myself. I gave myself the power to love myself. I "pretended" I was big and strong and could do that. And the stand "I belong" gained power in the saying of it, and as the child part of myself believed me and looked up to me, she empowered me even more.

Creating a place for me to stand called "I belong" caused a major shift in the world. Neither my parents nor Jessica changed. My fundamental belief about who I was shifted and *that* altered the way I saw the world. Standing up for Jessica became a natural, although not always easy, extension and expression of my stand for my own absolute belonging. I have found my family to be deeply feeling, accepting, and loving. I am also much more free to ask that Jessica be included when I feel she is being left behind.

I am convinced that the issue of belonging is at the heart of the considerable pain there is in relation to disability, and is probably close to the heart of what it is to be a human being today. Yet belonging is hardly ever acknowledged as an issue. The urgency of my desire to have a happy life forced me to give myself the gift of belonging. In the process, I discovered that we *do* have the power to bestow that gift on ourselves, and, in the process, to affirm the humanity and belonging of others.

NOW THE WORLD

Lao Tsu is said to have linked courage to love. I believe that it does take great love—of ideas, of people, of life—first, to perceive the possibility of a reality not expressed in the common-sense view of the world, and second, to question the accepted reality with courage. Jessica has granted me the gift of great love. The common-sense reality would have been for me to "accept" the tragic view: to care for her as a burden, to love her privately, but to accept the world's view of her as a defective little creature. My own early years of questioning and rejecting the common-sense assumptions about disability did require courage. But this was only a hint of the courage I imagine parents 30 or more years ago must have had, who, when advised, even ordered, to institutionalize their babies with disabilities, said, "No."

Obviously, if going into the world with a disability and insisting on a place, on belonging, requires courage, things in the world are not all that wonderful. Once I had arrived at the views that nothing was inherently wrong with Jessica, that the disability did not diminish her worth as a human being, and that nothing was wrong with me and that I was not "unbelongable," the tendency was to view the world as the place where things were wrong. Something had to be wrong somewhere.

A TV cooking class on making bread supplied an interesting metaphor that I have found useful for thinking about notions of disability in our society and where they come from. In fact, the anecdote has helped me think differently about what there is to cope with. In Europe, years ago, castles and homes were built with a small enclosed room used for making bread. Today, after generations of making bread in these rooms, it is unnecessary to add yeast to the bread dough. The yeast culture simply lives in the air and leavens any dough that happens to be placed there. For the most part, I have come to see our assumptions and presuppositions as invisible—like the yeast, part of the air we breathe. We do not consciously choose them or invent them: Philosophers have described them as "inherited." As I envision it, our "culture," instead of little yeast bacteria, is made up of millions of sentences, metaphors, and stories about life that we have learned to call true. And although the conditions that make the sentences and stories seem like the truth frequently change, they usually linger in the cultural atmosphere long after their usefulness has been exhausted.

Many people have traced the fear and hatred of people with disabilities to the eugenics movement, the desire to "perfect" the species through genetic control, that swept the country in the early decades of this century. As such, this prejudice has common roots with racism. I am convinced that the current social institutions, unfortunately, still reflect assumptions from that legacy. Even more insidious are the automatic inherited strains of that kind of thinking that still live in and are given expression in our culture. Others have noted that fear of "difference" is characteristic of primitive societies and that the conditions for tolerance and appreciation of diversity must be generated intentionally and nurtured.

In terms of sheer survival, the automatic interpretation of disability as a tragedy was a reasonable response when gauged against a backdrop of a rugged frontier land or a time before we had the modern conveniences we take for granted now. I shudder to think of what life with Jessica would be like without indoor plumbing, electricity, roads and sidewalks, and health and family supports. But now—and I believe it *is* only a very recent phenomenon—we are lucky enough to live in a society based on democratic values and in a time of technological and material advancement that makes contribution and participation for people with disabilities a real possibility beyond what was previously even thinkable. However, like the rising loaves in the bread room, we also dwell in a cultural environment that has a profound effect on us. The sentences, or assumptions, we inherited about disability are part of an inappropriate and outmoded vocabulary.

An interesting research project reported in the July/August/September 1990 issue of the *Journal of Rehabilitation* illustrated the pervasiveness of the assumptions and how they affect our day-to-day perceptions. Entitled "Stresses as Perceived by Children with Physical Disabilities and their Mothers," the article examined the results of a study that compared the reports from 20 children with physical disabilities (ages 8 to 15) of what stressed them with their mothers' beliefs about what stressed their children. There was a wide gulf between mothers' and children's perceptions of what is stressful. With the exception of one response from one child, the children did not express concern about "being different" nor did they dwell on things they couldn't do. They were stressed most often by aversive events they *did* experience.

The mothers' concerns were with how their children differed from the norm, and they frequently identified the disability itself as the source of stress. Not surprisingly, this same perspective was shared by many of the professional helpers as the researchers learned that the study was begun:

Similarly, a group of medical and mental health professionals predicted that the research presented here would be a waste of time because "*everyone already knows* [italics added] that the disability itself is what causes the children's stress." Further, they believed that any stresses other than those arising from the physical difficulty itself would be trivial and unimportant. They speculated that the children, in particular, might fail to understand what is their "real" problem. (Tackett, Kerr, & Helmstadter, 1990, pp. 33–34)

I had a similar experience and revelation about Jessica. Not that long ago, I realized that I believe that Jessica must be sad not to be able to walk. So much a part of me was this belief that I didn't even really know I had it lurking there in the background. I just *knew* it was true. Since, like most parents, I hurt when my child hurts, there was an appropriate sadness that went with the thought. Once I became aware of the assumption, I thought I would ask her, but I was afraid to. I was so certain that not walking *must* be a source of pain for her that I felt it would be a cruelty to ask her, that the asking would call to mind her limitation and thus cause her pain. When I finally did summon the courage to ask, "Jessica, don't you wish you could walk?" her response was a nonchalant "No." When I asked why, she simply said, "I fall down." There was not a shred of suffering about it, or regret, or anything.

CREATING A NEW CULTURE

Going back to the bread room for a moment, it is easy to grasp the pervasiveness and inescapability of the "culture." At the same time, though, there is a hint of a very exciting possibility: Regardless of how much they are presented as true, the assumptions and presuppositions are only sentences. With regard to disability, the children in the study cited earlier seemed to grasp this reality much more profoundly than did the adults in their lives. They did not automatically attach stigma and suffering to the fact of a particular physical condition. Were they wrong not to do so? Were they deluding themselves or in denial? Were they unaware of what was "really wrong" with them, as suggested by the professionals?

Richard Rorty, professor of humanities at the University of Virginia, offered this thought on the relationship between the way things are and what we say *about* the way things are in his book *Contingency, Irony, and Solidarity* (1990): "Only *descriptions* [italics added] of the world can be true or false. The world on its own—unaided by the describing activities of human beings—cannot" (p. 5). Descriptions and interpretations of meaning are really the essence of what we are talking about when we say "cognitive coping." To separate the circumstance from the meaning associated with it is the first step. Next is to realize that the concern with the truth or falseness of what a situation means is not all that important or useful. What is useful is to ask whether the meanings we attach are empowering. Do they offer more freedom? Rorty wrote that "revolutionaries and poets of two centuries ago [began to realize that] . . . anything could be made to look good or bad, important or unimportant, useful or useless, by being redescribed" (p. 7). It is the sentences we say to ourselves about what things mean that make the difference. And sentences can be re-placed with new ones.

Realizing that we have some power to choose interpretations is empower-ing because it enables us to try on many different personal redescriptions. It also points to a way to have an effect on the kind of sentences that will make up the "bread-room bacteria" for future generations.

> The method is to redescribe lots and lots of things in new ways, until you have created a pattern of linguistic behavior which will tempt the rising generation to adopt it, thereby causing them to look for appropriate new forms of non-linguistic behavior, for example, the adoption of new scientific equipment or new social in-stitutions. (Rorty, 1990, p. 9)

There are many to whom it is still most obvious and "commonsensical" that loss and tragedy are inherent in disability, that the people so affected are truly outside the norm of what it is to be a full and complete human being, that they do not belong. To those who hold this view, the parents and others who do not are in what some label a *denial stage*. Or perhaps they are bravely or cleverly coping with this tragedy by concentrating on the so-called positive as-pects. (Of course, we all know that the only things needing a positive veneer or attitude are things that are really negative.)

It now seems to me that nothing could be more obvious and self-evident than that people differ from each other, that nature is full of variation, that het-erogeneity is the norm, and that chance and contingency could disable any of us at any time, that the vulnerability that comes with disability is a gift. A funda-mental belief about the tragic nature of the situation informs one world view. Acceptance of disability as a legitimate part of life informs another. The view that has disability as a tragedy is not "wrong"; neither is the other view "right." The accuracy or truthfulness of the view—whether it corresponds accurately to the real, inherent meaning—is not as interesting or fruitful a question to pursue as the question of whether the interpretation is useful or empowering. (Espe-cially since, if you take Rorty's [1990] perspective, there is no true inherent meaning!)

If disability is an ordinary part of life, there is no longer a need to *cope* with the obvious and inherent tragedy of disability. But that most certainly is not the vocabulary with which I began my adventure with Jessica, nor do I believe these assumptions are the ones our culture bestows on us simply by virtue of being born in a particular place and time. Not yet, anyway. Families, even if they have managed to invent or discover a new description of the situa-tion for themselves, are still living in a world of inherited meaning.

COPING

Coping can be empowering or disempowering. If the source of the problem is that *the person* is defective, coping, even at its best, can only convey a sense of putting up with a situation that is inherently bad and about which nothing really can be done. What one is left with is to be brave and courageous, or to find humor, or to adopt any number of other strategies to help deal with this unassailable fact. Since, obviously, most people with disabilities are not going to get magically fixed, and the source of the problem *is* the disability, all there is left to do is cope.

How can coping be empowering? The "cognition" about the possibility that maybe things are not wrong was ultimately empowering to me. It gave me a new freedom to act and participate more fully in actual, as distinct from feared or made-up, scenarios. I prefer to think of that kind of cognition as something other than coping. To be actually empowered, to cope because of a presuppositional shift, is very different from coping by resigning oneself to putting up with or enduring a miserable reality. When sailors and explorers thought the world was flat, they coped with that fact. That knowledge structured everything about how sailors thought and behaved. When word got out that the world was round, this news caused a shift in behavior and in people's perceptions of what was possible. The world did not change, but what was thought to be true about it changed and people went about sailing their boats very differently based on the fact that the world was round. I am interested in giving parents access to the kind of thinking that allows the "world" to change from flat to round.

Current Coping Strategies

1. *Be aware of the power of presuppositional meaning attached to a particular situation.* When I experience distress, I ask myself what meaning and significance I attach to the situation. The degree to which people have access to the assumptions that shape their world view determines the degree to which they are free to interact with varying situations.

2. *Identify what there is that I need to cope with.* What is the source of stress? Have I made a judgment that the situation is simply wrong and should not be the way it is? Is it that Jessica is not able to walk, or is it the flight of stairs that prevents access? If Jessica were already viewed as beautifully and perfectly human, if she really belonged and knew it, even if she had to face physical barriers every day, inside a vision of total belongingness and a commitment to making the world accessible, would that be a tragedy or an opportunity for committed action?

3. *Distinguish Jessica's experience of life from my own assessments of what her life must be like.* In other words, I try not to assume that I know how Jessica feels—instead, I ask her to tell me. This one deserves to be taken on as a discipline, with vigor.

4. *Don't worry so much about being right or wrong.* I trust myself and my instincts. I have substituted my concern for "truth" with a concern for freedom, self-expression, and participation.

5. *Try on a variety of interpretations for a situation.* Taking a victim stance is automatic—I am already familiar with what that perspective allows for. Sometimes I find it empowers me. Often we are victimized by the way society is organized. There are inequities; life is not fair. Given that reality, what is my commitment in the matter? I also like to try on other perspectives. Sometimes I pretend that, if I were God, what might I want to gain from things being the way they are? It's just a silly pretense, but sometimes it empowers me to try on all kinds of different perspectives, all sorts of meanings. If I hit on one that speaks to me, that enables me to act on things in a more powerful way, I keep it.

6. *Ask, "What am I building?"* For me, the answer is always something grand and glorious. My vision takes me back to the bread-room metaphor. If, even through my everyday actions and conversations, I can help change the "culture," if I can add strength and vitality to certain sentences and metaphors such that they replace the ones that make up the current environment, that possibility empowers me. I want to replace our current story about who belongs and who doesn't with a story of increasing willingness to live with plurality. My vision for an inclusive society extends way past my own and Jessica's lifetimes.

7. *In times of upset and stress, remind myself what it is I am committed to.* If I were not committed to belonging and participation as a natural part of Jessica's life, there would be no occasion for me to be upset when she was excluded or not respected as a valid participant. And so it goes for education, health, employment, and recreation. Seeing the upset as an expression of vision lets me first of all be upset when I am upset, and it provides powerful access to the vision.

8. *Be on the lookout always for ideas, thoughts, stories, and poems that empower me in designing a new view of the world.* The following are some that I have recently collected (Safransky, 1991, p. 40):

> One cannot be deeply responsive to the world without being saddened very often. [Seeing people left out, marginalized, or suffering for any reason is painful. Sadness is an appropriate response to that suffering and can be a powerful motivator.] —Erich Fromm

> It is slow, painful, and difficult for an adult to reconstruct a radically different way of seeing life, however needlessly miserable his preconceptions make him. —Peter Marris

> The greatest and most important problems of life are all fundamentally insoluble. They can never be solved but only outgrown. —Carl Jung

There are only two ways to live your life. One is as though nothing is a miracle. The other is as though everything is a miracle. —Albert Einstein

The reasonable man adapts himself to the world; the unreasonable one persists in trying to adapt the world to himself. Therefore, all progress depends on the unreasonable man. —George Bernard Shaw from "Reason," in *Maxims for Revolutionists*

Most Promising for Other Families

1. *Help families create a vision that empowers them*. These words are from a poem by Darrell Bolender, a father from Iowa (*Looking to the Future II*, 1991):

A Simplified Tale of An Ongoing Story

From family groups to conference gatherings,
Out of our uniqueness,
And unifying experiences
We create visions "Looking to the future."

Toward what future are we moving?
As parents of children with special needs,
We often hear,
Take it one day at a time.
The future, tomorrow,
Is many "one days" added
up to a today.
This day.

Tomorrow, the future,
The whole of what our children,
And families,
Will grow to be,
Is greater than just the sum of many days
Taken "one day at a time."

I love this poem's assertion of a wholeness beyond the constraints of what Shakespeare referred to as the petty, creeping pace of day-to-day living. It wasn't until I began to investigate contemporary management practices a few years ago that I even began to take the notion of vision seriously. I learned that what was characteristic of companies that had achieved incredible success was that they all had a vision from which they operated. I figured if Fortune 500 companies could make big bucks by having an empowering vision, it might be useful to me in generating my own wealth in terms of belonging and a network of support.

I agree with the poet that families of children with disabilities are not allowed—or at least not encouraged—to have a dream or a vision for their children's future. What the past has given as possible outcomes for people with disabilities is far less than inspiring. If all we have to look forward to is an extension of the past, I should think we would want to avoid the pain of that future as long as possible. But I have a motto: *Vision over visibility*. Having a vision is not just planning for a future we already know how to get to. It is daring to dream about what is possible.

It is one's vision that influences every detail. It is the vision that gives the tips. Creating a vision is very different from trying to follow tips. So many people start with the details—the day-to-day. One's intention, or vision, if it is powerful enough, automatically organizes his or her actions accordingly. What has helped me has been people asking me about my vision and encouraging me to talk about it. It can be true that even in the middle of the most dire circumstances, the vision can exist as a full and complete vision, as a possibility to be lived into. It is not something that will suddenly occur one day. It begins now, as a possibility to which one is devoted, and unfolds into the future as one takes action appropriate to the vision. One tip: Be ready for surprises!

2. *Learn to speak differently*. According to Rorty, "Speaking differently as opposed to arguing well is the chief instrument of social change" (1990, p. 9). In the area of disability we do need social change. We need to help create new possibilities for belonging and participation by how we speak about our dreams and visions of what is possible for our children and for society. People with differences have been marginalized in our country's imagination. We have made tremendous legal advances by focusing on a kind of speaking that emphasizes rights. Considerable grassroots advocacy efforts have helped ensure the right of all children with disabilities to an appropriate education alongside their peers without disabilities, a right that has been protected by federal legislation since the 1970s. With the passage of the Americans with Disabilities Act of 1990, there is now a federal law that guarantees the civil rights of people with disabilities and prohibits discrimination against them in all aspects of society. We are accustomed to encouraging parents to be strong advocates to stand up for their children's rights. Indeed, the conversation to further rights is basic and cannot ever be ignored. However, it does not allow the heart of the tale to be told. Perhaps the next era's unfolding will require parents to be strong poets and storytellers as well, helping to create communities where all belong.

Anticipated Future Stresses

The future is now. Jessica is 21, almost 22. Thanks to a lot of help from our friends, Jessica is no longer in a state school but is living on her own in the community and loving it. I had a meeting with the adult services agencies charged with Jessica's care. Some professionals and agencies are eager to help because they share the same vision of belonging. We are exploring and pushing the boundaries of the current system together. I have learned from the state rehabilitation agency that supported employment as practiced in my state is only available to people who will need it for up to 1 year. Furthermore, they do not consider people with mental retardation or severe disabilities their concern. This too shall change. I am interviewing business owners whom I know and asking them to consider the possibility of employing Jessica, and they have expressed a willingness at least to explore the possibility. The school system is contracting with an outside agency with a good record of success to create a job for Jessica and to support her in the long term. The state mental retardation agency has tentatively agreed to pick up the funding once the school year is complete and her entitlement to an education ends. There is a pervasive element of uncertainty and risk. Clearly we are making the path by walking it. Sometimes we bump into trees and brambles, and sometimes huge vistas open before us.

The sheer physical and mental effort required to make her life happen is enormous and stressful. Jessica has finally gotten an electric wheelchair, but it is impossible for us to get it into the apartment where we live because there are eight steps. It is a major effort simply to get her in and out of the house. Everywhere I turn, there are barriers.

There is no question that without the help of society, the sheer details of providing adequate care are overwhelmingly stressful. While life is not easy now, it is not more than I can bear. But it is possible that it could become so. The most effective form of cognitive coping with these tough realities is engaging in political and other forms of action that can help change unsuitable social structures. True access to equal opportunity for Jessica and many others must include accommodation and a range of supports. Yet even health care, a basic right in most industrialized countries, is a privilege in the United States of America. Preexisting condition clauses exclude people with disabilities from most health insurance plans. Also, for Jessica and others with severe disabilities, the new world of inclusion made possible by the ADA means nothing without the personal assistance they need simply to get up, get dressed, and get out of the door so that they *can* participate and contribute. Personal assistance of this nature should be part of basic health care. Our country's social policies, however, are designed such that billions of dollars go toward keeping people with disabilities restricted in nursing homes and institutions rather than making attendant services available. The latter would enable people to live and work in their own homes and communities.

People who have been excluded and stigmatized because of their difference need support to belong. They may need to be invited, to be shown hospitality, or simply to be viewed as regular people. Even though students with disabilities have a right to an education, the opportunity for an integrated education, where they can be truly part of their school communities, is still a rarity. People with disabilities generally say it is the attitudinal barriers that are the most oppressive. Unfortunately, I do not see these stresses vanishing any time soon.

FUTURE RESEARCH DIRECTIONS

People with disabilities regularly identify societal attitudes as the most potent and negative stressor in their lives. Yet, we still seem to lack powerful access to what it will take to alter those attitudes, or even much of a sense that they are alterable. There is a need to begin to explore the unknown, almost taboo arena of human relationships and the impact of difference. How do we shift these attitudes? How do we help families gain the tools they need to tell (and believe) a different story about disability and empower and ennoble themselves at the same time? How do we learn to speak differently about disability in such a way that our speaking will cause new social structures to take the place of the ones we have now? How do we all learn to tell the kind of stories that will help ameliorate differences and allow for a sense of belongingness? What would it take to equip professionals-in-training with a sense that learning to speak differently about disability is part of their job?

How can people with disabilities themselves play a role in rehabilitating our sense of community? Self-determination and self-definition go hand in hand. A worthwhile inquiry might be to ask what people with disabilities need to define themselves newly. Even more important, we should ask what it would take for everyone else to listen with new ears.

For ideas and stories that can help, we need to gain exposure. Perhaps we should conduct research, for example, on the effectiveness of television as a vehicle for transforming attitudes. What more can we learn by listening to people with disabilities themselves and by using every possible medium and forum for them to tell their own stories?

Even more than new research projects about what people think about disability, we need to give exposure to what we now know and have known for at least 20 years: People without disabilities usually have mistaken notions of what people with disabilities think and feel. We as parents and professionals committed to furthering the rights of citizenship for people with disabilities have a right to expect that the people working for them be aware of research findings that have a direct impact on the most critical issues of their lives.

The professionals who compared the mothers' and the children's perceptions in the research (Tackett et al., 1990) referred to earlier in this chapter thought it was irrelevant to inquire into what it was that caused the children stress—they already knew what the answer must be. One wonders how many questions are not asked because the answer is already supposedly obvious and self-evident. How much of what we "already know" do we know wrong?

CONCLUSION

On belonging, what empowers me every day is that I totally belong to Jessica and she to me. In that total handing over of my life to her, and in claiming her life for me in the utter, complete selfishness of all that, I find that I belong to the world. I find that state of being freeing and exhilarating. There is something about living at risk for one's dreams that, while certainly painful on occasion, is fun. I forget this all the time. Thanks for giving me the opportunity to remember.

ABOUT THE AUTHOR

Janet Vohs In addition to being the full-time mother of Jessica, I am the director of publications for the Federation for Children with Special Needs and editor of *The Coalition Quarterly: The Journal of the TAPP (Technical Assistance for Parent Programs) Project*, and *Newsline*, the Federation's regular newsletter. I am also involved in projects dealing with assistive technology, health care and school reform, transition and supported employment, and, in general, issues related to creating a society that works for everyone with no one left out. Jessica is now 21 years old and is integrated on a full-time basis at her local high school with a heavy focus on community-based supported employment. She also has her own two-bedroom apartment in the neighborhood in which she grew up. She pays rent with her SSI check and with assistance from Section 8, a federal rent subsidy program for people with low incomes. There are surprises—some thrilling, some terrifying—every day. But that's another story!

REFERENCES

Looking to the future II. (1991, February). [Conference brochure]. Fort Dodge: Iowa Parent to Parent, Iowa Pilot Parents.

Rorty, R. (1990). *Contingency, irony, and solidarity*. Cambridge: Cambridge University Press.

Safransky, S. (1991). Sunbeams. *The Sun: A Magazine of Ideas* (April), p. 40.

Tackett, P., Kerr, N., & Helmstadter, G. (1990, July/August/September). Stresses as Perceived by Children with Physical Disabilities and Their Mothers. *Journal of Rehabilitation*, pp. 30–34.

chapter 5

Beyond Chronic Sorrow
A New Understanding
of Family Adaptation

Corinne W. Garland

Ten minutes into the antics of the "Pink Panther," a neighbor appeared at my side, beckoning me away from my three children. It is some measure of the size of our town that I had not told anyone that we would be at the theater in search of distraction from the Thanksgiving dishes still piled in the kitchen and from the fact that my husband was already several minutes into a transatlantic flight.

"There's been a terrible accident," he said. ". . . a fire in your home."

"Thank God," I replied, leaving my friend baffled as I reframed the potentially devastating event—comparing the relative triviality of a house fire to the news of the airplane disaster I had, in that moment, anticipated.

It is clear that it is not life events but our perceptions of those events, filtered through our personal experiences, beliefs, and values, that give them meaning. The filtering process may be immediate, resulting in a *percept*—a split-second interpretation of the meaning of an event. Sometimes life gives us the opportunity to process more slowly, more slowly than we might like—to hold an object or event up for consideration in the light of our own cognitive schema or framework, to look for the place in which it might fit.

I have been privileged to stand beside many families as they have held the fact of a child's disability up for scrutiny in the light of their beliefs and values. I have watched fathers and mothers try to fit new information about an infant or toddler into an existing cognitive schema developed for the expected or "fantasy" child (Solnit & Stark, 1961). I have stood by as families have compared the caregiving and medical needs of their children to the perceived reality of their own resources and abilities, and have watched them cope. I have watched families modify their concepts in a Piagetian sense, assimilating and accommodating (Piaget, 1952), until new realities take on meanings with which families can live. For some families, this process of assimilation and accommodation, or *cognitive coping,* is repeated over time, with each new piece of diagnostic or developmental information, with each triennial eligibility meeting, with each medical crisis or unanticipated triumph.

The names of individuals discussed in this chapter have been changed.

Since most of my work has been with infants, toddlers, and preschool-age children, most frequently I see families who are just learning of the "difference in their families" (Featherstone, 1980). At this especially difficult time, many families are not yet coping cognitively, modifying feelings or understanding in order to lessen the negative impact of the diagnosis. Families whose children are in newborn intensive care units (NICUs) or are newly diagnosed with a developmental disability are, rather, engaging in daily struggles for survival. That they manage to get out of bed, dress and feed their other children, and meet numerous basic needs each day is testimony to their coping capacity. Other families have been engaged in struggles for survival long before the child with a disability entered the family. Such families continue their struggle with poverty, homelessness, and chronic underemployment or unemployment. For our work with those families, Maslow's (1970) theory of a hierarchy of human needs, beginning with basic needs for food, clothing, and shelter, provides more guidance than does the cognitive coping literature.

I remember a recently widowed father of 11, the youngest of whom had mental retardation. This man held his job, earned enough to provide food, shelter, and clothing for this family, and drank with regularity each night. I remember thinking that this was not an altogether bad coping strategy.

I developed a close personal relationship with Andrea, a mother whose preschool-age son and daughter both had profound physical and intellectual disabilities. Her preadolescent son was healthy and active; her husband had become seriously emotionally disturbed after the birth of the second child with disabilities. Andrea did 11 tube feedings a day for the two younger children, each taking 40 minutes. "Some days," she said to me, "I feel like taking both babies in my arms and walking into the river." I marveled that she did not.

Another mother of a terminally ill child with severe disabilities said:

> At first, I didn't know [how I felt], I just acted. When no support came during critical times, I did nothing. There were no silver linings and nothing funny about what I was faced with. The message from physicians was to wait for death. The stress was not knowing how long I could wait. We needed respite, or hospice, a visiting nurse to help with feedings. When that help did not come, our family just acted. We struggled to create our own care within the family, by trial and error, with little purposefulness, organization or focus . . . just anger at knowing there had to be a better way and that it was not available to us.

The same mother recently spoke at a state board hearing. She held up a sock, not 1½ inches from heel to toe.

> My son was so small, even at his death when he was three years old, that even newborn socks were too big. I could never find anything to fit him until these. Once I understood that my son's life would be so short, our family's goal became to make our life with him and our older child as normal as possible. But I had to keep looking for services the same way I looked for socks . . . because nothing fit our family.

EVOLUTION OF EARLY
INTERVENTION AND FAMILY COPING

When I reflect on the major milestones in early intervention related to family coping, I think of all the families who have had to search for services "that fit." Certainly for the first 10 of the 20 years I have worked in early intervention, programs were involved with designing and implementing a variety of strategies for families that professionals believed would be helpful and supportive. Only within the last 3–5 years has the notion of family-centered services (Chandler, Fowler, & Lubeck, 1986; Johnson, McGonigel, & Kaufmann, 1989; McGonigel & Garland, 1988; Shelton, Jeppson, & Johnson, 1987; Trivette, Deal, & Dunst, 1986) surfaced, profoundly changing the ways in which we interact with families to support and enhance their coping skills.

Professionals who began programs for preschoolers, infants, and toddlers in the late 1960s and early 1970s did so without a substantive body of literature to guide their early innovative efforts. The theoretical rationales on which such programs were based were, for the most part, limited to developmental theory governing interactions with children. Programs using developmental prescriptive, Piagetian, or behavioral approaches with children tried to design training programs for families that would give them the skills needed to use the same approach in teaching their children at home.

Initially, the theoretical base for work with families was influenced by the early work of Farber (1959, 1960), Olshansky (1962), Solnit and Stark, (1961), and others who described the negative impact of a child with a disability on the family. Kubler-Ross (1969) provided another theoretical framework for understanding the feelings of families of children with developmental disabilities. She offered an explanation—anger or denial—when families were less than excited at the prospect of carrying out the behavioral training programs designed for parents to use at home in the mid-1970s (Heward, Dardig, & Rossett, 1979; Kroth, 1975). Those whose training was psychoanalytic could easily apply an understanding of ego defense mechanisms to families who seemed to be rationalizing, substituting, or intellectualizing.

> If the parent is militantly aggressive in seeking to obtain therapeutic services for his child he may be accused of not realistically accepting the child's limitations. If he does not concern himself with efforts to improve or obtain services he may be accused of apathetic rejection of this child. If he questions too much he has a "reaction formation" and may be overprotective and oversolicitous. (Barsch, 1968, pp. 8–9)

The distinction between ego defense mechanisms as repressive and unconscious and cognitive coping as a conscious function, seems unimportant as families find strategies that work and that let them survive with egos and families relatively intact. Marla's mother read everything she could find about cerebral palsy, therapy techniques, and alternative communication, and then brought the literature to school for teachers and therapists to read. Was she intellectualizing, or using strong cognitive coping strategies of mastery and control? Marla, who is nonambulatory and has an immune deficiency disease, is now a university student who communicates with a computer and voice synthesizer. Her mother has continued to study and master the public education and health insurance systems.

Brenda had cerebral palsy and was nonambulatory. She had not had services until after she was 8 years old. She showed none of Marla's intellectual promise. At a parent conference, I asked Brenda's parents what their hopes for their daughter were. Brenda's father responded that he hoped some day she would live apart from them, either with support or independently, as an adult, holding a job. In 1975, we sincerely believed that Brenda's father was unable to accept the severity of her disability and the limits of her potential. He may have been, rather, a visionary. In the cultural and service context of today, I would respond differently.

FAMILY-CENTERED SERVICES

The changes in early intervention since the early 1980s have been dramatic. Family systems theory has been influential in helping early interventionists design and deliver services (Dunst, 1985; Trivette et al., 1986; Turnbull, Summers, & Brotherson, 1984). Early intervention services are beginning to be driven not by system needs or child needs, but by family needs, as families perceive and articulate those needs (Bailey, 1987; Johnson et al., 1989; McGonigel & Garland, 1988; Trivette et al., 1986; Turnbull & Turnbull, 1986). Work bridging between research related to family coping and actual practices in early intervention has resulted in a new attention to the strengths and resources that families have and can use in meeting their own needs (Affleck, Tennen, & Gershman, 1985; Dunst & Trivette, 1985; Dunst, Trivette, & Cross, 1986; Healy, Keesee, & Smith, 1985; Summers, Behr, & Turnbull, 1989; Zeitlin, 1985) and in living their lives in the absence of chronic sorrow described by Olshansky (1962, p. 190). The Infant and Toddler Program (Part H) of the Individuals with Disabilities Education Act, formerly known as PL 99-457, is a direct response to that attention.

Regulations for Part H require that participating states provide a multidisciplinary team assessment of the child's strengths and needs and of family strengths and needs related to the development of the child. Families play a major role in defining their own strengths and needs. Further, all eligible infants and toddlers must have written individualized family service plans (IFSPs), designed by a team on which the family participates. The IFSP must specify the family's desired outcomes or goals for themselves and for their child, and the services they will receive to help them reach those goals. This legislation hurtles early intervention programs forward to the point at which families whose infants and toddlers have disabilities should not have to shop for services that fit. Services will be designed specifically to meet the needs of each individual family, helping them build on their unique strengths to reach their goals.

Many early intervention providers are apprehensive at the thought of being responsible for such a broad brush of services. Some are concerned that they lack the skills needed to help families articulate their own needs, strengths, and priorities. Others are concerned that families will do too well at the task and will overburden the system with demands for services.

For the most part, however, we find our current work infinitely more satisfying and successful than the systems-centered work of the past. We are working to develop our own skills at finding and following families' leads, rather than trying to force-fit the rich diversity of family life into one program approach. We are trying to learn from each family how that family works and how we can support them in their coping styles and skills, rather than trying to reinvent families using our blueprints for failure.

The model of early intervention services used at Child Development Resources (CDR) in Lightfoot, Virginia, is designed to provide each family with the information, support, and skills they need to enhance their child's development and to lessen any negative effects of the disability on the child and on the family. Families serve on the agency board, ensuring that policies support family-centered services. Assessment, IFSP planning, and service coordination are guarantees of the system. Case management serves as the link or bridge between the family and the service system, providing assistance, to the extent a family feels necessary, in obtaining, organizing, and coordinating the array of community services needed by the child and the family. Families choose from an array of services that might include home visits, or center-based developmental play groups, parent groups, therapies, and others.

Whether fortuitously or by design, each of these services offers families the opportunity to enhance the cognitive coping strategies and skills described by Summers et al. (1989): that is, causal attribution, establishing mastery, and enhancing self-esteem. The early intervention team assessment process provides a vehicle for the search for causal attribution in its most literal sense; for the understanding of a child's medical or other diagnoses. The team works with the family during assessment, during the process of collecting and reviewing records, during consultation with our medical staff, and during regular home visits to ensure that families have and understand the information they need to make informed decisions. Several parents with whom I spoke in preparing to write this chapter described themselves as becoming experts during the diagnostic period. They gained both mastery and self-esteem by reading—sometimes selectively, sometimes everything they could find. This was true for families for whom diagnoses were slow in coming as well as for those who were given diagnoses of their child's disability immediately after birth.

Laurene was told shortly after now 3-year-old Molly's birth that her daughter had trisomy 18 and would live only a few days. Laurene and her husband chose not to read or seek any more information than they could use at any one time, finding that some information was helpful, but that too much was stressful. The implication here is that interventionists must determine how to be simultaneously sensitive and responsive to both the need for information and the need for hope.

Many families find that the sometimes frustrating search for funds to support the services that their children require increases the urgent need for them to become experts about their own children, about diagnostic information, about medical care and routines, about medications and their effects, about therapy approaches, and about the technicalities of early intervention and special education legislation. They learn to discuss seizure control medications with neurologists with ease and come to IFSP and individualized education program (IEP) meetings prepared for their roles as team members.

The opportunity to participate to the level and extent they desire as members of the early intervention team offers families an opportunity to use the mastery they acquired of necessity as a powerful and satisfying coping strategy. Many families have said that when they became involved in early intervention programs they felt at last they "were doing something" for their children. Other families see their involvement in early intervention as changing their role in relation to their child from nurturer to teacher. That role change interferes with parents' definition of themselves and their role relationships within their families.

In the rural South, many families find meaning not in the diagnostic process, but in their faith, in a divine plan for their families. "I know God sent her to us for a reason," one parent said, "although I am still struggling to find that reason." Developing an early intervention system that is respectful of each family's culture and values is a major challenge in our increasingly pluralistic society. Carol, the mother of a school-age child with autism who is now in a fully integrated placement and at grade level in almost every subject, cautions about letting the search for meaning become a stressor in itself, or even, "buying magic."

In the last few years, the most profound change in my own work and that of my colleagues in supporting and enhancing family coping is that we now know to follow the parents' lead rather than to impose our notion of what families must learn and do in order to cope.

SUPPORTING FAMILIES' COPING STRATEGIES

Choosing the coping strategy that will work in a given context is an art. Parents have talked with me about finding the balance between mastery as a successful coping strategy and as a stressor in itself. We see parents weigh their strategies and make elegant choices. Three parents whose children defied medical prognoses of death in the neonatal period talked of the time when the search for diagnostic information was no longer useful: "We learned material that could help us day to day, and not to bog down." "We learned to let her write her own biography." "Professionals can leave the door open for possibilities." Professionals can, indeed, leave the door open for hope. Charisse told of a turning point at her child's first birthday. "I decided," she said, "to let Amy be Amy. I don't want a diagnosis. I don't care. There is no sense in my running to clinics." Another said, simply, "There are issues that, at times, need to get put on the back burner."

Professional responses to families who choose mastery as a coping strategy are unfortunately not always positive. Service providers are sometimes threatened by a parent whose expertise exceeds their own. The medical community in particular has not given reinforcement to the roles families have chosen as informed medical consumers. In fact, it has been in the hospital setting that mastery has been the least effective coping strategy for many with whom I have worked. Parents recount being left out of the medical decision-making process regardless of the extent to which they were prepared to participate knowledgeably. Said one mother, "You have to have a variety of [coping] strategies to draw on. If you get to the hospital and control is the way you cope, you're out of luck!" Another echoed the need for multiple coping resources: "If you use just one [coping strategy], when that one doesn't work, you have a big hole in your life raft."

When mastery does work as a strategy, when providers respond to families as knowledgeable and important decision-makers on the team, self-esteem is also enhanced. Many parents report learning to "trust their instincts" or even their "guts." One parent said, "I certainly don't talk about trusting my instincts as a strength in an IFSP meeting . . . but it is . . . and I choose professionals who trust me."

When families join the early intervention team and are received as respected experts on the subject of their children, they are more likely to believe that the demands of the task do not exceed their resources to cope. One service provider described this as a cyclical process that can enhance family coping. Families seek information, and practice using it in the early intervention setting, getting reactions and testing a variety of strategies. When they find mastery and know they have the respect of the team, they are encouraged to continue to grow and to use those coping skills.

For early interventionists, respect for families does not derive from the information or skills they have acquired but from a professional approach to working with people. Early intervention providers see families when the initial diagnosis and the fact of their children's disabilities have dealt a harsh blow to self-esteem. Providing not only services but an environment that inherently enhances self-esteem is central to the relationship between the early intervention system and the family.

The ways in which the early intervention environment can be structured to support families in their use of coping skills are as rich and varied as the families themselves. Many families find that the early intervention center is one place in which their babies are uniformly greeted with the aahs, oohs, and coos of appreciation that other families find in every supermarket and on every playground. Early intervention providers comment on pretty skin tone, hairdos, and outfits—not purposefully to enhance parents' self-esteem but because early intervention staff are trained to appreciate children in their infinite variety. Tracheostomies, shunts, congenital facial or digital anomalies, and prostheses all fail to distort their perceptions of children as beautiful and welcome visitors to the center. As one mother said candidly: "This is the only place I come where no one asks what's wrong, and everyone tells me how cute she looks." Said another parent, "I choose to surround myself with people, personal friends and professionals, who reinforce my self-esteem. The parent group is a place where I can pour out my feelings. Just the concern alone is supportive." In parent groups, or through parent-to-parent networks, parents compare notes and find they are not alone, "not the only one in the world." Parent groups offer settings in which families can share coping strategies with one another, and can offer suggestions ranging from how to deal with the unrealistic expectations of the extended family to how to find a good dentist.

Wally, the father of a mildly retarded boy, was himself being treated for mental illness. He sat each week in a parent group without speaking. He eventually became comfortable enough to walk, unsteadily, through the halls to get a cup of coffee, to respond to staff who greeted him, and sometimes to initiate an interaction. Surely psychotherapy and medication played a role, but Wally was accepted by parents and staff in the same ways that each child is accepted. When he left the program he wrote to his case manager, "Before I came here I was a nothing—a nobody. Now, I am a real person."

A mother described another way in which the coping success of one parent fostered her belief in her own eventual control over her situation. She described meeting, in a parent group, Masie, the mother of a blind man and the custodial grandparent of his blind son. This woman was calm, competent, and at peace with her role as a parent. Masie was "the light at the end of the tunnel," offering encouragement by her very example as a coping mechanism.

The search for "the silver lining" seems almost universal. Families watching one another's children in developmental play group find comparisons that support cognitive coping. They see their own child's disabilities as less stressful than another's, all the while realizing that the other parent probably feels the same way. Other families see the impact of the child on the family as having positive aspects. One family member told of an interfaith wedding ceremony that was boycotted by one side of the family. The estrangement persisted until after the birth of the child with a disability. "At least," she said, "the baby brought the family together."

Carol, the mother of the school-age child with autism, talked about reading an Anna Quindlen column in which Ms. Quindlen reportedly said that of all disabilities, she would find being the parent of a child with autism the hardest. "I wanted to call her and say, 'They can be a lot of fun!' "

Emily Pearl Kingsley likened her experience as parent of a child with a disability to having planned a trip to Italy and stepping off the plane to find herself in Holland without benefit of guidebooks or road map.

> "Holland!?!?" you say. "What do you mean, Holland?? I signed up for Italy! All my life I've dreamed of going to Italy. . . . "
>
> But they've taken you to Holland. It's slower-paced than Italy, less flashy than Italy. But after you've been there for a while . . . you begin to notice that Holland has windmills. . . . and Holland has tulips. Holland even has Rembrandts.
>
> But everyone you know is busy coming and going from Italy. And for the rest of your life, you will say, "Yes, that's where I was supposed to go. That's what I had planned."
>
> And the pain of that will never, ever, ever, ever go away . . . because the loss of that dream is a very very significant loss.
>
> But . . . if you spend your life mourning the fact that you didn't get to Italy, you may never be free to enjoy the very special, the very lovely things . . . about Holland. (Kingsley, 1981)

Early intervention can help families acquire the roadmaps and the guidebooks, and can serve as traveling companion, supporting families as they let go of the dreams of Italy and free themselves "to enjoy the special things in Holland" (Kingsley, 1981).

As families acquire new skills in handling, feeding, or teaching, the pleasure and satisfaction they take in even very small developmental gains are real and measurable—more easily measurable at times than the gains themselves. Early intervention and medical personnel reinforce coping through mastery and self-esteem by providing positive reinforcement, but remain wary of the trap of tying a parent's self-esteem to the developmental progress of the child.

If there is one coping skill or strategy that varies most widely among family members it certainly seems to be humor. The ability to laugh at oneself or at the awkward or uncomfortable moments in life is not only a coping strategy but a gift. While no one would find anything funny about having a child with a disability, many family members are able to find humor in their life situations on a daily basis. One mother of a child with Down syndrome who was born in Asia told of the doctor who, upon seeing the unusually shaped eyes and lids, asked if the child's father were Asian. However, parents whose humor takes a particularly wry, sarcastic, or Addams-esque flavor, are frequently met by startled looks or shock—even by their own family members who are less given to wit.

DETERMINING FAMILIES' NEEDS

The home context in which many family-centered early intervention services take place colors the relationship between family and service provider with a unique intimacy. It may also be a crucial element in getting to know each family and its coping style. Overwhelmingly, parents confirm the feeling of one mother that home-based services give providers a "sense of family reality. No one can say to you, 'What are your coping skills?' . . . In your home they see your style and they learn how to use what you have to help." Another talked about the intimacy of the home visit. Her home visitor "saw how we interacted, saw the dance" that allowed her to tailor services to meet their needs.

Recently, a group of mothers talked openly about similarities and differences in coping styles within a family, citing their own or friends' spouses who "didn't cope," who were in "constant denial," or who "wouldn't seek support." One mother described herself, cheerfully and accurately, as the "head coper." Their observations and those of early intervention staff are less of unified family coping style, than of the interaction or "dance" among family members. "He was *today*," one mother said. "I was *future oriented*." Parents stress how important it is for providers to understand the impact of events on all family members so that they can help minimize family stress and help enhance family coping.

Parents have often talked of their other children's concerns about the differences of their siblings. They have described older children and adolescents as worrying about their own chances of having children with disabilities. "You can't expect other children to skip developmental stages because of one child," said Justine, the mother of a large family. Parents have often spoken of grandparents' difficulties in seeing "the good things about our family," of wanting to rescue or help when "we think things are really all right," or of not knowing how and when to help. Parents have reported knowing they can change the ways in which extended family and friends perceive their family's stress by "being able to handle it." However, they also come back to the need to surround themselves with family and friends who support their families and see the good things about their families.

Providers trying to support and enhance family coping skills are challenged to address the multiple and varied needs of the whole family. Women offer suggestions about how to reach out to their husbands, describing the differences between them. "They don't want support. They want control." "They need to feel capable and needed." Fathers choosing among options for participation in CDR's early intervention program have been most enthusiastic about family recreation activities or programs that offer very specific and concrete information. They have requested such information as genetic counseling or estate planning. They have responded readily to requests for their help with building or equipment maintenance and repair, or with other skills "that early intervention staff may lack."

Individual family members must be free to choose the early intervention services that meet their individual and collective needs, and those of their other children. "Early intervention is more for me than for my child," one parent said. Another spoke of the integrated developmental play group: "My older children probably get a lot more out of it than the child who is enrolled in the program," referring to their opportunity to meet other children whose siblings are developing atypically. As we plan early intervention services that are family-centered and that reinforce and enhance coping skills, we need to learn what each family member needs from the system and find creative ways to meet those needs.

DIRECTIONS FOR FUTURE RESEARCH

Early intervention programs look to theorists and researchers to help us find answers to our many questions about enhancing family coping. How can we learn from families what cognitive coping strategies they find helpful? How can we design programs that enhance the coping styles and strategies that families already use? Does a family want or need alternate strategies and can we offer help in developing coping mechanisms? Perhaps most of the important questions have to do with the extent to which it is possible to help adults who come to early intervention with few, if any, coping skills. (Most assuredly, we can't teach humor and its use to the humorless.) When and how are cognitive coping skills learned? Is there a critical period in the development of cognitive coping skills, and what happens when it is missed?

We encounter regularly in our work the adolescent mother who comes to early intervention with extremely poor self-esteem. Her choice to have a child, if a conscious choice was made, has frequently been related to needs for peer approval and for unconditional love. When that child has a disability, a strategy seen as a sure formula for success and acceptance has failed. For many of these young women, nothing in their early lives, in their nurturing, or in their education has equipped them with the cognitive coping skills that they need in order to believe in their ability to succeed as parents. When, if ever, is it too late to acquire cognitive coping skills? Can they be taught? By whom and how?

We have had occasional success stories—Dennie, a teen-age mother of three who went on to get her general education development (GED) diploma, to parent with love and skill, to write creative and beautiful poetry. What, however, did she bring to us that we nurtured, and what did we do that worked?

For those of us who see families of children with developmental disabilities in the diagnostic period the research agenda is urgent. Each of our interactions is with a family who needs *today* the skills to cope and who will need *tomorrow* the ability to transfer those skills to the many stressful situations they have yet to face. While the families I know can hardly be characterized by the chronic sorrow paradigm, I do know that the health care, educational, and daily care needs of their children will place them in stress, if not in crisis, repeatedly over the course of their children's lives.

Can we help families involved in early intervention develop coping skills that they can transfer to other, later life situations as they leave our services? Can we help families evaluate a situation and choose the most effective coping skill? Is it possible that we can learn from families and share with other families useful strategies? Can families do that for each other?

Early intervention programs that respond to the intent of recent legislation by developing IFSPs based on family needs, values, preferences, and priorities can provide a therapeutic milieu that fosters the development of family coping and that reduces to the extent possible the stress associated with early identification of a disability. Discovering what precisely it is that we do that is successful or how we can be more supportive is less easy. While the potential for answering important questions related to family coping is inherent in the service setting, few community-based programs have the financial or personnel resources necessary to carry out field-based research. Money and skills are not the only barriers. Methodology and protocol designed in the research environment are often perceived as intrusive and potentially damaging to the relationships service providers so carefully cultivate with families. Early intervention programs that greet each child and family with unconditional acceptance and appreciation are understandably reluctant to engage in an interview protocol that asks such questions as: "Were you depressed when you came home from the hospital?" "Have you ever wished your child had not been born?"

CONCLUSION

The dialogue among family members, service providers, theorists, and researchers at the Conference on Cognitive Coping (held in Lawrence, Kansas, in June 1991) is a healthy and necessary first step to including the pressing questions of service providers in the research agenda and to the development of research methodology that is appropriate for use in a service setting. This dialogue has the potential to enhance the now fragile connections between research and practice, and to speed the information from theory to practice so that those of us engaged in daily work with families can support and enhance their coping skills in the most effective ways.

ABOUT THE AUTHOR

Corinne W. Garland, M.Ed. My experience has been as a developer and an administrator of programs for children with disabilities and their families. In my work, families have been generous in sharing their stories and their perceptions of the ways in which they and other families have adapted to having members with disabilities. Their experiences, more than any education or training I have received, now influence my work in program and policy development.

REFERENCES

Affleck, G., Tennen, H., & Gershman, K. (1985). Cognitive adaptations to high risk infants: The search for mastery, meaning, and protection from future harm. *American Journal of Mental Deficiency, 89*(6), 653–656.

Bailey, D.B. (1987). Collaborative goal setting with families: Resolving differences in values and priorities for services. *Topics in Early Childhood Special Education, 7*(2), 59–71.

Bailey, D.B. (1988). Considerations in developing family goals. In D.B. Bailey & R.J. Simeonsson (Eds.), *Family assessment in early intervention* (pp. 229–250). Columbus, OH: Charles E. Merrill.

Barsch, R.H. (1968). *The parent of a handicapped child: The study of child-rearing practices.* Springfield, IL: Charles C Thomas.

Chandler, L., Fowler, S., & Lubeck, R. (1986). Assessing family needs: The first step in providing family-focused intervention. *Diagnostique, 11*(3–4), 233–245.

Dunst, C.J. (1985). Rethinking early intervention. *Analysis and Intervention in Developmental Disabilities, 5,* 165–201.

Dunst, C.J., & Trivette, C.A. (1985). *Measures of social support, parental stress, well-being and coping, and other family-level behavior* [Monograph of the Technical Assistance Development System]. Chapel Hill: University of North Carolina.

Dunst, C.J., Trivette, C.A., & Cross, A.H. (1986). Mediating influences of social support: Personal, family, and child outcomes. *American Journal of Mental Deficiency, 90,* 403–417.

Farber, B. (1959). Effects of a severely mentally retarded child on family integration. *Monographs of the Society for Research in Child Development, 24*(2).

Farber, B. (1960). Family organization and crisis: Maintenance of integration in families with a severely mentally retarded child. *Monographs of the Society for Research in Child Development, 25*(1), Serial No. 75.

Featherstone, H. (1980). *A difference in the family.* New York: Basic Books.

Healy, A., Keesee, P.D., & Smith, B.S. (1985). *Early services for children with special needs: Transactions for family support.* Iowa City: University of Iowa.

Heward, W., Dardig, J., & Rossett, A. (1979). *Working with parents of handicapped children.* Columbus, OH: Charles E. Merrill.

Johnson, B.H., McGonigel, M.J., & Kaufmann, R.K. (Eds.). (1989). *Guidelines and recommended practices for the individualized family service plan.* Washington, DC: Association for the Care of Children's Health.

Kingsley, E.P. (1981, November). *Welcome to Holland.* From "Kids Like These," CBS-TV Movie of the Week, Nexus Productions.

Kroth, R. (1975). *Communicating with parents of exceptional children.* Denver: Love Publications.

Kubler-Ross, E. (1969). *On death and dying.* New York: Macmillan.

Maslow, A.H. (1970). *Motivation and personality* (2nd ed.). New York: Harper & Row.

McGonigel, M.J., & Garland, C.W. (1988). The individualized family service plan and the early intervention team: Team and family issues and recommended practices. *Infants and Young Children, 1*(1), 10–21.

Olshansky, S. (1962). Chronic sorrow: A response to having a mentally defective child. *Social Casework, 43,* 190–193.

Piaget, J. (1952). *The origins of intelligence in children.* New York: W.W. Norton.

Shelton, T., Jeppson, E., & Johnson, B. (1987). *Family-centered care for children with special health care needs.* Washington, DC: Association for the Care of Children's Health.

Solnit, A.J., & Stark, M.H. (1961). Mourning and the birth of a defective child. *Psychoanalytic Study of the Child, 16,* 523–537.

Summers, J.A., Behr, S.K., & Turnbull, A.P. (1989). Positive adaptation and coping strength of families who have children with disabilities. In G.H.S. Singer & L.K. Irvin (Eds.), *Support for caregiving families: Enabling positive adaptation to disabilities* (pp. 27–40). Baltimore: Paul H. Brookes Publishing Co.

Trivette, C.M., Deal, A., & Dunst, C.J. (1986). Family needs, sources of support, and professional roles: Critical elements of family systems assessment and intervention. *Diagnostique, 11,* 146–267.

Turnbull, A.P., Summers, J.A., & Brotherson, M.J. (1984). *Working with families with disabled members: A family system approach.* Lawrence: Kansas University Affiliated Facility.

Turnbull, A.P., & Turnbull, H.R. (1986). *Families, professionals, and exceptionalities: A special partnership.* Columbus, OH: Charles E. Merrill.

Zeitlin, S. (1985). *Coping Inventory: Self-rated form.* Bensenville, IL: Scholastic Testing Service.

chapter 6

Lessons Learned
Cognitive Coping Strategies of Overlooked Family Members

Donald J. Meyer

My friends said to me: "Robert, what's with your sister? She's really screwed up! Her eyes are crossed, she drools, she can't talk, she wears diapers and she can't feed herself. She can't do anything."

So I told them: "That's not true! She can do a lot! My parents are always trying to keep Traci from going downstairs. They put up gates and all sorts of stuff. And no matter what they put up, she *still* climbs over the top!" (Robert, age 12, about his sister Traci, age 8)

For both of us, Nigel is probably the most marvelous experience in our lives. Raising our own children was rich and fulfilling, but it was also patterned and predictable. Nigel is an adventure into the unknown, a journey toward an uncharted destiny . . . . Each day is a new phenomenon, each night thresholds tomorrow's blossoming. (June Click, about her grandson Nigel; Click, 1986, p. 1)

Before Eric came along, I was on what you might call the corporate fast-track. Not anymore. My family is more important to me now. (John Oldenburg, about his son, Eric)

Like Robert, like June, and like John, most siblings, grandparents, and fathers of people with disabilities have learned to cope with the reality of a family member's disability. Unfortunately, much of that learning has been solitary. Most fathers, siblings, and grandparents have learned what they know without the benefit of talking to a peer who has shared similar experiences.

Things are changing, however. Increasingly, these traditionally underserved family members are being served by peer support and education programs designed especially for them. Service providers, over the years, have learned much about cognitive coping from the family members who attend these programs. More importantly, these family members have learned a great deal about coping from one another.

This chapter provides an overview of support and education programs for

---

Preparation of this chapter was supported by Project No. MCJ-535077-01-0 from the Maternal and Child Health Program (Title V, Social Security Act), Health and Human Services Administration, Department of Health and Human Services.

fathers, siblings, and grandparents and suggests how these programs can encourage cognitive coping among the participants. Current issues and future directions as they pertain to this population are also discussed. Throughout this chapter, there is an attempt to share with the reader what these family members have to teach service providers and each other about cognitive coping.

PROGRAMS FOR FATHERS, SIBLINGS, AND GRANDPARENTS

Since 1977, I have had the good fortune to meet, work with, and learn from these overlooked family members in programs designed specifically for fathers, siblings, and grandparents of children with special needs. The Fathers Program, which began at the University of Washington's Child Development and Mental Retardation Center in 1978, provides fathers with opportunities for peer support, education, and direct involvement with their children with disabilities (Meyer, Vadasy, Fewell, & Schell, 1985). Fathers' interests—often different from mothers' interests—set the agenda for the program.

The success of the Fathers Program encouraged us to reach out to other family members who are overlooked by traditional family programs. In 1981, the SEFAM (Supporting Extended Family Members) Program was created with funding from the U.S. Department of Education's Handicapped Children's Early Education Program. Besides the ongoing Fathers Program, SEFAM staff implemented Sibshops, which provide peer support and information to siblings—the family members who will likely have the longest lasting relationship with the person with the disability. Among the goals of the Sibshop model are to provide brothers and sisters with an opportunity to meet other brothers and sisters in a relaxed, recreational environment, and to learn how others handle situations commonly experienced by siblings of children with special needs (Meyer, Vadasay, & Fewell, 1985).

Grandparents Workshops, the third SEFAM program, were initiated in 1983. At these workshops, participants meet other grandparents of children with special needs, discuss concerns that they have about their children and grandchildren, and seek information on a wide range of disability-related issues (Meyer & Vadasy, 1986).

Although simple in design, peer support and education programs can be powerful in their ability to help all family members cope with the impact of a child's disability. Programs for fathers, grandparents, and siblings can provide forums for participants to seek information that is of immediate use to them. These programs can provide an emotional environment that emphasizes wellness, mutual encouragement, and empowerment. Most programs have similar goals. Examples of goals of programs for fathers, siblings, and grandparents are presented in Table 1.

Table 1. Goals of programs for specific family members

Programs for fathers[a]	Programs for brothers and sisters[b]	Programs for grandparents[c]
Fathers programs provide participants with opportunities:	Sibshops provide participants with opportunities to:	Grandparents workshops provide participants with opportunities to:
Peer support	Peer support	Peer support
To meet other men in a similar situation	To meet other siblings in a relaxed, recreational setting	To meet other grandparents of children with special needs
To discuss common joys and concerns	To discuss common joys and concerns with other brothers and sisters	To discuss common concerns, and develop peer supports
To examine the impact of the child's disability on the entire family		
To explore the changing role of the father in today's society		
Education	Education	Education
To learn more about the nature of his child's disability	To learn more about the implications of their sibling's special needs	To learn more about the nature of the grandchild's disability
To learn to read his child's cues and interpret his child's behavior	To learn how other brothers and sisters handle situations commonly experienced by siblings of children with special needs	To learn about programs and services available for children with special needs
To develop an awareness of activities, materials, and experiences suitable to his child's current age and abilities	To provide parents with information about sibling issues	To discuss helpful strategies that enable grandparents to be supportive of their children and families
To develop an awareness that he will be his child's primary educator and advocate		To discuss and better understand the impact of the child's disability on the entire family
Involvement		
To practice his skills as the child's primary caregiver		

[a]From Meyer, D.J., Vadasy, P.F., Fewell, R.R., & Schell, G. (1985). *A handbook for the Fathers Program: How to organize a program for fathers and their handicapped children* (pp. 25–28). Seattle: University of Washington Press; reprinted by permission.

[b]From Meyer, D.J., Vadasy, P.F., & Fewell, R.R. (1985). *Sibshops: A handbook for implementing workshops for siblings of children with special needs* (pp. 11–13). Seattle: University of Washington Press; reprinted by permission.

[c]From Meyer, D.J., & Vadasy, P.F. (1986). *Grandparents workshops: How to organize workshops for grandparents of children with handicaps* (p. 13). Seattle: University of Washington Press; reprinted by permission.

Cognitive coping, as described by Behr and Murphy (chap. 11, this volume), is thinking about a situation in ways that enhance a sense of well-being. These ways may include: 1) finding meaning in an otherwise negative event, 2) regaining mastery or control following the negative event, 3) perceiving that the impact of the event has ultimately been small, or 4) perceiving that one has eventually profited from it. Cognitive coping, however powerful, is only one means of adapting successfully to the demands of a disability. Coping, according to Antonovsky (chap. 8, this volume), is a "many-splendored sword." Besides cognitive coping strategies, family members will need to develop effective instrumental, physical, and logistical coping strategies.

Programs for family members have enormous potential to enhance a family member's ability to develop a wide range of adaptive coping strategies:

- At the *Fathers Program,* participants discuss how their views of work and family have changed in the wake of the child's diagnosis. Fathers (who bring their children to the program) practice caregiving skills, thereby increasing mothers' opportunities for future respite. Participants learn information about the implications of the disability, relieving the mother of the strain of being the child's sole "expert."
- During a *Sibshop,* brothers and sisters express the "good and not-so-good" aspects of having a sibling with a disability. Participants share strategies to address common sibling concerns, such as what to do when classmates make insensitive comments about people with disabilities or when siblings embarrass them in public.
- Grandparents share their deep concerns and the special joys they have for their children and grandchildren during a *Grandparents Workshop.* Participants discuss what has and has not worked in their attempts to provide practical and emotional support for their families.

These programs become a place where coping strategies—cognitive and otherwise—are discovered, shared, modeled, and discussed.

LESSONS LEARNED

Fathers, siblings, and grandparents have much to teach us and especially each other about coping—if they are given a chance. Behr and Murphy (chap. 11, this volume), found that construing positive contributions from the experience of having and raising a child with a disability was a major cognitive theme identified by parents and other relatives. These family members felt that persons with disabilities enrich and enhance the quality of life for family and friends.

The next sections provide a brief review of the following positive contributions as expressed by fathers, siblings, and grandparents of people with disabilities:

Pride in things the child can do
Personal strength and family closeness
Feelings of happiness and fulfillment
Personal growth and maturity
Sense of control or influence over events

These contributions are not intended to trivialize the very real concerns and challenges experienced by these family members that have been well-documented elsewhere (Meyer, 1986a; Powell & Ogle, 1985; Vadasy, Fewell, & Meyer, 1986). Instead they provide perspectives of families who have struggled, persevered, and even thrived—despite the presence of a disability in the family.

Pride in Things the Child Can Do

The comments of Robert, the brother quoted in the beginning of this chapter, are typical of those heard during sibling workshops. Brothers and sisters frequently express pride in their siblings' accomplishments and view their sibs in terms of what they *can* do. Siblings, like the archetypal Peace Corps volunteer, view the glass as half full, not half empty. Nondisabled siblings frequently complain about people who view their sibling *as* the disability. These people, they say, never get to know the "neat kid" who has many abilities and just happens to have a disability. Melissa, age 16, wrote the following about her sister Kim:

> [People] just don't understand. Because they have only had the opportunity to see mentally retarded people, many never get the chance to talk and get to know the heart of someone like Kim. They probably never get past the fear of, or feeling sorry for them. All they see is a person who maybe moves strangely or talks slow and maybe makes uncivilized noises. It is really a shame. (Hansen, 1985, p. 9)

Jennifer, age 10, wrote:

> Sometimes kids at school look at Elizabeth and say, "Is that your sister?" "Who is she?" They think because she looks different that she's different inside. But she's just like us inside. And she doesn't want to be stared at and laughed at or ignored. ("Jennifer," 1990, p. 2)

Like brothers and sisters, fathers and grandparents also express pride in the accomplishments of the child with a disability. One grandfather reported at a workshop: "You begin to appreciate the child for who he is, despite the disability."

A father's pride in his child's abilities can have second-order effects, increasing the pride he has in his abilities as a parent. A father of two children, one of whom has Down syndrome, wrote: "It's exciting, working with Danny. I feel much closer to him than I do to Caroline. Caroline is doing things in spite of me; Danny is doing things because of me—it's exciting" (McConachie, 1982, p. 157). And another reported:

> Forcing myself to take Laura to museums, stores, and even the dreaded playground
> has helped make me a better parent by giving me the confidence I need. . . . I feel
> proud of her and even proud of myself—that I'm a damn good father. The irony is
> I probably wouldn't have been if I didn't have a special needs child. (May, 1991,
> p. 12)

Personal Strength and Family Closeness

For many men, becoming a father is a profound experience. During this developmental milestone, fathers frequently take stock of their accomplishments and
their satisfaction with their careers, families, and marriages. The diagnosis of a
disability will make this reassessment even more complex. Fathers, such as the
father quoted in the beginning of this chapter, who can reframe the stressful
event of a child's diagnosis may experience a reassessment of values and personal growth (Meyer, 1986b). At Fathers Programs, fathers offer hard-won
words of advice to fathers of newly diagnosed children: "Your life will not end,"
one father said. "You can have a child with a disability and thrive."

A "difference in the family," as Featherstone (1981) called it, also can inspire other family members to reassess what it means to be in a family. Brothers
and sisters express appreciation for the efforts their parents have made:

> I really admire our family for how well we accept Kim like anyone else. . . . My
> parents give Kim everything she needs: love, acceptance, understanding, pa-
> tience, discipline, proper hygiene, entertainment. Everything any other child
> needs. That's not to say she isn't spoiled, but who does not spoil their children?
> [My brother] Kevin and myself have never rejected her, only the opposite.
> (Hansen, 1985, pp. 5–6)

Similarly, Grandparents Program participants frequently discuss what
they have learned from their children and grandchildren about unconditional
love, acceptance, and support. The child's disability, they say, can help all family members appreciate how dependent they are on one another. One Grandparents Program participant said: "I see myself as an extension of Danny's parents—to be there when needed by *both* Danny and his parents" (Meyer &
Vadasy, 1986, p. 8).

Feelings of Happiness and Fulfillment

Family members frequently acknowledge what the member with the disability
has taught them about unconditional love. Wrote one grandmother: "He is so
full of love and responsive to love that the joy of his companionship is almost
overwhelming." Another grandfather offered:

> I never realized I would derive so much pleasure from this "special" grandchild.
> Instead of feeling pity, I am happy for her—for the way she's developing, for her
> part in decision-making, for her accomplishments, and for the fun she has every
> day. She makes me feel good about myself because I feel part of her life. (Behr,
> 1986, p. 2)

That people who have disabilities can enrich all our lives is a theme noted by many family members. This father shared what his son taught him about happiness:

> What can you say about a six-year-old, mentally retarded boy who smiles the first thing on getting up in the morning? What do you say about a boy who thinks getting hugs is better than getting Christmas presents? I sometimes think my other kids should follow his example. Perhaps we all should. (May, 1991, p. 13)

Personal Growth and Maturity

In the early 1970s, when life with a family member with a disability was assumed by many to be a pathological condition, young adult brothers and sisters let professionals know otherwise. Approximately 45% of the college-age siblings Grossman (1972) surveyed reported that they had benefited from growing up with a brother or sister with mental retardation. Among the benefits they cited included: increased understanding of other people, more tolerance and compassion, and greater appreciation of their own good health and intelligence.

These family members frequently noted that, despite the challenges caused by the child's disability, there are benefits, often unanticipated, that have contributed to their lives. Some have developed lifelong friends whom they have met through the family member with a disability. Others have embarked on unanticipated careers or learned specific skills. One grandfather wrote: "I learned that if I wanted to communicate with her [his granddaughter], I would have to learn signing—and I'm proud of that accomplishment" (Behr, 1986, p. 2).

Other family members identify the insight, personal growth, and maturity they have acquired as a result of living with a relative who has a disability. Josh Greenfeld, in *A Place for Noah*, wrote:

> It's ironical: If Noah has proven debilitating to our dreams, he also has provided the material for a kind of realization of ourselves. It's not the realization either one of us anticipated or wanted, but then one cannot predetermine the scenario one is destined—or doomed—to act out either. (1979, p. 286)

Brothers and sisters frequently cite growing up with a sibling who has a disability as the inspiration for personal growth:

> My experience with my sister has been one of the most important in my life. It has at times been stressful but ultimately a very positive influence. It has definitely shaped my life and channeled my interests in ways I would otherwise have not pursued. (Itzkowitz, 1990, p. 4)

Sense of Control or Influence Over Events

A natural response to a crisis in the family (such as the diagnosis of a disability) is the desire to do something that will ameliorate the situation. Early intervention programs and related services are now generally available as a result of PL

99-457, the Education of the Handicapped Act Amendments of 1986. These programs usually involve mothers, but other family members may not be included and thus have few opportunities to contribute toward relieving the crisis. Without opportunities to contribute, family members may feel powerless: Cummings (1976) wrote that fathers of children with special needs wanted to do something directly helpful, something that provided concrete evidence of their loving, caring, and benevolent concern.

Other family members also may wish to contribute. A Grandparents Program participant wrote: "I am devastated by this and want to learn and do anything that will help my grandchild." By providing these overlooked family members with opportunities for support and information about issues of deep concern (e.g., services, therapies, future concerns) fathers, siblings, and grandparents can increase their sense of control over the crisis of the child's disability.

Programs that provide family members with concrete ways of ameliorating the family's situation also may promote mental well-being. Men who participated in the Seattle-area Fathers Program reported less sadness, fatigue, guilt, and stress due to the child's disability, and less pessimism over future concerns than did fathers in similar situations who had not participated. These fathers also reported more satisfaction, greater feelings of success versus failure as a person, fewer total problems, and better decision-making ability.

Among the most compelling reasons to address the concerns of individual family members will be the reverberating positive effects on other family members. Wives of men who were involved in the Fathers Program reported fewer feelings of failure, less stress resulting from their children's disabilities, and more satisfaction with the time that they had to themselves than women in similar situations whose husbands were not involved in programs for fathers (Vadasy, Fewell, Meyer, & Greenberg, 1984).

CURRENT ISSUES AND FUTURE DIRECTIONS

Need for More Programs

Since the early 1980s, there has been a growing recognition that a child's disability or illness will affect more than the child and his or her mother. In the professional literature and in practice, the term *family* has increasingly replaced *parents* (and before that, *mothers*). This broader focus acknowledges the reciprocal effects a family member's disability or illness can have on all family members. However, despite changes in the terminology, too frequently the word *family* still refers to "parents and child with a disability or illness." Grandparents, aunts and uncles, and siblings are still largely excluded.

Despite the tremendous success of common-sense efforts like the Parent-to-Parent and Pilot Parent Programs, there continues to be a dearth of programs offering peer support and education for other family members. According to preliminary data from the national survey of Parent-to-Parent programs conducted by the Beach Center on Families and Disability at the University of Kansas, only 28% of the responding Parent-to-Parent programs offer support programs for siblings or other family members. Of the community agencies that sponsor Parent-to-Parent programs, only 6% have support activities for siblings or other family members. Brothers and sisters, who will likely have the longest lasting relationship with the person with the disability, deserve to have their peer support and education needs addressed.

There are similarly compelling reasons to offer increased services for fathers and grandparents. A father's attitude toward a child's disability frequently sets the tone for the family's attitude (Frey, Fewell, Vadasy, & Greenberg, 1989). Mothers of children with disabilities as well as professionals acknowledge the need for more paternal involvement (Gallagher, Cross, & Scharfman, 1981). By providing forums specifically designed to address fathers' concerns and interests, the child with a disability will benefit from having two informed advocates and the mother will feel supported in her role (Lamb & Meyer, 1991). Said one Fathers Program participant: "I think participating in the Fathers Program is one of the most important things fathers can do for mothers" (Meyer, Vadasy, Fewell, & Schell, 1985, p. 5).

Grandparents who lack information and support may actually burden their children with unwanted, inaccurate, or outdated advice about what they should do for the grandchild. Grandparents also may feel so consumed by their own sense of grief or loss that they are unable to offer support to their children when they need it most. When grandparents lack access to information and emotional support, it is easy to see why a grandparent's needs will affect an entire family's ability to cognitively cope with the child's disability.

Increasing the availability of programs that address the interests and concerns of specific family members is a current need identified by parents and other professionals throughout the country. Two federally funded projects are designed to make these programs more available for family members. The Sibling Support Project, at Seattle's Children's Hospital and Medical Center and supported by a U.S. Department of Health and Human Services Maternal and Child Health grant, provides on-site training, demonstration, and technical assistance to agencies throughout the United States wishing to add peer support programs for brothers and sisters of children with special health and developmental needs to their existing matrix of services. The Fathers Network, at Merrywood School in Bellevue, Washington, and supported by the Association for the Care of Children's Health, provides training and technical assistance on creating programs for fathers of children with special needs. Currently there are no similarly funded national projects to encourage agencies to create peer support and education opportunities for grandparents. However, there are curricula designed to provide guidance to agency staff who wish to implement programs for fathers, siblings, and grandparents of children with special health or developmental needs (see Table 2).

Need for More Research on Cognitive Coping

Cognitive coping strategies employed by traditionally underserved family members warrant further inquiry. Facilities such as the Beach Center have recognized the need to study the cognitive coping strategies employed by parents, grandparents, and other family members. Comparable studies exploring strategies used by brothers and sisters across the life span would provide information that would enrich existing data and provide information useful for siblings of all ages, as well as parents and professionals.

Also, the Beach Center has described the status of Parent-to-Parent (or Pilot Parents) programs throughout the United States. These programs are invaluable for helping parents learn and discover coping strategies. With programs for specific family members (i.e., fathers, siblings, and grandparents) growing in number, similar studies would appear warranted.

Need for Programs Targeting Other Family Members

In addition to research, there are areas of service to specific family members that deserve the attention of providers. One such population is adult brothers and sisters of people with special needs.

Increasingly, adult children with disabilities of the baby-boom and post–baby-boom generation are living and working in the community. As their parents age and die, their nondisabled brothers and sisters will be involved in their

Table 2. Curricula for programs for grandparents, siblings, and fathers of children with disabilities

Grandparents

Meyer, D., & Vadasy, P. (1986). *Grandparents Workshops: How to organize workshops for grandparents of children with handicaps.* Seattle: University of Washington Press.

Siblings

Lobato, D.J. (1990). *Brothers, sisters, and special needs: Information and activities for helping young siblings of children with chronic illnesses and developmental disabilities.* Baltimore: Paul H. Brookes Publishing Co.

Meyer, D., Vadasy, P., & Fewell, R. (1985). *Sibshops: A handbook for implementing workshops for siblings of children with special needs.* Seattle: University of Washington Press.

Nollette, C. (1985). *Autism . . . A family affair: A curriculum for use with siblings of special needs children.* Minneapolis: Minneapolis Children's Medical Center.

Usdane, S., & Melmed, R. (1988). *Siblings Exchange Program: A support program for brothers and sisters of the disabled.* Phoenix: Phoenix Children's Hospital.

Fathers

Meyer, D., Vadasy, P., Fewell, R., & Schell, G. (1985). *A handbook for the Fathers Program: How to organize a program for fathers and their handicapped children.* Seattle: University of Washington Press.

lives in significant ways. Many adult nondisabled siblings will struggle with seemingly incompatible loyalties that they have toward their brothers and sisters and loyalties that they have toward their own families. Most will be affected by the lack of residential services and career opportunities for their adult brothers or sisters.

Adult siblings of people with disabilities continue to be an extraordinarily overlooked population. Few agencies are reaching out to provide these family members with the support and information that will address their concerns and help them make appropriate decisions. Programs for adult siblings of people with special needs can help participants gain needed information and share concerns they have about their siblings, their parents, and their own families.

Programs for young siblings are a relatively recent innovation; therefore, most adult siblings of people with disabilities grew up without the opportunity to discuss their concerns with peers. Consequently, participants in adult siblings programs express an interest in discussing common childhood experiences: the stares they felt as they went into the community with their siblings; the distinctive sense of humor that their family developed as a result of coping with the siblings' disabilities; or the problems they faced with their friends, classmates, and parents. These opportunities, say adult participants, can help put their childhood experiences and their understanding of their families into perspective.

Programs for adult and younger siblings can provide yet another service: advocacy. Adult sibling participants who become more informed about issues facing adults with disabilities can become needed and effective advocates for their brothers and sisters. The information younger siblings receive about their brothers' and sisters' future during a siblings workshop can lay the groundwork for an understanding of the issues they will eventually address as adults. Besides ensuring a better life for participants' brothers and sisters, these advocacy and preadvocacy activities can also foster coping strategies: 1) obtaining needed information may moderate the anxiety participants have about their and their siblings' future, and 2) learning the tools of advocacy can help participants feel that they have an influence in their brothers' and sisters' lives.

CONCLUSION

When given a chance, fathers, brothers, sisters, grandparents, and other family members have much to teach each other and the professional community about cognitive coping. Clearly, there is a need for increased opportunities. As programs that provide support and education for these family members increase in number, it will be important to study their impact not only on the participants, but on other family members as well, to determine possible second-order effects.

As the professional community attempts to learn from these family members it will be essential to plan program evaluations carefully in order to capture the strengths and effective coping strategies these individuals possess. As McConachie (1982) has noted:

> Most [scales] do not evaluate positive traits. Where the researcher has given parents greater freedom to comment, they tend to demonstrate their strength, resilience, and sense of humor in coping with their own reaction . . . and also with the reactions of their family and neighbors. (p. 161)

It should be noted that programs for these family members do not and have never attempted to appeal to *all* grandparents, siblings, or fathers. They are also not a panacea. Many family members will have needs that cannot be served by such programs.

However, their existence in the community will provide a valuable service for those choosing to use them. They also will be a constant reminder that all fathers, grandparents, and brothers and sisters of people with special needs are an integral part of the family, deserving of providers' consideration and attention. These programs will remind us that within the family are subgroups having concerns and interests that are both similar to and different from other family members. Finally, these programs can remind us that each individual in the family is a resource to the whole, too important and too valuable to squander.

ABOUT THE AUTHOR

Donald J. Meyer, M.Ed. For the past 14 years, I have had the good fortune to design and implement services for fathers, siblings, and grandparents of people who have special health and developmental needs. In my current position as director of the Sibling Support Project, I have been able to pursue my long-standing interest in creating peer support and education programs for brothers and sisters of all ages. In addition to developing curricular and awareness materials, our project provides training, demonstration, and technical assistance to agencies throughout the United States.

REFERENCES

Behr, B. (1986). Would you like to see a picture of my granddaughter? *Especially Grandparents, 1*(5), 1–3.
Click, J. (1986). Learning to be special. *Especially Grandparents, 2*(2), 1–4.
Cummings, S.T. (1976). The impact of the child's deficiency on the father: A study of mentally retarded and chronically ill children. *American Journal of Orthopsychiatry, 46*, 246–255.
Featherstone, H. (1981). *A difference in the family: Living with a disabled child.* New York: Penguin.
Frey, K.S., Fewell, R.R., Vadasy, P.F., & Greenberg, M.T. (1989). Parental adjustment and changes in child outcome among families of young handicapped children. *Topics in Early Childhood Education, 8*, 38–57.

Gallagher, J., Cross, A., & Scharfman, W. (1981). Parental adaptation to a young handicapped child: The father's role. *Journal of the Division for Early Childhood, 3*, 3–4.

Greenfeld, J. (1979). *A place for Noah.* New York: Pocket Books.

Grossman, F.K. (1972). *Brothers and sisters of the retarded children: An exploratory study.* Syracuse, NY: Syracuse University Press.

Hansen, M. (1985). *Straight from the heart.* Saskatoon: Saskatchewan Association for the Mentally Retarded.

Itzkowitz, J. (1990). Siblings' perceptions of their needs for programs, services and support: A national study. *Sibling Information Network Newsletter, 7*(1), 1–4.

"Jennifer." (1990). Mailbag: a column for siblings to speak out. *Sibpage: A newsletter for and by brothers and sisters of children with special needs, 2*(4), 2.

Lamb, M.E., & Meyer, D.J. (1991). Fathers of children with special needs. In M. Seligman (Ed.), *The family with a handicapped child* (pp. 151–179). Boston: Allyn & Bacon.

Lobato, D.J. (1990). *Brothers, sisters, and special needs: Information and activities for helping young siblings of children with chronic illnesses and developmental disabilities.* Baltimore: Paul H. Brookes Publishing Co.

May, J. (1991). *Fathers of children with special needs: New horizons.* Bethesda, MD: Association for the Care of Children's Health.

McConachie, H. (1982). Fathers of mentally handicapped children. In N. Beal & J. McGuire (Eds.), *Fathers: Psychological perspectives* (pp. 144–173). London: Junction.

Meyer, D.J. (1986a). Fathers of children with special needs. In M.E. Lamb (Ed.), *The father's role: Applied perspectives* (pp. 227–254). New York: John Wiley & Sons.

Meyer, D.J. (1986b). Fathers of handicapped children. In R. Fewell & P. Vadasy (Eds.), *Families of handicapped children* (pp. 35–73). Austin, TX: PRO-ED.

Meyer, D.J., & Vadasy, P.F. (1986). *Grandparents Workshops: How to organize workshops for grandparents of children with handicaps.* Seattle: University of Washington Press.

Meyer, D.J., Vadasy, P.F., & Fewell, R.R. (1985). *Sibshops: A handbook for implementing workshops for siblings of children with special needs.* Seattle: University of Washington Press.

Meyer, D.J., Vadasy, P.F., Fewell, R.R., & Schell, G. (1985). *A handbook for the Fathers Program: How to organize a program for fathers and their handicapped children.* Seattle: University of Washington Press.

Nollette, C. (1985). *Autism . . . A family affair: A curriculum for use with siblings of special needs children.* Minneapolis: Minneapolis Children's Medical Center.

Powell, T.H., & Ogle, P.A. (1985). *Brothers & sisters—A special part of exceptional families.* Baltimore: Paul H. Brookes Publishing Co.

Usdane, S., & Melmed, R. (1988). *Siblings Exchange Program: A support program for brothers and sisters of the disabled.* Phoenix: Phoenix Children's Hospital.

Vadasy, P.F., Fewell, R.R., & Meyer, D.J. (1986). Grandparents of children with special needs: Insights into their experiences and concerns. *Journal of the Division of Early Childhood, 10*(1), 36–44.

Vadasy, P.F., Fewell, R.R., Meyer, D.J., & Greenberg, M.T. (1984). Supporting fathers of handicapped young children: Preliminary findings of program effects. *Analysis and Intervention in Developmental Disabilities, 5*, 151–163.

chapter 7

Cognitive Coping at Parents Helping Parents

Florene Stewart Poyadue

Strategies for coping with all of the various aspects of family life are as individualized as the life events that we each experience every day. Sometimes our coping responses are behavioral—we count to 10, we go for a long walk, we scream and shout. Sometimes our coping responses are cognitive in nature—we think about a situation in a way that will enhance our sense of well-being. We may compare our own situation to someone else's and feel better that we have our set of circumstances to deal with rather than another's; or perhaps we look ahead to someone further along in life's journey and feel a sense of hope about our own future. Considering that there may be positive benefits to an event may make an otherwise stressful situation seem less so. Sometimes simply gathering information so that a sense of mastery or control over a situation becomes possible is helpful. Working to understand why an event has occurred and what it may mean is another way of coping cognitively with the adventures, both easy and difficult, that life sends our way. The use of humor often facilitates the successful resolution of a difficult situation and reduces stress. At Parents Helping Parents (PHP), a parent-directed family resource center (PDFRC) in San Jose, California, parents of children who have special needs are provided with many opportunities to enhance and utilize their own style of cognitive coping.

To families who are meeting the challenges of a disability within the family, PHP provides the opportunity to grow, to be realistic, and to still hold on to all of the positive thinking and hope that they create for themselves. Committed to the right of children to achieve their full potential, and to receive coordinated, community-based health care, education, social, and legal services with respect and dignity, through family and professional empowerment, PHP began providing emotional and informational support to families in 1976.

PHP enhances each parent's personal coping skills by assuming a foundation of family wellness. At Parents Helping Parents, all families are considered to be well families, and the presence of a family member with a disability doesn't change a family's wellness. Regrettably, what does change is how families are viewed by society when one of the family members has special needs.

The pervasive societal view that families who are challenged by disability are less well and are overwhelmed by so many additional burdens in itself *creates* a need for coping. At PHP, the assumption is that all families are functional and the challenges that families face from time to time result not so much from the presence of a disability, but rather from a society that is sometimes less than supportive and understanding.

Indeed, at PHP, there is great discomfort with the whole notion of coping. The word *coping* strikes a negative chord and the concept of coping conjures images of weakness, constant sorrow, and a sense of just hanging on, tolerating, or making the most of a bad situation. Since we do not want to think of our children as a "bad situation," the word *coping* is seldom heard at PHP. Parents know full well the need to be able to cope when necessary; yet they want other parents to know that coping does not have to become a way of life after a child with special needs is born.

The philosophy of PHP is that there is no one right way to build upon personal coping strategies—but through self-help services that increase knowledge, parent-to-parent contacts that model and share marathon skills that are so important for life's journey, and mutual problem solving, parents are encouraged to discover, use, and appreciate their own personal coping skills.

One of the cornerstones of PHP, and one of the most powerful coping supports it offers to parents, is the mentor visiting parent (MVP) program. An MVP is matched with another parent whose child and family experiences are similar to his or her own. The role of the MVP is to facilitate self-discovery. The MVP listens, supports, serves as a role model for, and encourages the newly referred parent as together they travel on their own family journeys. The story of a woman I'll call Susan illustrates how well this process works.

SUSAN'S FAMILY STORY

Part 1

Four years ago, I celebrated a graduation with Susan. This special occasion marked both the end and the beginning of an era—for Susan and for me, and we both shed tears of sadness and of joy as we shared our mutual memories. Susan's graduation marked her completion of a 9-hour training course for becoming a mentor visiting parent at PHP. For 5 years I had served as Susan's MVP, and now she was going to share that same unique gift with other parents whose children had special needs. The torch had been passed—parent to parent.

Susan and I first met via the telephone over 8 years ago. She called PHP in the desperate hope that somehow she, as a single parent, could keep going— keep meeting the needs of her infant daughter with Down syndrome, and keep holding down her job despite weeks of sleepless nights and a child-care situation that she knew was not ideal. As I hung up the phone after listening to and talking with Susan, I felt both emotionally depleted and emotionally energized.

This young mother was at the end of her rope—her limits having been reached by the challenges of infancy, disability, and single parenthood all rolled into one. Her daughter was on a heart monitor and was having trouble eating, meaning that most of Susan's interactions with her were difficult and filled with anxiety. Susan's own employment situation was precarious due in large part to the many times she had to come in late or miss a day entirely to respond to her daughter's needs. Susan believed that the woman who was providing child care was so nervous about possible medical complications that she was afraid to interact at all with her daughter. Sobbing, she readily admitted to the appeal of simply abandoning her daughter in a motel room, so that for once she herself could get some much needed rest and go back to work without the constant interruptions. It was, to say the least, a difficult situation for both Susan and her daughter. And it was an emotionally draining conversation for me.

And yet, I felt energized, because as I listened to and talked with Susan, I was able to validate her frustration, anger, and need for support—because I too am a parent of a child with Down syndrome. Our common bond, I believe, made it easier for her to share openly with me the intensity of her feelings and the urgency of her need for added supports. As an MVP, I was able to help her acknowledge her own feelings, explore options, and make the best possible decisions for her family. Together we mapped out a plan to request some emergency respite care for her daughter. Of the 24 hours that Susan had while her daughter was being provided with alternative care, Susan spent 18 of them sleeping and the other 6 talking with me.

We talked about a variety of options as a part of our "situation-solving" process. At PHP, "problem solving" is reframed to become "situation solving" in recognition that, with or without a child with special needs, life naturally offers many complex adventures that need to be addressed. Viewing these adventures as situations rather than problems is an example of the cognitive coping strategy of finding a more positive way of interpreting life and its many happenings. Sometimes this simple positive emphasis makes all the difference in the mind of a parent. It certainly did for Susan. Susan and I observed that usually there is no one solution that works; many times there is no final solution, whether or not one is dealing with a disability-related issue. Each diverse family uniquely solves its own situations cloaked in the fabric of the previous events of its life. The art of decision making and cognitive coping are natural aspects of life that go on and on for all human beings.

As Susan's MVP, I was the first person to approach her family from the wellness perspective that is the hallmark of PHP. My confidence in the wellness of her family was a source of strength for Susan day in and day out, and she too began to believe in her own wellness. Viewing her family as a well family was an important coping strategy for Susan, allowing her to focus on the positives that existed in her own family situation. Susan no longer needed to cope with her own doubts, but now had only to deal with the coping that society expected that she needed to do.

Susan, in the supportive environment that often can be facilitated only by another parent who has walked in the same shoes, connected with some of her intense feelings—confusion about Down syndrome, guilt about having to work, anxiety about losing control, the loneliness and isolation that often accompany the birth of a child with a disability, and the exhaustion that comes with sleepless nights. As we talked, I could feel Susan looking to me as a role model, as someone to whom she could compare herself and gain a sense of hope that if I had "made it," then so could she. I was Susan's window on the future, and through me, perhaps for the first time, Susan dared to consider that there might be a happy future for herself and for her daughter. I was Susan's social comparison and, as such, I served as the vehicle that helped Susan to get in touch with her own capacity to use the cognitive coping strategy of social comparisons. As an MVP, my simply being there for Susan was a powerful stimulus for her own self-awareness about her own strengths. Susan herself validated this for me when she said, "Boy, if you can do it, then so can I."

At PHP, we have found that the more information and resources families have, the less need they have for support and coping. Providing families with information—about available community resources, about the disability, about their legal rights, about financial supports, about other families who have walked before them—empowers them to negotiate for the supports and services that will best meet their needs. When families are informed, then they are the masters of their own destinies. Families at PHP report that this sense of mastery and control is a powerful cognitive coping strategy for managing the day-to-day, as well as the long-term, logistics of life itself.

As Susan and I continued to talk during our early contacts 8 years ago, her many questions to me suggested her great need for information. We explored all of the existing avenues of support for her need to protect her employment status, and yet feel understood and supported in her role as a new parent of a child with Down syndrome. As options were uncovered, Susan slowly became convinced that she had alternatives to her early desperate plan to abandon her daughter in a motel room. Each new bit of information became a part of the "road map" that Susan was now able to construct herself. As an MVP, I served as the source of this information initially, modeling for her the many ways to obtain information. PHP provides in addition to the one-to-one matched opportunity, an extensive library of resources—information about disabilities, about available local services, about national resources—and a series of workshops and training sessions around legal, medical, financial, educational, and parenting issues. As Susan became her own master of information, I became merely her traveling companion. She now had an awareness of her own coping skills to identify and locate the information she needed to plan the best possible route for her daughter and for herself.

Susan decided to develop a three-pronged approach to meeting her daughter's needs as well as her own. Using the directory of community services and resources that was available through PHP's Special Needs Library, Susan discovered that there was an integrated day-care program that provided child care for children with special needs and offered a sliding scale for the payment of fees. She and I talked first about questions that she might ask about the center, and then we went together to talk to the director. Because Susan had prepared in advance, she felt quite comfortable advocating for her daughter, and again was coping through her use of mastery and control.

Susan was also interested in learning more about her daughter's feeding difficulties and the heart surgery that loomed ahead. Despite the fact that Susan and I had been matched based upon similarity of disability and family issues, my son had not needed heart surgery, and so my experiences with this aspect of Down syndrome were limited. Working through PHP, however, a second match was made for Susan, pairing her with a mother whose 2-year-old had undergone a similar surgery. This mom was enormously helpful to Susan and shared with her a great deal of medical information about the procedures, as well as some of her own personal coping strategies for getting through this stressful time. Susan also began to attend PHP's Family Rap or Guidance Sessions (FROGS) so that she could talk with other parents about ways to simplify her daughter's feeding sessions. FROGS are informal morning or evening sessions for several families to discuss common issues, concerns, and feelings. Guidance is provided by an experienced parent or professional speaking on a specific topic, with plenty of time allowed for the sharing of ideas. Parents have an opportunity to learn new information, thus increasing their sense of mastery, as well as a chance to make social comparisons as a way of coping cognitively with their own set of circumstances. Humor is very much a part of FROGS (indeed the name has a humorous derivation—FROGS are so named because just as the princess had to fall in love with the frog in order to see that he was really a prince, so too do people merely need to fall in love with children who have special needs to begin to see the beauty in them), and the sessions are often filled with the special laughter that comes from common understandings and issues.

In order to be sure that Susan's own needs were being met, so that she could then meet her daughter's needs, respite care opportunities were explored. PHP maintains a roster of "family friends," volunteers who are willing to provide respite care when primary caregivers need a break. Scheduling a few hours a week when she could have some time to herself gave Susan a new outlook on her role as a parent of a child with special needs. Strengthened by this opportunity to nurture herself, Susan's perspective began to change. She was

more able to see that, along with the challenges, there were some positive benefits that came with parenting a child with special needs—not the least of which
were the special bonds she formed with her "family friends."

Susan and I had successfully worked through a difficult situation for her
family. Through PHP, Susan was provided with opportunities to build upon her
own strengths and coping strategies, and to do so surrounded by other parents
who knew firsthand her issues and challenges. These connections with other
parents through the MVP program and the many training workshops provided
Susan with an important support network that significantly reduced her isolation, and surrounded her with many examples of cognitive coping strategies.

Another chapter in Susan's story offers a wonderful example of how
parent–professional collaboration can work to enhance the coping strategies
that families already have in place.

Part 2

Despite the fact that Susan is now an MVP to other parents who come into PHP
for emotional and informational support, she and I still benefit immensely from
our continuing relationship with each other. In many ways, I continue to be her
MVP, as she serves as an MVP to others. Her capacity to cope and to know that
she can cope comes in part from the nurturing she receives from me—
likewise, she nurtures and supports the referred parents with whom she is
matched and provides a safe environment in which they are free to explore their
own coping skills.

Life marches on, though, for Susan and her family. Susan's daughter began to have seizures when she started the 2nd grade, and there had been several
times when she had a seizure while at school. These public seizures were terrifying for her daughter as well as for the other children in the classroom. Susan
called to share her concern with me and to brainstorm possible solutions. Together we coped by considering the fact that at least Susan's daughter was capable of telling us about how she felt so that we knew where to start (making a
social comparison). We gathered in as much relevant information as we could to
assist us with the development of our action plan (gaining a sense of mastery
and control). The next day, Susan called the school to request a meeting with
the principal, the school nurse, and her daughter's classroom teacher. Susan
suggested that, as a staff person at PHP, I come into the classroom to talk about
how people are alike and different and the fact that there are differences over
which we have no control—some people are left-handed, some have asthma,
some have seizures—but people are people just the same.

As we carried out our plan, the response from the children in the classroom was heartwarming. They easily volunteered information about their own
differences. One child raised her hand and wanted the other children to know
that she had a hard time understanding math and that she hoped that they
wouldn't laugh at her. Another hand went up: "I have allergies and sometimes

have to use an inhaler." Still another child volunteered that his uncle had multiple sclerosis and shared his concern that he too might develop his uncle's illness. The highlight of the afternoon came when Susan's daughter raised her hand and shared that she sometimes has seizures, and that it's scary but it's okay. The relief on her face that came with her pronouncement was a powerful testimony to the importance of parent–professional collaboration that enhances and makes the most of everyone's own individual coping styles.

Part 3

Just last year, Susan joined the Directing Board at PHP—a role that she feels will allow her to give back to the agency a small piece of the invaluable support she herself has received during her 8-year association with our organization. By providing Susan with this opportunity to work side by side with community leaders, parents, and service providers, PHP is continuing to contribute to and enhance Susan's coping strategies. She feels empowered by her co-equal role with professionals, and her own sense of well-being is certainly strengthened by her knowledge and recognition that she herself has much to give—to PHP, to other parents, and to professionals.

CURRENT EFFORTS OF PHP

Provides Comprehensive
Services for Families and Professionals

One of the most important components of PHP has been the evolution of the support services that are available to families. The mentor visiting parent program, providing the one-to-one matched opportunity between trained veteran parents and newly referred parents, continues to be at the heart of our organization. PHP is one of 55 statewide federally funded PTIs (Parent Training & Information Centers). In recognition of the fact that there are many different ways to enhance and expand upon individual coping styles, PHP now offers a comprehensive array of support services to families:

Parent-to-parent contacts
Information and referral
Training opportunities
Care service coordination, or case management assignments
Respite care
Sibling support groups
Special needs library
Newsletter
FROGS (Family Rap or Guidance Sessions)
Specific disability groups (parent support groups)
Gifts for infants up to 12 months who are referred

Information packets on services and disabilities
Speakers bureau

Thus, PHP is a one-stop shop that serves families from before birth and throughout the life cycle. Families either receive direct supports and services at PHP, or they are referred to the appropriate service agency in the local community. The MVP moves with the family and serves as the "guide at the side" to ensure that referrals to other agencies are successful. The strategy of supporting the successful navigation of the sometimes confusing service system is one that contributes a great deal to an overall sense of family well-being.

The recognition that professionals are important members in the circles of support that surround families has led to a comparable evolution of participation opportunities for professionals. In the same way that efforts to enhance a sense of well-being for parents have a positive impact on the child, similar efforts on behalf of service providers may have a positive impact on parents. Providing support to families happens in many different ways, including supporting the professionals who work with families. The following services are available at PHP for professionals:

Annual symposium on children with special needs
Workshops for medical professionals taught by parents themselves on better
    ways to deliver the diagnosis
Internships for professionals interested in establishing a parent-directed family
    resource center in their local community

PHP is a conduit that connects families and the professional community while offering a cornucopia of services directly to families and practitioners.

Serves as Model for Other
Parent-Directed Family Resource Centers

Since 1990, PHP, as a model parent-directed family resource center, has been offering replication training nationwide to parents and professionals interested in establishing a PDFRC in their communities. Currently, 10% of the inquiries that we receive come from other states and countries seeking technical assistance on how to start a PDFRC. There is now a recognition that a one-stop-shop opportunity (as delivered by a PDFRC) to receive appropriate, individualized support is extremely useful for families. Families need only to make one telephone call to be connected to the whole arena of family supports offered in their home community. The family-centered philosophy of recognizing and building upon family strengths, respecting individual differences, building trusting relationships, and empowering families to direct the service delivery system are at the heart of the PDFRC (Shelton, Jeppson, & Johnson, 1992).

Families and professionals alike are supported at PDFRCs in their coping efforts on behalf of family members who have special needs. Families are provided with a supportive environment for acknowledging their own reactions and feelings and exploring the causes and meaning of the disability, for gathering information to strengthen their own sense of control, for comparing their situation with others' in ways that add to their own sense of well-being, for being supported in seeing the positive benefits of their experiences with disability and in envisioning great expectations for the future, and for using humor to find the fun. Professionals report that the presence of a PDFRC in their community enhances their own capacity to cope with their personal and professional challenges of finding the most meaningful ways to support families. As one service provider related, "It's such a relief to know that you [Parents Helping Parents] are there to provide the support that only other parents can. Your presence makes it easier for me to fulfill the responsibilities that our agency *can* fulfill."

Fosters Parent–Professional and Interagency Collaboration

Developing parent–professional collaboration is another important effort of PHP. Collaboration between and among families and those providing professional services to them leads to a service system that is truly seamless in the delivery of family-centered care.

Another major effort of PHP has been the interagency, intercommunity collaboration that has occurred as PHP has developed into an integral part of the San Jose community. As an agency, PHP is basically no different from any other private, not-for-profit organization. We operate professionally, utilizing a staff and board members that have the appropriate education and credentials for the positions they hold. All of our staff also have personal experience, in the role of parent of a child with special needs. Staff members are joined by other parents, representatives from various service agencies, and community leaders to sit and work together as members of the several different boards at PHP.

Encourages New Ways of Understanding the Adjustment Process

Much has been written about the stages that parents move through as they adjust to all of the new roles and responsibilities that accompany the presence of a family member with a disability (Moses, 1983; Seligman, 1979). Typically, these various stage theories describe a series of reactions, beginning with shock and confusion and ending with acceptance, as the family comes to terms with their new reality.

At PHP, we believe that there is a stage beyond acceptance, and we call it the "appreciation" or the "all right" stage. During this stage, coping is no longer a necessary part of the family's daily living, and life is really okay. Parents experiencing the appreciation stage not only accept the fact that their children have mental retardation, but they feel that the presence of this disability is really all right. Many parents report developing "a new set of normals" for their child, no longer comparing the growth and development of their son or daughter with children who do not have a disability. Instead of asking, "What is he *not* doing that other normal kids his age *are* doing?" parents in the appreciation stage are more apt to ask, "What is he doing today that he couldn't do last month?" Parents are now looking for the positives in their children and using the cognitive coping skill of social comparisons—but only in reference to their children themselves. Parents report that there is a world of difference in the peace, love, abiding happiness, and deep-seated joy that is felt when one transcends from the level of acceptance to the level of appreciation. Susan, the woman discussed earlier in this chapter, acknowledged her own transition to this stage of appreciation when she completed the MVP training and began to be an emotional and informational resource for other parents.

Professionals need to be aware of this all right stage as well. Without an understanding of the depth of appreciation that parents feel for the strengths within their family, some professionals may think that these parents have suddenly lost sight of their child's diagnosis or at least the prognosis. They may describe this as being "in denial." They may be tempted to give out a double dose of negativism to bring the parent back to their professional view of reality—a reality that unfortunately includes some form of ongoing/chronic sorrow and coping. As an MVP, Susan reported to me that on one of her visits to the home of her referred parent, she found this parent to be unusually sad and depressed as compared to the last several contacts. Through her empathetic listening, Susan discovered that this parent had had several contacts with a professional who, through a general misunderstanding of the adjustment/appreciation process, kept trying to point out what he saw to be the harsh reality of her set of circumstances.

When service providers try to talk parents out of their feelings, they are interfering with the parents' own naturally developing coping strategies. Recognizing the importance of and being aware of and validating individual coping styles that parents bring with them is one of the most important roles that a support person can play.

FUTURE DIRECTIONS FOR PHP

PHP will continue to provide emotional, informational, and logistical support to families who have a member with special needs, and consulting and educational services to the professionals who are providing services to families. Our efforts will continue to be guided by our belief in the wellness of families, our commitment to a family-centered philosophy, and our dedication to the importance of parents helping other parents.

Enhance Parent-to-Parent Contacts

The one-to-one matched opportunity is the very foundation of PHP, and we will be exploring our opportunities to increase the diversity of our MVPs, so that our requests for specialized matches can be more easily met. Particularly, we will be making efforts to involve as MVPs more fathers, more parents for whom English is a second language, and more parents who are traditionally under-represented in the service system because they are socially, economically, edu-cationally, occupationally, and/or geographically challenged. We will also in-crease our outreach efforts to include more siblings and grandparents in the mentor role.

We intend to increase the amount of support we provide to our MVPs as they support their matched parent, so that we are indirectly providing additional support to referred families. Opportunities for MVPs to come together for mu-tual ongoing support—so that information, helpful strategies, and humor can be easily shared—will be explored. One MVP commented on the importance of getting together with other MVPs by saying, "I'm just a Dad, and all that I bring to my match is myself. When I can meet and talk with other MVPs, why then I benefit from all of their experiences and wisdom as well."

For many parents, becoming an MVP is the stepping stone to many other activities and roles. Strengthened by their own successes as an MVP, parents often seek additional ways to be involved on behalf of families. This additional involvement can be a great source of personal pride and may be seen as a posi-tive benefit of their own family situation. By supporting the interests and efforts of parents to become involved in such arenas as legislative advocacy and policy reform or preservice training for professionals, we will be offering parents an-other avenue for enhancing their sense of well-being.

Because matches cannot always be activated at the precise time of need, we will work to increase opportunities for drop-in parent-to-parent contacts. If a parent needs to talk with another parent, and the matched MVP is not avail-able, a staff member at PHP would be readily available to fill in. The timing of parent-to-parent contacts is often critical to successful coping.

Expand Parent Training Programs

Information often contributes to the ability of parents to cope with the chal-lenges of life, and at PHP we will be building on our repertoire of educational training sessions for parents. Workshops in such content areas as early inter-vention, situation solving, full inclusion, advocacy, family-centered care, educational and financial rights, and permanency planning will be added and/or expanded. We will also investigate alternative delivery styles for our workshops—audio and video cassettes and interactive technology will be ex-plored as options for facilitating the learning opportunities.

We will also be working with a humorist and/or cartoonist to infuse more humor into our training activities and materials. So often humor is such a powerful coping strategy, and sometimes it is the only coping strategy that is available. By including humor in our training sessions, we hope to model for parents the use and value of humor as a coping device.

Enable Parents To Be Equals in Partnership

Through preservice and inservice training opportunities in personnel preparation programs, we will work to involve parents as co-faculty. When parents are involved in the design and implementation of coursework that emphasizes family-centered approaches, then the providers of tomorrow benefit from both the modeling of parent–professional partnerships and the firsthand experiences of the parents. Who better to teach about what parents prefer than the parents themselves? The collaboration opportunities between PHP and universities hold so much potential for changing attitudes, while at the same time offering parents a chance to feel that they are indeed making a significant difference.

Parents, too, need the experiences of professionals as they begin to be presented with more opportunities to work in partnership with professionals. As programs hire parents as family service coordinators, and as parents begin serving in greater numbers on state and local interagency coordinating councils, transition councils, and advisory boards, their own coping strategies for managing these new opportunities will be enhanced by some awareness and skill-building information.

Yet professionals must recognize the enormous amount of information about their family and the service system that parents acquire on their journey. And professionals must receive administrative support for encouraging parents to bring this knowledge with them and to share it confidently at all planning meetings on behalf of the child and the family. When parents are truly accepted as credible members of the planning team and as co-partners with professionals, then a significant reason for parents feeling as if they have to cope will have been reduced.

Broaden Perception Scopes

In all of PHP's interactions with parents and with professionals, we will emphasize the importance of viewing the family and the child with a wide scope. Only through a conscious shift in perceptions and in attitudes will it be possible for all families to be seen as whole and functional, and for all children to be viewed holistically as well. At PHP, we will work to take a leadership role in solidifying this perceptual shift. Through seminars and institutes that are planned and implemented by teams of parents and professionals as true partners, we will continue to share this important message.

Develop International Networks

There is a growing interest internationally in the whole area of family support and finding better ways to enhance family well-being. At PHP, we are beginning to build an international network so that we can share information and training materials worldwide. In 1991, we hosted visitors from Africa, India, New Zealand, England, France, and Russia, and we expect that our international efforts will continue to expand. Perhaps just as experienced MVPs are matched with newly referred parents for support, so too, "veteran" PDFRCs or family support programs can be matched with folks in other countries who are interested in developing such a program.

FUTURE DIRECTIONS IN
RESEARCH ON COGNITIVE COPING

There seem to be three different directions that research on disability and cognitive coping might take in the future: 1) studies that would help to determine why some people seem better able to cope than others, 2) studies that examine the relationship between the quality of parent coping and outcomes for the children in the family, and 3) studies that explore the impact of the disability experience on various members of the family.

Factors that Enhance Coping

At PHP, one of the primary ways that we help families to cope is by matching an MVP with a parent newly referred to the program. We firmly believe that this one-to-one match is a significant support to parents and strengthens their overall ability to cope. However, there are as yet no firm data to confirm our beliefs. A study examining the relationship between the one-to-one matched experience and a parent's use of coping strategies would serve to validate our assumptions, and to strengthen the credibility of parent support efforts that utilize the parent-to-parent match.

A related research effort that would examine other varieties of family support and their impact on parent coping would also be useful. Can coping strategies be taught, and if so, what are the best ways to teach cognitive coping?

Studies that seek to examine individual factors that may or may not determine overall coping styles would be useful in designing support efforts. For example, there might be significant differences in the coping strategies of fathers, mothers, siblings, and/or extended family members of a child with special needs. What are these differences? How might these differences be taken into account when developing family support activities?

Outcomes of Successful Coping

A research effort that explores the relationship between successful parent coping and the adult life experiences of a child with a disability would lend credibility to the whole notion of enhancing parent coping as a way of providing quality supports for the child. How interesting it would be to discover that strong parent cognitive coping skills lead to a more satisfying adult life for the child with special needs. Might the same be true for siblings?

A whole line of research might be devoted to looking at the impact of the use of cognitive coping skills on the life and career choices that parents of children with special needs make across the life span. Does the use of cognitive coping determine marital or job stability? Does enhanced cognitive coping minimize child abuse?

Impact of the Disability Experience

Since societal attitudes toward disability are often mentioned by parents as a primary reason for having to cope, research that would look into how societal attitudes are determined (and how they might be changed) might teach us about ways to reduce some of the negative societal influences on families who have children with special needs. Often parents have to cope with the demands and pressures created by a society that imposes its degrading attitudes on those with special needs; thus research aimed at ameliorating this negative view might reduce the parents' need for coping. For example, does the full inclusion of children with disabilities into educational programs determine the attitudes that children (both with and without disabilities) have as adults toward individuals with special needs? What are some strategies for changing adult attitudes?

Until recently, most of the studies that look at the impact of disability have focused on either the individual with the disability or on the parents. Studies that examine the impact of the disability experience and of parental expectations on siblings would be useful in determining best practices for supporting siblings (see Meyer, chap. 6, this volume).

CONCLUSION

At PHP, we do not directly teach cognitive coping skills. We teach situation solving, planning, and negotiation skills, and we provide information, resources, and knowledge—all within the caring environment of parents helping other parents. These skills provide an infrastructure and an environment that is conducive to the acquisition of cognitive coping skills. Through the skills that we do teach, we stimulate, promote, and initiate the reframing of thinking in ways that enhance a sense of well-being. Clearly the need for all forms of coping decreases with increased respect, choices, and resources—all of which are provided at PHP.

ABOUT THE AUTHOR

Florene Stewart Poyadue, R.N., B.V.E., M.A., M.F.C.C.   It was an intriguing challenge to maintain my perspective as a service provider while writing this chapter, since I am also the parent of a child who has Down syndrome. My background as a legal secretary and my education and training as a nurse, teacher, and marriage and family counselor prepared me to develop the Parents Helping Parents (PHP) program, for which I have served as chief executive officer for the past 15 years. My thinking has been most influenced by what I've learned from the thousands of families I have counseled and trained, and especially by Mary Ellen Peterson and the late Georgette Strohm, who have been co-developers of PHP with me. My present passion is convincing others that there is as much diversity within any racial group of individuals as there is in the general population.

REFERENCES

Moses, K.I. (1983). The impact of initial diagnosis: Mobilizing family resources. In J.A. Mulick & S.M. Pueschel (Eds.), *Parent-professional partnerships in developmental disability services* (pp. 11–34). Cambridge, MA: Ware Press.
Seligman, M. (1979). *Strategies for helping parents of exceptional children.* New York: Free Press.
Shelton, T.L., Jeppson, E.S., & Johnson, B.H. (1992). *Family-centered care for children with special health care needs.* Bethesda, MD: Association for the Care of Children's Health.

chapter 8

The Implications of Salutogenesis
An Outsider's View

Aaron Antonovsky

It is generally wise to avoid neologisms. In developing the theory that has shaped my research over the past 15 years, however, I felt compelled to coin a new word—*salutogenesis*—to express what I saw as a radically new orientation. I, no less than all of my colleagues in biomedical and sociopsychological research, had studied the origins of diseases (i.e., used a pathogenic orientation). In my 1979 book, and more fully in the one that followed, I proposed that it was at least as important to understand the *origins of health*, and discussed in detail the serious and exciting implications of adopting a salutogenic orientation (Antonovsky, 1987, pp. 1–14).

A salutogenic orientation facilitates seeing things that experts in a given pathology might well fail to see. Bronfenbrenner (1986, p. 738) described the body of family research as:

> curiously one-sided, for its predominant focus is on . . . family disorganization and developmental disarray. Yet, for every study that documents the power of disruptive environments, there is a control group that testifies to the existence and unrealized potential of ecologies that sustain and strengthen constructive processes. . . .

Why have these "constructive processes" been ignored? I suggest that it is because the experts have been trained to think primarily about "germs," breakdown, and diseases—that is, to think pathogenically. At least some of the major implications of thinking salutogenically are explored in this chapter.

Why has it taken so long, in so many fields, even to begin to realize the limitations of the pathogenic orientation? How did I come to do so? I submit that it is in good part precisely because I am not an expert in disability, family, or cognition, and because I am no longer an expert in social class or coronary heart disease, as I once was, that I was open to the idea of salutogenesis. Feeling constrained at being an expert in a specific field, I came to read and think about work and alienation; about the health care systems of preliterate societies, and about utopian communities that survive; about cancer and heart disease; about children of schizophrenic parents; and about retirement. I even read the *Disabilities Studies Quarterly*.

Over and over again, a common problem emerged from this reading, one that is best put, on the most general level, as "order out of chaos" (Prigogine & Stengers, 1984). Or, to put it another way: How do living systems cope with omnipresent entropic, disorder-producing forces? I am not more learned, creative, or profound than most of my colleagues. But given my work habits, I came to see that the real mystery common to wherever I looked was survival in the face of Murphy's Law. My seemingly scatterbrained work habits gave birth to the idea of salutogenesis. The salutogenic orientation, in turn, given its concern with the broad, integrative concept of successful coping, reinforces the work habits. This is in contrast to the pathogenic orientation, which leads one to be an expert in a narrow field and, in that field, particularly if there are pressing problems of service, to concentrate on the coping failures.

Please do not misunderstand. I am not urging anyone to abandon a profound commitment to the field of developmental disability. I do suggest that it will be fruitful if specialized expertise is tempered with an openness to what is going on in seemingly unrelated fields, in an attempt to consider the underlying problems shared by many, and, above all, to learn from coping successes. Let me give a few concrete illustrations. Is it farfetched to suggest that you can learn much from understanding how some concentration camp survivors have successfully rebuilt their lives? Or how a teen-age single mother successfully raises her child? Or how, to refer to the days in which I originally wrote this chapter, Israeli society went on functioning with some normalcy while Iraqi Scud missiles landed in the Tel Aviv area? Once insights from other fields begin to emerge, they can be applied to one's own field.

PROBLEMS WITH TERMINOLOGY

What can a nonexpert with a salutogenic orientation offer that might be of value to the theme of the conference on Cognitive Coping in Families who have a member with a Developmental Disability (which was the impetus for this book)? A pathogenic orientation fits comfortably into a biomedical model, focusing narrowly on the particular diagnosed disease entity, the particular developmental disability (note, not even on developmental disabilities). A salutogenic orientation compels one to see a far broader picture, both in terms of defining the problem and in searching for coping resources. This view has led me to feel discomfort with each of the three main terms of the conference title: 1) *cognitive coping*, 2) *member with a developmental disability*, and 3) *in families*.

Cognitive Coping

First, what is meant by *cognitive* coping? The concept was defined by the conference planners as "thinking about a particular situation in ways that enhance a sense of well-being." Five examples of cognitive coping strategies were then given. In part, these strategies appeal to my common sense. But is there not, in this approach, an unstated assumption that the core, or even the totality, of the problems confronted by a family with a member with a developmental disability is *cognitive*? More important, does it not imply that *cognitive* coping strategies are the major resources to be used? Such implications would be most unfortunate. The problem set of such a family is a complexity of inextricably intertwined cognitive, affective, and instrumental issues. Does not the family have to deal with physical fatigue? with finding a good teacher? with guilt, anger, and blame? with anticipated and unanticipated expenses beyond its means? with the dangers of scapegoating and jealousy?

I am well aware of the ascendance of cognitive psychology in recent years. Over half a century ago, W.I. Thomas coined what has become one of sociology's important epigrams: "If men [sorry, but this was in the 1920s] define situations as real, they are real in their consequences" (quoted in Merton, 1957, p. 426). A situation may initially have to be defined and appraised cognitively. (For a discussion of the primacy of cognition, see Lazarus, 1984, and, in the context of coping with stressors, my discussion of this issue in Antonovsky, 1987, p. 149.) But then the affective and instrumental issues still have to be handled. What salutogenesis teaches us is that successful coping is a many-splendored sword, dealing simultaneously with the entire problem complex. To think that cognitive strategies alone are adequate is, I am afraid, quite naive.

Member with a Developmental Disability

This final term in the conference title likewise troubles me. If interpreted pathogenically, it poses the danger of seeing the very serious chronic stressor of developmental disability as the only or, at any rate, the major problem. Much as the oncologist sees only the tumor and the cardiologist only the artery blockage, so this phrase implies focusing only on the stressors directly associated with the disability, with the "index case." But do not families with members with developmental disabilities also have members who lose their jobs, women who are frustrated at having to stay home, women and men who hate their jobs and teen-agers who hate their schools, and elderly parents to take care of? Do they not also confront all the daily hassles, acute and chronic stressors other families confront, only some of which are directly linked to the disability? If one is disease or disability oriented, one focuses on dealing with the particular pathology; if one is health oriented, one focuses on coping with the stressors of living.

In order to avoid misunderstanding, I should make it clear that I am fully aware of the need to set priorities, to give attention to issues that at a given time are more burning than others. In the same way, there is undeniably a need for experts, in research and service. Yet I would insist that if there is not, at least on the conceptual level, an understanding of the broader picture, and the development of concepts and tools appropriate to the entire canvas, there will be limited success in the long run.

I have suggested, in discussing the first and third main terms of the conference title, that a salutogenic orientation leads us, first, to encompass the cognitive, emotional, and instrumental complexities of the developmental disability
problem; and second, to see that problem in the context of the overall set of
problems faced by many other families. In making these points, it may well be
that I am, as we say in Hebrew, "bursting through an open door"; that is, I am
only formulating explicitly what is implicitly clear or at least readily acceptable.
If this is the case, then at least no damage has been done.

In Families

It is the middle term in the title, *in families*, that troubles me most. What I have
to say may not be easily acceptable, to the extent that many professionals are
blinkered by pathogenesis. There is no way of getting away from the reality that
it is the family that, day in and day out, bears the main burden (or faces the
challenge—I return later to the meaning of which phrase is appropriate) of
coping with the chronic problem. It has been said that the salutogenic perspective
enables individuals to learn how to use their own resources to their best advantage when dealing with life's challenges. True, but it does far more than that!

A salutogenic orientation implies learning how to use the resources of the
family member with a disability and the resources of other family members.
But is also means learning how to use the resources of others as well. What
does this last phrase mean? It is easily understood in terms of social supports or
the use of experts, that is, resources to which the family turns. I submit, however, that once one starts searching for resources, one discovers that there are
potential resources that may be decisive in successful coping but over which no
individual family has direct control. I refer to the sociocultural context in which
family coping takes place. The foremost example of such a resource, or, rather,
in the present case, the absence of a resource, follows.

In American society, with its individualistic ethos, there is a void that is
incredible to the rest of the Western world. I refer to the fact that the United
States has no form of a national health insurance system. Of course there is
Medicaid, Aid to Families with Dependent Children (AFDC), and a wide and
complex network of community services. But in contrast to the commitment, at
least in theory, that every American child will have an equal chance to receive a
decent education, that every American home will have police protection, and so
on, as elementary rights, the United States has not adopted the same principle
with respect to health care. Many American families with a member with a
developmental disability are not able to count on the availability of crucially
needed resources as a right rather than as a function of their own ability to buy
resources or of a voluntary or governmental "Lady Bountiful." Of course no
society is so affluent that it can provide adequate resources to meet all needs. I
am sure that families with disabled members in Sweden or Britain or Canada,
not to mention Israel, have complaints. But at least they know that their so-

cieties have accepted the moral and legal responsibility for providing the resources to the best of their abilities.

This is one aspect of paying attention to the broader context within which family coping takes place. Consider two further examples. It may be of little direct comfort and aid to families with members with developmental disabilities that the society be committed to preventive activities designed to avoid an increase in the number of such families. I refer, of course, to the shocking inadequacies of prenatal services in general and in particular of assistance to pregnant women who are HIV positive or who have been caught in the net of substance abuse. A salutogenic orientation calls attention to the issue of who or what is "pushing people into the river" and not only to asking how to help "people who are struggling to keep afloat downstream." And perhaps such preventive action can help avoid the birth of a second child with a disability.

A third example of the importance of the sociocultural context is more directly related to coping. I refer to the question of stigma. I am afraid that I must be skeptical about the chances for successful coping with the stigma of disability by means of cognitive redefinition within the family or even within a self-help group, as important a first step as such redefinition is. Until the stigma prevailing in the culture in which one lives is erased, the individual family can only go so far. In fact, I suggest that taking part in a public, organized campaign to fight the stigma is one important, effective way for a given family to redefine its own situation successfully.

INTERIM SUMMARY

One way of summing up what I have discussed so far is to say that a pathogenic orientation focuses on the more immediate problem of the individual and on the appropriate therapy. A salutogenic orientation, concerned with overall health, pressures one to think in systems terms. It leads one to seek to understand and deal with all the entropic (disorder-promoting) forces and, more particularly, the negentropic (order-promoting) forces, the strengths not only within the system—in this case, the individual and the family—but also in the suprasystems within which the family functions. Seymour Sarason (as well as other psychologists, like George Albee) has for many years tried to call our attention to the issue, most recently phrasing it very succinctly and pointedly: "Any conception of the individual that is blatantly asocial and ahistorical . . . will get us to where we are: nowhere, a dead end" (1990, p. 1064).

I have, then, suggested that a salutogenic orientation goes much further than emphasizing cognitive family strengths in coping with the problems directly associated with the problems of developmental disabilities. I have tried to avoid abstractions, and have given concrete examples of what I mean. But if I were to integrate in one sentence the core of what I have said to this point, it would be: Much as a pathogenic orientation has led, with considerable success, to the formulation of theories of specific diseases, the salutogenic orientation opens the way to formulating a theory (or competing theories) of overall successful coping and health, or, rather, of moving toward the healthy end of the illness–health continuum. It is to this issue that I now turn.

THEORY OF SUCCESSFUL COPING

Having reached the stage in my own thinking of asking what prevented what I called "breakdown" (see Antonovsky, 1972 and 1974, for the initial formulation, and Antonovsky, 1990, for an overview of this development), I gave my attention to what I called *generalized resistance resources* (GRRs).

Generalized Resistance Resources

In my 1974 chapter, I defined a GRR as "the power which can be applied (by an individual) to resolve the tension expressive of a state of disturbed homeostasis" (p. 246). I discussed three GRRs in detail: 1) homeostatic flexibility, 2) ties to concrete others, and 3) ties to the total community. I proposed that each of these could make a valuable contribution to successful coping with a wide variety of stressors. A few years later, the study of social supports came into vogue. Health researchers, particularly in the mastery-oriented culture of the United States, became enamored of Rotter's (1966) internal locus of control. Here and there, the unusual clinician, or the family struggling with coping, distilled an idea from personal experience. Empirical studies produced promising findings (see, for example, Hinkle, 1974, on "insulation"). In good measure, however, this period was still in the spirit of pathogenesis. Consider my own GRRs: they referred to buffering, ameliorating, or mediating mechanisms, thought of as blunting the invariably negative impact of stressors and thus preventing breakdown.

New Questions

It is, however, only when one takes the paradigmatic leap of asking not "What prevents breakdown?" but the initial salutogenic question "What promotes health?" that one is open to new concepts and questions. We are all familiar with the concept of a *risk factor*. Can we then not think of the concept of a *salutary factor*? Concomitantly, once one realizes that the outcome of a stressor is not preordained, one can see that even undesirable stressors can have salutary outcomes. Likewise, a coping resource can be reconceptualized not merely as a buffer, which it undoubtedly can be, but as directly salutogenic. More important, we begin to search for coping resources that are available as potentials but that have not been actualized.

There is, however, a fundamental problem with this approach. Once this problem is confronted, we are led to what I believe is the most important contribution of the salutogenic orientation. Although I would not say that bright ideas are a dime a dozen, unless one has some criterion, some culling rule, for separating wheat from chaff, some basis for predicting that a given characteristic, situation, cognition, or action is likely to promote health, the enterprise becomes hit or miss. Or, to put it more accurately, the ideas should derive from a theory and, in turn, be tested with a view to refining the theory. It was this realization that led me to the formulation of the sense of coherence (SOC) construct.

Sense of Coherence Construct

The SOC construct refers to an integrated way of looking at the world in which one lives. As long as I thought in terms of GRRs, as did most of my colleagues who had become interested in coping, I was limited to the level of bright ideas, testing each one, and accounting for this or that fraction of the variance. It was only when I began to ask *why* we think of GRRs such as social supports, a mastery orientation, cultural stability, and money were all useful in coping with stressors, or, to put it a better way, *what successful coping resources have in common*, that I was able to move ahead.

What the availability of a resource meant, I realized, was that it strengthened one or more of the three prerequisites for coping successfully with any problem. I call these prerequisites *comprehensibility, manageability,* and *meaningfulness*. To optimize the chances of successful coping with a stressor, one must believe that one *understands* the problem and that one has at one's disposal the *resources* that are needed, and one must *wish* to cope with the problem. A family that sees its world as comprehensible, as manageable, and as meaningful is a family that has a strong SOC and will, the theory predicts, have a good chance of coping well.

As Applied to Disabilities

A major determinant of the capacity of a family with a member with a developmental disability to cope successfully with the complex of problems it faces is the strength of its SOC. (For discussions of individual and family SOC, see Antonovsky & Sourani, 1988, and Sagy & Antonovsky, in press.) If this hypothesis is correct, then we are provided with both a systematic source of bright, practical ideas and a clear criterion for judging whether a given coping idea makes sense. A family with a strong SOC will develop and employ cognitive, affective, and instrumental strategies that are likely to facilitate coping. This in turn raises the question of how families, service personnel, and researchers can strengthen the SOC of the family. Perhaps no less important, one has a criterion for avoiding strategies that may weaken the SOC.

Space does not allow spelling out in detail how the SOC construct can be translated into concrete proposals. But let me give just one example, brought to my attention by a colleague with whom I discussed this chapter. She not only is familiar with the SOC theory, but also works with children with disabilities.

She pointed out that, in her emphasis on her own value of autonomy, she had urged a mother to invest the necessary energy and time to help her child learn to eat by himself. "I have six other children and a house to take care of," the mother replied. The expert was damaging the mother's sense of comprehensibility and manageability. I am loathe to try to give further examples, because my experience has been that the experts in a given field, once the theory is understood, are far more competent than I am at getting such ideas. I would, however, like to make three comments aimed at clarifying the SOC construct.

Coping

It is absolutely essential to understand that, as I have put it (Antonovsky, 1987, p. 138):

> A strong SOC is *not* a particular coping style. . . . The stressors life poses are many and varied. . . . To consistently adopt one pattern of coping . . . is precisely to fail to respond to the nature of the stressor and hence to decrease the chances of successful coping. . . . *What the person with a strong SOC does is to select the particular coping strategy that seems most appropriate to deal with the stressor being confronted.*

The availability of a wide repertoire of coping strategies, then, and flexibility in choice at any given time are crucial. This point is, I believe, of particular importance in American culture, with its emphases on action, mastery, and individual self-reliance. These culture traits may often lead to useful coping strategies, but they may just as often be inappropriate or even boomerang.

Meaningfulness

The more I have thought about the SOC, the more have I come to see the meaningfulness component as primary. Earlier, I referred to seeing a developmental disability as a burden or challenge. This is the motivational heart of the matter. Let me be clear that I am not speaking of pain or sadness. The SOC is not a panacea for happiness; it does not do away with tragedy. But given reality, the initial question becomes: Do I, or we, *wish* to cope? Starting from hopelessness, one can only despair about gaining understanding or mobilizing resources. Starting from seeing coping as desirable, whatever the difficulty in being assured of a positive outcome, increasing comprehensibility and manageability is more likely. Providing explanations and support, in the absence of motivation, is likely to be of little help.

SOC as a Dependent Variable

My final point refers to the nature of the SOC as a dependent variable. In discussing the development of a strong SOC (Antonovsky, 1987, chap. 5), I argued that by the end of young adulthood, one's location on the SOC continuum, barring major and lasting changes in one's life situation, is more or less fixed. The imprint of childhood, educational, and work experiences is powerful in shaping how one has come to see the world. If this is correct, two conclusions follow. First, it is essential to structure, from very early childhood on, life experiences of the family member with a developmental disability that contribute to a strong SOC. The core characteristics of these experiences are *consistency*, which strengthens comprehensibility; an *overload–underload balance*, which strengthens manageability; and *participation in socially valued decision making*, which strengthens meaningfulness. What a wide variety of GRRs have in common is that they make such experiences more likely. These cannot be discussed in detail here (for an in-depth discussion, see Antonovsky, 1987, chap. 5). I can only say that these concepts provide us with guidelines for structuring and evaluating experiences.

The second conclusion that follows from the idea that the SOC is shaped in good part by early life experiences may be discouraging. It suggests that the task of significantly strengthening the SOC of adult family members is well-nigh insurmountable. Only incurable and self-deceptive optimism denies that "it is too late or too hard" in some cases. Is there, then, nothing to be done? I think there is, at two levels. In some cases, it may be possible to transform radically the life situation of one or more family members, with particular regard to their major life activity. The very first issue I would raise with a family member is: "Is your work an ongoing, daily complex of experiences that strengthens or weakens your SOC?" If the answer is that the SOC is being weakened, then the question becomes how this situation can be changed. At a second, more limited level, there are small changes that can be made that can just slightly increase the strength of the SOC. Thus, for example, the adoption of family rituals (see Boyce, Jensen, Sherman, & Peacock, 1983) provides consistency. Only adolescents or diehard revolutionaries disdain steps that make life a bit more bearable without fully solving problems. Most of us are grateful for such ease.

Testing the Theory

I believe that the salutogenic model all too briefly presented here makes a good deal of sense. It provides, first and foremost, a fundamental way of thinking and a rich program of research. I also think that it is a systematic source of guidelines to action. As a researcher, however, I must be cautious. As persuaded as I am that I am on the right track, the evidence is very far from being all in. Since the full model, including an instrument to measure the SOC, was only published in 1987, there is as yet no basis for saying that there are strong data that support and few data that refute the theory. But to my knowledge, there are some 115 ongoing studies, and more than 40 published papers, dissertations, and theses. These are being conducted in 20 countries and cover a wide range of ages and health issues. I here refer briefly only to a few studies that have focused on disability, conducted under the direction of Malka Margalit of the Department of Special Education at Tel Aviv University.

Four findings are noteworthy. First, both the mothers and fathers of children with severe disabilities have lower SOC scores than do the parents in control groups. This was true in a case-control study of 67 kibbutz families with children who had severe or moderate disabilities (Margalit, Leyser, Avraham, & Lewy-Osin, 1988), as well as in Bargteil's (1989) study of 83 urban families with children with chronic severe disabilities. Further, the mean SOC score in a study of 34 young adults with cerebral palsy (Margalit & Cassel-Seidenman, 1987) was substantially lower than that of most other samples for whom data were available. Second, in both the Margalit et al. and the Bargteil studies, the SOC scores of mothers were lower than those of fathers, the difference being slightly greater in the study than in the control groups. Third, in both studies the SOC was found to be closely related to the relationships dimension of Moos' Family Environment Scale (Moos & Moos, 1986). Finally, in the Margalit and Cassel-Seidenman study it was found that of the three components of the SOC, meaningfulness accounted for a major part of the variance on a measure of life satisfaction. None of these are longitudinal outcome studies, testing the SOC–successful coping hypothesis. Nor do I wish to present the results of other studies here, although these are beginning to become available. My purpose, rather, was simply to hint at the rich research possibilities offered by a salutogenic model.

CONCLUSION

The thesis of this chapter is that a salutogenic orientation has far wider implications than simply providing a directive to focus on the health rather than on the pathology of persons with developmental disabilities and to study those who have coped successfully. It has been pointed out that there is much to learn from studies that deal with the "order out of chaos" problem in a wide variety of fields. The perspective directs us to define the problem-coping complex of disability as one that includes cognitive, affective, and instrumental problems and modes of coping; to see the directly disability-linked issues in the context of the totality of family problems; and to see the issue of coping not only in the family context, but in the far broader social structural and cultural context of community and society.

Further, I have tried, albeit telegraphically, to show how the salutogenic orientation opened the possibility for me to develop the construct of the sense of coherence as the core of a theory of successful coping. This theory, if borne out by research, will provide a systematic, parsimonious set of guidelines for programs of action. Such programs will, with careful evaluation, feed back into improving the theory.

As one who sits in the ivory tower of research, let me close by saluting the courage of those who, in service or as family members or both, are daily in the front lines. If my thoughts and work are of any use to you, I am well rewarded.

ABOUT THE AUTHOR

Aaron Antonovsky My attention as a researcher in stress and coping was caught some 20 years ago by the extraordinary capacity of some concentration camp survivors to rebuild their lives and health. This eventually led me to propose the crucial significance of understanding the *salutogenic* process (versus the pathogenic focus) and the construct of sense of coherence. Gratifyingly, these concepts have stimulated considerable research in some 20 countries and in many health domains. As a teacher of medical and nursing students, I have tried to train them to be salutogenic forces. And, as a citizen of a stressor-ridden region, I try to understand the pathways of successful coping.

REFERENCES

Antonovsky, A. (1972). Breakdown: A needed fourth step in the conceptual armamentarium of modern medicine. *Social Science and Medicine, 6,* 537–544.
Antonovsky, A. (1974). Conceptual and methodological problems in the study of resistance resources and stressful life events. In B.S. Dohrenwend & B.P. Dohrenwend (Eds.), *Stressful life events: Their nature and effects* (pp. 245–258). New York: John Wiley & Sons.
Antonovsky, A. (1987). *Unraveling the mystery of health.* San Francisco: Jossey-Bass.
Antonovsky, A. (1990). A somewhat personal odyssey in studying the stress process. *Stress Medicine, 6,* 71–80.
Antonovsky, A., & Sourani, T. (1988). Family sense of coherence and family adaptation. *Journal of Marriage and the Family, 50,* 79–92.
Bargteil, D.M. (1989). *Personal and familial resources among parents of disabled children.* Unpublished master's thesis, Department of Psychology, Tel Aviv University, Tel Aviv.
Boyce, W.T., Jensen, E.W., Sherman, A.J., & Peacock, J.L. (1983). The Family Routines Inventory: Theoretical origins. *Social Science and Medicine, 17,* 193–200.
Bronfenbrenner, U. (1986). Ecology of the family as a context for human development research perspectives. *Developmental Psychology, 22,* 723–742.
Hinkle, L.E. (1974). The effect of exposure to culture change, social change, and changes in interpersonal relationships on health. In B.S. Dohrenwend & B.P. Dohrenwend (Eds.), *Stressful life events: Their nature and effects* (pp. 9–44). New York: John Wiley & Sons.
Lazarus, R.S. (1984). On the primacy of cognition. *American Psychologist, 39,* 124–129.
Margalit, M., & Cassel-Seidenman, R. (1987). Life satisfaction and sense of coherence among young adults with cerebral palsy. *Career Development for Exceptional Individuals, 10,* 42–50.
Margalit, M., Leyser, Y., Avraham, Y., & Lewy-Osin, M. (1988). Social-environmental characteristics (family climate) and sense of coherence in kibbutz families with disabled and non-disabled children. *European Journal of Special Needs Education, 3,* 87–98.
Merton, R.K. (1957). *Social theory and social structure.* Glencoe, IL: Free Press.
Moos, R.H., & Moos, B.S. (1986). *Family Environment Scale manual* (2nd ed.). Palo Alto, CA: Consulting Psychologists Press.
Prigogine, I., & Stengers, I. (1984). *Order out of chaos: Man's new dialogue with nature.* Toronto: Bantam.

Rotter, J.B. (1966). Generalized expectancies for internal versus external control of reinforcement. *Psychological Monographs, 80*(1).
Sagy, S., & Antonovsky, A. (in press). The family sense of coherence and the retirement
transition. *Journal of Marriage and the Family.*
Sarason, S. (1990). [Review]. *Contemporary Psychology, 35,* 1064.

chapter 9

Coping with Stress
The Beneficial Role
of Positive Illusions

Jonathon D. Brown

Coping is a complex affair. Behaviors that provide benefits in one situation may prove ineffective in another. Even within the same experience, temporal changes may alter the adequacy of attempts to manage stressful events. Adaptability, rather than inflexibility, is the key to successful coping.

This chapter explores the role that illusions play in promoting effective coping behaviors. The term *illusions* refers to a characteristic manner in which many individuals view themselves and their ability to act on the environment. Three illusions are particularly prominent. These involve tendencies on the part of individuals to: 1) possess unrealistically positive views of themselves, 2) overestimate their ability to control environmental events, and 3) entertain views of their future that are more optimistic than probability estimates can justify (Taylor & Brown, 1988). Beliefs like these were once thought to be symptomatic or promotive of psychological dysfunction (see, for example, Jahoda, 1958). Increasing evidence suggests, however, that people who exhibit illusions enjoy better psychological and physical health than do those in whom these illusions are absent (Alloy & Abramson, 1988; Brown, 1991a; Sackeim, 1983; Taylor, 1983, 1989; Taylor & Brown, 1988). These benefits are most apparent when people struggle to cope with stressful life circumstances (Brown, 1991a; Taylor, 1983; Taylor & Brown, 1988).

Illusions typically involve a modicum of distortion. For instance, people who believe their chances of being involved in a fatal car crash are lower than actuarial data support are not being realistic (Weinstein, 1982). At the same time, it is often difficult to establish when any given individual is being unrealistic; after all, most individuals will not die in an automobile accident. For these reasons, it is best to view illusions simply as a characteristic way of viewing the world that accentuates the positive and is not necessarily grounded in reality.

The preparation of this article and some of the research reported herein was supported by National Science Foundation Grant No. BNS-8958211.

I thank Shelley Taylor for her many contributions to this project.

STRESS AND COPING

Understanding how illusions promote well-being under stress requires a familiarity with the stress process itself. Lazarus and his colleagues (Lazarus & Folkman, 1984; Lazarus & Launier, 1978) have provided a comprehensive account of this process. As shown in Figure 1, the model begins with the occurrence of a significant environmental event. The event triggers a process of primary appraisal. Here people (implicitly) ask themselves whether the event has implications for their well-being. If they answer affirmatively, they proceed to define these implications as positive or negative. Purely positive appraisals are apt to be rare (Brown & McGill, 1989; Lazarus & Folkman, 1984). Negative appraisals take one of three forms: 1) harm/loss (in the case where damage to well-being has already been sustained), 2) threat (in the case where damage to well-being appears imminent), and 3) challenge (in the case where damage to well-being, though impending, is seen as offering the potential for growth).

Secondary appraisals follow these assessments. During secondary appraisal, people attempt to define what can be done to manage a stressful experience. Here, individuals inventory the resources they command to offset or handle a stressful event. These resources include psychological factors (e.g., perceived characteristics such as perseverance or creative problem-solving abilities) and material factors (e.g., money), and can derive from self or others. Secondary appraisals combine with primary appraisals to affect the nature and intensity of the person's response to a stressful event.

Coping is the next stage in the stress process. Coping can be defined as the actual strategies people employ in their efforts to manage stressful life events. Lazarus and Folkman (1984) distinguished two kinds of coping strategies—problem-focused coping and emotion-focused coping. Other investigators have identified additional coping strategies (Billings & Moos, 1984; Carver, Scheier, & Weintraub, 1989; Endler & Parker, 1990).

Coping Dimensions

A synthesis of this research reveals two important dimensions regarding the manner in which people cope with stressful events (Table 1). The first dimen-

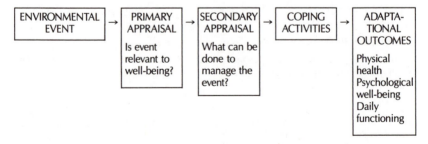

Figure 1.   Conceptual model of the stress process. (Adapted from Lazarus & Folkman, 1984)

Table 1. A conceptual framework of the coping process

Type of coping effort	Coping aim		
	Alter event	Transform implications	Manage consequences
Behavioral	Seek a reconciliation	Establish alternative relationships	Seek social support
Cognitive	Plan a reconciliation	Reinterpret event	Daydream

sion concerns the type of coping activities people initiate. This dimension pertains to whether the coping activity is behavioral or cognitive in nature. The second dimension concerns the immediate aim of the coping effort. Coping efforts can be targeted toward: 1) directly altering the precipitating event, 2) transforming the implications of an event for well-being, and 3) reducing the negative emotional consequences of a stressful event.

To illustrate these distinctions, consider the case of a man who is undergoing a painful divorce. Actively seeking a reconciliation or planning to initiate a reunification with his estranged wife are examples, respectively, of behavioral and cognitive attempts at directly altering the source of distress.

Attempts to transform the implications of the event can also take two forms. Behaviorally, the man can try to replace his wife by establishing alternative romantic involvements. Substitute activities like these, although leaving the source of distress intact, reduce stress by modifying the implications an event has for well-being. Essentially, getting on with his life enables the man to put the negative event behind him.

Cognitive attempts to transform the implications of an event also occur. These efforts typically involve reinterpreting an event in order to extract a more positive meaning (Taylor, 1983). Upon reflection, the man may decide that his marriage was actually ill conceived and that, in many ways, a divorce is preferable to an unhappy marriage.

Finally, coping includes attempts to reduce feelings of distress and depression that often accompany stressful events. For example, rather than taking instrumental action or seeking to reinterpret the stressful event, the man undergoing a divorce may simply try to put the event out of his mind. This might be accomplished behaviorally, by seeking social support from others, or cognitively, through the use of daydreaming or distraction.

Two important points about these strategies need to be made. First, people typically use more than one of these techniques in their attempts to manage a stressful encounter (Folkman & Lazarus, 1985). Second, the effectiveness of these strategies often depends on properties of the precipitating event (Vitaliano, DeWolfe, Maiuro, Russo, & Katon, 1990). Whether active attempts to alter the source of stress are adaptive, for example, partly depends on whether the source of stress is modifiable. Timing is also a critical factor. Effective action often requires a cool head. During the initial stages of a stressful encounter, attempts to manage the emotional consequences of stress—even if they involve escape and withdrawal—may be a necessary first step toward solving the problem (Lazarus, 1983).

Adaptational Outcomes

Returning to Figure 1, it may be seen that adaptational outcomes define the endpoint of the stress process. These outcomes include measures of physical health (e.g., blood pressure), psychological well-being (e.g., positive emotion, ability to think clearly), and daily functioning (e.g., resumption of social activities).

Summary

To summarize, environmental events trigger a process of cognitive appraisal. During primary appraisal, people classify the event in terms of its relevance to well-being; during secondary appraisal, they assess their ability to cope with the event. Coping itself consists of behavioral and cognitive attempts to: 1) alter the source of stress, 2) transform the implications of an event for well-being, and 3) reduce the emotional consequences of a stressful event. Collectively, these activities determine people's ability to adapt to a stressful encounter.

Although the preceding discussion has painted the stress and coping process in a linear fashion, an important feature of the process is its recursive nature. Primary appraisals, secondary appraisals, and coping strategies feed back into one another. To illustrate, cognitive reinterpretation (a coping mechanism) may lead one to conclude that an event was not as threatening as it initially seemed (a primary appraisal). In this manner, the component processes of the model are joined in reciprocal, rather than unidirectional, relations (Lazarus & Folkman, 1984).

ROLE OF ILLUSIONS

Having outlined a model of the stress and coping process, we are now ready to consider the role that illusions play in this process. As indicated earlier, illusions refer to the overly (and somewhat unrealistically) positive manner in which most individuals regard themselves, their capacity to effect desired changes in the environment, and their likelihood of experiencing a bright future. The evidence supporting the prevalence of these illusions has been documented elsewhere (Brown, 1991a; Taylor, 1989; Taylor & Brown, 1988) and is not reviewed here. Instead, the present focus is on the application of illusions to coping with stress.

Illusions and the Appraisal Process

First, consider how illusions affect the primary appraisal process. Beliefs in one's ability to control events affect whether a potentially stressful event is perceived primarily in terms of challenge or threat. People who believe they are efficacious and capable of surmounting obstacles are more apt to regard an event as a challenge to be mastered rather than a threat to be endured (Bandura, 1989; Dweck & Leggett, 1988). Appraising events as challenges, instead of threats, reduces stress reactions (Lazarus & Folkman, 1984). Feelings of personal control are therefore linked to lower levels of experienced stress.

Illusions influence the secondary appraisal process in a similar manner. The more resources individuals believe they can enlist to counter a potentially troublesome event, the less stress they experience. People with positive attitudes toward the self, a belief in their ability to control the course of environmental events, and an optimistic orientation toward the future tend to believe they possess more, and more effective, resources than do those who lack these characteristics (Taylor et al., 1991). In this fashion, positive illusions reduce stress reactivity by fostering the perception that one possesses the means necessary to meet environmental demands.

Illusions and Coping

Illusions also foster effective coping techniques. Active attempts to alter the source of a stressful situation require a "can-do" attitude; this attitude is the virtual embodiment of the illusions under consideration. People with high self-esteem, strong beliefs of personal efficacy, and an optimistic attitude are more likely to initiate active coping behaviors targeted toward altering the source of stress than are those who lack these characteristics (Aspinwall & Taylor, 1991; Scheier & Carver, 1987; Taylor et al., 1991). They are also more apt to sustain these coping efforts in the face of initial obstacles and ultimately to cope more successfully.

Several factors contribute to the success-promoting effects of positive illusions. For example, when people are confident of success they are able to conjure up a clear image of themselves achieving a goal; the ability to image success vividly, in turn, makes goal attainment more likely (Markus, Cross, & Wurf, 1990). When people are confident of success they also maintain concentration in the face of obstacles and do not allow their thoughts to be clouded by anxiety and doubt. The capacity to remain focused on the task at hand further increases the likelihood of successfully completing difficult activities (Dweck & Leggett, 1988). In these ways, then, beliefs in one's ability, even if illusory, can promote goal attainment.

Illusions also promote coping activities aimed at altering the implications of an event for well-being. Taylor's (1983) theory of cognitive adaptation is particularly relevant here. Taylor argued that in their efforts to adjust to threatening events, people often transform the implications of a negative experience in ways that minimize damage to well-being. One way to do this is by finding meaning in their experience. For example, people who survive traumatic events often emerge from their experience with a newfound appreciation for life. In this manner, an originally negative experience is transformed into a positive one.

Selective valuation provides a related means by which people may construe benefit from despair. Here, people may decide that a formerly desired outcome is not as important as previously believed. By way of illustration, Taylor (1983) reported that many persons with cancer rearrange their priorities in response to their illness, deciding, for example, that time spent with family is far more important than time spent at work.

In a similar manner, a process of compensatory self-enhancement can work to minimize the adverse implications of a negative experience. With compensatory self-enhancement, individuals respond to a negative event by exaggerating their capabilities or virtues in other, unrelated domains (Baumeister, 1982; Baumeister & Jones, 1978; Brown & Smart, 1991; Steele, 1988). For example, persons with cancer may concede that their health is not what it once was but believe that their psychological character has been significantly strengthened by their experience. In so doing, they are able to regard their cancer as a mixed blessing rather than a purely negative experience.

An additional strategy for altering the meaning of one's situation is to engage in downward social comparison (Wills, 1981). Here, individuals reduce the seriousness of their own situation by drawing a comparison with others who really are or are imagined to be worse off than themselves. Many cancer patients report feeling that things could have been a lot worse and that they were a good deal better off than many other cancer patients (Taylor & Lobel, 1989; Wood, Taylor, & Lichtman, 1985).

Illusions and Managing Distress

Thus far, illusions have been linked to coping efforts targeted toward altering a stressful situation and those geared toward transforming its implications. Illusions may also foster effective use of coping aimed at reducing the emotional consequences of a negative experience. Attempts to minimize emotional distress are sometimes associated with avoidance or denial; these terms are value laden and connote an inability to cope successfully (Haan, 1977). As noted earlier, however, reducing anxiety, fear, or depression is often a prerequisite for effective action. This is the case because the capacity to formulate and execute complex plans is enhanced when emotional distress is diminished. Further, some events are not amenable to change; in these cases, the best one can do is minimize the intensity of negative emotions (Rothbaum, Weisz, & Snyder, 1981). Distancing and distraction, when used in moderation, may therefore be an adaptive response to a stressful experience (Brown, 1991b; Lazarus, 1983).

The evidence linking illusions to the effective control of emotions is currently sparse. Brown and Mankowski (1991) have found that people with high self-esteem are better able to manage negative moods than are those with low self-esteem. Negative mood states lead people with low self-esteem to engage in self-deprecation; when sad, these individuals tend to believe they are incompetent, unworthy, and unloved. The effects of negative moods are far more limited among people with high self-esteem. These individuals do not engage in severe self-deprecation when sad; they also take more active steps to alleviate sadness. These findings provide preliminary evidence that illusions (in the form of positive views of the self) play a role in the self-regulation of mood states.

Summary

To summarize, illusions can promote effective coping through several routes. A positive attitude toward the self, a belief in one's ability to master environmental events, and the conviction that the future will be bright and rosy can reduce stress by: 1) leading individuals to appraise negative events in terms of challenge rather than threat, 2) fostering active attempts to alter stressful situations, 3) promoting the effective use of cognitive reinterpretation in which individuals are able to construe stressful events in a manner that renders them less threatening, and 4) helping individuals to manage emotional distress.

ADDITIONAL ISSUES

Potential Liabilities

The potential liabilities of illusions need to be considered (Baumeister, 1989). Unrealistic optimism, for example, may lead people to ignore risks associated with their actions and undermine the practice of appropriate preventive health behaviors (Weinstein, 1982). There is some evidence that these effects occur, particularly before a threatening event has been experienced (Weinstein, Sandman, & Roberts, 1991).

At the same tme, the liabilities of unrealistic optimism may be tempered by an accompanying belief in one's ability to control the environment. To illustrate, although unrealistic optimism may diminish the chances that people will initiate preventive health behaviors, a strong sense of mastery and the belief that one can control events may aid them in maintaining proper health habits once they are begun (Bandura, 1988). Consistent with this analysis, recent research suggests that people who are optimistic are more likely to adopt active coping strategies once a threatening event has occurred (Scheier & Carver, 1987; Scheier et al., 1990; Taylor et al., 1991). These findings suggest that the liabilities of illusions may be modest. However, further research is needed and this issue remains an important topic for future investigations.

Distinguishing Illusions from Defense Mechanisms

Historically, the use of illusions was treated with disdain (Haan, 1977). Parents who insisted that caring for a child with a disability was an enriching and positive experience, for example, were regarded as immature and unable to face the realities of their situation. Even today, when the benefits of illusions are conceded, they are seldom lauded and rarely encouraged.

Some of the ambivalence many people exhibit toward illusions is based on a belief that illusions are merely defense mechanisms in disguise. This perception is misleading. Illusions differ from defense mechanisms in a number of important ways. The most important of these concern their basis in conscious rather than unconscious processes and their level of distortion.

In classic psychoanalytic theory, anxiety arises when individuals perceive that unacceptable instinctive impulses are not being satisfied in a socially acceptable manner. Anxiety, in turn, initiates attempts to keep these threatening impulses from gaining expression. These attempts involve mental strategies called defense mechanisms (Freud, 1915/1957). Examples include: 1) projection, which involves attributing repeated unacceptable impulses, wishes, or characteristics to others; 2) displacement, which involves transferring feelings or thoughts from an unacceptable source to a socially acceptable source; 3) denial, which involves refusing to acknowledge the existence of some threat; and 4) sublimation, which involves redirecting forbidden impulses toward the pursuit of socially acceptable goals.

Repression—the process of keeping unconscious impulses from entering consciousness—underlies all mechanisms of defense. Hence, in order to be effective, defense mechanisms must operate outside of conscious awareness. This is not true for illusions. For example, an individual may deliberately decide to quit dwelling on the negative aspects of an experience and start accentuating the positive. This kind of cognitive reinterpretation is not founded in the unconscious; as a consequence, it is subject to control should the need to revise it arise. For this reason, illusions are more responsive to environmental changes than are the mechanisms of defense (Brown, 1991a; Taylor, Collins, Skokan, & Aspinwall, 1989).

Another, related difference between illusions and defense mechanisms concerns the degree of distortion each involves. Extreme cases of denial involve gross distortions of reality. Illusions, in contrast, do not involve major distortions of reality. Instead, they often involve important variations in how reality is interpreted or represented. To return to an earlier example, a man undergoing a divorce may console himself by belittling the importance of marriage as a lifestyle, by reminding himself of the number of other couples who have also separated due to marital difficulties, by comparing himself with those who are helplessly trapped in unhappy marriages, and so on. All of these strategies are likely to make him feel better but none involve a major distortion of reality.

FUTURE RESEARCH DIRECTIONS

Two related tasks face researchers interested in the link between illusions and well-being. First, the conditions under which illusions are beneficial need to be more clearly specified. To elaborate, although turning one's attention away from a stressful experience may be an appropriate response for facing an intractable situation, it may prove maladaptive when confronting situations that are more immediately amenable to change. The effectiveness of illusions as a function of the match between them and the properties of stressful experiences requires additional attention.

A second issue is whether illusions are effective for all individuals. Although they have been linked to effective functioning across diverse samples (Taylor & Brown, 1988), whether everyone benefits from the use of illusions has not been determined. Individual differences here are probable. For example, comparing oneself with less fortunate others is unlikely to console everybody. Whether everyone can learn to use illusions when confronting a stressful experience also needs to be examined. These issues must be resolved before successful interventions can be designed and implemented. Effective coping will be maximized when a fit is achieved between the features of the person, the situation, and the particular illusion being employed. The task of future researchers is to identify these relations.

CONCLUSION

To paraphrase a popular aphorism, "negative events happen." The ability to manage them effectively is one of the most critical tasks that individuals face. This chapter has explored how a set of illusions involving overly favorable views of the self, an exaggerated sense of one's ability to control environmental events, and a naive belief in the brightness of one's future facilitates adaptive coping. The judicious use of these illusions enables many people to weather negative events with their self-esteem and well-being relatively unscathed. It would seem that much as the immune system has evolved to protect the body from outside invaders, so, too, have people's cognitive capacities developed to insulate the self from threatening experiences.

ABOUT THE AUTHOR

Jonathon D. Brown, Ph.D.   As a social psychologist, I am interested in the strategies people use to maintain psychological well-being in the face of negative life events. My research has found that a set of positive beliefs about oneself and one's ability to change the environment promote adjustment even if these beliefs are somewhat illusory or overly optimistic. My future research will explore how best to instill these perceptions in people as a means of aiding adjustment to negative events.

REFERENCES

Alloy, L.B., & Abramson, L.Y (1988). Depressive realism: Four theoretical perspectives. In L.B. Alloy (Ed.), *Cognitive processes in depression* (pp. 223–265). New York: Guilford Press.

Aspinwall, L.G., & Taylor, S.E. (1991). *Individual differences, coping, and adjustment to college: A longitudinal study.* Manuscript submitted for publication.

Bandura, A. (1988). Self-efficacy mechanism in physiological activation and health-promoting behavior. In J. Madden IV, S. Matthysse, & J. Barchas (Eds.), *Adaptation, learning, and affect.* New York: Raven Press.

Bandura, A. (1989). Self-regulation of motivation and action through internal standards and goal systems. In L. Pervin (Ed.), *Goal concepts in personality and social psychology* (pp. 19–86). Hillsdale, NJ: Lawrence Erlbaum Associates.

Baumeister, R.F. (1982). Self-esteem, self-presentation, and future interaction: A dilemma of reputation. *Journal of Personality, 50,* 29–45.

Baumeister, R.F. (1989). The optimal margin of illusion. *Journal of Social and Clinical Psychology, 8,* 176–189.

Baumeister, R.F., & Jones, E.E. (1978). When self-presentation is constrained by the target's prior knowledge: Consistency and compensation. *Journal of Personality and Social Psychology, 36,* 608–618.

Billings, A.G., & Moos, R.H. (1984). Coping, stress, and social resources among adults with unipolar depression. *Journal of Personality and Social Psychology, 46,* 877–881.

Brown, J.D. (1991a). Accuracy and bias in self-knowledge. In C.R. Snyder & D.F. Forsyth (Eds.), *Handbook of social and clinical psychology: The health perspective* (pp. 158–178). New York: Pergamon Press.

Brown, J.D. (1991b). Staying fit and staying well: Physical fitness as a moderator of life stress. *Journal of Personality and Social Psychology, 60,* 555–561.

Brown, J.D., & Mankowski, T. (1991). *Self-esteem and the cognitive consequences of mood states.* Manuscript in preparation.

Brown, J.D., & McGill, K.L. (1989). The cost of good fortune: When positive life events produce negative health consequences. *Journal of Personality and Social Psychology, 57,* 1103–1110.

Brown, J.D., & Smart, S.A. (1991). The self and social conduct: Linking self-representations to prosocial behavior. *Journal of Personality and Social Psychology, 60,* 368–375.

Carver, C.S., Scheier, M.F., & Weintraub, J.K. (1989). Assessing coping strategies: A theoretically based approach. *Journal of Personality and Social Psychology, 56,* 267–283.

Dweck, C.S., & Leggett, E.L. (1988). A social-cognitive approach to personality and motivation. *Psychological Review, 95,* 256–273.

Endler, N.S., & Parker, J.D.A. (1990). Multidimensional assessment of coping: A critical evaluation. *Journal of Personality and Social Psychology, 58,* 844–854.

Folkman, S., & Lazarus, R.S. (1985). If it changes it must be a process: A study of emotion and coping during three stages of a college examination. *Journal of Personality and Social Psychology, 48,* 150–170.

Freud, S. (1957). Repression. In J. Strachey (Ed. and Trans.), *The standard edition of the complete psychological works of Sigmund Freud* (Vol. 14, pp. 143–158). London: Hogarth Press. (Original work published 1915)

Haan, N. (1977). *Coping and defending: Processes of self-environment organization.* New York: Academic Press.

Jahoda, M. (1958). *Current concepts of positive mental health.* New York: Basic Books.

Lazarus, R.S. (1983). The costs and benefits of denial. In S. Breznitz (Ed.), *Denial of stress* (pp. 1–30). New York: International Universities Press.

Lazarus, R.S., & Folkman, S. (1984). *Stress, appraisal, and coping.* New York: Springer.

Lazarus, R.S., & Launier, R. (1978). Stress-related transactions between person and environment. In L.A. Pervin & M. Lewis (Eds.), *Perspectives in interactional psychology* (pp. 287–327). New York: Plenum.

Markus, H., Cross, S., & Wurf, E. (1990). The role of the self-system in competence. In R.J. Sternberg & J. Kolligan, Jr. (Eds.), *Competence considered* (pp. 205–225). New Haven, CT: Yale University Press.

Rothbaum, F., Weisz, J.R., & Snyder, S.S. (1981). Changing the world and changing the self: A two-process model of perceived control. *Journal of Personality and Social Psychology, 42,* 5–37.

Sackeim, H.A. (1983). Self-deception, self-esteem, and depression: The adaptive value of lying to oneself. In J. Masling (Ed.), *Empirical studies of psychoanalytical theories* (Vol. 1, pp. 101–157). Hillsdale, NJ: Analytic Press.

Scheier, M.F., & Carver, C.S. (1987). Dispositional optimism and physical health: The influence of generalized outcome expectancies on health. *Journal of Personality, 55,* 169–210.

Scheier, M.F., Matthews, K.A., Owens, J., Magovern, G.J., Sr., Lefebvre, R.C., Abbott, R.A., & Carver, C.S. (1990). Dispositional optimism and recovery from coronary artery bypass surgery: The beneficial effects on physical and psychological health. *Journal of Personality and Social Psychology, 57,* 1024–1040.

Steele, C.M. (1988). The psychology of self-affirmation: Sustaining the integrity of the self. In L. Berkowitz (Ed.), *Advances in experimental social psychology* (Vol. 21, pp. 261–302). New York: Academic Press.

Taylor, S.E. (1983). Adjustment to threatening events: A theory of cognitive adaptation. *American Psychologist, 38,* 1161–1173.

Taylor, S.E. (1989). *Positive illusions: Creative self-deception and the healthy mind.* New York: Basic Books.

Taylor, S.E., & Brown, J.D. (1988). Illusion and well-being: A social psychological perspective on mental health. *Psychological Bulletin, 103,* 193–210.

Taylor, S.E., Collins, R.L., Skokan, L.A., & Aspinwall, L.G. (1989). Maintaining positive illusions in the face of negative information: Getting the facts without letting them get to you. *Journal of Social and Clinical Psychology, 8,* 114–129.

Taylor, S.E., Kemeny, M.E., Aspinwall, L.G., Schneider, S.G., Rodriguez, R., & Herbert, M. (1991). *Optimism, coping, psychological distress, and high-risk sexual behavior among men at risk for AIDS.* Manuscript submitted for publication.

Taylor, S.E., & Lobel, M. (1989). Social comparison activity under threat: Downward evaluation and upward contacts. *Psychological Review, 96,* 569–575.

Vitaliano, P.P., DeWolfe, D.J., Maiuro, R.D., Russo, J., & Katon, W. (1990). Appraised changeability of a stressor as a modifier of the relationship between coping and depression: A test of the hypothesis of fit. *Journal of Personality and Social Psychology, 59,* 582–592.

Weinstein, N.D. (1982). Unrealistic optimism about susceptibility to health problems. *Journal of Behavioral Medicine, 5,* 441–460.

Weinstein, N.D., Sandman, P.M., & Roberts, N.E. (1991). Perceived susceptibility and self-protective behavior: A field experiment to encourage home radon testing. *Health Psychology, 10,* 25–33.

Wills, T.A. (1981). Downward comparison principles in social psychology. *Psychological Bulletin, 90,* 245–271.

Wood, J.V., Taylor, S.E., & Lichtman, R.R. (1985). Social comparison and adjustment to breast cancer. *Journal of Personality and Social Psychology, 49,* 1169–1183.

chapter 10

Cognitive Adaptation to Adversity
Insights from Parents of Medically Fragile Infants

Glenn Affleck and Howard Tennen

More than a decade ago, we initiated a research program at the University of Connecticut School of Medicine on coping with major medical problems. What has made our investigations possible has been the enthusiasm and generosity of its participants—couples who had given birth to a sick or premature infant, had a child with diabetes, or had difficulty conceiving a child; men who were recovering from a heart attack or were facing surgery to repair coronary arteries; and individuals who had lost their sense of taste or smell or were living with chronic pain from rheumatoid arthritis. The population that we have studied most extensively, and who are the focus of this chapter, are parents of medically fragile infants who begin life in a newborn intensive care unit (NICU) and are at risk for chronic illness, developmental disability, and learning problems in school (Affleck, Tennen, & Rowe, 1991).

In several independent studies, we have chronicled the psychological challenges of newborn intensive care and its aftermath; examined how parents' appraisals of this unfolding crisis aided or impeded their adaptation; documented strategies parents used to mitigate the stresses of the hospitalization; and identified situational, intrapersonal, and interpersonal factors that contribute to parents' well-being during the hospitalization and months and years later. We also learned how parents' initial reactions to their child's intensive care make a difference in their child's later development. Each of the studies was longitudinal, with the first interview conducted when the infant was discharged from the NICU.

In this chapter, we summarize what these parents taught us about cognitive adaptation to threatening events. Our principal aim is to demonstrate how parents' cognitive restructuring of the newborn intensive care crisis can help them restore a sense of control and find meaning in their misfortune. We also discuss comforting alternatives to personal control beliefs and the delicate issues involved in others' attempts to supply parents with meaningful interpreta-

135

tions of this event. Finally, we highlight a new direction we are following in our research, one that pursues individual differences through intensive time-sampling designs and within-person analysis. Before doing so, we underscore how the birth of a medically fragile newborn threatens parents' comforting assumptions about themselves and the world.

VIOLATION OF CHERISHED ASSUMPTIONS

> My pregnancy was great. I had no morning sickness. I felt fine and had a lot of energy. I never missed a day's work. I had been doing everything to make sure that things would turn out all right. Then one night while we were getting ready to go out to dinner, I went into the bathroom, and all of a sudden, blood was pouring out of me. My husband called the doctor, who said I should go to the hospital right away. The doctor had me transferred to the medical center. They weren't willing to wait, so they delivered the baby by C-section. And only 4 hours earlier, I had been thinking about going out to dinner. That's what was so weird about it . . . that it happened so suddenly without warning.

Like 70% of the mothers who participated in one of our studies (Affleck et al., 1991), this woman had no warning of a premature or hazardous delivery. Her pregnancy had been progressing uneventfully, and she had been doing all the right things to make sure it would stay that way. Yet her expectations were abruptly violated. Half the mothers in this study had never imagined when they were pregnant that their baby would need intensive care. And virtually all recounted things they had done to prevent complications of pregnancy and delivery, such as avoiding alcohol, quitting work, and eating more nutritious foods. Many fathers also spoke of their own efforts to help ensure an uneventful pregnancy and their expectations of a good outcome. Feelings of control and positive expectations were not the only assumptions threatened by this experience. Some parents, instead of questioning their presumption of personal control, questioned the control they had accorded their obstetrician. As one father said: "What happened to my child should not have happened. . . . My son's problem is something that should have been prevented . . . [Our obstetrician] missed something, he knew better. I don't think I'll ever get over this fact." And many questioned the meaningfulness, even fairness of events: "It's just not fair. Here I did everything I was supposed to do. And this woman in the bed next to me, who was a heavy smoker, had this moose of a kid. So why me and not her?"

Janoff-Bulman and Frieze (1983) stated that "from day to day . . . [we] operate on the basis of assumptions and personal theories that allow [us] to set goals, plan activities and order [our] behavior" (p. 3). These assumptions include seeing ourselves as having control over events and being relatively invulnerable to harm; viewing the things that happen to us as orderly, predictable, and meaningful; and regarding ourselves as worthy and other people as benevolent. The centrality of these assumptions in our lives is rarely apparent; the minor disappointments and failures of everyday life seldom bring them to light. But they are revealed when a personal catastrophe challenges their validity.

A growing body of research shows that people have an extraordinary capacity to restore their assumptive world in the wake of traumatic events. By appraising the event or its consequences in certain ways, individuals are able to regain a sense of mastery over their lives and bring meaning to their misfortune. It is these post-trauma appraisals that Shelley Taylor (1983) has made the centerpiece of her theory of cognitive adaptation to threat. (See Brown, chap. 9, this volume, for further discussion of this theory.)

A major thrust of our own research concerns how parents' beliefs about the intensive care crisis can mitigate feelings of helplessness and victimization and, even more, can impart a sense of privilege and purpose in life. Appraisals of stressful events should be distinguished from conscious strategies of coping with these events. Coping strategies, as currently conceptualized and measured, refer to conscious cognitive or behavioral *efforts* by the individual to alleviate the distress stemming from the event (Lazarus & Folkman, 1984). Although we have studied the strategies parents use to cope with newborn intensive care, including their efforts to find emotional support, to minimize the problem, and to employ other tactics directed at problem resolution or emotional regulation (Affleck et al., 1991; Affleck & Tennen, 1991a), we reserve our discussion here to *beliefs* that assist cognitive adaptation.

FINDING MEANING

In this section, we illuminate three pathways to finding meaning in the newborn intensive care crisis: discovering a purpose, construing benefits or gains, and making comforting comparisons. We also suggest caveats to those who would use this information to help parents reframe their situation in a positive light.

Discovering a Purpose

> We know that seven out of every 100 babies are born prematurely. We know that a problem with my uterus was the cause. But that doesn't help me answer the question, "Why us and not someone else?"

This mother acknowledged, as did many, that learning the cause of premature deliveries fails to answer a more pressing question: "Why *me*? Why was I the one whose baby had to be hospitalized on a newborn intensive care unit?" Most parents we have interviewed admitted having asked themselves this question before taking their baby home from the hospital, and most were able to answer it, at least in a tentative way. Most commonly, they concluded that God has a plan for them; some said the answer to the question has yet to be revealed; others called the situation a test of their faith; and still others found themselves privileged to have been chosen to be the parent of a child with special needs.

Those who were able to find some purpose in this event before NICU discharge displayed greater responsiveness to their child's needs in the first months of caring for their child at home (Affleck et al., 1991).

On balance, one in four of our research participants maintained that the question "Why me?" never came to mind. Thus, an active search for meaning, although a common response to this crisis, is not a universal one, and much the same conclusion can be reached from studies of other so-called victimizing events. What's more, the second most frequent answer to the question "Why me?" is to counterpose the question "Why *not* me?" A sizable proportion of parents apparently do not view this event as purposeful; rather, they write it off to chance. What prompts or undercuts the search for meaning and what leads people to find a purpose in their plight is unclear from our research, and there are few clues from theory or studies reported by other investigators.

Construing Benefits or Gains

> The good that came out of this was how we reacted as a couple. Something like this could tear a marriage apart . . . but instead, it has brought us closer.

> Right after she was born, I remember this revelation. She was teaching us something . . . how to keep things in perspective . . . to realize what's important. I've learned that everything is tentative and that you never know what life will bring.

> I've learned that I'm a much stronger person than I had thought. I look back, see how far I've come, and feel very pleased.

> The good that's come from this is that I marvel at what a miracle she is . . . what a miracle that she's alive and that we are going to take her home.

Reappraising a threatening experience as beneficial or advantageous is another way in which people bring meaning to adversity (Taylor, 1983; Thompson, 1985). The majority of parents we have studied—mothers and fathers—are able to describe at least one benefit from their infant's intensive care. As the preceding quotes convey, many parents believe that this crisis brought them closer to their spouse, other family members, and friends; taught them what's important in life; increased their empathy for others; engendered personal growth; and made them cherish their child even more than if he or she had been born healthy. We learned that the perception of benefits is not necessarily shared by spouses, with one exception. When one partner believed that the marriage was strengthened, the other was likely to agree (Affleck et al., 1991).

Mothers who construed benefits from this event—any benefits—at NICU discharge displayed less psychological distress in the months after discharge (Affleck et al., 1991). Further, the comparatively few mothers who were unable to find any benefits had children who developed less optimally during their second year of life. This predictive relation was independent of mothers' emotional well-being at discharge and the severity of their child's perinatal medical problems. This specific connection with an objective outcome echoes an important finding of our research with survivors of a myocardial infarction: Men who had found benefits soon after their heart attack were significantly less likely to have another attack in the ensuing 8 years, regardless of the severity of their attack (Affleck, Tennen, Croog, & Levine, 1987). Evidence like this commands attention; yet we are still unable to explain these relations through conceivable intervening processes measured in our studies.

Are parents who find the "silver lining" in what many would view a personal tragedy turning away from reality? Are they "denying" the painful truths of this traumatic experience? These are key questions that are difficult to resolve empirically, but get at the heart of the meaning of these beliefs. We do have evidence from a questionnaire study that parents who find more benefits from this situation are no more or less likely than parents finding fewer benefits to endorse statements about the harmful aspects of this experience (Affleck, Tennen, & Rowe, 1990). Thus, perceiving benefits does not imply denial of threat.

We assume that it is the perception of benefits—the appraisal itself—that helps parents maintain a sense of well-being. Nonetheless, when parents identify family harmony as an unexpected gain, might any consequences for their well-being (or their child's) simply be due to improvement in social support? If so, then this "cognitive adaptation" may be just an epiphenomenon, of interest only as a marker of an influential change that has occurred. This is a complicated question that has not been adequately researched.

Our working hypothesis is that the accuracy of the benefits construed from misfortune is less critical for one's well-being than the belief that valued changes have occurred. When individuals construct a benefit, they create a reality to which they respond. This constructivist position implies that positive connotations supply plausible realities, rather than essential truths (Tennen & Affleck, 1991). And it leads us to ask why some efforts to bring meaning and order to one's misfortune might help the individual to rebuild his or her assumptive world whereas others might make it harder to do so.

To illustrate an instance of the latter, consider parents whose attempts to explain their child's premature delivery leads them to conclude that their obstetrician was incompetent. Many researchers have found that when individuals blame their medical problems on other people, coping problems are compounded, in part because this attribution may raise troubling questions about others' benevolence, trustworthiness, or competence (Tennen & Affleck, 1990). We have found that blaming physicians for a premature delivery is associated with emotional upset and can generalize to distrust of other physicians who are caring for the child on the NICU (Affleck et al., 1991).

Downward Comparison

The first time I saw my baby, he looked wonderful compared with some of the other babies on the unit. He was very tiny and attached to all these wires and tubes, but the other babies looked a lot worse. Their skin seemed translucent, all full of blotches, and discolored.

I remember standing at the door of the unit, worried to death about what my baby would look like. When I walked over to the isolette, I just fell apart completely. But then I looked around and saw several babies who were smaller than mine. And there was one baby whose head was bigger than his body. In a way that helped calm me down.

Sometimes the meaning of a threatening event is weighed by comparing it with alternative circumstances: It may not have been purposeful or beneficial, but it could have been worse. Theory and numerous studies point to the value of making downward comparisons when coping with adversity, especially its importance for self-esteem maintenance (Wills, 1987). Our research has revealed that parents of medically fragile infants also make downward comparisons with less fortunate others and situations (Affleck & Tennen, 1991b; Affleck et al., 1991; Affleck, Tennen, Pfeiffer, Fifield, & Rowe, 1987).

When given free rein to describe the crisis of newborn intensive care, many parents compared their child with other infants observed on the NICU. For some, including the two mothers whose comments opened this section, the ability to make a downward comparison brought them a shred of comfort during the stressful first visit to the NICU. Interestingly, mothers who said they were more interested in the medical condition of other infants were more likely to conclude that their infant was relatively better off. Thus, a more active search for comparison information may increase the likelihood of drawing a downward comparison. Several mothers told us that the nursing staff had expressly discouraged their curiosity about other infants' medical conditions. Ironically, what staff fear, we learned later, is that parents might make upsetting upward comparisons.

Parents' unprompted statements reveal the extraordinary flexibility of the downward comparison process. When offering comparisons, they tended to compare their infant selectivity with others on severity dimensions that made their child's condition appear less worrisome. For example, mothers of the smallest babies tended to compare their child with those who needed more technological support to survive. Conversely, mothers of infants who were larger, but in some ways sicker, compared on the size attribute. Parents also offered downward comparisons about their own coping abilities, for example:

> I would carefully watch how other parents would react to bad news about their baby. I must have been better informed because they seemed not to be upset by the news. If you really knew what was happening, you would have to be upset!"

This mother's remarks are noteworthy in revealing how a potentially demoralizing upward comparison (being more *upset* than others) can be mitigated by a downward comparison concerning its meaning (being more *informed* than others). Again, the resilience of the downward comparison process is most impressive.

A telling illustration of the lasting significance of downward comparison comes from our inquiry into the content and affective quality of mothers' remembrances of their child's hospitalization, months after discharge (Affleck et al., 1991). Many remarked how the comparisons they had made before discharge remained a key feature of their long-term memories. As one mother confessed:

> Some days when I'm watching her sleep, I'll begin to remember what a rough time we had. I'll begin to wonder why this had to happen. And then I'll think about how some of the other babies were worse off, and how lucky I really was.

New opportunities for downward comparison appear after discharge as well. Interesting, it was mothers of children who were exhibiting developmental delays, having recurring illness, or were especially difficult to care for who were most apt to offer downward comparisons in describing their situation. Could it be that when objective circumstances are harder to endure, the ability to make a downward comparison takes on greater importance?

Directing the Search for Meaning

Before we turn to our findings on perceptions of control and related appraisals, we must caution that nothing summarized to this point implies that deliberate attempts by family, friends, or helping professionals to direct parents' search for meaning will be helpful. The evidence we have is that at least some parents may well resent others' efforts to reframe their situation for them (Affleck et al., 1991). When mothers described the things other people did or said that helped them and upset them while their baby was on the NICU, a few volunteered that they appreciated being reminded to "trust in God's will" or to "try to look at the good that's come from this." But others objected to such entreaties from family and friends. A sizable proportion of parents were glad to hear stories about how other premature infants eventually thrived, but others resented these stories because they appeared to minimize their baby's unique problems. Implicit in mothers' evaluations of these support gestures is the motivation they impute to the other person. Both the message and the intent of the messenger are taken into account. This may explain why family members, who may have an apparent self-interest in seeing parents recover quickly from this crisis, seemed to be resented most for attempting to reframe the experience.

Helping professionals seem less inclined than informal support providers to offer parents' meaningful interpretations of their plight. At least, few parents we have interviewed commented on this practice. Professionals, however, are often placed in the position of supplying information that could be used by parents to make upward or downward comparisons. The available evidence (Affleck & Tennen, 1991b), tentative as it may be, suggests that the "safest" approach would be to emphasize the ways in which parents are displaying comparatively good adjustment (few would resist such a compliment). How might parents react to hearing about other parents who have coped superlatively with a special needs child? Taylor and Lobel's (1989) findings suggest that exposing people to information about similar others who have overcome difficulties does not necessarily prompt a demoralizing upward comparison but may inspire confidence and hope. The desire for "upward contacts" can coexist comfortably with, rather than undercut, the use of downward comparisons for self-evaluation.

A riskier strategy in our opinion would be to offer parents downward comparisons about the severity of their child's problems, for example, by mentioning other parents whose children are far worse off. We suspect that some would find this an unwelcome attempt to minimize the unique burdens and challenges that have been and may still need to be overcome. A second reason for avoiding such comparisons is especially compelling in the case of parents of children with chronic diseases or disabilities. Presenting parents with what may be interpreted as a worse case could serve as a troubling reminder of what the future might hold (Taylor, Wood, & Lichtman, 1983).

REGAINING A SENSE OF MASTERY AND CONTROL

> Going to the hospital all the time and being allowed to touch him, get close to him, and hold him was good for both the baby and me. It was a terrific confidence builder. It also gave us a lot of hope that his problems were controllable.

> Even though he's still having some problems, I feel like I'm more in control now. In the hospital, I was just a bystander. It was the hospital's baby, not mine. It's very tiring taking care of him, but I'm enjoying the feeling of being the one who can make a difference in his life.

> I'm the one who has the say now. When she was in the hospital, other people were calling the shots. Now it's up to me. I have the control over what happens to her.

Regaining a sense of mastery is another goal of cognitive adaptation to threatening circumstances (Taylor, 1983). Perceptions of personal control figure in many accounts of adaptive appraisals of stressful events (e.g., Miller, 1980; Rothbaum, Weisz, & Snyder, 1982; Thompson, 1981), and there is substantial evidence that people adjust more successfully to stressful events when they perceive control over their consequences (see Affleck et al., 1991).

As we stated previously, one of the more demoralizing consequences of the birth and hospitalization of a medically fragile newborn is the loss of a sense of control. How then do these parents restore a sense of control in this very context? We asked parents about ways they had found to assist their child's recovery in the hospital. Frequent visiting, providing social stimulation, supplying breast milk, performing caregiving tasks, praying, and diligent monitoring of their child's medical care were mentioned frequently as activities that afforded parents a sense of control. For several, including the mothers who were the sources of the second two quotes at the beginning of this section, the restoration of control came only after they were able to take their baby home.

Generally, these retrospective appraisals of personal control are associated with emotional well-being in our studies. Our research, however, suggests that not all control-related cognitions are associated with less distress. We found that when mothers about to take their baby home from the hospital were more certain that their child's future health and development would depend on their personal actions, they displayed greater emotional distress in the ensuing months (Affleck & Tennen, 1991a). Thus, the emotional benefits of perceiving control "after the fact" do not appear to extend to the anticipation of control. Neither were mothers expecting more control those who perceived more control over their child's health and development after months had passed. We learned that several mothers expecting considerable control over their child's well-being subsequently made many burdensome accommodations to see this through, at some cost to their own well-being and family harmony. For example, as one mother said:

> I became almost obsessed with protecting her when she came home from the hospital. I wouldn't let anyone come into the house. I wouldn't let anyone breathe on her. I was constantly disinfecting my hands. Maybe this isn't worth it, raising her in a bubble, worrying about the slightest thing that might happen. What kind of life is this for her? What kind of life is it for me?

Alternatively, some mothers' control expectancies may not have been matched by their self-efficacy (Bandura, 1977). They may have been distraught to find that appropriate actions were not within reach. Or, in view of the fact that a control orientation seems to heighten one's attention to the desired outcome (Burger, 1989), they may have become demoralized by even minor problems with their child, viewing them as instances of personal failure. As one mother herself expressed this point:

> The hardest part is realizing that this person is totally dependent on me for whatever his future brings. This has put tremendous pressure on me to do the right things. But I'm very upset that I haven't been getting much in return, that there's been very little response to my best efforts.

COMFORTING ALTERNATIVES
TO PERCEPTION OF CONTROL

Burger (1989) noted a paradox in the literature on personal control. Research documenting the benefits of perceived control suggests that people will choose to retain control rather than to abandon it. But other studies show that people sometimes prefer to abandon control or react adversely to situations in which they are expected to exert control. Miller (1980) has proposed that surrendering control is especially likely in health care settings because of the perception that health care providers are better able to produce desired outcomes.

Mothers clearly differed in their felt *need* to assert personal control over their child's medical care in the hospital (Affleck et al., 1991). One group appeared to value their active participation in health care decisions, but they were not pursuing primary control over these decisions. Rather, they were seeking what Reid (1984) has termed *participatory control*, a form of control that emphasizes a cooperative partnership between parents and health care providers, a concession of the providers' expertise and competence, and the providers' willingness to impart information and to solicit parents' active involvement in decision making. We have telling evidence of the devastating consequences for parents who failed to obtain the participatory control they desired. Not only was this reflected in the anger with which parents described staff members' resistance to their desire to be actively involved in all care decisions, but this conflict remained a distressing feature of the intrusive memories they went on to experience long after the child's discharge from the NICU (Affleck et al., 1991).

Yet another group of parents seemed uninterested in gaining even participatory control. Instead, they appeared willing to cede control of their child's treatment decisions to the NICU staff, stressing the great confidence they had in these individuals, in their competence to make the right decisions. Apparently, they were comforted by a sense of "vicarious control" (Rothbaum et al., 1982). As two parents stated:

> Things didn't really bother me, because I knew he was in the best place in the state. I just kept reminding myself that the doctors would be able to take care of it all, and they did.

> After seeing what went on in the unit—the monitors, the respirators, the tube feedings—I became convinced that they could and would do what needed to be done, so I stopped feeling anxious.

There is also mounting evidence that what people expect from the future does not necessarily depend on their perceived control over events. Some individuals—"dispositional optimists"—expect good things to happen, whether or not they believe it's necessary to make them happen (Scheier & Carver, 1987). We asked mothers at NICU discharge to estimate the probability that their child's future health and development would be normal in all respects (Affleck & Tennen, 1991a). One in five were absolutely certain of a normal outcome, and less than one in 10 believed that there was greater than a 50/50 chance of problems. Interestingly, the children whose mothers were more optimistic about the future in fact displayed superior cognitive and behavioral development in the second year after discharge, regardless of the severity of their risk status from medical variables measured before discharge.

If mothers' positive outcome expectancies derive from dispositional optimism, this latter finding might be explained by the resources that optimists bring to threatening events (Scheier & Carver, 1987). These include more reliance on solutions to problems, less denial, and a reluctance to dwell on negative emotional responses to the problem. Each of these resources could enhance parents' ability to weather and find solutions to the problems of rearing medically at-risk infants who are often temperamentally difficult and pose extraordinary challenges to parents' sense of competence.

Research on the "fragile child syndrome" supplies an alternative explanation (Perrin, West, & Culley, 1989). Prematurely born infants are often viewed by their parents as fragile and in need of extraordinary protection, even when they enjoy good health. This can limit the child's developmental opportunities through vacillating patterns of overprotection and reluctance to set age-appropriate limits. We would not be surprised to learn that mothers who expect their children to develop normally are less apt to perceive them as fragile and vulnerable. As a result they may provide more optimal conditions for their infants' exploration and self-regulation. Of course, most of the mothers who expected a positive outcome in this instance were correct: Only one fourth of their infants were diagnosed as developmentally delayed or disabled in the second year of life (Affleck & Tennen, 1991a). A key question in extrapolating this finding to parents of children who have disabilities from birth is whether optimistic but patently unrealistic expectations have similar consequences both for parents and for their children.

NEW DIRECTIONS IN COGNITIVE ADAPTATION AND COPING RESEARCH

We cannot emphasize too strongly the need for detailed, prospective studies of coping and cognitive adaptation to threatening events or chronic stressors. If we have learned anything from our and others' research it is that appraisal and coping are processes, meaning simply that they change over time. Much more work needs to be done to document the natural histories of coping with threat, illuminating individual differences, and resisting unwarranted assumptions about the "staging" of grief and other common misconceptions that have poorly served patients, their families, and helping professionals (Allen & Affleck, 1985; Silver & Wortman, 1980). Such inquiries will not only provide the necessary descriptive base for further research but will help answer important questions about the origins of cognitive adaptational processes. For example, when do people initiate the search for meaning? From what sources does meaning derive? When and why do people turn from the search for meaning to devote limited resources to other coping pursuits? Cross-sectional studies that seek correlations between appraisal and coping processes and well-being at some moment in time rarely reveal, and may even mislead.

We are following this recommendation to study individual differences and change to its logical end in moving to intensive time-sampling studies of the daily lives of individuals with chronic illnesses (Affleck, Tennen, Urrows, & Higgins, 1991b; 1992; Tennen, Affleck, Urrows, Higgins, & Mendola, 1992). The daily process paradigm (Larsen & Kasimatis, 1991; Tennen, Suls, &

Affleck, 1991b) emphasizes the psychological significance of everyday stressors, the ways people appraise and cope with them, and the proximal consequences of these daily processes for emotional well-being and health.

The research findings summarized in this chapter ignore the day-to-day processes of coping with, or appraising, chronic stressors. We have concentrated our attention on newborn intensive care as a major life event, but we have learned little of its impact or manifestations in daily life. The daily process paradigm allows us to test new models of how major life events influence well-being. It has been argued, for example, that the impact of major life events is mediated by its influence of everyday affairs (Kanner, Coyne, Schaefer, & Lazarus, 1981; Rowlinson & Felner, 1988). Thus, the birth of a seriously ill newborn is not only a significant threat itself, as we have seen, but also leads to the disruption of established family patterns and day-to-day social relations, which itself is threatening. An interesting variant of this point of view is found in the depression literature. Investigators have noticed that although depression is associated with major life events (Brown & Harris, 1989), depressive episodes are often preceded by what appear to be everyday tribulations (Brown & Harris, 1978; Paykel, 1978). Thus, a seemingly mundane occurrence, such as an argument with a spouse or a minor setback at work, may serve for a parent of a hospitalized newborn as a trigger of a depressive episode.

A major methodological advantage of prospective daily research is that it permits unusually powerful causal inferences from the temporal sequencing of variables—far more so than can be gained from traditional longitudinal designs with even several waves of data (West & Hepworth, 1991). What's more, because each participant serves as his or her own "control" in this design, the differences between individuals that always complicate the interpretation of between-person correlations between coping, appraisal, and adaptational outcomes become irrelevant. The daily process approach also enables exploration of the sources of individual differences in the relations between stressors, appraisals, coping strategies, and well-being. We can determine, for example, whether people who differ in stable personality dispositions such as optimism or negative emotionality respond differently to daily stressors stemming from major life changes (Bolger & Schilling, 1991). (Readers interested in further discussion of the daily process paradigm can consult a recent special issue of the *Journal of Personality* devoted to personality and daily experience [Tennen, Suls, & Affleck, 1991a]. Through historical analysis of the daily event literature, empirical inquiry, and methodological and statistical commentary, the contributors to this issue conveyed both the possibilities and problems of studying everyday life, and elucidated in particular how people's dispositions, personal goals, and commitments influence their emotional well-being and health, their reactions to events, and even which disturbing events they will encounter from day to day.)

In one study that is germane to the topic of this chapter, we are assessing both beliefs about benefits from living with chronic pain from rheumatoid arthritis and the day-to-day occurrence of efforts to reappraise the pain so as to make it more bearable (Affleck, Tennen, Urrows, & Higgins, 1991a). The daily use of a positive reappraisal strategy appears bimodal: while most participants rarely employ this tactic, a few rely upon it almost every day as a way of contending with their daily pain. However, those who use this strategy more frequently do not differ from those who use it rarely, as reflected in their scores on a questionnaire assessing benefits from living with chronic pain. This underscores once again the distinction between beliefs and coping strategies. Construing benefits from the illness did predict an important daily outcome, however: Those who had construed greater benefits from their illness and subsequently experienced more intense pain were less likely to limit their daily activities because of their pain (Tennen et al., 1992). It may be that finding benefits promotes perseverance in the face of uncontrollable threat, a process that Rothbaum et al. (1982) described as a form of *secondary control.*

Although we are unaware of daily process research with families of children with disabilities, we believe that fresh insights would be derived from this strategy. Above all, this approach would lead us away from unrevealing studies of the vague stressor of "parenting a child with a disability" to discover the contextual day-to-day stressors of rearing a child with a disability and to discern how they may (or may not) differ from the daily demands of rearing children without disabilities. A particularly fruitful strategy would be to design daily studies covering periods of stressful transitions, for example, the child's entry into school or the time surrounding medical or psychoeducational assessments that may present parents with new and threatening information about their child.

CONCLUSION

We find it hard to imagine a richer privilege than to have learned about cognitive adaptation to adversity from the hundreds of families whose experiences are chronicled in our research on newborn intensive care. We do not wish to dismiss the magnitude of these parents' disappointment and pain, but in retelling their stories we have concentrated on their progression from "victims" to "survivors" of trauma. The documentation of distress and disintegration during newborn intensive care and other childbearing and childrearing crises is an all too familiar research enterprise. We have tried instead to illuminate the recovery process, and more than that, the opportunities this crisis affords for personal transformation and growth. In our efforts to isolate the basic ingredients of cognitive coping and adaptation, it has been easy to lose sight of each family's unique experiences. For this reason, we look forward with enthusiasm to studies that will preserve the integrity of individual differences in the cognitive adaptation process.

ABOUT THE AUTHORS

Glenn Affleck, Ph.D., and Howard Tennen, Ph.D. Our studies on parents' cognitive adaptation to the unfolding crisis of newborn intensive care are a key component of a stress, coping, and health research program that we have been developing. Our general interest is in the interaction between psychological states and illness, including how people adapt to medical problems in themselves or loved ones and how illness is influenced by psychological processes. Most recently, we are pursuing answers to these questions in the context of daily life experience. It is our hope that our findings will not only advance stress-and-coping theory, but will appeal to helping professionals, patients, children with developmental disabilities, and families.

REFERENCES

Affleck, G., & Tennen, H. (1991a). Appraisal and coping predictors of mother and child outcomes after newborn intensive care. *Journal of Social and Clinical Psychology, 10*, 424–447.

Affleck, G., & Tennen, H. (1991b). Social comparison and coping with major medical problems. In J. Suls & T.A. Wills (Eds.), *Social comparison: Contemporary theory and research* (pp. 369–394). Hillsdale, NJ: Lawrence Erlbaum Associates.

Affleck, G., Tennen, H., Croog, S., & Levine, S. (1987). Causal attribution, perceived benefits, and morbidity following a heart attack: An eight-year study. *Journal of Consulting and Clinical Psychology, 55 ,* 29–35.

Affleck, G., Tennen, H., Pfeiffer, C., Fifield, J., & Rowe, J. (1987). Downward comparison and coping with serious medical problems. *American Journal of Orthopsychiatry, 57,* 570–578.

Affleck, G., Tennen H., & Rowe, J. (1990). Mothers, fathers, and the crisis of newborn intensive care. *Infant Mental Health Journal, 15,* 12–20.

Affleck, G., Tennen, H., & Rowe, J. (1991). *Infants in crisis: How parents cope with newborn intensive care and its aftermath.* New York: Springer-Verlag.

Affleck, G., Tennen, H., Urrows, S., & Higgins, P. (1991a, November). *Daily coping with rheumatoid arthritis pain: Patterns and correlates.* Presented at the annual meeting of the Arthritis Health Professions Association, Boston.

Affleck, G., Tennen, H., Urrows, S., & Higgins, P. (1991b). Individual differences in the day-to-day experience of chronic pain: A prospective daily study of rheumatoid arthritis patients. *Health Psychology, 10,* 419–426.

Affleck, G., Tennen, H., Urrows, S., & Higgins, P. (1992). Neuroticism and the pain-mood relation in rheumatoid arthritis. Insights from a prospective daily study. *Journal of Consulting and Clinical Psychology, 60,* 119–126.

Allen, D., & Affleck, G. (1985). Are we stereotyping parents? A postscript to Blacher. *Mental Retardation, 23,* 200–202.

Bandura, A. (1977). Self-efficacy: Toward a unifying theory of behavioral change. *Psychological Review, 84,* 191–215.

Bolger, N., & Schilling, E. (1991). Personality and the problems of everyday life: The role of neuroticism in exposure and reactivity to daily stressors. *Journal of Personality, 59,* 335–386.

Brown, G., & Harris, T. (1978). *Social origins of depression.* New York: Free Press.

Brown, G., & Harris, T. (1989). *Life events and illness.* New York: Guilford Press.

Burger, J. (1989). Negative reactions to increases in perceived personal control. *Journal of Personality and Social Psychology, 56,* 246–256.

Janoff-Bulman, R., & Frieze, I. (1983). A theoretical perspective for understanding reactions to victimization. *Journal of Social Issues*, *39*, 1–17.

Kanner, A., Coyne, J., Schaefer, C., & Lazarus, R. (1981). Comparison of two modes of stress measurement: Daily hassles and uplifts versus major life events. *Journal of Behavioral Medicine*, *4*, 1–39.

Larsen, R., & Kasimatis, M. (1991). Day-to-day physical symptoms: Individual differences in the occurrence, duration, and emotional concomitants of minor daily illnesses. *Journal of Personality*, *59*, 387–424.

Lazarus, R., & Folkman, S. (1984). *Stress, appraisal and coping*. New York: Springer.

Miller, S. (1980). Why having control reduces stress: If I can stop the roller coaster, I don't want to get off. In J. Barber & M. Seligman (Eds.), *Human helplessness: Theory and applications* (pp. 71–95). New York: Academic Press.

Paykel, E. (1978). Contribution of life events to causation of psychiatric illness. *Psychological Medicine*, *8*, 245–253.

Perrin, E., West, P., & Culley, B. (1989). Is my child normal yet? Correlates of vulnerability. *Pediatrics*, *83*, 355–363.

Reid, D. (1984). Participatory control and the chronic illness adjustment process. In H. Lefcourt (Ed.), *Research with the locus of control construct: Extensions and limitations* (Vol. 3, pp. 361–389). New York: Academic Press.

Rothbaum, F., Weisz, J., & Snyder, S. (1982). Changing the world and changing the self: A two-process model of perceived control. *Journal of Personality and Social Psychology*, *42*, 5–37.

Rowlinson, R., & Felner, R. (1988). Major life events, hassles, and adaptation in adolescence: Confounding in the conceptualization and measurements of life stress and adjustment revisited. *Journal of Personality and Social Psychology*, *55*, 432–444.

Scheier, M., & Carver, C. (1987). Dispositional optimism and physical well-being: The influence of generalized outcome expectancies of health. *Journal of Personality*, *55*, 169–210.

Silver, R., & Wortman, C. (1980). Coping with undesirable life events. In J. Garver & M. Seligman (Eds.), *Human helplessness: Theory and applications* (pp. 279–375). New York: Academic Press.

Taylor, S. (1983). Adjustment to threatening events: A theory of cognitive adaptation. *American Psychologist*, *38*, 624–630.

Taylor, S., & Lobel, M. (1989). Social comparison activity under threat: Downward evaluation and upward contacts. *Psychological Review*, *96*, 569–575.

Taylor, S., Wood, J., & Lichtman, R. (1983). It could be worse: Selective evaluation as a response to victimization. *Journal of Social Issues*, *39*, 19–40.

Tennen, H., & Affleck, G. (1990). Blaming others for threatening events. *Psychological Bulletin*, *108*, 209–232.

Tennen, H., & Affleck, G. (1991). Paradox-based treatments. In C. R. Snyder & D. Forsythe (Eds.), *Handbook of social and clinical psychology: The health perspective* (pp. 624–643). New York: Pergamon Press.

Tennen, H., Affleck, G., Urrows, S., Higgins, P., & Mendola, R. (1992). Perceiving control, construing benefits, and daily processes in rheumatoid arthritis. *Canadian Journal of Behavioral Science*, *24*, 186–203.

Tennen, H., Suls, J., & Affleck, G. (Eds.). (1991a). Personality and daily experience [Special issue]. *Journal of Personality*, *59*.

Tennen, H., Suls, J., & Affleck, G. (1991b). Personality and daily experience: The promise and the challenge. *Journal of Personality*, *59*, 313–338.

Thompson, S. (1981). Will it hurt less if I can control it? A complex answer to a simple question. *Psychological Bulletin*, *90*, 89–101.

Thompson, S. (1985). Finding positive meaning in a stressful event and coping. *Basic and Applied Social Psychology*, *6*, 279–295.

West, S., & Hepworth, J. (1991). Statistical issues in the study of temporal data: Daily experiences. *Journal of Personality, 59,* 609–662.

Wills, T.A. (1987). Downward comparison as a coping mechanism. In C.R. Snyder & C. Ford (Eds.), *Coping with negative events: Clinical and social psychological perspectives* (pp. 243–268). New York: Plenum.

chapter 11

Research Progress and Promise
The Role of Perceptions in Cognitive Adaptation to Disability

Shirley K. Behr and Douglas L. Murphy

> If science is to tell us anything about the world, if it is to be of any use in our dealings with the world, it must somewhere contain empirical elements . . . it is in the empirical component that science is differentiated from fantasy. . . . it is precisely the accumulation of empirical evidence which shapes a welter of opinions into scientific knowledge common to many minds.
> —Abraham Kaplan (1963, pp. 34–36)

In 1987, our research team began a 3-year study on family perceptions—a topic that, until recently, was explored by few researchers in the disability field. The majority of family studies have examined family dysfunction, negative impacts, and disability-related stressors. Indeed, parents' affirmations of benefits derived from the presence of their child with a disability all too frequently have been discounted as fantasy or denial, or subjected to unscientific post-hoc interpretations.

The purpose of our research was to develop empirically based instruments for investigating variables associated with successful coping among parents of children and adults with disabilities. The inspiration for the study came from our work as professionals with and on behalf of children and adults with disabilities and their families, as well as from personal experiences coping with disability and chronic illness in some of our own families.

We were further inspired by a paper entitled "Who Are These Researchers and Why Are They Saying These Horrible Things About Me?" by Patty Gerdel (1985), the mother of a child with cerebral palsy in Topeka, Kansas. Gerdel called attention to the unwarranted nature of the conclusions reached by many

The research reported in this paper was supported by the National Institute on Disability and Rehabilitation Research, Grant #G008720074.

151

studies, which suggested that families of children with disabilities tend to be dysfunctional and at risk for failure. She observed that these families are, in most respects, like other families, with their share of difficulties as well as their share of joys.

The vehicle for our exploration was the Family Perceptions Research Project (Summers, Behr, & Murphy, 1991), designed to develop and validate questionnaires that would enable the further study of four perceptions associated with cognitive adaption to threatening events. We anticipated that information collected with these instruments would contribute to the understanding of these perceptions and their roles as cognitive coping strategies. The study was completed in September 1990; this chapter provides a welcome opportunity to share some highlights of where we have been, how we got here, what we have learned, and what we believe are the major milestones of our empirical work. Finally, we reflect on some intriguing questions that emerged from our study.

WHERE WE HAVE BEEN

Among the reasons for the limited number of studies on cognitive coping are the absence of a clear conceptual framework for understanding perceptions as a phenomenon and a lack of valid and reliable instruments to measure them. The challenges inherent in a study of this nature were aptly described by Jan Spiegle-Mariska (1990), who is the parent of a child with a disability:

> Each parent faces a supreme and very personal challenge to reach acceptance; how each parent finally comes to acceptance is very much a matter of personal coping style. The contributions that a child with handicaps brings to a family are substantial, yet they defy quantification by their very nature. For the most part they are intangible, and they are easily overlooked or hard to focus on when you live nearly every day in a crisis mode.

Families differ in their responses to stressful events, such as having a child with a disability. The ABCX family crisis model (Hill, 1949, 1958; McCubbin & McCubbin, 1987; McCubbin & Patterson, 1983) is an attempt to explain these differential responses. In the model, Factor A refers to events that have been an impact or have the potential to have an impact on the family system. Factor B refers to the family's resources to meet the challenges of these events. Factor C, the family's perception or definition of the events, indirectly influences the degree of crisis (Factor X) that might occur in the family. Crisis is defined as a change in the family system for which the family's previous patterns of response are not adequate.

We have been interested particularly in the role played by Factor C, perceptions, in the process of adaption. Besides the definition of stressful events, Factor C might also include a cognitive reappraisal of the situation to make it more manageable or to maintain an optimistic outlook or acceptance. Examples of cognitive reappraisal are present in many parent-written manuscripts that describe how their lives have been enriched and made more meaningful because of having parented their child with special needs (Mullins, 1987).

HOW WE GOT HERE

We based our work on the cognitive adaptive theory (Taylor, 1983; Taylor, Lichtman, & Wood, 1984), which proposes that individuals respond to personally threatening events in their lives through a process of adjustment involving the resolution of three cognitive themes and their respective cognitions or perceptions. A *search for meaning* is associated with finding positive meaning from a negative experience, with the negative experience serving as a catalyst to restructure one's life along more meaningful lines. An *attempt to gain mastery or control* is associated with the belief that one can take active steps to control directly the course of the event or to prevent it from recurring, or that the event can be directly controlled by others. A combination of direct and indirect control is considered to be strongly associated with positive adjustment. *Enhancing self-esteem*, or selectively evaluating oneself in ways that are self-enhancing, is a means of minimizing feelings of victimization, perceiving instead that the impact of the event has been small or that one has profited from it. Through this process, individuals focus on the beneficial qualities of the situation and engage in active coping efforts that foster positive changes related to adjustment or adaption.

We developed four questionnaires related to these cognitive themes:

1. Construing positive contributions for the parent and family from the experience of having and raising a child with a disability, theoretically associated with the search for meaning and the enhancment of self-esteem
2. Attributing a cause for the child's disability, theoretically associated with the search for meaning and the attempt to gain mastery or control
3. Believing that one has direct or indirect control over short- and long-term outcomes for the child with a disability, theoretically associated with an attempt to gain mastery or control
4. Comparing oneself favorably, unfavorably, or similarly with others, theoretically associated with enhancing self-esteem

Figure 1 illustrates theoretical relationships between perceptions and cognitive adaptation themes.

Empirical evidence of positive contributions was initially reported by Turnbull, Guess and Turnbull (1988), who analyzed letters submitted by individuals with disabilities, their parents, and other family members to the U.S. Department of Health and Human Services (HHS; 1983). The letters were written in response to the departments' Proposed Rule, July 5, 1983, which sought

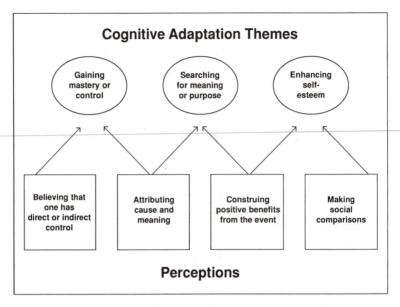

Figure 1.   Theoretical relationships of four perceptions to cognitive adaptation themes.

to invoke the authority of HHS to regulate the medical treatment of newborns with severe disabilities. A consistent theme for supporting the regulations was that persons with disabilities enrich and enhance the quality of life for family members and friends. The findings of this study laid the groundwork for developing the Positive Contributions Survey (Behr, 1990) to measure the positive benefits associated with having in the family a child or an adult with a disability. Measures of the other three perceptions were developed along dimensions indentified by attribution, control, and social comparison theories.

After developing initial versions of the questionnaires and testing them with a regional sample of almost 400 parents, Summers et al. (1991) revised the questionnaires and used them in a national mail survey study. The primary purpose of the study was to validate the instruments, but we also hoped to collect some data that would enable us to explore further the relationship between our measures of perceptions and outcome measures of family well-being (The Family APGAR, Smilkstein, 1978) and stress (Comprehensive Computerized Stress Inventory, Press & Osterkamp, 1986).

Over 1,200 birth parents, foster and adoptive parents, and legal guardians of children with disabilities participated in the national study. Ages and types of disabilities of these respondents' children varied widely, although a sizable proportion reported that their children had mental retardation. As is common in many mail survey studies, respondents in our study were overwhelmingly white and represented middle to upper socioeconomic levels.

WHAT WE LEARNED

Evidence of Validity

We believed that each of the four perceptions associated with cognitive adaption could actually be thought of as a cluster of related perceptions. For example, we believed that a parent might construe several distinct types of positive contributions from having and raising a child with a disability and that several categories of causes for the child's disability could be detected. Therefore, the main focus of the construct validity study was to identify the underlying dimensions of the perceptions.

The factor analysis of the data supported our hypotheses. We identified nine different dimensions of positive contributions, five dimensions of causal attributions, four dimensions of mastery or control over outcomes, and four dimensions of social comparisons (Summers et al., 1991). The dimensions are listed in Table 1.

Relationships Between Perceptions and Well-Being and Stress

A secondary purpose of the study was to explore relationships between parental perceptions and measures of stress and family well-being. It is outside the realm of this chapter to report in detail findings related to this purpose. Some of those results have been reported elsewhere (Murphy, Behr, & Summers, 1990a,

Table 1. Underlying dimensions of the four perceptions

Positive contributions	Social comparisons	Attributing a cause	Mastery or control
Learning through experience with special problems in life	Similar comparison	Fate or chance	Personal control
Happiness and fulfillment	Downward comparison	Special purpose	Professional control
Personal strength and family closeness	Upward/favorable comparison	Physiological cause	
Understanding life's purposes	Upward/unfavorable comparison	Professional blame	
Personal growth and maturity		Self-blame	
Awareness of future issues			
Expanded social network			
Career or job growth			
Pride and cooperation			

1990b; Murphy, Behr, & Tollefson, 1990). Instead, we wish to report themes in our findings that have relevance to further research into cognitive coping among families of children with disabilities.

One of the assumptions of the study was that parents of children with disabilities are not necessarily more at risk for dysfunction than are other parents. Therefore, we selected two outcome measures normed on ordinary, well-functioning adults: 1) the Comprehensive Computerized Stress Inventory (Press & Osterkamp, 1986), designed as a stress and coping check-up for "normal," healthy adults or people dealing with typical lifestyle problems, high levels of stress, or similar difficulties; and 2) the Family APGAR (Smilkstein, 1978), a measure of general satisfaction with one's family as a nurturing and supporting unit.

Data revealed a great deal of variability in perceptions, stress and well-being among the parents we sampled. In general, they reported stress and well-being levels similar to those of adults in the general population. In other words, we found little evidence that the parents in our study were operating in the "crisis mode" (Summers et al., 1991).

As a group, our respondents said that their children with disabilities made contributions to their families as sources of learning through experiences with disabilities, happiness and fulfillment, and strength and family closeness. They were less likely to say that their children were sources of career or job growth or that they took pride in their children's accomplishments.

These parents did not attribute their children's disabilities to any of the five categories of causes we had identified. It is noteworthy that a substudy group of about 100 parents of children without disabilities believed that parents of children with disabilities would have significantly higher scores on causal attributions measures than was actually observed.

In general, parents compared themselves favorably with other parents who had children with disabilities. This assessment was reached by comparing themselves, their families, and their children with others who were similar to themselves, and with others who were worse off or better off.

There were, however, marked differences in perceptions within the sample. Some individuals reported high levels of positive contributions from their children while others reported low levels. Some attributed the cause of their children's disabilities to specific causes (e.g., physiological factors) and others did not. Some compared themselves favorably with others and some compared themselves unfavorably. Clearly, we believe it is not possible to characterize perceptions of "the family of a child with a disability" as a unitary phenomenon.

We did find that one factor—the age of the child—appeared to be related to some of the differences noted above. For example, parents of younger children reported significantly higher levels of stress and lower perceptions of some kinds of positive contributions (e.g. source of pride and cooperation). These differences were robust, even when the severity of the disability was taken into account. It was enlightening to find similarly high levels of stress for parents of young children with disabilities and those who had young children *without* disabilities, suggesting that raising young children is accompanied by stressors, regardless of the child's disability or nondisability status.

A second theme in the findings is that patterns in relationships between the measures of perceptions and the outcomes varied, depending on the particular outcome studied. To illustrate, several perceptions were significantly related to the measure of overall stress. Parents who had lower levels of stress reported that they compared themselves favorably with others who were better off or worse off than they. They also reported that their child contributed to strength and family closeness.

Different perceptions were significantly related to the measure of satisfaction with family relations. Parents who reported high levels of satisfaction with family relations compared themselves with others who were similar and compared themselves favorably with others who were worse off. They also reported that their children contributed to the expansion of their social network, happiness and fulfillment, strength and family closeness, and pride and cooperation.

A third theme in the findings has implications for theory, research, and practice. At best, the set of perceptions we measured and explored had only a modest relationship with stress and family well-being. This suggests that we must look further to identify factors critically related to these outcomes. However, our analyses showed that the perceptions consistently had a stronger relationship with the outcomes than family variables traditionally studied in this connection. These variables included the age of the child, the severity of the child's disability, the marital status of the parents, family income, and education.

In summary, we applied a theory developed to explain cognitive adaption among individuals who are themselves victims of such threatening events such as chronic illness or accidents, to individuals who experience the long-term challenges associated with parenting children with disabilities. The results of our study (Summers et al., 1991) provide moderate support for the theory, but the weak to moderate relationships found between perceptions and outcomes suggested that more research is needed to explore further the process of cognitive adaption in families of children and adults with disabilities.

MAJOR MILESTONES OF OUR EMPIRICAL WORK

Dewey (1933) suggested that reflective thinking is best accomplished by "climbing a tree" to get a more commanding view of the situation, looking at additional facts, and deciding how the facts stand related to one another. Metaphorically speaking, we sat in the treetops to gain a view of the milestones and to ascertain the direction in which our work seems to be heading.

We believe one major milestone of our empirical work has been the development of psychometrically sound instruments for measuring some perceptions related to cognitive adaption. Several researchers have already used or adapted these instruments in studies of mothers and siblings of children with severe and profound disabilities in Costa Rica, caregivers of persons with Alzheimer's disease, persons with heart disease, parents of children with emotional disabilities, and parents of preschool age children with and without disabilities. As a knowledge base builds with the increased use of these instruments, we anticipate a better understanding of the dynamic relationship of perceptions and various adjustment-related outcomes, refinement of theory on cognitive coping, and direction for the training of service providers who work directly with the families of children with disabilities.

A second milestone stems from the exploratory nature of our study and the findings about the relationships among perceptions, various individual and family variables, stress, and family well-being. However, the contribution of this milestone lies not so much in solid conclusions, but in questions that arise from the tentative conclusions, taken together with findings of other researchers. We discuss two of the most provocative questions next.

FUTURE DIRECTIONS FOR
RESEARCH ON COGNITIVE COPING

Our work in cognitive coping among parents of children and adults with disabilities has concentrated on developing measures of perceptions associated with cognitive adaptation. We believe that these tools will contribute to empirical research in this field as they are used to deepen understanding of coping processes in families. Further, we have explored relationships between perceptions and various outcomes, and found moderate relationships among them. While these findings support some predictions from theory, as in all research, their value lies in the questions they stimulate for reseach. Two major questions for our future work relate to the application research findings and the refinement of theory.

Application: How Are Cognitive Coping Strategies
Learned and Can Their Learning Be Enabled or Enhanced?

To introduce this question, let us review the logic of the study we have discussed in this chapter. The rationale was straightforward: Cognitive coping strategies lead to the attainment of certain adaptation goals. Like most cognitive strategies, these are probably learned and applied by individuals when these goals become salient. If the strategies can be understood and described, then it might be possible to help people learn them and use them to enhance their own adjustment or adaptation.

Therefore, it seemed reasonable to develop a means of teaching these strategies to parents of children with disabilities. We chose a workshop-type format in which parents would be introduced to the strategies we had identified, have opportunities to discuss their own use of the strategies, and practice in a secure setting strategies not necessarily in their "coping repertoire." At the outset, we had determined that the target population should be parents of very young children as these parents, according to our findings, are most at risk for experiencing stress and frustration.

We pilot-tested the workshops with members of parent-to-parent groups who served in the role of "veteran" parents with newly referred parents. With few exceptions, these pilot-test participants expressed concern and caution about the potentially negative impact that attending a workshop of this nature might have on parents of very young or newly diagnosed children who might not be sufficiently far enough along in the adjustment process or ready to learn about using cognitive coping strategies.

They suggested, instead, that the workshop would be most useful for veteran parents, by helping them retrospectively affirm the coping process they had already been through and by helping them recognize how they learned to use cognitive coping strategies naturally and incidentally over time. These observations and suggestions were consistent with many comments from parents who took part in the validation study (Summers et al., 1991). These parents told us that their answers to our survey would have been very different had they completed it several years earlier; acceptance of their child's disability had been the result of growth and experience. Work by Affleck and Tennen (chap. 10, this volume) and Singer (chap 16, this volume) has shown that some individuals are very resistant to well-intentioned attempts by others to have them look at their distressing circumstances in a more positive light or to reframe them to be more acceptable or meaningful.

Given these reactions and findings, the question is: If it is not possible to teach these strategies directly to parents of children with disabilities, how *are* they learned, or are they learned at all? Taylor (1989) made the eloquent argument that the tendency for interpreting negative life events in an overly optimistic manner is "inherent in the way that the mind processes and ascribes meaning to information" (p. 245), but her argument does not necessarily extend to specific strategies. We suspect that strategies are learned in the same ways as values, attitudes, beliefs, and other cognitive processes. It is probable that some strategies are acquired through social learning processes, and others are acquired through formal means. For example, there is anecdotal evidence that parents of children with disabilities learn to view their families' lives more positively by participating in mutual support groups with other parents. Does this learning occur incidentally or by more intentional means?

Because we believe these questions are so important, we have directed our current research efforts toward addressing some of them. Our revised workshop, Coping with Change, will be presented to a sample of parents of young children with disabilities who are members of a support group. We will follow these parents for several months, using repeated measures, to explore their cognitive coping strategies and the perceived antecedents and consequences of the strategies. A control group of parents who belong to a support group but do not attend the workshop will be included in the study for comparison purposes. Such longitudinal work is essential to developing an understanding of how individuals learn to use cognitive strategies in the constantly changing processes of adaptation. Knowing how this learning can be enhanced might be a great advance in designing services for families of children with disabilities.

Theory: Is Cognitive Coping a Strategy or a Goal?

When cognitive coping is defined as a strategy or as a process used to attain a goal, as in the validation study, researchable questions focus on the nature of the process and the nature of the goals. Much of the research in cognitive coping has described the various strategies. We find it intriguing that many of us who have taken the strategy perspective tend to be less than explicit on the topic of strategic goals. For instance, according to the cognitive adaptation theory (Taylor, 1983), the goal of cognitive coping strategies is adjustment or adaptation. However, the theory is not definitive about these goals. For parents who are coping with the challenges of their child's disability, a goal of adjustment might be to exercise instrumental control by finding a competent speech-language therapist. Other goals might be to reduce feelings of distress by finding humor in difficult circumstances or to reappraise the situation by realizing the benefits of the child's presence in the family.

We believe that creative research is needed to clarify the nature of goals of cognitive coping strategies. Are these goals in the realms of instrumental control, emotional adjustment, or cognitive adaptation, or combinations of these, in tandem? Promising theoretical work in this direction has been started by Ortony, Clore, and Collins (1988).

Reflecting on our work from the "treetops" makes it possible to view elements from various perspectives and to reverse assumptions mentally. It occurred to us midway through our work that what we had been regarding as strategies might, indeed, more properly be considered goals. If, as Taylor and her colleagues argued (Taylor, 1989, Taylor & Brown, 1988), people have an inborn tendency to interpret events in wildly optimistic terms, then perhaps perceiving positive contributions, comparing oneself favorably with others, or developing objectively unrealistic illusions about one's mastery over events are the end product, the goal, of a yet-to-be-understood process.

This alternative view raises intriguing research questions. For example, Hill (1949, 1958) distinguished among three types of definitions of the stressor event: those developed by impartial observers, those developed by the community, and those developed by the family. Recalling Hill's ABCX Model, Factor C refers only to the family's subjective definition of the event. If the goal, or outcome, for the individual is positive perceptions that mark successful coping, the other definitions proposed by Hill could be considered independent variables. In that case, one might ask: How does the community's definition of disability influence the parent's ability to attain an optimum level of positive perceptions? How is the community's definition manifest in the support and services it provides to families? In institutional resources or barriers that either enable or inhibit the development of positive perceptions within the family? What is the relationship between these manifestations of the community's definition of disability and the family's attainment of the goal?

There is a clear difference between the strategy and the goal points of view. When perceptions are viewed as strategies, the tendency is to focus on the individual's and family's learning and use of strategies and how to intervene with the family. This assumption is not without merit. In contrast, regarding the perceptions as goals focuses attention on factors, both inside and outside the family, that influence the development of the perceptions. These factors might include communication within the family, family cohesion, or problem-solving capabilities. They might also include availability of services, societal attitudes, supports for the family, economic constraints and opportunities, and other community factors.

CONCLUSION

Our research on cognitive coping among parents of children and adults with developmental disabilities began as a result of our personal observations and interest in evidence that many families not only cope successfully with the challenges associated with disabilities, but seem to make a transition to higher levels of well-being (Mederer & Hill, 1983). With family stress and coping theory and cognitive adaption theory as the framework for research design and instrument construction, we embarked on a course of empirical study to measure perceptions and investigate their relationship to successful coping outcomes.

We recognize the need to study the development of perceptions over time. We recognize, as well, the need to study perceptions among family members of individuals who have a variety of physical and mental impairments, across the life cycle. We anticipate that the adaptation and use of the *Kansas Inventory of Parental Perceptions* (KIPP) (Behr, Murphy, & Summers, 1992) will assist other researchers in such efforts.

We are also engaged in research that addresses the current need in the disability field for empirically based interventions that can support families and enhance their efforts to cope successfully. Toward that end, we are conducting a study to investigate the immediate and longer-term effects of a workshop, Coping With Change, among parents of young children (birth to age 5) with disabilities of a lifelong nature (e.g., mental retardation, spina bifida, cerebral palsy). The context for this workshop emerges from the research described in this chapter, and it is designed to provide parents with an enhanced awareness of perceptions and naturally occurring cognitive coping strategies.

Finally, we have highlighted the need for further research to refine cognitive coping theory and to address questions related to the application of knowledge about cognitive coping to helping families cope sucessfully with disability-related challenges.

We believe that research on cognitive adaptation has the potential for helping us understand better how individuals and families cope with challenges associated with disabilities. If greater understanding can be incorporated into the training of those who work with these individuals and families, it is possible that services can be planned and provided that are more sensitive to natural coping processes and that encourage positive adaptation.

ABOUT THE AUTHORS

Shirley K. Behr, Ph.D., O.T.R., and Douglas L. Murphy, Ph.D.   Our research has been inspired and strengthened by personal experiences coping with disability and chronic illness in our own families and by our work with families of children with disabilities. At the Beach Center on Families and Disability, we focused on the cognitive resources parents use to cope successfully with disability-related challenges. We now look forward to expanding this work to investigate cognitive coping processes in other populations and to examine helping professionals' perceptions of positive adaptation among parents who use cognitive coping strategies.

REFERENCES

Behr, S.K. (1990). *The underlying dimensions of positive contributions that individuals with developmental disabilities make to their families: A factor analytic study*. Ann Arbor, MI: University Microfilms.

Behr, S.K., Murphy, D.L., & Summers, J.A. (1992). *Users manual: Kansas Inventory of Parental Perceptions (KIPP). Measures of perceptions of parents who have children with special needs.* Lawrence: University of Kansas, Beach Center on Families and Disability.

Department of Health and Human Services. (1983). Proposed Rule, July 5, 1983. *Federal Register, 48*, 30846–30852.

Dewey, J. (1933). *How we think: A restatement of the relation of reflective thinking to the educative process*. New York: D.C. Heath.

Gerdel, P. (1985). *Who are these researchers and why are they saying these horrible things about me?* Unpublished manuscript, Topeka, KS.

Hill, R. (1949). *Families under stress*. New York: Harper & Row.

Hill R. (1958). Generic features of families under stress. *Social Casework, 49*, 139–150.

Kaplan, A. (1963). *The conduct of inquiry: Methodology for behavioral science*. New York: Harper & Row.

McCubbin, H.I., & McCubbin, M.A. (1987). Family stress theory and assessment: The T-Double ABCX Model of Family Adjustments and Adaption. In H.I. McCubbin & A.I. Thompson (Eds.), *Family assessment inventories for research and practice* (pp.3–34). Madison: University of Winsconsin–Madison.

McCubbin, H.I., & Patterson, J.M. (1983). Family transitions: Adaption to stress. In H.I. McCubbin & C. Figley (Eds.), *Social stress and the family: Advances and development in family stress theory and research* (pp.1–6). New York: Haworth Press.

Mederer, H., & Hill, R. (1983). Critical transitions over the family life span: Theory and research. In H.I. McCubbin, M.B. Sussman, & J.M. Patterson (Eds.), *Social stress and the family: Advances and developments in family stress theory and research* (pp.39–60). New York: Haworth Press.

Mullins, J.B. (1987). Authentic voices from parents of exceptional children. *Family Relations, 36,* 30–33.

Murphy, D.L. Behr, S.K., & Summers, J.A. (1990a, May). *Social comparison strategies and their relationship to self-reported stress in parents of children with mental retardation.* Paper presented at the annual meeting of the American Association on Mental Retardation, Atlanta.

Murphy, D.L., Behr, S.K., & Summers, J.A. (1990b, August). Do something about it—Think! Cognitive coping strategies and stress and well-being in parents of children with disabilities.. In A.L. Quittner (Chair), *Critical events and contexts in family adjustment to disability.* Symposium conducted at the annual meeting of the American Psychological Association, Boston.

Murphy, D.L., Behr, S.K., & Tollefson, N. (1990, June). *Social comparisons and self-esteem of fathers and mothers of children with disabilities.* Paper presented at the annual meeting of the American Psychological Society, Dallas.

Ortony, A., Clore, G.L., & Collins, A. (1988). *The cognitive structure of emotions.* Cambridge, England: Cambridge University Press.

Press, A.N., & Osterkamp, L. (1986). *Comprehensive Computerized Stress Inventory.* (Available from Preventive Measures, Inc., 1115 West Campus Road, Lawrence, KS 66044).

Smilkstein, G. (1978). The Family APGAR: A proposal for a family function test and its use by physicians. *Journal of Family Practice, 6,* 1231–1239.

Spiegle-Mariska, J. (1990, March). *One mom's perceptions.* Keynote address presented at the opening session of the Early Intervention Training Workshop, Calgary, Alberta, Canada.

Summers, J.A., Behr, S.K., & Murphy, D.L. (1991). *The Family Perceptions Research Project: An investigation of the role of perceptions in coping among parents of children with disabilities including those with mental retardation.* Unpublished final report, University of Kansas, Beach Center on Families and Disability, Lawrence.

Taylor, S.E. (1983). Adjustment to threatening events: A theory of cognitive adaption. *American Psychologist, 38,* 1161–1173.

Taylor, S.E. (1989). *Positive illusions.* New York: Basic Books.

Taylor, S.E., & Brown, J. D. (1988). Illusion and well-being: A social psychological perspective on mental health. *Psychological Bulletin, 103*(2), 193–210.

Taylor, S.E., Lichtman, R.R., & Wood, J.V. (1984). Attributions, beliefs about control, and adjustment to breast cancer. *Journal of Personality and Social Psychology, 46*(3), 489–502.

Turnbull, H.R., Guess, D., & Turnbull, A.P. (1988). Vox populi and Baby Doe. *Mental Retardation, 26*(3), 127-132.

chapter 12

Individual and Interpersonal Influences on the Use of Cognitive Coping

Suzanne C. Thompson

There are many types of misfortune that could befall one in life: the loss of a loved one, physical disability, crime victimization, the diagnosis of a serious illness, and so on. These situations seem particularly important to study because they have the power to transform lives. On an applied level, knowledge about adaptive ways to cope may provide guidance for families and individuals who are faced with these events themselves. The support given by counselors in these circumstances will also be more effective if it is informed by accurate views of how people successfully negotiate serious trauma. In addition, these extreme circumstances can reveal what is critically important about human lives and human behavior, and thus can broaden and deepen theories that were developed to explain more mundane circumstances. There is another, more personal, reason for studying the serious losses that many people will face in life: It arises from knowing that none of us is immune to similar misfortunes ourselves. For me, this has led to a deep interest in how people handle difficult circumstances; I am especially intrigued by those individuals who seem to do it exceptionally well.

The questions that have guided my research in the past 5 years concern how people react to and cope with these extreme circumstances. In particular, what cognitive strategies help people successfully deal with traumatic events? Why are some people more likely than others to use the successful strategies? How do interpersonal factors (e.g., quality of relationships, communication, caregiving style) affect the use of cognitive strategies?

DEMONSTRATING UTILITY OF COGNITIVE STRATEGIES

The first studies that I did in this area tested the idea that certain cognitive coping strategies are associated with good coping. This research was intended to build on Bulman and Wortman's (1977) study of persons with spinal cord injuries—one of the first studies to interest social and health psychologists in the social cognitive factors involved in reactions to a "real-world" event. Bulman and Wortman found that quadriplegic and paraplegic accident survivors who were coping successfully tended to blame themselves for the accident. The explanation for this counterintuitive finding focused on the issue of control— taking personal responsibility for the accident contributed to a sense of control and future avoidability. In addition to questions about self-blame, the study included open-ended questions about how participants found meaning in this experience. Some of the intriguing answers fell into categories such as "re-evaluating the event as positive," "God has a reason," and "fate." The authors suggested that finding meaning in such a traumatic experience helped people to cope with their losses; however, because close-ended scales to measure these concepts were not included, it was not possible to test this idea nor to examine the adaptiveness of particular meanings.

The Bulman and Wortman (1977) study raised the possibility that a particular way of finding meaning in a traumatic experience—focusing on the positive—was associated with good coping. It seemed likely that it would be helpful for those experiencing a negative event to focus on what was beneficial or esteem enhancing about it. To test this idea, I began a study of fire survivors (Thompson, 1985). Close-ended questions were devised to measure five ways of taking a positive focus on a traumatic experience: 1) comparing oneself to others who are worse off, 2) comparing one's situation to worse situations, 3) forgetting the negative, 4) getting a positive side benefit, and 5) redefining goals (i.e., changing what one wants to fit with what one is likely to get). These five positive focus techniques were highly intercorrelated and were associated with good psychological outcomes both immediately following the fire and a year later. Even more important, the relationship between using positive focus techniques and good coping did not depend on the extent of the loss. This ruled out a troublesome alternative interpretation that those who used positive focus had better outcomes because they had lost less.

I have since done several other studies with a similar theme—demonstrating with close-ended scales that cognitive coping strategies are associated with good psychological outcomes, even when the effects of the severity of the event are controlled for. For example, stroke patients and their caregivers were less depressed when they had a sense of meaning and purpose and perceptions of control even when severity of the stroke, site of the stroke, and the financial consequences of their situation were controlled for (Thompson, Sobolew-Shubin, Graham, & Janigian, 1989). Cancer patients with high perceptions of control were less depressed, even when the seriousness of their condition was taken into account (Thompson, 1990).

EXPLAINING INDIVIDUAL
DIFFERENCES IN USING COGNITIVE ADAPTATION

A second purpose of my research has been to try to explain why some people use adaptive cognitive strategies and others do not. Presumably, these ways of looking at the experience would provide the same benefits and assistance in the coping process for most people. However, it is clear that not everyone adopts the useful strategies, such as finding a positive focus, generating a sense of control, and finding meaning in the experience. Based on my studies, I would estimate that 40%–60% of respondents report using adaptive cognitive strategies (Thompson, 1985; Thompson et al., 1989). One answer to why the others do not might be that those whose losses are greatest find it particularly difficult to use these techniques; however, this idea has been ruled out by the studies reported above. Many of the individuals most severely affected used cognitive coping and the strategies were still associated with coping even when the effects of extent of loss were controlled for.

I have explored two further explanations. One is that the use of adaptive coping strategies is dependent on *long-term views* about oneself and the world that were developed before the misfortune took place. For example, those who have an optimistic style would find it easier to focus on the positive when a tragedy occurred; in contrast, those who see the world in ways consistent with Ellis's (1977) irrational beliefs—perfectionistic, cynical about other people, and ready to see every setback as a catastrophe—could find it especially difficult to find meaning and control in a traumatic experience. The second explanation is that *interpersonal factors* can make it easy or difficult to adopt useful cognitive techniques. For example, important others may model successful techniques, or may provide a supportive environment that makes the discovery of these techniques on one's own more likely. The effects of long-term views and interpersonal factors are discussed next.

Long-Term Views

Are those who have psychologically healthy world views before the event better able to use adaptive cognitive techniques? Thompson and Janigian (1988), for example, suggested that those who have less materialistic goals—which would be less likely to be challenged by a traumatic event—will find it easier to find meaning in an extremely negative experience. To test this idea, we had cancer patients retrospectively report on their prediagnosis and current goals and world views. Contrary to the hypothesis, current goals and world views predicted current adjustment, but prediagnosis goals and world views did not. This study is, of course, limited by the use of retrospective data. However, if it does present an accurate picture of prediagnosis beliefs, it suggests that some people *change* their goals and views in adaptive ways in the face of a major misfortune, rather than have pre-existing views that determine whether or not they use adaptive cognitive techniques. Unfortunately, we still have little information about why some people change goals and views while others do not.

Interpersonal Environment

A second influence on the use of coping strategies might come from one's social network. Network members may influence the use of cognitive coping by modeling ways of looking at the situation that help those who experience a trauma to generate a sense of control, find meaning, and adopt a positive focus. If this is the case, then one would expect that the cognitive assessments of those undergoing a trauma would be similar to the views of their families and close friends because positive-thinking and hopeful intimates may influence others to adopt similar views. This should be especially true for marital partners whose close association over a long period of time and numerous opportunities to discuss an important experience seem likely to lead to similar approaches to important life events. However, in two tests of this idea, I found little support for the idea that marital partners influence each other's views in this direct manner. Stroke patients and their spouses agreed on a number of dimensions—the patient's level of functioning, and the financial stress caused by the stroke, for example—but there was very little correspondence in the extent to which they had found meaning in the event or in their perceptions of control (Thompson et al., 1989). Similarly, cancer patients and their spouses had very similar perceptions of the amount of financial stress the illness had caused and of the quality of their relationship, but there was no correlation between their perceptions of control, the extent to which they had found meaning, their adherence to "irrational" beliefs, or their sense of optimism (Thompson, 1991). Thus, there is little evidence that one source of the ability to use adaptive cognitive approaches comes from modeling the reactions of intimate others.

A second way in which network members might have an influence on the use of adaptive cognitive techniques is through indirect messages that reflect their views of the person who has experienced the trauma. Traumatic events, especially those that result in greater dependence on others, can threaten a sense of mastery and positive self-esteem. Some individuals may find it difficult to generate feelings of control, maintain high self-esteem, and remain optimistic if the implicit message from family and friends is that they no longer see the individual as an autonomous adult (or in the case of a child, as capable as other children that age). In a series of studies, my colleagues and I investigated the effects on chronically ill adults of feeling overprotected by family members.

A caregiving style of overprotection seems particularly important to examine because of the possibility that doing too much for an ill individual and restricting him or her from usual adult activities is likely to send the message that the individual is seen as incompetent, which could make it difficult for him or her to maintain a sense of control. Consistent with this idea, stroke patients, cancer patients, and adults with other chronic illnesses had lower perceptions of control and were more depressed when they felt overprotected by family members (Thompson & Sobolew-Shubin, 1990; Thompson, Sobolew-Shubin, Galbraith, Schwankovksy, & Cruzen, in press; Thompson et al., 1989). On the positive side, cancer patients who reported that they received good emotional support from their spouses felt that they had higher levels of personal control (Thompson et al., in press). Persons with chronic illness whose caregivers were emotionally supportive, treated them as adults, and were not overprotective found it easier to maintain a sense of control in their lives. Thus, the social environment may be one explanation for why some people are able to generate feelings of control and others are not.

FURTHER INVESTIGATIONS OF CAREGIVING STYLES

A final issue my research has investigated is why some adults with chronic illness feel overprotected. In a study of 60 stroke patients and their caregivers, we found that the functioning level of the patient, and discrepancies between patients and caregivers in their ratings of how well the patient was functioning, did not predict patients' feelings of being overprotected (Thompson & Sobolew-Shubin, 1990). However, overprotected patients tended to be those whose caregivers reported more resentment toward the patient and the caregiving role. This finding suggests that an overprotective caregiving style may, in part, be an indirect reflection of negative attitudes toward the recipient. Perhaps, as some writers have proposed, the caregivers may sometimes overprotect the ill family member as a way of expressing frustration or exerting control (Watzalawick & Coyne, 1980).

CURRENT ISSUES RELATED TO FAMILY COPING

Research on cognitive coping confirms the idea that such cognitive approaches as finding meaning, generating a sense of control, and focusing on the positive are associated with successful adjustment. This suggests that families who do not use these perspectives on their own may be helped by interventions to encourage their application. In order for those interventions to be optimally effective, it is important to understand the factors that prompt some individuals to engage in cognitive adaptation while others do not seem able (or, perhaps, willing) to do so.

Some promising results along these lines are the findings that the interpersonal environment has an effect on the use of cognitive techniques. As discussed above, individuals do not seem to directly model the cognitive coping strategies of intimates. However, cancer patients who have good emotional support from their spouses have stronger perceptions of control, and both stroke and cancer patients who do not feel overprotected also feel more in control and are more likely to have found meaning in the event. This suggests that intimate others may provide an environment that makes it easier to use adaptive strategies (emotional support) or one that makes it more difficult (overprotective care).

Good Support from Family Members

Although most of the research described above was done with chronically ill adults and their spouses, it speaks to the issue of how family members dealing with any misfortune might help each other cope more successfully with a stressful event. The receipt of good support (i.e., that allows the recipient to express feelings and feel valued by a friend or family member) seems to be associated with such cognitive strategies as generating perceptions of control. Overly controlling, restrictive, or smothering treatment, however, is correlated with low use of successful coping techniques by the recipient. It is interesting to note that we found that the correlations between negative support styles such as overprotection and poor coping are generally much stronger than those between positive support and good coping (Thompson & Sobolew-Shubin, 1990). This is consistent with other research that finds that the negative aspects of social interaction have more effects on coping than do the positive aspects (e.g., Manne & Zautra, 1989; Rook, 1984). Thus, those who are undergoing a stressful event will find it easier to adapt successfully if their support network provides appropriate but not controlling or demeaning help, and avoids negative behaviors and interactions that increase coping difficulties.

Reducing Caregiver Burden

Because this research has found that overprotecting caregivers tend to be those with higher levels of resentment toward the recipient of their care, another implication is that issues of caregiving burden and resentment need to be addressed. Some examples of how feelings of burden and resentment could be lessened are:

- Support groups where caregivers can discuss difficulties and receive validation for their feelings
- Respite care that provides some relief for those giving continual care
- Interventions to enhance communication and the quality of the relationship between the care provider and recipient and within the family

Reciprocity in Relationships

My current research is examining other solutions through the study of how care providers and recipients successfully "balance" their relationship. Social exchange theories of close relationships suggest that people tend to be more satisfied with relationships that are balanced—each partner's contributions to the relationship and benefits from the relationship are fairly evenly matched (Hatfield, Traupmann, Sprecher, Utne, & Hay, 1985). This type of reciprocity may become an issue when one partner is unable to provide the types of benefits for the other that he or she once did (in the case of an adult with a chronic illness) or that might be expected in that type of relationship (accomplishments or help around the house from a child). One issue I am pursuing in a group of persons with coronary heart disease and their spouses is how relationships become balanced under these circumstances of patients' reduced opportunities to provide benefits. Some couples may handle this issue by focusing on past benefits from the patient, emphasizing future expected benefits, referring to role requirements ("I'm doing this because this is what husbands do"), or providing as many opportunities as possible for the ill partner to make a contribution (asking him or her for help). This line of work suggests that finding ways to establish reciprocity may reduce some of the burden and resentment associated with the caregiving role.

Life Schemes and Storytelling

Another promising way to understand how people cope with a stressful life event is to examine the stories or accounts they relate about the experience. Thompson and Janigian (1988) proposed that each individual has a cognitive representation of his or her life, much like a story, that organizes world views, goals in life, and events relevant to those goals. These life schemes may be changed by a traumatic event to accommodate the new experience. In my current research on patients in cardiac rehabilitation, patients and their spouses are asked to tell their "life story" and also their story of the cardiac incident and its effects on their marriage. These accounts will be analyzed to identify themes that are related to good or poor adjustment. For example, I expect that a story that mentions benefits and lessons learned from the incident or a theme that one is a survivor will be associated with better adjustment than will be a theme of irretrievable loss. In my future research, the effects of being able to tell one's story and the changing themes in stories over time will be examined.

CONCLUSION

The benefits of cognitive coping techniques have now been established by a variety of studies. My continuing interest in this area focuses on the individual factors that are associated with the use of cognitive coping and the effects of relationships and network members on the use of these adaptive strategies. Family members and friends clearly are in a position to have dramatic effects on the coping of people facing a misfortune. The challenge is to understand how this influence works and to identify successful ways that families handle stressful life events.

ABOUT THE AUTHOR

Suzanne C. Thompson, Ph.D. My training in health psychology and social psychology led to an interest in how people cope with very stressful life experiences, such as being chronically ill or caring for an ill family member. In my current position as associate professor of psychology, I teach and do research on these topics. My recent studies have focused on the effects of cardiac problems on the marital relationship, how cancer patients and their spouses maintain a sense of control and meaningfulness, and the adaptive coping processes of people who are infected with the human immunodeficiency virus (HIV).

REFERENCES

Bulman, R.J., & Wortman, C. (1977). Attributions of blame and coping in the "real world": Severe accident victims react to their lot. *Journal of Personality and Social Psychology, 35,* 351–363.

Ellis, A. (1977). The basic clinical theory of rational-emotive therapy. In A. Ellis & R. Grieger (Eds.), *Handbook of rational-emotive therapy* (pp. 3–34). New York: Springer.

Hatfield, E., Traupmann, J., Sprecher, S., Utne, M., & Hay, J. (1985). Equity and intimate relations: Recent research. In W.J. Ickes (Ed.), *Compatible and incompatible relationships* (pp. 91–117). New York: Springer-Verlag.

Manne, S.L., & Zautra, A.J. (1989). Spouse criticism and support: Their association with coping and psychological adjustment among women with rheumatoid arthritis. *Journal of Personality and Social Psychology, 56,* 608–617.

Rook, K.S. (1984). The negative side of social interaction: Impact on psychological well-being. *Journal of Personality and Social Psychology, 46,* 1097–1108.

Thompson, S.C. (1985). Finding positive meaning in a stressful event and coping. *Basic and Applied Social Psychology, 6,* 279–295.

Thompson, S.C. (1990, November). *The search for meaning and control: Lessons from stroke and cancer patients.* Paper presented at the National Council on Family Relations Annual Conference, Seattle.

Thompson, S.C. (1991). [Cancer patients and their spouses: Living with cancer]. Unpublished data.

Thompson, S.C., & Janigian, A. (1988). Life schemes: A framework for understanding the search for meaning. *Journal of Social and Clinical Psychology, 7,* 260–280.

Thompson, S.C., & Sobolew-Shubin, A. (1990). *Overprotective relationships: A nonsupportive side of social networks.* Manuscript under review.

Thompson, S.C., Sobolew-Shubin, A., Galbraith, M., Schwankovsky, L., & Cruzen, D. (in press). Maintaining perceptions of control: Finding perceived control in low-control circumstances. *Journal of Personality and Social Psychology.*

Thompson, S.C., Sobolew-Shubin, A., Graham, M., & Janigian, A. (1989). Psychosocial adjustment following a stroke. *Social Science and Medicine, 28,* 239–247.

Watzalawick, P., & Coyne, J.C. (1980). Depression following stroke: Brief, problem-focused family treatment. *Family Process, 19,* 13–18.

chapter 13

Coping Strategies Among Older Mothers of Adults with Retardation
A Life-Span Developmental Perspective

Marty Wyngaarden Krauss
and Marsha Mailick Seltzer

> The hardest part is at night, when he's lying there peacefully and you're thinking the 100,000 thoughts of what could have been and all the reasons why this happened. You think that from day one, and I think you ask that all your life. And it goes on 24 hours. It does not end. (A 72-year-old mother of a 49-year-old son with mental retardation)

It has been observed that a single event has the power to transform not just one life, but many lives and to change not just one stage of life, but an entire lifetime. Some events, such as graduation from school, marriage, and the birth of children are predictable, expected, and occur at roughly the same time for most people. These events are often called *normative* events. Other events, however, are *nonnormative*, in that they do not occur to most people, are unplanned and unanticipated, and usually are not wanted or desired (Baltes, Reese, & Lipsitt, 1980; Brim & Ryff, 1980). Common examples include temporary unemployment, divorce, traumatic injury or illness, and chronic disability. While both normative and nonnormative events have the potential to transform lives, the nonnormative events do so in less predictable ways.

Research on nonnormative events has focused on their impact on the individual, and to a lesser extent, on the family as a unit. This research is characterized by its short-term focus (i.e., the specific patterns of reactions and accommodations to the nonnormative event within a relatively distinct time period) and by its cause–effect perspective (i.e., a stressor–response orientation) (Endler & Parker, 1990; Folkman & Lazarus, 1980; Pearlin & Schooler, 1978). What have been less well studied are the adaptations of individuals and families to nonnormative events that are of lifelong consequence, such as the parenting of a child with mental retardation (Seltzer & Ryff, in press). The quotation at the beginning of this chapter reveals the powerful and enduring impacts of a nonnormative event. Our goal in this chapter is to apply a developmental perspective to what we have learned about the ways that mothers, in particular, cope with the experience of parenting a child with mental retardation throughout the mother's adulthood.

Our research is designed to contribute to an understanding of how families manage and feel about their efforts to provide lifetime in-home care for a member with retardation. We have brought a life-span developmental perspective to our research, a perspective that is based on three critical assumptions (Baltes et al., 1980):

1. We view human development not as the province of the chronologically young, but as a characteristic phenomenon of individuals over their entire lives. Thus, we anticipate that coping is a mechanism through which human development and learning occurs.

2. We view human development as deeply affected by the historical period in which it occurs. Thus, we anticipate that the coping strategies and beliefs of the parents we study who are in their 60s, 70s, and 80s may differ in important ways from those of younger cohorts of parents who are rearing their child with retardation in a vastly different social and political context than was experienced by earlier generations of parents.

3. We view human development as an interplay between individual characteristics, life-span tasks, and life-span contexts. This suggests that while there are normative tasks associated with different ages or stages of human development, the nonnormative context in which such tasks are pursued may affect the accomplishment of the life-span tasks. Thus, we anticipate that one consequence of the continued role of *parent* for a group of women who "should be" (chronologically speaking) retired from active parenting roles may be the development of more finely honed, personally effective coping skills than might be evident in like-age cohorts of women who have not experienced the nonnormative event of parenting a child with retardation.

This chapter reviews the basic questions that drive our research, presents qualitative and quantitative information about the coping strategies used by aging mothers either currently or over their many decades of caregiving, and describes some of the questions we will continue to pursue in our future studies.

CORE QUESTIONS ADDRESSED IN OUR RESEARCH

Since 1988, we have followed a sample of 462 families in Massachusetts and Wisconsin that had two central characteristics at the time of study enrollment: The mother was at least 55 years of age and she had a son or daughter with mental retardation at home with her. (See Krauss, Seltzer, & Goodman, 1992, and Seltzer & Krauss, 1989, for a more detailed description of study design and methods.) By the time the study ends, we will have met four times with each family in our sample, with each visit occurring 18 months after the preceding one.

Our initial analyses, conducted after the first round of visits, were designed to assess the current well-being among mothers in our study (Seltzer & Krauss, 1989). While our research collects information from fathers, siblings, and the sons and daughters with retardation, the analyses conducted to date have focused primarily on information from the mothers. Our preliminary analyses used a multidimensional perspective on well-being, which we defined as physical health, life satisfaction, perceived burden of care, and parenting stress. We found considerable evidence that the mothers in our sample had at least as high a level of well-being as several relevant comparison groups. Specifically, mothers in our sample reported: 1) better physical health in comparison to other women their age with and without significant caregiving responsibilities, 2) greater life satisfaction in comparison to other women who provided daily care to an elderly relative, and 3) no greater burden or stress associated with parenting an adult child with retardation in comparison to younger mothers of children with mental retardation or women providing care to an elderly relative.

These positive outcomes, at first glance, were puzzling to us. The mothers in our study averaged 66 years of age; the youngest mother was 55 years old, while the oldest mother was 85 years old. Most of their sons and daughters with retardation had lived at home their entire lives and had received minimal educational or other support services when they were children. Their mothers reported having had considerable difficulty getting competent professional help and had experienced many instances of the social insensitivity and discrimination that was particularly prevalent in the 1940s through the 1970s. Most mothers also had poignant accounts of the often heroic efforts they had expended to raise their child with retardation along with their other children. The objective facts of their histories, diverse and unique as each one was, conveyed a common theme—the arduous task of parenting a child with retardation in an era in which little public and often spotty private support was available. Their subjective perspectives on their histories also conveyed a common theme— these women felt like pioneers, opened up new opportunities for their children, used their situations to forge a "career" as a parent, and now gamely recounted the successes they achieved. It was clear that, at this stage in their lives, they had developed a framework for their experiences; a set of beliefs about what had happened to them; and a personal view of what this nonnormative event had taught them about themselves, their families, and about people with disabilities.

PREVALENT COPING STRATEGIES

Among other issues, we delved more deeply into these personal frameworks in our second set of interviews (conducted 18 months after the first) and, at that time, we probed the coping styles and strategies reported by the mothers in our sample using both quantitative and qualitative methods. Specifically, the mothers were asked to complete a standardized coping questionnaire (the *Coping Orientations to Problems Experienced* [COPE] scale by Carver, Scheier, & Weintraub [1989]). This measure is multidimensional, is based on the Lazarus Model of Coping (Lazarus, 1966), includes cognitive and behavioral strategies that are generally considered to be both adaptive and maladaptive, and covers the most commonly identified ways in which people respond to or cope with stressful events. The mothers also responded to a series of open-ended questions about their experiences as a parent of a child with mental retardation. The questions focused both on current appraisals of their lives and on how they had coped and made decisions about the care of their son or daughter with retardation in earlier stages of the family's life.

Given the great diversity in their individual circumstances and personalities, we anticipated diversity in their cognitive and behavioral coping styles and their spontaneously described experiences (McCrae & Costa, 1986; Ryff & Dunn, 1985). Indeed, we found that most mothers reported that they used *all* of the strategies covered in the COPE instrument (Carver et al., 1989) to some extent, although the use of maladaptive strategies was much less common than the use of adaptive strategies. Maladaptive strategies included mental disengagement (psychological withdrawal from the goal with which the stressor is interfering), denial (an attempt to reject the reality of the stressful event), or behavioral disengagement (giving up, or withdrawing effort from the attempt to attain the goal with which the stressor is interfering). Adaptive strategies included acceptance (acknowledging the fact that the stressful event has occurred and is real), positive reinterpretation and growth (making the best of the situation by growing from it or viewing it in a more favorable light), turning to religion (increased engagement in religious activities), and planning (thinking about how to confront the stressor, mapping out one's active coping efforts). These results were consistent with other research on older individuals, which reported an infrequent use of denial strategies in coping with stressful events (Aldwin, 1991). One hypothesis advanced by Aldwin for the low rate of escapist or denial strategies among older people is that experience has taught them that such strategies are ineffective techniques for coping with stress. Thus, from a developmental perspective, age-related differences in the use of coping strategies may reflect the effects of learning via trial and error about helpful and effective ways to manage the challenges presented by their son or daughter with mental retardation.

In order to move beyond characterizing the mothers by the range of coping strategies they used, we examined the coping strategies on which each mother relied primarily. We defined reliance based on maternal responses regarding the frequency with which a mother used a specific strategy or set of strategies. We found most mothers in our sample relied on a core set of coping strategies that were confirmed both empirically (Krauss, 1991) and anecdotally. The cognitive coping strategies relied upon by over 75% of the mothers in our sample were: acceptance of the situation, positive reinterpretation and growth, turning to religion, and planning. Very few mothers relied primarily on negative strategies, although most used some negative strategies at times.

In order to amplify the ways in which the four most commonly used coping strategies contributed to how these mothers framed their lives, we have culled from the interviews a variety of accounts and examples. These are presented next.

Acceptance

Most discussions about an individual's adaptation to an unexpected and negatively perceived event include the importance of coming to terms with the event or of accepting it as real and as something with which to contend. The mothers in our sample confirmed that the struggle to accept their child with retardation for the person he or she is represented a major task for them personally and for their families. As one mother said, "From the time I *did* accept her, things have been a lot easier."

The intensity of the struggle to achieve some measure of acceptance is not necessarily a time-bound process. One mother expressed well the sentiments of many regarding the pain of accepting the limitations of their children:

> In the beginning, it was very hard to take. As soon as it starts, you would like it to be ended. But then, you just learn to take it. I'm blessed the way it is now. She's a great help. It's become positive. I know in the beginning that I was thinking that this was the worst thing that could happen to anybody. But now I would love to tell other ones that it happened to that it isn't the worst thing.

Positive Reinterpretation and Growth

From a developmental perspective, the appraisal of a nonnormative event may undergo significant changes over time. While most agree that the initial diagnosis of a child as having mental retardation constitutes a major threat to personal and family equilibrium, it is clear from the mothers in our sample that many reinterpretations of the *meaning* of this event have been woven into their life schemes or frames as they acquired experience as individuals and as parents. What is particularly remarkable is the salience of positive reinterpretations among mothers in our study, and of the attribution of individual growth and development to the challenges they have faced and mastered. As one mother said:

It all depends on how you look at the situation. There could be two people living in the same house—one could be happy, the other miserable. I look at this as my lot in life and I did it and I still do it. He's made a greater person out of me.

Other mothers reflected on the fundamental transformation that the experience of parenting a child with retardation has had on their lives. For some, this non-normative event jolted them into seeing themselves, and life, with a new lens. As one mother said:

When I was growing up, I was very good, top of my class. Everything I did was the best, and if it wasn't, it was done over again. When my daughter took sick, I had to face up to the fact that here was something I could not throw away and start over again. That built a lot of character. I had to pick up the pieces and keep on going. I had to face life as it is.

Another mother reflected on the family-level impacts of retardation from a developmental perspective:

I remember my mother's neighbor saying that Mother's attitude had changed a lot after my daughter [with retardation] was born. Before that, Mother thought things happened to people because of their own efforts, their own doing. She was impatient with other people's frailties. She learned something and I suppose I did, too.

Finally, one mother summarized succinctly her personal growth as an accomplishment: "It makes you more determined to survive and more stubborn to fight for your kids. From a meek little soul I became a lion, a tiger."

Turning to Religion

Many mothers noted that their spiritual lives have been enhanced by their experiences as a parent of a child with retardation. The need to have an explanation, a cause, or a meaning for unexpected events has been noted by other researchers (Taylor, 1983). Part of the frame the mothers in our study used to describe their experiences included an acknowledgment of the strength they have derived from their religious beliefs. As one mother said, "It's made me more compassionate toward anyone with physical defects and it's made me more patient to listen to other people. It has brought me close to God." Others attribute their ability to handle their parenting roles to personal qualities that they perceive as gifts from God. One mother told us, "I feel God gave me the strength to turn around and say, 'She's mine and I like her the way she is and if you don't— tough!'"

Planning

In addition to the cognitive coping strategies just described, these mothers recounted the immense efforts they have expended throughout their children's lives to ensure the best care and services possible. In doing so, they discovered or nurtured the ability to plan, to take action, and to advocate for their children.

Their effectiveness as planners, as creators of new services, and as organizers of their families' needs helped to create a sense of personal fulfillment that may well contribute to the general level of positive well-being we found in our initial analyses. As one mother recounted:

> The first two years [1943–1945] were bleak, with institutional placement the recommendation of professionals. How did we cope? Well, first we formed a parents' group. Then we helped to establish a special kindergarten class and turned it over to the school board. Also, we worked to develop our local sheltered workshop and most recently, we promoted the infant stimulation program for young parents. The best way to cope is to join with other parents early on, learn together, and then you can help to provide the best possible future for all retarded children.

Summary

Our initial investigation of the coping strategies used by older mothers of adult children with retardation yielded several conclusions. First, we were struck by the adaptive quality of their coping skills—their reliance on acceptance, positive reinterpretation and growth, religion, and planning. However, we cannot say whether these constructive strategies are attributable to their comparatively atypical parenting careers or, alternatively, are perhaps typical of older women, or even older men and women, in the general population. Nevertheless, two facts stand out: These mothers used a range of strategies, and the ones they tended to rely on required their active engagement with life's problems. These facts suggest that their nonnormative parenting careers have not resulted in a diminished or unwilling capacity to cope with new problems and may have been an unexpectedly positive experience in developmental terms.

FUTURE DIRECTIONS FOR RESEARCH

The study of the effects of nonnormative life events on individual and family development raises new challenges for research on coping strategies. The use of a life-span developmental perspective assumes explicitly that there is change over time in the responses, attitudes, and beliefs of individuals for whom a nonnormative stressor represents a lifetime, rather than time-bound, challenge. Clearly, the careful study of the use, effects, and refinement of specific cognitive and behavioral coping strategies over time constitutes a major research agenda for us and, we hope, for others. Our preliminary cross-sectional analyses provide a stimulating glimpse into the cognitive appraisals of older mothers of adult children with retardation. Our next step involves a longitudinal investigation of change in cognitive appraisals—how it occurs, why it occurs, and the effect of its occurrence. This will be critical to extending our knowledge about appropriate interventions for families and individuals living with lifelong challenges.

Our research, and that of others, suggests that how one copes with events that have a resolution (e.g., situational unemployment) may well differ from how one copes with events that have no endpoint (e.g., parenting a child with retardation). In this sense, the context of our research provides fertile ground for exploring the developmental processes that explain changes in coping strategies over time to specific nonnormative events. Making careful distinctions about the nature of the event to which a person responds seems particularly important. Clearly, the reactions that characterize the individual's initial response to a nonnormative event may not be sustained over time as a result of increasing expertise in coping and positive reinterpretation. Thus, from a developmental perspective, it is expected that there is a learning process that results in a more cogent and personally efficacious set of responses or cognitive coping strategies.

The narratives of the older women in our sample regarding how they have coped with the experience of parenting a son or daughter with mental retardation exposes the fact that our questions may have provided an opportunity for them to engage in and articulate a life review. It also suggests that life reviews, or what we have called earlier the frames used by these women to view their experiences, focus quite sharply on the specific beliefs, strategies, or actions that they *think* made a critical difference in their lives. Their cognitions about their experiences serve as explanations for why they have prevailed as parents, despite the enormous odds they may have faced initially. Taylor's (1983) articulation of the *illusions* that people facing major threats develop about the meaning the threat has for them (see Brown, chap. 9, this volume) may have particular relevance in our future research on cognitive appraisals within our sample.

We are also intrigued by the idea that the keys to success—the effective coping strategies—described by the mothers in our sample to the issue of parenting a son or daughter with retardation may be generalizable to other domains of their lives. Most of these women face, either currently or imminently, a variety of other major life changes or crises. Given their age, many are or will be widowed, will experience declines in their health or in the health of loved ones and friends, and/or will confront the need to make specific plans for the future care of their son or daughter with retardation when they can no longer continue in this role. We may learn a great deal about how they approach these other normative and nonnormative events by our understanding of how they have mastered prior events. While this raises the question of the trait (i.e., a dispositional characteristic of the individual's general personality) versus process (i.e., affected by the specifics of the stressful event) orientation to coping (Kobasa, Maddi, & Kahn, 1982; McCrae & Costa, 1986; Parkes, 1984), we suspect that exploring the interaction between individual characteristics, prior experiences, and current events may be a compelling framework for explaining the adaptation of these mothers to new challenges.

ABOUT THE AUTHORS

Marty Wyngaarden Krauss, Ph.D. My research has focused on the effects of mental retardation on family members—mothers, fathers, siblings—across the life span. As a senior investigator on a longitudinal study of families entering the early intervention system and as co-director of a longitudinal study of aging families of adult children with mental retardation living at home, I have had opportunities to study how different generations interpret, adjust to, and evaluate the meaning of retardation to themselves, their families, and their society.

Marsha Mailick Seltzer, Ph.D. My research spans the areas of aging and mental retardation. I am interested in how the family is affected by a member with a disability, including disabilities due to problems associated with development and with the aging process. I am co-principal investigator of a longitudinal study, funded by the National Institute on Aging, of aging families who have an adult child with mental retardation living at home with them. Through this study, I am able to investigate the independent and reciprocal effects of disability on all the members of a family, including the mother, the father, the adult with mental retardation, and his or her siblings. In addition, this study affords me the opportunity to understand how family members cope with the inevitable transitions that accompany aging.

REFERENCES

Aldwin, C.M. (1991). Does age affect the stress and coping process? Implications of age differences in perceived control. *Journal of Gerontology, 46,* P174–180.

Baltes, P.B., Reese, H.W., & Lipsitt, L.P. (1980). Life-span developmental psychology. *Annual Review of Psychology, 31,* 65–110.

Brim, O.G., Jr., & Ryff, C. (1980). On the properties of life-span events. In P.B. Baltes & O.G. Brim, Jr. (Eds.), *Life-span development and behavior* (Vol. 3, pp. 368–388). New York: Academic Press.

Carver, C.S., Scheier, M.F., & Weintraub, J.K. (1989). Assessing coping strategies: A theoretically based approach. *Journal of Personality and Social Psychology, 56,* 267–283.

Endler, N.S., & Parker, J.D.A. (1990). Multidimensional assessment of coping: A critical evaluation. *Journal of Personality and Social Psychology, 58,* 844–854.

Folkman, S., & Lazarus, R.S. (1980). An analysis of coping in a middle-aged community sample. *Journal of Health and Social Behavior, 21,* 219–239.

Kobasa, S.C., Maddi, S.R., & Kahn, S. (1982). Hardiness and health: A prospective study. *Journal of Personality and Social Psychology, 42,* 168–177.

Krauss, M.W. (1991, May). *Coping styles among mothers of adults with mental retardation.* Paper presented at the 24th Annual Gatlinburg Conference on Research and Theory in Mental Retardation, Key Biscayne, FL.

Krauss, M.W., Seltzer, M.M., & Goodman, S. (1992). Social support networks of adults with retardation who live at home. *American Journal on Mental Retardation, 96,* 432–441.

Lazarus, R.S. (1966). *Psychological stress and the coping process.* New York: McGraw-Hill.

McCrae, R.R., & Costa, P.T. (1986). Personality, coping, and coping effectiveness in an adult sample. *Journal of Personality, 54,* 385–405.

Parkes, K.R. (1984). Locus of control, cognitive appraisal, and coping in stressful episodes. *Journal of Personality and Social Psychology, 46,* 655–668.

Pearlin, L.I., & Schooler, C. (1978). The structure of coping. *Journal of Health and Social Behavior, 19,* 2–21.

Ryff, C.D., & Dunn, D.D. (1985). A life-span developmental approach to the study of stressful events. *Journal of Applied Developmental Psychology, 6,* 113–127.

Seltzer, M.M., & Krauss, M.W. (1989). Aging parents with mentally retarded children: Family risk factors and sources of support. *American Journal on Mental Retardation, 94,* 303–312.

Seltzer, M.M., & Ryff, C. (in press). Parenting across the life-span: The normative and nonnormative cases. In D.L. Featherman, R.M. Lerner, & M. Perlmutter (Eds.), *Life-span development and behavior* (Vol. 12). Hillsdale, NJ: Lawrence Erlbaum Associates.

Taylor, S.E. (1983). Adjustment to threatening events: A theory of cognitive adaptation. *American Psychologist, 38,* 1161–1173.

chapter 14

Family Functioning When Rearing Children with Developmental Disabilities

Laraine Masters Glidden, Michael J. Kiphart,
Jennifer C. Willoughby, and Beverly A. Bush

A major shift has occurred in the thinking of many people involved with families who are rearing children with mental retardation or other developmental disabilities or disabling conditions. An almost monolithic conception of the inevitability of distress, crisis, and pathology has been replaced by a recognition of the extreme variability of family response and an understanding of the importance of identifying the antecedent causes of that variability. This identification, and the subsequent delineation that should follow it, has scientific value for theory on stress, coping, and adaptation, as well as service value for intervening with families who want and need intervention.

This "new look" in families and disabilities is the result of many factors. For instance, there is much greater interest in families now than there was even 10 years ago. This interest is manifested in both research about and services for families. For example, in 1988, 21% of the articles published in the *American Journal on Mental Retardation* were about family issues, as contrasted to only 1% in 1978 (Glidden, 1989a). In the service domain, the passage of PL 99-457 ensured that families would be the core unit around which young children would receive interventions. Perhaps it was inevitable that with this much focus on families a more complex and multidimensional portrait of them would begin to emerge.

This greater interest and visibility undoubtedly stems, at least in part, from the empowerment movements that began in the 1950s and continue today. With deinstitutionalization, more children with disabilities stayed with their families, giving rise to a greater need for information about families and provi-

This chapter was supported, in part, by Grant No. HD 21993 from the National Institute of Child Health and Human Development and by the School of Social Welfare, University of California–Berkeley.

sion of services for them. Demographics play a role as well. The high birth rate that led to the baby boom generation initially meant that there were more children and today, as the boomers are in middle life, that there are more families.

Finally, psychological theory and research about families and about stress, coping, and adaptation have become much more sophisticated, with complex models about how individuals and families adjust to potentially stressful events (e.g., Crnic, Friedrich, & Greenberg, 1983; Lazarus & Folkman, 1984; McCubbin & Patterson, 1983; McCubbin, Thompson, Thompson, & McCubbin, chap. 18, this volume). These new models emphasize the cognitive determinants and concomitants of coping, the macro-environment in which the family lives, and the long-term results of any potential stressful event.

STUDY OF ADOPTIVE FAMILIES

The work described in this chapter began with the recognition that the negative impact of rearing a child with a developmental disability was being emphasized to the exclusion of other outcomes. We knew, anecdotally, that regardless of whether or not "chronic sorrow" characterized family reaction, it was not the only characterization. That is, it was quite possible to live with the sorrow that our child with Down syndrome, for example, would never go to college, and also to feel joy and pride in what that child could and would do. We believed that initially it might be easiest to explore the positive outcomes for families of having a member with a developmental disability by investigating those families that had made a voluntary decision via adoption to rear children with developmental disabilities.

That it was possible to study such families reflects a major change in the adoption field, a change that had its roots in the 1950s, but gained considerable momentum in the 1960s and 1970s as social, economic, and demographic trends coalesced to create a powerful push toward the adoption of children with special needs (Cole, 1990). This push was given weight by both rhetoric and resources directed toward individuals with disabilities, as well as a decline of healthy, white infants available for adoption. Currently, it is estimated that as many as half of the children available for adoption in the United States have developmental disabilities (Loef, undated). Thus, it became possible to study families who had made a voluntary commitment to rearing a child with a developmental disability. Our initial hypotheses were that these families, as a group, would express somewhat different, and more positive, beliefs and attitudes about this rearing than the typical birth family, and that these more positive cognitions would result in more effective coping.

Positive Outcomes for Adoptive Families

The results of our first study of 42 families who had adopted 56 children with mental retardation demonstrated that, as a group, the parents viewed the adoptions positively, and would almost certainly do them again, if they had the chance to remake the decision (Glidden, 1986, 1989b). Many benefits were cited by adoptive mothers and fathers in interviews about the impact of the child on the family. For example, 62% of mothers responded that they had changed for the better, becoming less selfish and more compassionate and tolerant. Moreover, maternal perceptions of positive impact were not limited to self-impact, but extended to other family members. Most mothers reported that the impact of the adoption was positive for the other children in the family, citing greater flexibility and happiness in support of these positive perceptions. Overall, only 5% of the adoptions were seen by mothers as having a negative impact that outweighed the positive impact (Glidden, Valliere, & Herbert, 1988).

This portrait of positive impact was conveyed both in responses to a series of semistructured interview questions and in the pattern of answers to the Holroyd Questionnaire on Resources and Stress (QRS; Holroyd, 1985), a 285-item true–false format instrument. Maternal and paternal responses to the QRS indicated a pattern of coping and adaptation that was more typical of birth families whose children had no developmental disabilities than of birth families whose children had developmental disabilities. When we compared these adoptive mothers to a control group of mothers of children with no disabilities that had been studied by Holroyd, we found that they did not score significantly differently on 8 of 10 scales relating to parent problems or family functioning (Glidden, 1989b).

Longitudinal Follow-Up of Adoptive Families

A mail questionnaire follow-up of this adoptive sample approximately 3 years after the initial interviews confirmed the original results (Glidden & Pursley, 1989). Only 2 of 44 children were no longer living with their adoptive families because of adjustment difficulties, and 12 of 31 families had adopted 12 additional children, 11 of whom had disabilities. Furthermore, responses to both the QRS (Holroyd, 1985) and other measures of the child's impact on the family conveyed a predominantly positive portrait of family functioning. This portrait was vividly painted by maternal responses to two open-ended questions about the rewards and benefits and the problems and difficulties that had arisen as a result of the child's becoming part of the family. Mothers described more than twice as many benefits as difficulties. The benefits that were described were quite varied, ranging from pride and pleasure in the child's accomplishments to an increase in religiousness.

Conclusions

In sum, both the original study and its 3-year follow-up confirmed our hypothesis: Families who had voluntarily chosen to rear children with developmental disabilities would adjust well to the task. In addition, several characteristics of these adoptive families provided important clues as to what variables might be important for predicting good adjustment. Specifically, as a group, the adoptive families had extensive familiarity and experience with disabilities prior to the child's entrance into the family. In only 14% of the families did parents have merely minimal knowledge of or experience with handicapping conditions. In many of the remaining 86% of families, the experience was extensive, including rearing other children with disabilities, or working professionally with individuals with disabilities (Glidden, 1989b).

In addition to their experience with disabilities, a set of beliefs, commitments, and attitudes typified these families. For example, more than half of the respondents indicated that a primary motivation for the adoption was their view that all children, regardless of characteristics, were entitled to a happy home life. Sometimes this belief was expressed in a religious context, but for other respondents it was secular. Regardless, it was an important motivator, and may be a predictor of adjustment (Glidden, 1989b).

In addition, we hypothesized that the relationship between beliefs and adjustment may be mediated by cognitive coping. Specifically, beliefs, commitments, and attitudes can be viewed as a kind of cognitive substrate or ideology that influences an individual's specific coping responses. Many researchers and theorists have emphasized the importance of these substrates; they undoubtedly play a role in the development of the family schema (McCubbin, Thompson, Thompson, & McCubbin, chap. 18, this volume) or family paradigm (Reiss, 1981). These constructs of schema and paradigm are similar, and refer to the relatively stable views that family members hold regarding their relationships to each other and of the family's interactions with people and systems external to it. (For a more extensive discussion, see McCubbin, Thompson, Thompson, & McCubbin, chap. 18, this volume.)

Two illustrations from interviews with adoptive parents demonstrate how a person's way of viewing the world can have a powerful influence on behavior. In each case, the response was in answer to a query regarding why the person/family wanted to adopt a child. An adoptive father said:

> The main reason was because we've been very fortunate and there have been times in our life when we didn't have two coins to rub together and for whatever reason our bills were always paid. I guess it was a payback, basically. God was good to us and we felt that this is something we can help out with. I think we benefit from it more than anything.

And an adoptive mother from a different family said:

> I just feel like if you have the capability and ability to give something back or to give something to someone or a community or whatever, that it's a moral responsibility that we have. Somebody may opt to do that in a different way, and I think that I could best do that by means of adoption.

In each case, the respondent has described a way of looking at the world that can be a powerful motivator; it also undoubtedly filters other events, creating a link between ideology and behavior, between values and adjustment.

This relationship between beliefs and values on the one hand and adjustment on the other has important theoretical and applied value. For example, if beliefs and values were found to be an important predictor of parental and/or family adjustment, then theoretical positions that emphasized the role of cognitive appraisal would be strengthened. If, however, a variable such as family income played an important role in determining outcome, then theories emphasizing tangible resources would gain in credibility. Similarly, the approach to intervention and provision of services might differ considerably depending on which of these two results were obtained. If cognitive appraisals are highly predictive of outcome, then intervention programs designed to change them if necessary and possible, or at least be aware of their role, would presumably be efficacious. In contrast, a strong relationship between family income and adjustment would suggest that providing financial help or the kinds of services that money can buy would be the intervention of choice. In 1987, we began a research program with the ultimate goal of exploring this relationship between beliefs and values and long-term adjustment. This research is described in detail in the next section.

ADOPTIVE AND BIRTH FAMILIES COMPARED

The specific aims of our research included a direct comparison of adoptive and birth families that were each rearing at least one child with a diagnosis of developmental disability or at risk for developmental disability. Our predictions were based on a model of adjustment (Glidden, 1989b) that is presented in Figure 1. This model is based on the belief that as soon as the child enters the family, two types of adjustments must be made: *Existential issues* must be resolved and *reality burdens* must be incorporated into the family's daily life. Existential issues tap the very meaning of life and the understanding and acceptance of self. Parents who experience feelings of grief, isolation, lowered self-esteem, shame, and a "pervasive sense of meaninglessness and despair" (Glidden, 1989b, p. 19) are undergoing existential crises. Regardless of the severity of these crises, however, reality burdens that frequently entail time and energy commitments and consequent lifestyle changes are major adaptational tasks for the family. Although both adoptive and birth families may experience both existential and reality crises, for the adoptive family these crises are more likely to be buffered by a number of mediating variables. Among them are the six listed in Figure 1.

Briefly, the adoptive family has made a conscious commitment to rear a child with a disability, and that commitment is present when the child enters the family. Similarly, the adoptive parents are relatively prepared for the child. They are familiar with his or her needs and characteristics. In contrast, the birth family does not expect a child with a disability and is not prepared for one. Thus, when that diagnosis is made, existential crises are likely to be intense, arousing feelings of loss, fear, anger, loneliness, self-doubt, and depression. Further-

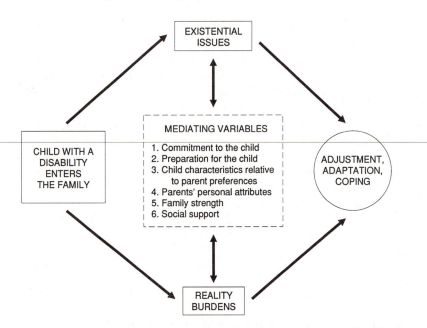

Figure 1. Adjustment model for families with children with disabilities. Mediating variables affect the relationship between existential and reality crises. (From Glidden, L.M. [1989b]. Parents for children, children for parents: The adoption alternative. *Monographs of the American Association on Mental Retardation, 11*, 171; reprinted with permission.)

more, adoptive parents usually are involved in deciding what "kind" of child they will adopt, whereas birth families must accept whoever is born to them, regardless of the fit between the child and their lifestyle and characteristics.

Parental personal attributes, family strength, and social support are also more likely to be buffers for adoptive families than for birth families. The adoption of a child with a disability is a task undertaken by families who may be more suited to it, thus resulting in better outcomes for those families. And finally, both formal support via the adoption agency and informal support because of the positive regard and attitudes of others is likely to be a strength for adoptive families.

For all these reasons then, the prediction was that adoptive parents would demonstrate better functioning than birth parents immediately after the child's entry or diagnosis as well as in the long term. This prediction, however, was simple, and not the primary interest of the research. The *process* of adjustment, and what variables were predictive of it, was the more important goal and is a primary focus of the remainder of this chapter.

Adjustment was examined in a comparison of 87 adoptive and 85 birth families. At least one primary caregiving parent from each family participated in a semistructured interview that provided most of the information for the study. Because all but two of the primary caregivers were mothers, only mothers' data are described here. The adoptive and birth families were matched on characteristics such as family income, occupational status, parent educational level, marital status, and so on. On average, the parents were middle class with mean family incomes approaching $40,000 per year. About 80% were married couples, and almost all were Christian in their religious affiliation. Each of the families had at least one child with a developmental disability or at risk for a developmental disability. Birth and adoptive children were also matched on characteristics such as age and level of functioning. The average age of the children at the time of the families' participation in the study was 6½ years.

Results of the Comparison

Our comparison of these adoptive and birth families yielded many similarities and some differences. Not unexpectedly, we found a major difference in their initial reaction to the child and his or her disability. Ratings of existential crises derived from interview responses demonstrated that birth mothers experienced more intense crises of longer duration than did adoptive mothers.

This finding was corroborated by the results of the Beck Depression Inventory (BDI; Beck, Ward, Mendelson, Mock, & Erbaugh, 1961), which was administered during the semistructured interview. Each respondent completed the BDI twice, once retrospectively for the time immediately after child entry (adoptive families) or diagnosis (birth families), and once for current functioning. Depression scores were initially quite high for birth mothers but low for adoptive mothers. However, birth mothers adjusted over time, being no more depressed than adoptive mothers at the time of interview (Figure 2).

Some other measures of family and mother responding also showed no differences in current functioning between birth and adoptive mothers. For example, each parent completed the QRS–Short Form (Holroyd, 1985), consisting of 11 scales describing the respondent's perception of family, parent, and target child functioning. No significant differences between adoptive and birth mothers emerged on 8 of these 11 scales, indicating similar perceptions of their child's characteristics, of the personal reward they derived from caring for their child, on the degree of harmony and disharmony in their family, and other categories.

Despite these similarities in current functioning between adoptive and birth mothers, there were notable differences. Three of the QRS scales (Holroyd, 1985) showed that birth mothers perceived more stress relating to limits on family opportunities, to life-span care for their child, and to how the burden of care affected them personally.

Furthermore, adoptive mothers scored significantly higher on a measure of respondent perception of family strength consisting of subscales of family pride and family accord (Olson et al., 1985). A similar pattern was found for ratings of marital adjustment (Locke & Wallace, 1959).

As predicted, then, adoptive families appeared to be better adjusted than

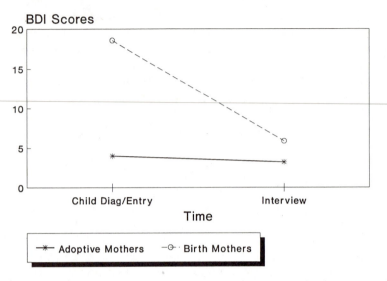

Depression in Birth and Adoptive Mothers

Figure 2. Beck Depression Inventory (BDI; Beck, Ward, Mendelson, Mock, & Erbaugh, 1961). Scores for birth and adoptive mothers at time of child diagnosis or entry into family and at interview approximately 5 years later. Higher scores on the BDI indicate higher levels of depression.

did birth families. However, it is important to note that there was substantial overlap between the scores of the two samples on many variables, and that no significant differences emerged on some scales where they might have been expected (e.g., the Family Disharmony and Lack of Personal Reward scales of the QRS [Holroyd, 1985]) given the large differences in initial experiences for these mothers.

Adjustment and Its Relationship to Cognitive Coping

In order to understand more about the relationship between parental adjustment and beliefs and values, we conducted additional analyses. Factors of the QRS (Holroyd, 1985) that primarily tapped family and parent functioning were selected as measures of adjustment. Based on previous empirical findings and theoretical issues relating to beliefs and values, we chose four measures to reflect the individual's cognitions, beliefs, and values: the BDI (Beck et al., 1961), the existential crisis score, a religiousness measure of strength of personal belief, and a religiosity measure of participation in and support received from religious organizations. Several demographic variables were also included.

Based on the results of these analyses, it appears that the role of cognitive variables in the coping process is pervasive for both adoptive and birth families rearing children with developmental disabilities. Depression, existential crises, and religiousness were generally more predictive of long-term adjustment than various demographic indicators such as family income or maternal education. Birth mothers reported less stress and better adjustment if they were less depressed when the child was first diagnosed, if they were better educated, and if they were actively involved with and derived support from religious organizations and activities. Adoptive mothers shared some features of this portrait, but were also quite distinct. They reported less stress and better adjustment if they were less depressed when the child first came to live with them, if they suffered less intense or shorter existential crises, if their child was less severely retarded, if they had higher income, if they were married, and if they reported stronger religious beliefs.

These data point to cognitions and to values as important determinants of adjustment. What they fail to elucidate, however, is the process by which the values and cognitions mediate coping and adjustment. For example, an adoptive mother was quoted earlier in this chapter as wanting to adopt because she felt that it was a moral responsibility to give something back to someone or to the community. Clearly, this ideology was important in her decision to adopt a child with a disability. Was it also important in mediating her long-term adjustment to this child? Does the sense of coherence (SOC) that Antonovsky (chap. 8, this volume) has hypothesized to be so critical in leading a fulfilled life derive from the consistency of her values, her sense of purpose, and her actions? Does this consistency operate on a day-to-day basis to transform threats into challenges, hassles into opportunities? These questions expose how little we know about the coping process and the cognitive underpinnings that influence it.

CONCLUSIONS AND FUTURE RESEARCH DIRECTIONS

The aforementioned questions and the empirical work of this project also point to directions for exploration in the next several years. The most important conclusions from this comparison of adoptive and birth families are: 1) most birth families rearing a child with a disability cope quite well with this task, and 2) cognitions and values are significant determinants of adjustment and need to be part of future research programs. Religiousness, especially, is a variable that needs thorough investigation. It has received only scant attention from researchers studying families rearing children with developmental disabilities. Results from different studies have been somewhat inconsistent, with some data finding religiousness to be related to good adjustment in families rearing children with developmental disabilities (Fewell, 1986; Zuk, Miller, Bertram, & Kling, 1961) and other data not supporting this conclusion (Friedrich, 1979). Given that religiousness has been measured differently in different studies and that different outcome variables have been used, this divergence of findings is perhaps not surprising. Clearly, the present findings indicate a need to focus more attention on religiousness, to determine its important components, and to begin to explore how it might act as a buffer in ameliorating stress and perhaps operate as a method of coping.

This focus on religiousness needs to be broad given the fuzziness and complexity of what religiousness is. It is certainly characterized by multidimensionality and undoubtedly correlated with many other variables that, themselves, may influence adjustment. For example, scientific studies of religiousness have identified two largely uncorrelated dimensions, intrinsic and extrinsic religiousness. Intrinsic religiousness is a measure of the individual's internalizing of religion, of the level of commitment to religious beliefs. Examples of statements that would be affirmed by people high in intrinsic religiousness are: "My religious beliefs are what really lie behind my whole approach to life" and "I try hard to carry my religion over into all my other dealings with life."

In contrast, an extrinsic orientation is more characteristic of those who use religion for instrumental and utilitarian ends. Such individuals are more likely to endorse statements such as: "The purpose of prayer is to secure a happy and peaceful life" and "What religion offers most is comfort when sorrow and misfortune strike." Intrinsic religiousness tends to be associated with empathy, responsibility, and religious practice, whereas an extrinsic orientation tends to be associated with anxiety, low levels of subjective well-being and responsibility, and high scores on scales measuring prejudice and authoritarianism (Allport & Ross, 1967; Batson & Flory, 1990; Wulff, 1991).

An obvious hypothesis is that persons high in intrinsic religiousness would cope better with various stressful life events than persons high in extrinsic religiousness. This hypothesis is testable. If it were to be confirmed, then it would lead to questions regarding the nature of the relationship and the processes by which it is mediated. These processes might very well include extensive cognitive coping. For example, reframing might involve a parent's thinking of rearing a child with a developmental disability not as a crisis, but as an opportunity to pay back a benevolent God, as the earlier quoted adoptive father stated.

Finally, findings on religiousness and its relationship to cognitive coping have implications for enhancing the cognitive coping success of all families, whether religious or not. Religiousness is only one aspect of the importance of world view in shaping the actions and reactions of individuals. Understanding the role it plays will also further the understanding of secular world views and how they influence adjustment in families. This understanding is a first step to enhancing coping success. It would be naive to expect that education and training programs of the sort usually provided for families should or could change ideologies, beliefs, and values that have been a lifetime in formation. However, it is entirely reasonable that programs would understand these ideologies and use them in creating an individualized process of training to maintain and facilitate different methods of coping. An individual or a family with a strong religious orientation might, for example, use prayer as an effective method of coping, deriving strength and determination from it. In contrast, an individual or a family with a secular orientation would clearly use different methods to sustain commitment and energy. A thorough exploration of these individual differences and their impact on coping efficacy will occupy research agendas for some time to come.

ABOUT THE AUTHORS

Laraine Masters Glidden, Ph.D. As a professor of psychology and human development, I have been involved in research, writing, and teaching about persons with mental retardation and developmental disabilities for more than 20 years. I am optimistic that the current emphasis on families and adaptation will operate at many levels to improve the lives of people with disabilities, as well as those individuals associated with them.

Michael J. Kiphart, Ph.D. I received my Ph.D. in experimental psychology from Colorado State University in 1985 and have spent the subsequent 7 years at St. Mary's College of Maryland as an assistant professor of psychology and as the associate provost for academic services. My major areas of research have been in learning, memory, and cognition, particularly haptic and sensory memory. I have a special interest in the measurement and methodological questions relating to family issues and perceptions.

Jennifer C. Willoughby, B.A. As a recent graduate of St. Mary's College of Maryland, I am interested in pursuing a career working with children and their families in a pediatric setting. I first became interested in studying families rearing children with developmental disabilities when I learned about Dr. Glidden's ongoing research in the area. I have since been working with her on the project that served as the basis for this chapter.

Beverly A. Bush, M.A. I have long been involved in research concerning family functioning and adaptive response to stressful situations. I personally became involved in cognitive coping as a result of having a daughter who was on an infant apnea monitor for the first 25 months of her life. This experience gave me an opportunity to observe what appeared to be more efficient and positive coping techniques among parents who had children with chronic illnesses. I am currently working on my doctoral dissertation, examining humor as a cognitive and affective coping skill in families who have a member with brain injury.

REFERENCES

Allport, G.W., & Ross, J.M. (1967). Personal religious orientation and prejudice. *Journal of Personality and Social Psychology, 5,* 432–443.
Batson, C.D., & Flory, J.D. (1990). Goal-relevant cognitions associated with helping by individuals on intrinsic, end religion. *Journal for the Scientific Study of Religion, 29,* 346–360.

Beck, A.T., Ward, C.H., Mendelson, M., Mock, J., & Erbaugh, J. (1961). An inventory for measuring depression. *Archives of General Psychiatry, 4*, 561–571.

Cole, E.S. (1990). A history of adoption of children with handicaps. In L.M. Glidden (Ed.), *Formed families: Adoption of children with handicaps* (pp. 43–62). Binghamton, NY: Haworth.

Crnic, K.A., Friedrich, W.N., & Greenberg, M.T. (1983). Adaptation of families with mentally retarded children: A model of stress, coping, and family ecology. *American Journal of Mental Deficiency, 88*, 125–138.

Fewell, R.R. (1986). Supports from religious organizations and personal beliefs. In R.R. Fewell & P.F. Vadasy (Eds.), *Families of handicapped children* (pp. 297–316). Austin, TX: PRO-ED.

Friedrich, W.N. (1979). Predictors of the coping behavior of mothers of handicapped children. *Journal of Consulting and Clinical Psychology, 47*, 1140–1141.

Glidden, L.M. (1986). Families who adopt mentally retarded children: Who, why, and what happens. In J. Gallagher & P. Vietze (Eds.), *Families of handicapped persons: Current research, treatment, and policy issues* (pp. 129–142). Baltimore: Paul H. Brookes Publishing Co.

Glidden, L.M. (1989a, March). Keynote address: *Family research and developmental disabilities.* Invited opening theme lecture at the Gatlinburg Conference on Research in Mental Retardation/Developmental Disabilities, Gatlinburg, TN.

Glidden, L.M. (1989b). Parents for children, children for parents: The adoption alternative. *Monographs of the American Association on Mental Retardation, 11.*

Glidden, L.M., & Pursley, J.T. (1989). Longitudinal comparisons of families who have adopted children with mental retardation. *American Journal on Mental Retardation, 94*, 272–277.

Glidden, L.M., Valliere, V.N., & Herbert, S.L. (1988). Adopted children with mental retardation: Positive family impact. *Mental Retardation, 26*, 119–125.

Holroyd, J. (1985). *Questionnaire on Resources and Stress manual.* Unpublished manuscript, University of California–Los Angeles, Neuropsychiatric Institute.

Lazarus, R.S., & Folkman, S. (1984). *Stress, appraisal, and coping.* New York: Springer.

Locke, H.J., & Wallace, K.M. (1959). Short marital-adjustment and prediction tests: Their reliability and validity. *Marriage and Family Living, 21*, 251–255.

Loef, J. (undated). *Adopting children with developmental disabilities.* Washington, DC: National Adoption Information Clearinghouse.

McCubbin, H.I., & Patterson, J.M. (1983). Family transition: Adaptation to stress. In H.I. McCubbin & C.R. Figley (Eds.), *Stress and the family: Vol. I. Coping with normative transitions* (pp. 5–23). New York: Brunner/Mazel.

Olson, D.H., McCubbin, H.I., Barnes, H., Larsen, A., Muxen, M., & Wilson, M. (1985). *Family inventories* (rev. ed.). St. Paul: University of Minnesota, Family Social Science.

Reiss, D. (1981). *The family's construction of reality.* Cambridge, MA: Harvard University.

Wulff, D.M. (1991). *Psychology of religion: Classic and contemporary views.* New York: John Wiley & Sons.

Zuk, G., Miller, R., Bertram, J., & Kling, F. (1961). Maternal acceptance of retarded children: A questionnaire study of attitudes and religious background. *Child Development, 32*, 525–540.

chapter 15

Self-Efficacy Coping, Active Involvement, and Caregiver Well-Being Throughout the Life Course Among Families of Persons with Mental Retardation

Tamar Heller

People often say to me, "How do you cope? How do you do it?" I answer, "Do I have a choice?" I just do it. Just like a person handles any challenges in life, I continue living my life the best way that I can. There are some days that I cope very well and others when I have a hard time. There are some days when my child brings me a lot of joy and other days when I am overwhelmed by his needs. It all depends on what day you ask me. Now that my child is in school my major struggle is with the school system. I feel like I'm continually battling and advocating.

These words of a mother of a 10-year-old boy with mental retardation depict the dynamic nature of coping among families of persons with mental retardation throughout the life course. Her words reflect how coping strategies and feelings of competence fluctuate with family members' developmental phases, their social context, and their daily demands. This chapter focuses on cognitive coping strategies of families from a life-span perspective, drawing upon my past and current research of family adaptation to having a family member with mental retardation. A major goal of my research has been to examine how family reactions change throughout their life course. A second goal has been to examine how families plan for and adapt to transitions. In much of this research, families' cognitive coping strategies have played a major role in shaping how they have adapted to these changes. This chapter more specifically examines both the determinants and consequences of self-efficacy (mastery and control) cognitive coping strategies of family caregivers. It also examines life-course phase differences in stressors, in these cognitive approaches, in caregivers' involvement with their relative, and in caregivers' well-being.

RESEARCH ON SELF-EFFICACY COPING

In their theories of cognitive adaptation to a stressful event, Bandura (1982) and Taylor (1983) have emphasized the importance of perceived self-efficacy over the threatening event as a means of managing it or of keeping it from occurring again. According to Bandura, perceptions of self-efficacy affect how much effort people will expend in the face of obstacles and their cognitive and affective reactions to stress. When faced with stress, those who have low estimations of their ability to cope with upcoming situations and to control their outcomes tend to give up easily and experience high levels of anxiety or depression.

Affleck, Tennen, and Gershman (1985) found that mothers of newborns in intensive care who believed that they had more personal control over their child's recovery experienced less depression and fewer major stress reactions. Affleck, Allen, McGrade, and McQueeny (1982) also found that mothers with an internal locus of control tended to be better adjusted, to seek services more actively for their child, and to participate more in their child's treatment program. Other studies of parents of newborns (Cutrona & Troutman, 1986), of caregivers of elderly parents (Boss, Caron, Horbal, & Mortimer, 1990; Moss, 1988), and of women with cancer (Taylor, Lichtman, & Wood, 1984) found that self-efficacy beliefs were associated with better adjustment.

There has been little research examining which control strategies families of persons with mental retardation may choose (Summers, Behr, & Turnbull, 1990). Affleck and Tennen (chap. 10, this volume) noted that, among families of medically fragile newborns, the following activities are frequently mentioned as providing parents with a sense of control: frequent visiting, providing social stimulation, supplying breast milk, performing caregiving tasks, praying, and closely monitoring their child's medical care. Generally, parents who retrospectively reported more appraisals of personal control experienced less distress. However, some mothers who expected to have considerable control over their child's well-being made many burdensome accommodations, at some cost to their own well-being. Other mothers were distraught when their child had minor problems or when they realized that appropriate actions were not within their reach.

RESEARCH ON CAREGIVER SELF-EFFICACY COPING, INVOLVEMENT, AND WELL-BEING

My research conducted with Louis Rowitz and Bernard Farber (Heller, Rowitz, & Farber, 1992) examined the factors contributing to self-efficacy coping strategies and to active involvement and the effects of these coping strategies on caregiver well-being. The larger study from which this research was based included in-home interviews and written surveys with 489 primary caregivers (93% of whom were female) of persons with severe to moderate mental retardation, living at home or in out-of-home placement and ranging in age from less than 1 year to 63 years. The sample included a large number of African-American (25%) and Latin (13%) families.

The study assessed: 1) characteristics of the family (socioeconomic status [SES]) and the person with mental retardation (age, level of mental retardation, problem behaviors, and residential placement status); 2) caregivers self-efficacy coping strategies (coping mastery and control); 3) caregiver involvement (seeking professional support, time helping the relative, and involvement in mental retardation activities and programs); and 4) caregiver well-being (perceived burden and depression).

Caregiver coping mastery referred to the extent that caregivers felt that they were competent to cope with their relative's caregiving demands. *Caregiver coping control* referred to the extent that caregivers felt that what they do can help improve their relative's situation.

Determinants of Self-Efficacy and Involvement Coping

We first examined the influence of characteristics of the family and the person with mental retardation on caregivers' perceived self-efficacy in helping their relative with mental retardation (Heller et al., 1992). The findings indicated that the caregivers who were most likely to feel a sense of mastery and control had a relative with mental retardation who had fewer problem behaviors and who was living in their home. Also, caregivers who were of higher SES and whose relative was younger tended to have greater feelings of control.

We then examined the effect of the characteristics of the family and person with mental retardation and of self-efficacy coping on the caregiver's degree of active involvement with his or her relative (Heller et al., 1992). As we predicted, the caregivers' self-efficacy coping strategies were related to their degree of involvement. Caregivers who felt a sense of control were more likely to be involved in mental retardation activities, to spend more time with their relative, and to seek professional support; caregivers with a greater sense of mastery also tended to participate more in mental retardation activities (e.g., their relative's program, training activities, support groups, advocacy groups). For all three measures of involvement, the relative's older age was related to less involvement. Caregivers of higher SES tended to be more involved in mental retardation activities and sought more professional support.

Influence of Coping on Caregiver Well-Being

We then sought to assess to what extent these coping strategies influenced caregivers' well-being as measured by their degree of perceived burden and depression (Heller et al., 1992). As predicted by cognitive adaptation theorists (Bandura, 1982), the families who felt a greater sense of self-efficacy perceived less burden in caring for their relative with mental retardation and experienced less depression. However, unlike our expectations, active involvement (particularly seeking professional support and spending a lot of time helping the relative) increased perceived burden but had no significant effect on the caregiver's depression.

The following comments were made by respondents who were either very high or very low in their self-efficacy perceptions. These comments illustrate the effects of their cognitive coping on their degree of involvement and well-being more poignantly than do the quantitative data. The responses were to questions about how they cope with problems related to their relative and to a question regarding what advice they would give to other families with a member having mental retardation.

The following are comments made by some of the persons who scored low in self-efficacy in regard to their relative with mental retardation.

> The best way to cope is being away. We stopped bringing her home at the advice of a social worker; she hasn't been home in two years. They used to bring her home. I have no way of getting her. They think that it's best. (Mother of an older adult)

> I feel God mistreated me by giving me mentally retarded kids, because I can't have them all with me. It hits pretty hard sometimes. When I see a young man my son's age, I say that could have been my son, my grandchild. I'm not handling it too well. (Mother of a young adult)

> By her being in a nursing home it's not a problem. If she lived at home, I'd have a nervous breakdown. (Mother of an adolescent)

In contrast, the following are comments from caregivers who scored high in self-efficacy:

> When she gets bigger and if she doesn't learn to walk, how are we going to handle her, get her out and around? We will talk to a doctor about a wheelchair when we need one. (Mother of a young child)

> Hang in there. Believe your child can make it through. Make your spouse feel important; this will take stress off you. Limit stress; otherwise you won't be relaxed. Don't listen to old wives' tales. O.K., listen, but take it with a grain of salt. Everyone wants to help you . . . feel it out . . . don't believe everything they say. Don't be afraid to switch doctors. (Mother of a preschool child)

> I have to do everything for him. I cope because I'm a strong person. (Mother of a young adult)

> Just don't abandon them. Give them as much love as possible. It's hard work, but worth it. Get involved in teacher–parent groups. Participate when you can. Important personal and professional information is exchanged. (Mother of an adolescent)

> We are already looking into vocational programs and he'll be starting prevocational training as part of his school program. You have to be practical about this. Assess realistically what he needs and what you can provide. Then seek out ser-

vices for his other needs. Deal with them with your head—not your heart. (Mother of a young child)

You come to accept it. Stop crying, and find things for her to do. (Mother of a preschool child)

RESEARCH ON LIFE-SPAN COPING DIFFERENCES

It is logical to assume that there would be life-span differences in stressors related to the relative with mental retardation and life-span differences in caregivers' self-efficacy coping, active involvement, and well-being. However, the research on the life-span impacts of having a family member with mental retardation is sparse (Seltzer, Krauss, & Heller, 1991). It tends to focus on the first decade of the child's life or on the last decade of the parent's life. Overall, recent studies have found that the majority of parents of young children cope effectively and positively with the additional demands of caring for a child with mental retardation (e.g., Bristol, 1987; Singer & Farkas, 1989). Less is known about families of adults with mental retardation.

The mental retardation, family development, and gerontological literatures provide some theories for examining long-term coping of families. Family theorists have written about the stages that families pass through and the developmental tasks that families face. In the Double ABCX Model of family adaptation (McCubbin & Patterson, 1983; see also Patterson, chap. 17, this volume), the normative growth and development of family members is viewed as an important aspect of the family demands factor. In comparing family stress across life stages, McCubbin and Thompson (1987) found that adolescence is the most stressful stage for the family.

Birenbaum (1971) and Farber (1959) have written about the extent to which developmental life cycles of families with a member with mental retardation differ from other families. They have hypothesized that as the child with mental retardation gets older, coping by family members becomes increasingly more difficult. Although developmental stage theory suggests a shift of responsibility from parents to their offspring, parents of persons with mental retardation continue assuming caregiving over a longer time period. With increasing age, these families are faced with the challenge of readjusting their expectations. Researchers have reported that parents of older children with developmental disabilities were less supported and more stressed than parents of younger children (Bristol & Schopler, 1984; Suelze & Keenan, 1981). In an exploratory study, Wikler (1986) found that the transition periods—those in which persons with mental retardation were entering adolescence or adulthood —were the most stressful for families.

Researchers of caregiving among families of impaired elderly persons have proposed an adaptational model of long-term caregiving (Townsend, Noelker, Deimling, & Bass, 1989). This model suggests that the caregiving role can be an opportunity for psychological growth over time. The results of the Seltzer and Krauss (1989) study of 462 older mothers caring for an adult with mental retardation provide preliminary support for the adaptational hypothesis. They found that many of the mothers in their study were healthier, had better morale, and reported no more burden or stress than did mothers in studies of younger families of persons with mental retardation or of family caregivers of elderly residents.

RESEARCH ON ADAPTATIONS TO DEVELOPMENTAL PHASES AND TRANSITIONS

In my research, I have sought to learn more about how families' stressors change and how families cope with these changes over developmental phases and through specific transitions. Most specifically, the transitions I have studied include residential relocation and planning for the time when parents can no longer provide care. First I discuss some of the major stressors families have described at different age phases. Then I discuss life-course phase differences in coping approaches and in caregivers' well-being.

Major Stressors at Different Age Phases and Transitions

My discussion of major stresses at different age phases draws on qualitative and quantitative data gathered across several studies (Heller, Bond, & Braddock, 1988; Heller & Factor, 1991; Heller et al., 1992). For this discussion, I describe five age phases based on the age of the person with mental retardation: 1) preschool (0–5 years), 2) young child (6–12), 3) adolescent (13–20), 4) young adult (21–30), and 5) older adult (over 30).

In the life-span study described earlier (Heller et al., 1992) we asked families caring for their relative at home about their current stressors and problems regarding their relative with mental retardation. Younger families were more likely to report problems related to obtaining information on their relative's development and to obtaining family support services than were older families. Older families were more likely to report stressors related to finding appropriate services for their relative than were younger families. Generally, families of adolescents reported the greatest difficulties of all the age groups in finding adequate support services for both their family member with mental retardation and for other family members, with maintaining ongoing contact with staff, with finding information on their relative's development, and with participating in parent groups. The oldest families were most likely to feel stressed about future residential placement issues.

Comments of family members from this study (Heller et al., 1992) and my other transition studies (Heller et al., 1988; Heller & Factor, 1991) further describe the major demands and stressors faced by many families of persons with mental retardation. In the preschool years, major family demands relate to obtaining an accurate diagnosis and reaching acceptance regarding the diagnosis. Many families have noted their struggles with professionals and with their own personal feelings regarding their child. The following comments of mothers of infants and preschoolers aptly describe the nature of the demands and stressors at this stage:

> At first I was very depressed. I thought it was my fault. I started dealing with it and it has gotten better. Initially, I didn't know how to handle him. Now I know how to.

> At first I felt terrible about her diagnosis of mental retardation. My biggest problem now is dealing with her medical problems. You need to talk to professional people and get clear information about your child's disability. Go to at least three or four agencies for workshops. Don't underestimate your ability to do. Our daughter has made us more appreciative, more loving, and more understanding.

The major issues faced by families of young children often relate to their advocacy role with the school system and their dealings with professionals. As some parents stated:

> You have to push for what you want. Otherwise the school district will shove you around.

> At first I felt trapped. Now I don't, though I still grieve at times. Fighting for him is hard. I'm continually calling on the phone to correct things.

> We've adjusted and are happier now; we've learned not to believe everything the doctors say. In time things do work out.

As noted in the general literature and as found in our quantitative analyses (Heller et al., 1992), adolescence is the most challenging phase for families. In particular, families have noted difficulties related to behavioral challenges, sexuality, and transition out of the school system. For example, some parents said:

> I worry how he'll function after school is completed. We're already looking into vocational programs.

> It is becoming more difficult at home as he no longer wants a female to tell him what to do.

> I wonder, will he ever be able to be independent? It's important to encourage him to take care of himself.

Families of young adults are likely to face issues centered around leaving the family home and the young adult's search for greater independence. Another key issue affecting families is the lack of sufficient adult services once the young adult has left the school system. Examples of parents' thoughts on these issues include:

> I am teaching her to be more assertive and communicative; I'm accepting her as she is.

> You need to let them be as independent as possible and love them.

> We have looked into residential programs and they all have long waiting lists.

There should be some kind of counseling to prepare parents for when their child leaves home.

My biggest problem is getting him to go to the workshop.

The major concern expressed by families of older adults usually centers around future planning issues, particularly the worry over who will care for their relative when they are no longer able to do so. Related to this are issues surrounding potential out-of-home placements and the future caregiving roles of other family members. Our research (Heller & Factor, 1991) on older parents has documented the frustration that families often experience in attempting to make concrete plans. Consider the following statements:

My prayer when she was sick was that the Lord spare her for me. My prayer now is that she go before we go so that I know she's not going to be pushed around, taken advantage of, or hurt in any way, shape, or form.

I wish she could stay in a loving situation like we have. I don't want her imprisoned by government agencies.

She has been with us all of our life and we feel like she is our responsibility and as long as the Lord gives us strength we will like to keep her in our home and take care of her.

We have tried to find a placement for 30 years and until recently there were no appropriate facilities.

I do not want to burden my [other] daughter with her [sister's] constant care.

Across various age phases, transition points are often stressful periods that bring new demands with which families need to cope. Our studies have primarily focused on out-of-home placement transitions (Heller et al., 1988; Heller & Factor, 1991). These transitions have included moves from the family home and from institutions to other settings. Among older parents, an adult child's placement out of the family home is often more stressful for the parent than for the adult child. As one elderly mother stated, "She is part of our life and her leaving was upsetting; you just don't get over having a child move out. Her move is so final."

In our studies of facility closures (Heller et al., 1988), we found that families strongly objected to their child's transfer out of the institution. Over three quarters of the families noted feeling highly stressed when they first heard the closure announcement. Yet, a year after the transfers the majority of families were pleased with the closure outcomes. These transition studies highlight the importance of examining the developmental phases and situational demands with which families need to cope.

Age-Phase Differences in Caregiver Self-Efficacy, Involvement, and Well-Being

In the life-span study noted earlier (Heller et al., 1992), comparisons of the self-efficacy coping, active involvement, and well-being measures across different life-course phases found considerable differences in most of the measures. Caregivers of an adolescent or young adult were the least likely to perceive a sense of mastery in helping their relative. Feelings of control over their relative's situation progressively decreased with each older age phase. Overall, the families who experienced the greatest sense of self-efficacy were those who cared for a preschool child.

For all the involvement measures, the caregiver's involvement decreased with each age phase. This was particularly dramatic in the case of seeking professional support and in time spent helping the relative. This finding closely mirrors findings in families without a member with mental retardation.

Perceived burden was highest in families of adolescents followed by families of young children and young adults. The families who were least burdened were those of the youngest and oldest groups. Although depression did not differ significantly across the age phases, its pattern was similar to that of burden. Hence, as predicted by family developmental phase theorists (McCubbin & Thompson, 1987), adolescence seems to be a particularly tough time for families in general. Also, our data on life-stage stressors indicated that during adolescence families experienced the greatest difficulty obtaining needed services (Heller et al., 1992). Interestingly, both the gerontological theory of family adaptation over the long term (Townsend et al., 1989) and the Farber (1959) theory of increasing difficulty over time for families were supported in part. It seems that adaptation to having a relative with mental retardation is easiest when the child is very young and becomes more difficult as the child approaches adolescence. However, adaptation also seems to become easier for families at the latest phases. As they age, caregivers are less involved with their relative with mental retardation yet feel a greater sense of mastery and fewer burdens. Perhaps at that stage there is greater acceptance of the relative and greater reciprocity in caregiving. In most older families' retrospective accounts of their coping, more positive feelings are described over time. For example, two older mothers stated:

> At first I was sick and devastated when I found out my daughter had mental retardation. Now she's my best friend.

> At first I thought why me? What did I do? Now he's a blessing. I enjoy his company. You get to accept things.

Another possibility is that only the families who have adapted the best survive into old age, and hence the cross-sectional nature of the sample produces such a bias. Some support for this explanation was provided by Farber, Rowitz, and DeOllos (1987).

CONCLUSION: IMPLICATIONS AND FUTURE DIRECTIONS

Our research on life-span issues in cognitive coping and active involvement in families of persons with mental retardation emphasizes the importance of considering normative developmental transitions in understanding adaptation of families (Heller et al., 1992). With each age phase, there are different demands and functions fulfilled by families. One promising line of research that my colleagues and I are pursuing is to examine how different coping patterns help or hinder successful adaptation of various family members at different age phases. For example, active involvement may be more beneficial to the family of a younger child than to that of an older person, who requires more independence from the family.

An important finding of our research is that high active involvement of families with their relative having mental retardation and with service providers can potentially lead to greater burnout among caregivers (Heller et al., 1992). This serves as a caveat to families who make extraordinary efforts for their children, while sacrificing other aspects of their life and families. As one mother of an adolescent said:

> I've seen too many parents who've become martyrs for their kids. Remember you have a life to lead. Sometimes they don't take advantage of programs. They think they are the only ones that can do anything for their kid. Try to treat the kid as normal[ly] as possible; live your own life as normal[ly] as possible.

In our recent research on older parents (Heller & Factor, 1991), we have found that a high degree of parental involvement in caregiving for their adult child with mental retardation appears to lead to their child's lower degree of community integration. In a study of fathers of persons with mental retardation, Farber et al. (1987) found that fathers who had reported high caregiving burden were less likely to still be alive 25 years later. Further research is needed to examine the issues of balancing the needs of the person with a disability and the needs of other family members. From our research (Heller et al., 1992) it seems that approaches that increase families' feelings of competence and mastery improve their well-being and increase their involvement with their relative with mental retardation. What is less clear is why active involvement is related to burden. Since our research was cross-sectional, we cannot assume directions of causality. Hence, it is possible that families seek more professional help when they feel burdened. With longitudinal studies we can better examine the effect of cognitive coping and active involvement approaches over time.

Currently, I am conducting two longitudinal studies that can add to our understanding of cognitive coping. One is an intervention study of support groups for parents of persons with autism. I am assessing whether participation in these groups increases parents' self-efficacy coping and well-being. A second study examines how older parents cope with out-of-home placements over a 2-year period. In both of these studies, the measures of family well-being have been expanded to include positive aspects, such as caregiving satisfaction and caregiving reciprocity.

While most of the research discussed in this chapter focused on mothers' views, our life-span study included data from fathers and siblings (Heller et al., 1992). Analyses of their different coping styles and adaptations to having a family member with disabilities will add significantly to our understanding of these families.

ABOUT THE AUTHOR

Tamar Heller, Ph.D. My research focus is on how families and persons with developmental disabilities plan for and adapt to transitions and how family coping changes throughout the life span. My role is coordinator of the Family Studies and Services Unit, Illinois University-Affiliated Program in Developmental Disabilities at the University of Illinois at Chicago. I have developed a program that provides model programs and consultation to families, service providers, and policymakers regarding family support. My work on family coping has been shaped by my research and clinical experiences, and by my personal experience of being a sibling of a person with developmental disabilities.

REFERENCES

Affleck, G., Allen, D., McGrade, B.J., & McQueeny, M. (1982). Maternal causal attributions at hospital discharge of high-risk infants. *American Journal of Mental Deficiency, 86,* 575–580.

Affleck, G., Tennen, H., & Gershman, K. (1985). Cognitive adaptations to high-risk infants: The search for mastery, meaning, and protection from future harm. *American Journal of Mental Deficiency, 89*(6), 653–656.

Bandura, A. (1982). Self-efficacy in human agency. *American Psychologist, 37,* 122–147.

Birenbaum, A. (1971). The mentally retarded child in the home and the family life cycle. *Journal of Health and Social Behavior, 12,* 55–65.

Boss, P., Caron, W., Horbal, J., & Mortimer, J. (1990). Predictors of depression in caregivers of dementia patients: Boundary ambiguity and mastery. *Family Process, 29,* 245–254.

Bristol, M.M. (1987). Mothers of children with autism or communication disorders: Successful adaptation and the Double ABCX Model. *Journal of Autism and Developmental Disabilities, 17,* 469–486.

Bristol, M.M., & Schopler, E. (1984). A developmental perspective on stress and coping in families of autistic children. In J. Blacher (Ed.), *Severely handicapped children and their families: Research in review* (pp. 91–141). New York: Academic Press.

Cutrona, C.E., & Troutman, B.T. (1986). Social support, infant temperament, and parenting self-efficacy: A mediational model of postpartum depression. *Society for Research in Child Development, 57,* 1507–1518.

Farber, B. (1959). Effects of a severely mentally retarded child on family integration. *Monographs of the Society for Research in Child Development, 24,* (2, Serial No. 71).

Farber, B., Rowitz, L., & DeOllos, I. (1987) *Thrivers and nonsurvivors: Elderly parents of retarded offspring.* Paper presented at the annual meeting of the American Association of Mental Deficiency, Detroit.

Heller, T., Bond, M.A., & Braddock, D. (1988). Family reactions to institutional closures. *American Journal of Mental Deficiency, 92,* 336–343.

Heller, T., & Factor, A. (1991). Permanency planning for adults with mental retardation living with family caregivers. *American Journal on Mental Retardation, 96,* 163–176.

Heller, T., Rowitz, L., & Farber, B. (1992). *The domestic cycle of families of persons with mental retardation*. Chicago: Illinois University Affiliated Program in Developmental Disabilities and School of Public Health, University of Illinois at Chicago.

McCubbin, H.I., & Patterson, J.M. (1983). The family stress process: The Double ABCX Model of Adjustment and Adaptation. In H.I. McCubbin, M.B. Sussman, & J.M. Patterson (Eds.), *Social stress and the family: Advances and developments in family stress theory and research* (pp. 7–38). New York: Haworth Press.

McCubbin, H.I., & Thompson, A.I. (1987). Systematic assessment of family stress, strengths, typologies, coping, social support and adaptation. *Family assessment inventories for research and practice.* Madison: University of Wisconsin–Madison.

Moss, M.S. (1988, November). *Caregiving satisfaction and shifts in satisfaction with nursing home placement*. Paper presented at the Gerontological Society of America, San Francisco.

Seltzer, M.M., & Krauss, M.W. (1989). Aging parents with mentally retarded children: Family risk factors and sources of support. *American Journal on Mental Retardation, 94,* 303–312.

Seltzer, M.M., Krauss, M.W., & Heller, T. (1991). *Family caregiving over the life course*. In M.P. Janicki & M.M. Seltzer (Eds.), *Aging and developmental disabilities: Challenges for the 1990s* (pp. 3–24). Washington, DC: American Association on Mental Retardation.

Singer, L., & Farkas, K.J. (1989). The impact of infant disability on maternal perception of stress. *Family Relations, 38,* 444–449.

Suelze, M., & Keenan, V. (1981). Changes in family support networks over the life cycle of mentally retarded persons. *American Journal of Mental Deficiency, 86,* 267–274.

Summers, J.A., Behr, S.K., & Turnbull, A.P. (1990). Positive adaptation and coping strengths of families who have children with disabilities. *Support for Caregiving Families, 2,* 27–40.

Taylor, S.E. (1983). Adjustment to threatening events: A theory of cognitive adaptation. *American Psychologist, 38,* 1161–1173.

Taylor, S.E., Lichtman, R.R., & Wood, J.V. (1984). Attributions, beliefs about control, and adjustment to breast cancer. *Journal of Personality and Social Psychology, 46*(3), 489–502.

Townsend, A., Noelker, L., Deimling, G., & Bass, D. (1989). Longitudinal impact of interhousehold caregiving on adult children's mental health. *Psychology and Aging, 4,* 393–401.

Wikler, L.M. (1986). Periodic stresses of families of older mentally retarded children: An exploratory study. *American Journal of Mental Deficiency, 90,* 703–706.

chapter 16

When It's Not So Easy To Change Your Mind
Some Reflections on Cognitive Interventions for Parents of Children with Disabilities

George H.S. Singer

In this chapter, I review a program of research that my colleagues and I have conducted at the Oregon Research Institute (ORI) over the past 6 years. (The personal pronoun *we* is used throughout this chapter to refer to myself and my colleagues at ORI.) I then highlight some of the questions that have arisen as a result of this work.

With the help of a set of research and model demonstration grants, my colleagues and I at ORI established a Center for Caregiving Families devoted to providing empirically evaluated support services to families of persons with disabilities. We decided early in our work to focus on developing and testing interventions that draw upon the self-help movement and cognitive behavior therapy. Thus, we are primarily concerned with face-to-face helping interactions between family members and counselors, family consultants (formerly called case managers), social workers, and psychologists, as well as parent-to-parent, self-help groups. In working with families and preparing initial studies, I was amazed to find that there is almost no treatment research in the clinical literature concerning families, apart from an important body of work on behavioral parent training. While there are dozens of studies over a 30-year period documenting family stress, there is little empirical guidance in determining what can be done about it. We hope to make a contribution toward filling this remarkable void.

DEPENDENT VARIABLE SELECTION

We are devoted to the notion that scientific method ought to play a major role in elucidating effective ways of assisting families. Given this precept, it has been

This chapter was funded in part from Grant No. G008730149 between the U.S. Department of Education, Office of Special Education and Rehabilitative Services, and the Oregon Research Institute. The views expressed herein do not necessarily reflect those of the funders.

important to determine critical dependent variables and reliable ways of measuring them. Because the state of family research is rapidly evolving and represents the work of several largely nonconversant disciplines and theoretical schools, it has been no small task to select some critical variables and ways to measure them. Our approach to selecting critical variables has been to stay very close to the phenomena as we see and hear them in our interactions with families. Thus, when we began offering different support groups and private counseling, it became clear to us that an important percentage of people who came to us requesting help were feeling demoralized. They often expressed feelings that are associated with depression: fatigue, lack of energy, hopelessness, a pervasive sense of discouragement, and a general shortage of enjoyment in life (Link & Dohrenwend, 1989). People may feel demoralized because of financial obligations, a troubled marriage, worry about a child's health, lack of response from the community in trying to get help for a family member, or memories of an abusive childhood. In the medically oriented jargon of clinical psychology, this kind of demoralization is referred to as having "depressive symptoms." It is measured normatively by comparing the self-report of one person with the self-reports of a larger representative sample of a target population. There are several measures of depressive symptoms that have well-established psychometric properties (Beck, Ward, Mendelson, Mock, & Erbaugh, 1961). Thus, it is possible to quantify this global kind of unhappiness and measure it for comparative purposes.

Another reason for selecting demoralization as a key dependent variable is that it is consistent with our shared societal values, which embrace the pursuit of life, liberty, and happiness as primary human endeavors. There is little need to argue for social validity for an intervention when a family member voluntarily seeks help, says he or she is unhappy, and reports having better morale and maintaining it after receiving assistance. Furthermore, the presence of parental depressive symptoms has been shown repeatedly to be associated with reduced responsiveness in parenting (Downey & Coyne, 1990). Mothers with elevated levels of depressive symptoms are likely to be less responsive to their children, to be more irritable, to interact less, and to use more coercive forms of discipline than are mothers whose morale is higher.

Finally, there is much evidence that mothers of children with disabilities are likely to experience higher than normal levels of depressive symptoms. My colleague Paul Yovanoff and I recently examined 20 studies in which parents of children with disabilities were compared to parents of children without disabilities on measures of depressive symptoms (Singer & Yovanoff, 1992). Comparing across all studies, we found that the average score for depressive symptoms among the parents of children with disabilities was higher than the score for 70% of the parents of children without disabilities. Another way to compare prevalence of demoralization is to look at the percentage of people over a cutoff score for depression in groups of parents of children with and without disabilities. The study that I believe to have the best design, sufficient subjects, and adequate instrumentation was done by Breslau and Davis (1986). They found that 30% of the parents of children with disabilities had scores above the cut-off level for risk on the Center for Epidemiological Studies Depression Inventory (Radloff, 1977) compared to 15% in a general population sample.

It must be emphasized that 70% of the parents in this study were not demoralized (Breslau & Davis, 1986). I do not wish to contribute to the unfortunate myth that families of children with disabilities are inevitably troubled. A large majority are coping well. However, an important number of families do ask for help and do experience difficulties that lead to elevated levels of unhappiness. It is this group that is the focus of this chapter. I would, however, like to note that my colleagues and I are currently engaged in an intensive study of well-coping families and hope to contribute to the emerging literature on factors associated with positive family outcomes. I have increasingly come to believe that we should view our interventions along a continuum that addresses needs for promotion of well-being among people who are already coping adequately, prevention of future suffering among people who might be at risk, and amelioration of present suffering. Some of my current questions and interests grow out of a desire to frame our interventions in this larger context. However, before discussing these issues, I would like to summarize briefly a set of treatment studies that my colleagues and I have conducted.

TREATMENT STUDIES

In reading the literature and working with the families of my students, I became intrigued with a simple idea: If family members experience stress reactions, isn't it possible that stress management treatments developed for other populations might be effective for them? We developed an 8-week psychoeducational class and support group for gatherings of 12 parents at a time. The meetings were called "classes" rather than "therapy," and the skills were presented as useful coping techniques for healthy people. That is, we made an effort not to imply that the parents were experiencing pathology. In fact, we have tried to place our interventions in an entirely nonmedical context, although our dependent variables and the language of our technical reports, because they are often aimed at clinical practitioners, keep the trappings of the psychomedical world view. The skills taught in these classes include cognitive and behavioral coping skills such as self-monitoring of stressors, progressive muscle relaxation, monitoring and expanding social support, using relaxation in natural settings, covert rehearsal for stressful situations, cognitive reframing, increasing pleasant activities, and time management. An initial study (Singer, Irvin, & Hawkins, 1988) compared a treatment group and a nontreatment group of randomly assigned parents of children with moderate and severe mental retardation. The study found significant reductions in depressive symptoms in the treatment group.

The literature and our experience with families suggested that the problems of family members are often environmental as well as intrapersonal. Consequently, we assembled a package consisting of a wide array of intervention components. We added to the stress management class an 8-week class on behavioral parent training with an emphasis on increasing children's participation in home and community activities. We also linked parents to a direction service agency that provides information, referral, and advocacy assistance to families. In addition, we created a special friends program in which college volunteers committed to 6 months of weekly outings to integrated community activities with the children with disabilities. An evaluation of this package of interventions found significant reductions in psychological distress in parents, improved child problem behavior according to parent reports, and increases in children's participation in community activities (Singer, Irvin, Irvine, Hawkins, & Cooley, 1989). Improvements in parent morale were maintained at 1-year follow-up.

My colleagues and I soon discovered that in every group of parents who entered our program, there were families for whom our services were not sufficient to alleviate serious distress. We have seen four recurrent patterns of distress that require more intensive kinds of assistance: 1) severe depression, 2) severe marital discord, 3) severe child problem behaviors, and 4) abuse and neglect of children in multiproblem families. In each of these cases, our mixture of classes, support groups, respite care, direction service, and volunteers was not sufficient, and we found it necessary to devise individualized forms of counseling and in-home assistance. We have developed a clinic in which we offer up to 15 sessions of individual, couple, or family counseling, with return visits as needed. Usually, the problems of these families involve the pile-up of multiple stressors. Except in the case of children with very severe problem behaviors, the child with a disability is rarely the primary presenting problem.

In order to try to build an empirical basis for treatment, we have begun to conduct a series of more focused studies in which we group people with presenting problems that are much more narrowly delineated than our original broad construct of "stress reaction." For example, in working with individual parents who sought help for clinical depression we observed that some of these parents seemed to experience high levels of guilt, self-blame, and unreasonably demanding, self-imposed standards. Nixon (1989) designed a creative, short-term group treatment aimed at helping parents reduce levels of self-blame and guilt. An evaluation of the treatment using randomly assigned comparison groups found that it led to significant decreases in parent depression, self-blame, and changes in attributional patterns (Nixon & Singer, in press).

Depression clearly has multiple causes; it is not one unified condition, but rather a conglomeration of symptoms that takes different patterns in different people. Thus, for some people, treatment of depression necessitates probing into their ways of thinking about their roles as parents. There are other parents who are depressed, but for whom the center of their distress appears to be marital discord. At ORI, we have developed expertise in an approach to couples counseling that stresses communication and problem solving skills. Lichtenstein (1990) used this approach in her study of four distressed couples who were parents of children with mental retardation. She showed that communication skills training, combined with some attention to broader cognitive themes in the relationship, led to increases in marital satisfaction and observed reductions in negative affect during problem-solving interactions.

In the area of behavioral parent training, we have developed in-home interventions to assist families whose children exhibit severe problem behaviors. We have tried to build upon previous work, mostly by investigating issues of generalization of behavioral parent training and by developing antecedent interventions designed to prevent behavior problems. Powers, Singer, Stevens, and Sowers (1992) found that, with sufficient practice and coaching, parenting skills could be generalized to community settings including shopping malls, grocery stores, and churches. A study by Singer and Singer (1990) found that a mother was able to make generalized use of a set of behavior management procedures, planned play activities, praise, and redirection across her 4-year-old with autism as well as her infant and her 8-year-old without disabilities. A recent study by Bitner, Stoner, and Singer (1991) at ORI has shown that behavioral parent training can also be highly effective in promoting increased communication between parents and their young children with severe disabilities.

Our experience with behavioral interventions has led to the insight that many families—not all—require more than traditional behavioral parent training in order to maintain successfully the use of these techniques. Some require considerable attention to the other social and emotional issues that obstruct adherence to the behavioral regimens. Other families require extensive in-home and in-community coaching. The small number of parents who require intervention around child abuse and neglect clearly fall into the category of families needing very intensive forms of assistance. Because some families benefit from interventions that require a few resources such as a behavior management class whereas others may need months of intensive in-home assistance, we have attempted to design a service delivery system that can match needs to services in order to improve cost-effectiveness (Singer, Irvine, & Irvin, 1989).

CURRENT ISSUES AND FUTURE RESEARCH

I have come to realize that: 1) there exist a number of inadequacies in the current professional service delivery system, and 2) complex and paradoxical limitations affect the use of cognitive coping techniques. These two insights have led me toward developing some new approaches in psychosocial interventions for families. These new approaches explore the use of helping interactions and the nature of acceptance as a combination of meta-cognitive and, to coin a word, *meta-affective* skills.

Limitations of a Professional Service System

My colleagues and I have come up with some interventions that the data show can be helpful to people. Moreover, the approximately 150 families we have served have, with only a few exceptions, been enthusiastic consumers of these interventions. However, there have been only a few requests to replicate our work around the country. An "underwhelming" response to our work at ORI has prompted me to consider the limits of developing interventions aimed at professional counselors. I believe one explanation for our seeming failure to attract professionals to replicate our models is that there aren't many people currently employed in roles that allow them to offer the combination of services that we find to be effective. The problem of limited human resources is widespread in the field of psychological services delivery (Levine & Perkins, 1987). Simply put, there will never be enough psychologists, social workers, or other trained helpers to meet the needs of the approximately 30% of families of children with disabilities who are troubled.

The community psychology movement has impressed me with its efforts to strengthen informal helping networks and to encourage the formation of self-help groups (Levine & Perkins, 1987). Although I plan to keep chipping away at the professional services systems to impress upon professional helpers the efficacy of cognitive behavioral counseling and psychoeducational support groups, I've gotten interested in the possibility of infusing these skills into self-help groups. I wonder to what extent parents could become the instructors of coping skills. What should the relationship between a trained counselor and a self-help group look like? Could the instructional side of our support groups be presented via videotape and the discussion and therapeutic side be directed by experienced parents who, perhaps, receive some training in counseling skills? The work of organizations such as Birth to Three and peer counseling programs may offer some promising models. Is it possible that a hybrid of a psychoeducational support group, which emphasizes the learning of coping skills, and a parent-to-parent network, which emphasizes mutuality of experience, might be an effective way to disseminate these techniques?

Limitations of Cognitive Coping Techniques

Cognitive therapy involves teaching people to examine their own patterns of thought and to identify automatic modes of interpreting situations that may be dysfunctional. These disabling habits may include ways of thinking that are assumed to be immalleable. For example, a parent may believe that her child who uses a wheelchair feels badly that she cannot walk. As a result, the parent may attribute sorrow and regret to the child. This unspoken assumption can become habitual and can seem to be an objective fact rather than a belief. The role of the therapist is to teach the client that thoughts and perceptions can be overridden through the development of meta-cognitive skills. These meta-skills include: self-reflection, self-questioning, and posing alternatives. Cognitive modification assumes that mood is, in part, a product of thought and that it can be modified by choice. These approaches clearly work with many people. Thus, my colleagues and I have included cognitive techniques such as self-monitoring of cognition, self-questioning, and self-coaching in our stress management classes. Our interviews and evaluation measures indicate that in every group that we conduct, several parents find such cognitive approaches to be useful. At the same time, however, other parents are unimpressed with these methods and find them either irrelevant or, in some cases, somewhat offensive.

My colleagues and I are not the only ones who have noticed that some people do not respond well to cognitive counseling. A group of researchers in the field of behavior therapy has been working with people who do not respond to traditional cognitive-based counseling approaches. Steven Hayes at the University of Nevada and Marsha Linehan at the University of Washington have identified groups of people who have not done well in cognitive treatments. Hayes has worked with people who have received prior treatment for severe depression, and Linehan with people who have received prior treatment for attempted suicide and accompanying severe problems. In both cases, they report that their clients are very resistant to the idea that they ought to challenge their own habitual ways of thinking and modify how they interpret situations. This notion, that people can identify what they are thinking, think differently, and, consequently, feel better, is at the heart of cognitive therapy. So it's something of a problem when people don't buy it.

In searching for clues about why changing one's thought in order to alter mood is not helpful to some people, three kinds of objections to the method have arisen: 1) a perceived lack of real understanding, 2) the relation between self-control and affect, and 3) the risk of failure to deal with nonpsychological problems.

Perceived Lack of Real Understanding

Marsha Linehan (1990) eloquently described this objection. When her patients are asked to look at a situation differently, they respond, "But it truly is a terrible situation. Are you suggesting that the problem is only in my mind?" They hear the suggestion that their thinking may contribute to their unhappiness as a dismissal of the reality of their suffering. Parents of children with disabilities may have plenty of reason to react this way. Charlie Nixon and I have been collecting examples from parents of the helpful and unhelpful things that people say to them regarding their child with a disability (Singer & Nixon, 1990). A common thread in their responses is that they often hear statements that seem to discount and dismiss their concerns. For example, a parent who is feeling tired and exasperated may hear from a neighbor, "You must be so patient." Or a parent who is feeling discouraged about paying bills may be told by a well-intentioned friend or relative, "Oh, you'll get through this. Remember, every cloud has a silver lining." The discrepancy between how the parent is feeling and the somewhat flip response from others can give rise to feelings of isolation, to the sense that "nobody understands."

Self-help groups can be particularly helpful in this regard because people are much more likely to believe that other parents of children with disabilities genuinely understand their difficulties (Thoits, 1980). However, here again, the same kind of problem with synchrony between people can arise. If a participant in a self-help group feels that others are either much more distressed or much less distressed, they are likely to feel misunderstood and more isolated. A number of parents have said that parent groups can make them feel depressed or lonely, rather than giving them the hoped-for sense of inclusion and acceptance. I believe that the negative effects of a perceived lack of mutuality are relevant to the problem that some parents have with cognitive approaches to change. In a social context in which parents and siblings feel that their concerns are commonly minimized or misunderstood by others, suggestions from a counselor that they look at things from a different point of view may be heard as more of the same.

Relation Between Self-Control and Affect

A second problem may have to do with the sometimes paradoxical relationship between self-control and affect. Willful control works for most of us in most of the realms we encounter during daily life. We decide to tackle a problem and our work often pays off. We decide to exercise and, in time, we get in shape, for example. Decision and willful action lead to desired outcomes. However, for some kinds of internal processes, in some instances, efforts at willful control may have a paradoxical effect (Hayes, 1990). I call this the "try not to think of a blue elephant" phenomenon. The mind has no analogies for nothingness other than unconsciousness; that is, it is not possible to deliberately not think of something without calling into awareness the very object that we desire to banish. Similarly, some efforts at self-control evoke the very state that we try to banish. For example, a person with insomnia may try to will him- or herself to sleep. This struggle to force sleep may give rise to a heightened state of wakefulness. Similarly, effort to banish fear reactions can sometimes actually intensify them. Hayes (1990) explained this paradoxical effect of efforts at self-control through learning theory. He asserted that people who have made repeated and unsuccessful efforts to control and avoid negative feelings and thoughts create a kind of conditioned response in which the effort to control becomes a conditioned stimulus for the undesirable thoughts and feelings themselves.

Risk of Failure To Deal with Nonpsychological Problems

A third limitation to the cognitive approach is that, if it is overemphasized at the expense of more concrete environmental approaches to change, it can fail to deal with substantive real-world concerns that may not be psychological in nature at all. For example, a mother who must awaken hourly at night to check her child's ventilator may simply need time off or help at night so she can get some sleep. A parent who is dealing with collection agencies because of catastrophic medical bills may be much more helped by getting a reasonable alimony settlement from an ex-spouse than by learning to think about the situation differently.

The quintessential example of the power of cognitive change is Victor Frankl's (1983) work on finding meaning in the horrible world of the concentration camp. He emphasized the mentalistic act of will and daily thought that made life during and after these harrowing experiences livable. However, other accounts of survival *in extremis* in the camps emphasized also the social and active coping aspects of resilience (Dimsdale, 1974). It is clear from these accounts of survivors that almost all of their tactics for overcoming the dehumanization of the camps involved both actions upon the environment and social support, as well as assuming a cognitive stance. While I do not mean to minimize the importance of will and deliberate choice of a cognitive stance toward difficult circumstances, my point is that we also should not underestimate the importance of acting upon the environment and receiving social provisions. In point of fact, a fairly consistent pattern of findings has begun to emerge in the research on family adaptation to disability suggesting that environmental variables such as levels of community services, social support, and fiscal resources do play an important role in coping, along with cognitive processes such as attributions about the situation (e.g., see review by Singer & Irvin, 1991).

Cognitive coping strategies are intertwined with social communities to such an extent that they may be impossible to analyze separately. Take, for example, a father of a child who experiences muscular dystrophy. He interprets his son's condition in a Christian framework as an opportunity to develop an understanding of suffering and redemption. This parent's thinking is more than an internal, private event. He chooses words and symbols that place him in a relationship with a social community both past and present. He most likely is a member of a religious group and may have had religious instruction as a child. Thus, his cognitive coping with religious thinking ties him to a group of people, a private history, and to a network of social interactions. If we learn about the father's way of coping by asking him how he views his child's illness, we will probably think of his answer as a description of cognitive coping. But if we ask him who helps him and where he goes for support and he answers that it is the Church that sustains him, we are likely to think of this coping strategy as social support. The point is that cognitive coping should not be considered apart from a person's past and present social history. Venters (1980) reported that parents who coped the best with their child's chronic illness gave meaning to the condition. Usually this meaning was consistent with a philosophy or religion to which the parent subscribed prior to the child's diagnosis. If Venters had asked about parents' past and present social networks, I expect that he would have found that most parents had other people who were important to them who also subscribed to these beliefs. Cognitive coping should not be removed from the social context in which it arises.

FUTURE RESEARCH DIRECTIONS

These observations about the limits of cognitive interventions for family members of persons with disabilities suggest three kinds of questions I would like to explore in future research:

1. What kinds of interpersonal interactions facilitate positive reception of cognitive coping suggestions, and can these be taught to members of self-help groups?
2. Can meditative and contemplative disciplines be useful alternatives to promoting acceptance when cognitive change is blocked?
3. Do packages of interventions that attend to environmental and social conditions, as well as to cognitive interventions, work better than cognitive interventions alone? For whom?

The first question draws upon extensive work in the fields of counseling and social psychology on helping relationships. It seems likely from 20 years of work in this area that relationship variables are essential to any kind of behavior change, including cognitive behavior change (Bellack & Hersen, 1985). We know many of the behaviors and attitudes that make for effective counselors and therapists (Evans, Hearn, Uhlemann, & Ivey, 1984). But what about the skills of natural helpers? Who is helpful to parents and siblings in their informal social networks, and what do these helpful microsocial interactions look like? While they may contain some of the elements of effective active listening skills that are routinely taught to counselors, my hunch is that many also look very different. Can these kinds of informal, helping interactions be taught to friends, relatives, and neighbors as well as professionals? If so, do they facilitate cognitive coping?

The second set of questions concerns the role of what I would paradoxically call "active efforts to cope passively." Some of the helping procedures that have the oldest pedigree and the widest history of use across many cultures are traditions of contemplation and meditation. These are often aimed at what we would now call "cognitive behavior modification." In contemplative and meditative traditions, people learn meta-skills relevant to their own thoughts and feelings. Some of these involve changing thoughts. Others, however, involve the development of mental states that might be called meta-affective in that they are states of awareness and emotion that endure through more transient forms of emotion. For example, students of these traditions may learn to take a stance of compassion and understanding toward their own thoughts and feelings. Compare the effects of this underlying attitude with that of a person who views his own thoughts and feelings with a persistent sense of shame or self-hatred. It is interesting to note that both Steven Hayes (1987) and Marsha Linehan (1990), two real innovators in behavior therapy, have both borrowed extensively from the Buddhist tradition in developing therapies for people who have not responded to more traditional cognitive methods. Could these meditative and contemplative approaches be taught to parents in ways that would be culturally normative and thus palatable? Could their impact be measured? Would they be effective?

My interest in this approach to cognitive change through teaching people to let feelings arise and pass comes in part from a recent experience with a father whose 6-year-old child is rapidly experiencing the degenerative symptoms of muscular dystrophy. Soon after the son began falling down and having limitations on his usual activities, the father began to drink heavily. While I was interviewing him and his wife in some depth, he revealed that he drank when he thought about his son's illness. Alcohol was being used as a kind of numbing agent. In a few sessions, I worked with him to call up the worst of his feelings while maintaining a relaxed state. The procedure is a variant on a behavioral therapy technique called *implosion* and is very similar to instructions in some forms of meditation to allow any thought or feeling to arise and pass without resistance. He wept and described his feelings of helplessness and sense of the unfairness of his child's condition. We also discussed with him the role that alcohol was beginning to play and coached him and his spouse through discussions about both the effect of the drinking and his feelings about his child. He stopped getting drunk soon afterward. Interestingly, he also arrived at a different point of view about his child's illness soon afterward: He decided he would focus on what he could do for his son *now* instead of on the inevitable loss. The process of implosion is very close to a guided meditation in which the learner is coached to be like a receptive vessel of thoughts and feelings rather than an active change agent in regard to them. This accepting stance is different from the common cognitivist emphasis on changing thoughts and feelings as active work. I would like to test this approach more thoroughly in the future.

Finally, as a partially dyed-in-the-wool behaviorist, I am rather skeptical that cognitive techniques will be sufficient in most cases in which the problem that family members confront is chronic stress. I suspect that we will continue to be most successful when we pinpoint concrete problems and assist people to solve them as well as to address their thoughts and feelings about these problems. Also, my guess is that we will be most successful if we not only emphasize cognitive meanings but also help people to achieve successful social interactions in the communities that support these meanings. For example, the best way to help parents develop a philosophical stance toward their child's condition might be to help them to make friends with people who have that philosophy. These questions of the relative importance of social interaction, behavior change, and cognitive modification could all be empirically explored.

CONCLUSION

The majority of parents of children with disabilities grow to appreciate the special lessons and gifts that their children contribute to their families. This appreciation sometimes develops over time as families encounter challenges posed by the disability and master these challenges. Sometimes, this process does not unfold by itself. In these instances, a pile-up of stressors may make it difficult for parents to adapt. Cognitive behavioral psychology has developed a variety of methods for promoting cognitive adaptation. Some of the studies reviewed here indicate that these methods can help parents of children with disabilities. However, counseling approaches may not be sufficient by themselves when families encounter a number of challenges. Experience with cognitive behavioral counseling suggests that care must be taken in actively working with people to challenge their thought patterns. This chapter suggests that Parent to Parent programs and family support programs that take a comprehensive approach to family needs should also be utilized to facilitate the process of cognitive adaptation.

ABOUT THE AUTHOR

George H.S. Singer, Ph.D. I am the director of the Hood Center for Caregiving Families. I grew up in a family that was challenged by chronic illness and disability, and I have pursued a career of scholarship and direct service aimed at figuring out some ways to enhance the caregiving capacity of families and make it easier for people to be kind to one another in homes. I am primarily interested in intervention and action research in hopes of producing something of practical value to families.

REFERENCES

Beck, A.T., Ward, C., Mendelson, M., Mock, J., & Erbaugh, J. (1961). An inventory for measuring depression. *Archives of General Psychiatry, 4*, 561–571.
Bellack, A.S., & Hersen, M. (1985). General considerations. In M. Hersen & A.S. Bellack (Eds.), *Handbook of clinical behavior therapy with adults* (pp. 3–22). New York: Plenum.
Bitner, K., Stoner, G., & Singer, G. (1991, May). *Parent facilitation of the functional language acquisition of their preschool children with handicaps: Effects of environmental arrangement strategies.* Paper presented at the 17th annual conference of the Association for Behavior Analysis, Atlanta.
Breslau, N., & Davis, G.C. (1986). Chronic stress and major depression. *Archives of General Psychiatry, 43*, 309–314.

Dimsdale, J.E. (1974). The coping behavior of Nazi concentration camp survivors. *American Journal of Psychiatry, 131,* 792–797.

Downey, G., & Coyne, J.C. (1990). Children of depressed parents: An integrative review. *Psychological Bulletin, 108*(1), 50–76.

Evans, D.R., Hearn, M.T., Uhlemann, M.R., & Ivey, A.E. (1984). *Essential interviewing.* Pacific Grove, CA: Brooks/Cole.

Frankl, V. (1983). *Man's search for meaning.* Boston: Beacon Press.

Hayes, S. (1987). A contextual approach to therapeutic change. In N. Jacobson (Ed.), *Psychotherapists in clinical practice.* New York: Guilford Press.

Hayes, S.C. (1990, November). *The pervasiveness of emotional avoidance.* Presentation at the 24th Annual Association for the Advancement of Behavior Therapy Convention, San Francisco.

Levine, M., & Perkins, D.V. (1987). *Principles of community psychology.* New York: Oxford University Press.

Lichtenstein, J.F. (1990). *Support for couples with children with disabilities: Behavioral marital therapy treatment.* Unpublished doctoral dissertation, University of Oregon, Eugene.

Linehan, M.M. (1990, November). *Dialectical behavior therapy: A treatment for the chronic parasuicidal client.* Presentation at the 24th Annual Association for the Advancement of Behavior Therapy, San Francisco.

Link, B., & Dohrenwend, B.P. (1989). Formulation of hypotheses about the true prevalence of demoralization in the United States. In B.P. Dohrenwend, B.S. Dohrenwend, M.S. Gould, B. Link, R. Neugebauer, & R. Wunsch-Hitzig (Eds.), *Mental illness in the United States: Epidemiologic estimates* (pp. 114–132). New York: Praeger.

Nixon, C.D. (1989). *The treatment of self-blaming attributions and guilt feelings in parents of severely developmentally disabled children.* Unpublished doctoral dissertation, University of Oregon, Eugene.

Nixon, C.D., & Singer, G.H.S. (in press). A group cognitive behavioral treatment for excessive parental self-blame and guilt. *American Journal of Mental Retardation.*

Powers, L.E., Singer, G.H.S., Stevens, T., & Sowers, J. (1992). Behavioral parent training in the community. *Education and Training in Mental Retardation, 27*(1), 13–28.

Radloff, L.S. (1977). The CES-D scale: A self-report depression scale for research in the general population. *Applied Psychological Measurement, 1,* 385–401.

Singer, G.H.S., & Irvin, L.K. (1991). Supporting families of persons with severe disabilities: Emerging findings, practices, and questions. In L.H. Meyer, C.A. Peck, & L. Brown. (Eds.), *Critical issues in the lives of people with severe disabilities* (pp. 271–312). Baltimore: Paul H. Brookes Publishing Co.

Singer, G.H.S., Irvin, L.K., & Hawkins, N. (1988). Stress management training for parents of severely handicapped children. *Mental Retardation, 25*(5), 269–277.

Singer, G.H.S., Irvin, L.K., Irvine, A.B., Hawkins, N., & Cooley, E.C. (1989). Evaluation of community-based support services for families of persons with developmental disabilities. *Journal of The Association for Persons with Severe Handicaps, 14,* 312–323.

Singer, G.H.S., Irvine, A.B., & Irvin, L.K. (1989). Expanding the focus of behavioral parent training: A contextual approach. In G.H.S. Singer & L.K. Irvin (Eds.), *Support for caregiving families: Enabling positive adaptation to disability* (pp. 85–102). Baltimore: Paul H. Brookes Publishing Co.

Singer, G.H.S., & Nixon, C. (1990). *You can't imagine unless you've been there yourself: Interviews with parents of children with traumatic brain injury.* Unpublished manuscript, Dartmouth Medical School, Lebanon, NH.

Singer, G.H.S., & Yovanoff, P. (1992). *Demoralization in parents of children with disabilities: A meta-analysis.* Unpublished manuscript, Dartmouth Medical School, Lebanon, NH.

Singer, J., & Singer, G.H.S. (1990, February). *Generalization of behavioral parent training across siblings.* Paper presented to the Oregon Troubled Child Conference, Eugene.

Thoits, P.A. (1980). Social support as coping assistance. *Journal of Consulting and Clinical Psychology, 54,* 416–423.

Venters, M.H. (1980). *Chronic childhood illness/disability and family coping: The case of cystic fibrosis.* Unpublished master's thesis, University of Minnesota, Minneapolis.

chapter 17

The Role of Family Meanings in Adaptation to Chronic Illness and Disability

Joan M. Patterson

In this chapter, I focus on cognitive factors influencing the adaptation of families to the stressful experience of living with a chronic illness or disability. The focus is on *cognitive adaptation* instead of *cognitive coping* (this book's theme) because I view the former as a broader construct that incorporates several "levels of meaning," all of which are interrelated. Cognitive coping is one kind of abstraction within these levels of meaning. Adaptation is the superordinate construct (White, 1974), of which cognitive factors are one subset of adaptation processes and cognitive coping is another subset. In addition, I discuss the process by which beliefs and meanings come to be held and the role of these meanings in the adaptation process for the family. Of particular importance is the degree to which meanings are shared by all family members, as well as the degree to which they are congruent with or fit with beliefs of others in the community, especially providers of health and education services. To illustrate these concepts, examples are drawn from the findings of a recent study in Minnesota on the family impact of caring for a medically fragile child at home (Patterson & Leonard, 1993). In this study, the role of meanings in family adaptation received attention.

Throughout this discussion, I make an effort to distinguish between family constructs and individual constructs. The critical distinction between scholars who primarily study individuals and those who study groups is the unit of analysis being considered. To avoid confusion and a misuse of concepts, it is important to consider what is legitimately an individual property versus a group property. Since my focus in this chapter is on the family system, which is a group, I first provide a rationale for considering *family meanings*.

Preparation of this chapter was supported by the National Institute on Disability and Rehabilitation Research Grant No. H133890012.

INDIVIDUAL VERSUS FAMILY MEANINGS

Perception occurs at the individual level. Through receptors in an individual brain, stimuli are experienced either within the self or external to the self. Given the myriad stimuli constantly available to any given individual, some selection occurs regarding what is attended to. This configuration of what in the perceptual world is attended to by an individual has been referred to as *elementary controls* (Reiss, 1981). This selective perception is influenced by many factors, including biological capability (e.g., capacity to hear), developmental status (e.g., newborns cannot see well beyond 10 inches), and emotional status (e.g., rage or fear may block perceptions), as well as the social context (e.g., giving a lecture versus giving a gift). The social context also influences selective perception through the process of social learning whereby different attending behaviors are modeled and reinforced. For example, in traditional U.S. families, girls are taught to pay attention to personal feelings as well as to those of others and are reinforced for showing empathy and expressing affect. Many boys have been taught to ignore personal feelings and to pay more attention to things or ideas. In this way then, the family, as a primary group for the socialization of its members, has a powerful role in influencing which stimuli are perceived. This does not mean that the family as a group actually perceives, but that family members are likely to share an orientation about what should be attended to and by whom.

Further, when something is perceived, an interpretation or meaning is given to it. Those interpretations or meanings are socially derived (Berger & Luckman, 1966). The degree to which there is consensus about attributing meaning varies depending on the nature of what is perceived and the degree to which consensus itself is valued and espoused. For concrete objects such as a chair, there is widespread consensus. In fact, a chair is a chair because we agree that it is a chair. Reality is a social construction. For abstract concepts such as love, there is greater variability in meanings and attributions and much less consensus. However, persons who share time and space and interact on a regular basis tend to be more alike in their definitions. People survive by fitting in with one another in social space—what cybernetician Humberto Maturana called structural coupling in a surrounding medium (Dell, 1985). The family is one of the primary social groups characterized by this structural coupling. A social consensus emerges to coordinate complex action patterns. Through language, the family develops an implicit and shared set of assumptions and meanings about themselves in relation to each other, and about their family in relation to the community and systems beyond their boundaries. Reiss (1981), who has elaborated most eloquently the theoretical basis for shared family construing, emphasized that shared explanatory systems play a crucial role in organizing and maintaining group process. Shared meanings reduce ambiguity and uncertainty about a complex array of stimuli and make coordination of response among group members possible. This, in turn, contributes to group stability.

The family is not the only social context shaping meanings and beliefs. Within the community, individuals participate in many other social environments, such as the school, workplace, neighborhood, church, and so on. Participants in any of these groups have a set of relatively shared meanings and norms coordinating their actions. Furthermore, the culture in which these social groups function also influences meanings, beliefs, values, and norms (Goffman, 1974). In some cultures or subcultures, there is great unanimity across families such that they all share the same or similar explanatory systems for most experience. This is particularly true of more hierarchically organized systems where legitimate authority is vested in only a few (e.g., conservative religions). In other cultures, autonomy, individualism, and creativity are valued. In this latter case, the family unit is likely to play a greater role for the individual in shaping beliefs and meanings. Given the heterogeneity of family types and racial/ethnic groups in the United States today, coupled with the acceleration of social change, diversity in values and beliefs has increased. This, in turn, creates greater uncertainty for individuals, who often look to the family to provide guidelines for living and an existential set of meanings about life.

Kluckhohn (1960), in a comparative analysis of beliefs about human beings' relationship to nature, has emphasized that in mainstream American culture, there is a strong ethic favoring mastery and domination of the environment, with individualism and autonomy highly valued. The norm is for the nuclear family unit to be internally bonded and relatively isolated from kin, depending on itself for successful adaptation.

Whether we focus on culture, subculture, community group, or family, we can speak of meanings and beliefs as being convergent (or divergent) with those held by others. Given the propensity of individuals to live in famiy units and to develop an orientation to life from that experience, and given that disability and illness are managed primarily in a family context, it seems particularly relevant then to consider family meanings.

LEVELS OF MEANING

Theoretical Milestones in Stress and Adaptation Theory

My own work regarding family meanings and cognitive coping emerged in the context of elaborating family stress theory, specifically with regard to the development of the Double ABCX Model with Hamilton McCubbin (McCubbin & Patterson, 1982, 1983a, 1983b) and later as the Family Adjustment and Adaptation Response (FAAR) Model (Patterson, 1988a, 1989a). In the evolution of this theoretical work, the role of meanings in shaping a family's response to crisis and subsequent adaptation has been elaborated.

ABCX Model

In the original ABCX Family Stress Model of Reuben Hill (1949, 1958), the family's definition of the stressor was included as the "c" factor that interacted with the stressor event ("a" factor) and the family's crisis-meeting resources ("b" factor) to produce "x," the crisis. Here the appraisal was solely on the stressor event, what Lazarus (1966) has called "primary appraisal." For example, a mother who believes that her infant with a newly diagnosed chronic illness is going to die soon may make no effort to bond with the infant (to avoid feeling the loss). Or, conversely, she may blame herself for having caused the illness and invest more attention in the infant as a way to ease the guilt of the pending loss.

Double ABCX Model

When the Double ABCX Model was introduced to describe postcrisis adaptation in families, McCubbin and Patterson (1982, 1983a, 1983b) expanded the "c" factor to the "cC" factor and defined it as the family's perception of the original stressor event, plus the pile-up of other stressors and strains ("aA" factor), plus its perceptions of its resources ("bB" factor). In doing so, we were now including what Lazarus (1966) called *secondary appraisal*, that is, appraisal of capabilities or the ability to manage the stressors and strains. Coping in the Double ABCX Model included both cognitive and behavioral factors. For example, a mother, believing that her infant could live if given the best medical care, might search the country for the best specialist. In this model, a coping strategy that functioned to alter meanings so as to make a situation manageable was also emphasized (e.g., believing this is God's will for their family and they were chosen because they can handle it). In addition, a more generalized meaning construct was introduced in the Double ABCX Model: a sense of coherence. Influenced by Antonovsky's (1979) work, a family's sense of coherence was defined as the family's ability to balance control and trust—that is, knowing when to take charge and when to trust in or believe in the authority and/or power of others. A family's sense of coherence was operationalized and tested in a study of military family adaptation (Lavee, McCubbin, & Patterson, 1985) and was found to be a critical factor explaining a major portion of the variance in family adaptation.

FAAR Model

In an effort to emphasize the adaptation as the central construct, I have called this model the Family Adjustment and Adaptation Response Model (Patterson, 1988b, 1989a). It is a family adaptation model more than a family stress model. This renaming is also consistent with the emphasis on positive outcomes, which is the focus of much of the empirical work using this model. In Antonovsky's (1979, 1987) language, this is the *salutogenic perspective* (see chap. 8, this volume).

In the FAAR Model, the meaning factor has been differentiated into two levels of meaning used by families in the adaptation process: situational meanings and global meanings (Patterson, 1988b, 1989a). Situational meanings refer to the individual's and family's subjective definitions of their demands, their capabilities, and of these two factors relative to each other. Global meanings transcend any given situation and are a more stable cognitive set encompassing beliefs about the relationships of family members to each other, and the relationship of the family unit to the larger community. These global meanings are referred to as the *family schema* (see McCubbin, Thompson, Thompson, & McCubbin, chap. 18, this volume).

Let me digress a moment to describe the FAAR Model briefly to see where this two-level meaning construct fits (Figure 1). There are two phases in the FAAR Model, adjustment and adaptation, separated by family crisis. During both phases, families attempt to achieve a balance between demands (the sum of all the stressors, strains, and hardships experienced by the family unit and its members) and their capabilities for managing demands. Capabilities include both resources (individual, family, and community) and coping behaviors. Situational and global meanings shape both what constitutes demands and capabilities and the effort to achieve a balance between them. During the adjustment phase, families make only minor (first-order) changes to achieve balance. This means they reduce demands and/or increase capabilities, either objectively or subjectively by the way they define the situation. However, the structural organization of the family remains the same. Crisis emerges when demands exceed capabilities and this imbalance persists to produce disruption and disorganization in the family system. A second-order change, or a change in internal organization, is needed to restore balanced functioning. During adaptation, families do this restructuring by changing their boundaries, roles, and/or rules. This requires a change in their family schema, that is, the implicit rules defining who is in the family, what their respective roles are, and rules for how they should relate to each other and to the world outside the family. Thus, the two levels of meaning affect two types of change in the family (discussed later in this chapter).

Situational Meanings

Appraisals of the demands and capabilities are an integral part of the coping process (Lazarus, 1966). In some instances, demands exist only by virtue of the definition or meaning given to them. For example, setting unrealistic expectations for one's performance in a role (such as parenting a sick child) creates a role strain, which, by definition in the FAAR Model, is part of the pile-up of demands. (Demands include both stressor events and ongoing strains.) Coping with this kind of role strain may include setting more realistic role expectations (e.g., "I don't have to spend all of my free time doing infant stimulation") or selectively perceiving accomplishments versus failures (e.g., "I can read my

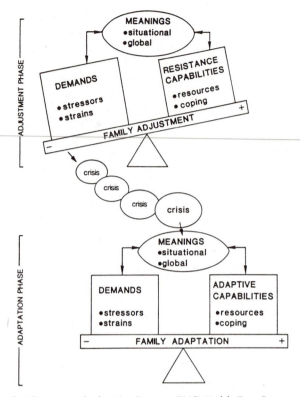

Figure 1. Family Adjustment and Adaptation Response (FAAR) Model. (From Patterson, J.M. [1988b], Families experiencing stress. The Family Adjustment and Adaptation Response Model. *Family Systems Medicine*, 6[2], 209; reprinted by permission.)

infant's cues more accurately now"). In other words, a cognitive coping strategy can be used to reduce demands (e.g., lower expectations) and/or increase capabilities (e.g., acknowledging one's accomplishments). In this way, cognitive coping could help restore balance between demands and capabilities. Furthermore, objectively experienced events (e.g., diagnosis of chronic illness) are subjectively appraised as to their degree of threat, harm, loss, or challenge (Lazarus, 1966). Similarly, some resources only exist because of perceptions (e.g., self-esteem) and even objective resources (e.g., money) are appraised for their adequacy relative to demands.

A system, whether an individual or family, faced with greater demands relative to its capabilities, will experience stress, which has been defined as "an actual or perceived demand-capability imbalance" (McCubbin & Patterson, 1983b, p. 9). Coping is a specific effort to reduce this imbalance, behaviorally and/or cognitively. In other words, coping is what you do and/or think. It may involve reducing demands objectively and/or subjectively through perceptions.

Saying "no" to requests for help, to a second job, or to longer work hours are objective examples. Setting realistic expectations for role accomplishments is a subjective example. Examples of coping to increase resources are finding and using a support group (objective), or seeing oneself as competent to do a task (subjective).

In families who have a member with a chronic illness or disability, there are numerous examples of the role of situational meanings in the coping and adaptation process. In our study of families with a child who is medically fragile (Patterson & Leonard, 1993), parents frequently reported the positive aspects of having a child with intense medical needs: 1) the child's warmth and responsiveness; 2) the tenacity and perseverance of the child to endure, which made the parents want to invest more of their effort; 3) the closeness felt in the family unit by pulling together to manage; 4) the assertiveness and skill that they as parents developed in response to caring for the child, as well as learning to deal with multiple providers and third-party payers; and 5) the growth in empathy and kindness in their other children. In other words, parents selectively attended to the positive aspects of their child's personality and behaviors while minimizing the limitations or health problems. In addition, many parents emphasized the growth and development of the self or the family unit in response to the challenges. These efforts at positive attributions are examples of situational meanings about capabilities and have been referred to by others as a kind of secondary control, or accommodating oneself to existing realities by maximizing perceived benefits of things that cannot be changed (Weisz, Rothbaum, & Blackburn, 1984).

Global Meanings: Family Schema

Over time and with experience, individuals and families acquire a set of meanings for orienting to their internal and external experience. The elements of sameness in experience create a kind of cognitive structure (Piaget, 1952), which is applied to new experiences until something is encountered that does not fit the existing structure. The mental structure either changes enough to incorporate this new element or ignores it. These processes of assimilation and accommodation occur in tandem throughout life (Piaget, 1952).

As discussed above, a cognitive structure can exist only in an individual mind, but social groups like a family develop a consensus about relationships to coordinate their interaction patterns. Using language and a process of interpolation (one member fills in what is missing for another) and extrapolation (generalizing from one experience to a similar one), the family develops shared beliefs, meanings, and values (Reiss, 1981). The regulatory process that emerges reduces uncertainty and maintains stability of relationships within and outside the family. This shared social construing, representing the intersection of individual family members' cognitive sets, is labeled the family schema. The family schema is a global orientation that transcends any one experience and provides a template linking repeated patterns of response to similar situations. Schema is more stable than situational meanings, and transcends and influences the latter. The family schema is not static and unchangeable, but rather is shaped, molded, and remolded over time in response to stressful experiences—particularly crisis situations when the family's balanced functioning is upset.

This way of thinking about a family's implicit assumptions and beliefs is consistent with the work of many scholars focused on individual and family adaptation to stressful life experience (Antonovsky, 1979; Fisher, Ransom, Kokes, Weiss, & Phillips, 1984; Kobasa, Maddi, & Kahn, 1982; Reiss, 1981). When the family schema was first introduced as a component of the FAAR Model, an effort was made to integrate these four theoretical orientations with qualitative findings from research on families experiencing the stress of chronic illness or from relocations associated with the military lifestyle (Patterson, 1988b, 1989a). Five dimensions of family schema were proposed: 1) shared purpose, 2) collectivity, 3) frameability, 4) relativism, and 5) shared control. In Table 1, definitions of these dimensions are presented, along with linkages to the dimensions identified by the other four theorists.

The data from our sample of families caring for a medically fragile child provides further evidence to support these dimensions of the family schema (Patterson & Leonard, 1993). In semistructured interviews, parents reported how meanings and beliefs influenced their ability to adapt. The beliefs and meanings they reported have been grouped along the five dimensions of the family schema:

1. *Shared purpose* Parents reported a deeper commitment to life, seeing it as precious. Priorities in the family were reordered with greater attention to "little things" and to people. Many families reported caring more about persons with disabilities and working for them.

2. *Collectivity* To care for the medically fragile child, family members worked more closely together and, as a result, felt greater affection for each other. Parents also communicated a trust in the doctors' and nurses' abilities, believing they had the family's best interests at heart. Parents realized in a new way that they needed the help of others to manage. Several parents reported that seeing how hard their spouse worked to care for their child made them want to do their part.

3. *Frameability* Many families reported developing a new outlook on life that was more optimistic. They were grateful for the quality of life they did have, knowing it could have been worse. They focused on the joy, beauty, and good in their children and saw their family as special.

4. *Relativism* Parents reported feeling more tolerant and less judgmental of others. They were more flexible. They lived life in the present, taking one day at a time.

5. *Shared control* Mothers and fathers reported a realization that they have less control over life than they previously thought. Many acknowledged

Table 1. Comparison of the dimensions of the family schema with other theoretical models of global meanings

Family schema: Conceptual dimensions	Family paradigm (Reiss, 1981)	Family world view (Fisher, Ransom, Kokes, Weiss, & Phillips, 1984)	Coherence (Antonovsky, 1979)	Hardiness (Kobasa, Maddi, & Kahn, 1982)
Shared purpose: Having family values, goals, and commitments that are shared and guide life activity; having a family ideology that provides continuity and identity			*Meaningfulness:* Having values and commitments of emotional significance	*Commitment:* vs. hopelessness and alienation; involved in life
Collectivity: Recognizing that both the individual and the family are part of something larger than themselves; a belief that there is orderliness and connection among the human elements of the universe; a "we" vs. "I" orientation	*Coordination:* Solidarity of unit; sensitivity to each other	*Consensus:* vs. toleration of differences	*Comprehensibility:* Belief that life is ordered and just; and has continuity	
Frameability: Viewing life situations optimistically and with hope while still retaining realism; seeing change and new demands as challenges versus impending disaster		*Optimism:* vs. pessimism		*Challenge:* Belief that change is normative and a growth opportunity, not a disaster
Relativism: Viewing life in the context of present circumstances, not in terms of absolutes that are prescribed and invariant; setting limits and expectations in accord with capabilities and accepting less-than-perfect solutions	*Closure:* Open to new information; here-and-now focus	*Variety:* vs. sameness		
Shared control: Balance of personal and family control with trust in others; sharing the burden of demands with others and still accepting responsibility	*Configuration:* Sense of mastery; belief that family can learn and gain control	*Security:* vs. insecurity	*Manageability:* Belief that things will work out by one's own efforts and with help from others	*Control:* Belief that one can influence experiences and not be powerless

From Patterson, J.M. (1988b). Families experiencing stress. The Family Adjustment and Adaptation Response Model. *Family Systems Medicine, 6*(2), 225; reprinted by permission.

the "higher power" in their lives. They also reported increased assertiveness in working with professionals.

New Theoretical Milestone: Three Levels of Meaning

In reexamining this global meaning construct with an awareness of the contributions of other authors of this book, it seems to incorporate two distinct levels of abstraction: one at the relationship level and one at a more teleological or existential level. When combined with situational meanings, I would propose that there are three levels of meaning that are important when considering adaptation to a stressful life experience such as disability. Furthermore, this differentiation brings into a clearer focus the interplay between the individual and the family system as distinct units of analysis and the issues of consensus and divergence between individuals.

Level One

The first level still involves situational meanings. The individual makes an appraisal of the situation, which involves primary appraisal of the stressor event or the pile-up of demands and secondary appraisal of capabilities for managing the demands. Family members may converge in their situational appraisals so that there is consensus or they may diverge with a resulting discrepancy in the situational meanings held. When an event first occurs, it may take time for a shared definition to emerge. This, in fact, is part of the process of family adaptation (McCubbin & Patterson, 1983b). It is highly unlikely that consensus will always occur among all family members, and it is probably not always necessary for families to function well. There are many domains of family life where individuals act independently (although families have implicit rules for how much independence is tolerated, which is part of the second level of meaning). However, when a coordinated family behavioral response is necessary for effective functioning, the need for consensus will be more important. For example, when appraising whether a child with asthma experiencing respiratory distress should be taken to the emergency room, parents who can arrive at a consensus quickly will be a more effective problem-solving unit. (In many cases, one parent defers to the other in making this decision because of perceived expertise. This reflects the couple's implicit rule for deciding—a second level of meaning.) In other words, in reality, situational meanings are arrived at individually, but because family members share social space, time, and experience, they influence each other in their ways of appraising situations. In cohesive families, joined by bonds of unity, there is likely to be mutual influence in arriving at these appraisals.

Level Two

The second level of meaning is defined as the rules of relationship describing how family members are to relate to each other and how they as a unit are to relate to the world outside the family. These rules are usually implicit and include: 1) definitions of external boundaries (who is in the family) and internal boundaries (e.g., encouraging subsystem alliances), 2) role assignments for accomplishing family tasks, and 3) rules and norms for interactional behavior. With regard to boundaries, Boss's (1987; 1988; chap. 19, this volume) work on boundary ambiguity is particularly relevant. She has advanced this concept as a critical aspect of the "c" factor in her Contextual Family Stress Model. She argued that both the physical and psychological presence of family members should be considered in defining boundaries. When both types of presence are congruent, there is less stress in the system. However, incongruence between physical and psychological presence creates ambiguity and increases family stress. For example, the birth of a premature infant who spends many months in a neonatal intensive care unit (NICU) is an example of psychological presence in the family system but with physical absence, which may be exacerbated by ambiguity about the infant's survival. The concept of boundary ambiguity is especially relevant when we consider the family member with a chronic illness or disability, particularly when there are functional losses. For example, is the person who has a cognitive impairment or dementia "in" or "out" of the family system?

Reiss's (1981) family paradigm dimensions of coordination and closure are also relevant to this second level of meaning in the family. Families have implicit rules for the degree of togetherness or apartness they tolerate among members. Developmentally, families strive for more togetherness (called *centripetal movement*) in the early stages of the life cycle as they add members to the family. Conversely, they tolerate more separateness (called *centrifugal movement*) as children move into adolescence and anticipate leaving home as young adults (Combrinck-Graham, 1985). Families also have implicit rules for the degree of change versus stability they will tolerate. For example, tradition-bound families strive for more stability by adhering to the rules of the past; modern family units prefer establishing new rules to fit the present social context.

A family system also establishes a role structure for accomplishing basic tasks, such as earning the family income, child care, meal preparation, household maintenance, and so on. Families vary in how segregated (each gender performing separate roles) or egalitarian (both genders sharing most roles) they are. When the family structure changes, either to include a new member or because someone leaves home or dies, these roles often have to be renegotiated. In our sample of families with a medically fragile child, many mothers had to leave the work force totally or partially to care for their sick child (Patterson & Leonard, 1993). In many instances, this led to fathers working longer hours to earn more income and/or to assure job security. In other words, bringing their child home led to reorganization in the family's roles and rules, or a change in this second level of family meaning.

It should be clear from this discussion that this second level of meaning is indeed a family construct. It defines the functional structure of the system. Most of the time it operates without the family being explicitly aware of it. Ordinarily, the rules of relationship in families are rather stable; they regulate family interaction process, and provide organization, continuity, and routine to family life. This functional structure may be threatened and break down in response to a crisis or major transition when second-order change (Watzlawick, Weakland, & Fisch, 1974) is needed. (I return to this idea when I discuss the process of adaptation and the relationship of meanings to behavioral change.)

Level Three

At the third level of meaning, we again move back to an individually held set of beliefs or meanings about existential issues such as the purpose and meaning of life—a world view. Again, however, at the family level, we are talking about consensus among individual beliefs rather than a family world view and whether consensus regarding world view is needed for family adaptation.

Many theorists have used the world-view perspective to explain the differing responses of persons to disastrous events or victimization. For example, Janoff-Bulman and Frieze's (1983) assumptive world-view perspective holds that persons see the world as benevolent and meaningful and the self as worthwhile. Disastrous events shatter this world view, which must be rebuilt to incorporate the negative event. In contrast, Taylor (1983) argued that persons who experience disastrous events adapt by selectively distorting negative views of self, relationships, and the world as a way to reduce the threat; instead they build illusions containing meaning, mastery, and self-enhancing cognitions. Thompson and Janigian (1988) proposed a life-scheme framework that provides a sense of order and purpose in life. When negative events challenge the life scheme, persons search for new meanings and purpose and change their life scheme.

In our own empirical work with families who have a medically fragile child (Patterson & Leonard, 1993), there is ample evidence that parents change their worldview regarding the meaning and purpose of their life so that it is consonant with the reality of their behavioral and emotional investment in their child. There would be too much cognitive dissonance for a parent to spend the time and energy caring for a medically fragile child while viewing the child as an undesirable person or the situation as an undesirable set of circumstances. Some parents have reported that having a medically fragile child has given them a new purpose in life. They join together with other parents of children with disabilities to advocate for their rights, to improve services, and to change social policies. Many have reported that the meaning of life changes, with more concern for living in the present, caring about people, and appreciating little things.

Clearly these three levels of meaning are interrelated. World view is made up of values and existential beliefs that influence how relationships with others are structured. Both of these will influence how a given situation is appraised. And moving in the other direction, a newly experienced event—especially one that is more severe, disastrous, or victimizing—is likely to lead to changed relationship structures and changes in one's world view.

PROCESS OF CHANGING MEANINGS

As already described, individuals come to hold a set of beliefs and assumptions about the meaning and purpose of life, about how relationships should be structured, and about ways to interpret experienced stimuli from their collective experience in social groups, particularly the family. When a couple begin dating and particularly when they move toward marriage, they begin to forge a new shared belief system and pattern of interacting that represents what each brings from earlier life experiences (especially from each of their families of origin). Over time and through shared experience, they develop a family schema for their relationship structure within the family and for the way they relate to others outside the family. In addition, there is likely to be some consensus about core values and existential beliefs (level three), as well as consensus about situational appraisals of experienced events. The degree of consensus or divergence is influenced by the implicit rule of relationship about how much they need to agree. In some families, individuality is highly valued and they agree to disagree. In other families, the implicit rule is that all must agree. Reiss (1981) called the latter "conscious-sensitive" families and the former "distance-sensitive" families. As already indicated, this rule about how much the family needs to see "eye to eye" changes normatively over the life cycle.

In addition to normative life-cycle transitions, changes in family meanings at all levels are likely to emerge when major nonnormative life events occur. The diagnosis of chronic illness or disability in a child is a prime example.

Disability and Level One Meanings

A diagnosis of disability or illness usually happens suddenly and unexpectedly. A first reaction may be one of disbelief or denial. This is an example of how someone else's situational definition of an event (e.g., the doctor's) doesn't fit a family schema for relationships (e.g., children are supposed to be healthy, grow up to be independent, and live longer than parents) or perhaps the parents' world view (e.g., we should be able to control what happens to us if we live right and work hard). Family members search for a cause—"Why did this happen?" Their present world view and their relationship schema will likely influence the definition they give this stressor: "I am being punished for misdeeds," "The doctors made a mistake," "You didn't take care of yourself during the pregnancy," and so on. These examples call attention to the important role of emotions in making cognitive attributions. Although it is beyond the scope of this chapter, the relationship between emotions, behaviors, and cognitions at the individual and the family level is critical to a full understanding of the coping and adaptation process (cf. Patterson, 1988a, 1991; Sargent & Baker, 1983).

In addition to beliefs about what caused the illness, the family also will have or develop beliefs about who is responsible for managing the illness. These two aspects of locus of control have been referred to as the *locus of cause* and the *locus of consequence* (Patterson, 1989b). Families' beliefs may vary from internal control, to external control via chance, to external control via powerful others (Wallston & Wallston, 1978). These beliefs have implications for behavioral compliance with treatment regimens and the relationship families develop with health care providers. Belief in chance may result in marginal connections to the health care system. Belief in powerful others may lead to searches for cures or to passivity in managing disease processes. High internal control may lead to more active management.

Disability and Level Two Meanings

The second level of meaning, the relationship schema, will be affected by the presence of illness or disability. Normal family regulatory processes will be disrupted (Steinglass, 1990). Routines for managing the illness tasks, role reallocations, and rule changes will need to occur. In the FAAR Model, this disruption to the family's organizational structure is viewed as a crisis, which is defined as persistent disruptiveness when the family's old structural organization is no longer adequate to meet the new demands. The nature of the change called for is at the second meaning level where rules of relationship need to be changed. In the FAAR Model, this has been referred to as the adaptation phase, that is, where second-order structural change in the family system is called for (Patterson, 1988b). The way in which the family restructures itself to accommodate the illness demands may have an impact on the family's identity and sense of purpose. Steinglass (1990) has emphasized that in some families faced with chronic illness, there may be a tendency to direct a disproportionate share of their resources toward the illness needs, reducing resources needed for normative family needs. This skew can lead to a family illness identity—for example, "the diabetic family" versus the family who has a diabetic member.

Disability and Level Three Meanings

If this skew toward the illness happens, family members may change their world view (the third level of meaning), redefining meaning and purpose for their lives. The illness becomes the centerpiece for organizing all family activity. It is possible, of course, that one parent may orient this way, making the child the central focus, while the other parent resists, trying to maintain more balance in family functioning. In this latter example when the parents' world views diverge, they could change their relationship schema to agree to disagree and to have less coordinated family behavior. Or this divergence in world views could extend to other values and beliefs, an inability to agree on a family relationship schema, and ultimately result in the dissolution of the family system. In essence, family breakdown and dissolution occurs when family members can no longer agree on a relationship schema. The structure becomes uncoupled and two separate family units result.

However, the opposite may occur and the family system restructures in a way that makes it stronger. It is a principle of physics that to "harden" steel, you place stress on it. Or to use a biological example, the healing of a wound results in tougher skin—a scar. In our sample of families with a medically fragile child (Patterson & Leonard, 1993), it was striking how frequently parents reported that having and caring for the child pulled their family unit together and made them stronger. This response may reflect the processes of coping and adaptation via shared social construing described in this chapter. Disastrous events shatter expectations and goals and perhaps world views. Uncertainty and ambiguity results. Individuals turn to their significant others in search of emotional comfort and explanation for what is happening. A loss of a sense of personal control leads to joining more closely with others. Steinglass (1990) reported that families often pull together, giving up individual world views for a shared one. Perhaps persons who are emotionally differentiated are less reactive and better able to do this. Support groups also serve this function for persons experiencing major illness. Part of the coping process involves enlarging the context—"I am not just an illness, but a person with an illness, who lives in relationship with significant others and in a world where others have this illness too."

Relationship Among Cognitions, Behaviors, and Emotions

It is in the social context of relationships that illness and disability are experienced and changes occur—changes in behaviors (actively living with and managing the illness) and changes in beliefs about self, relationships, work, priorities, and even the meaning of life. Whether meaning change precedes behavioral change or vice versa varies across individuals and circumstances. There are schools of therapy emphasizing one versus the other (e.g., cognitive-behavioral therapy emphasizes behavioral changes as a way to change beliefs). Acknowledging and facing emotional reactions is also critical to this process of change in behaviors and meanings.

Another observation about the coping and adaptation process in families who have a medically fragile child was that families experienced real limits in how much they could change the situation they were in (Patterson & Leonard, 1993). In other words, coping by reducing demands had its limits because they wanted their child at home and that meant an ongoing set of chronic care demands had to be managed. Coping by increasing resources also had its limits primarily because of policies that limited the amount and type of service providers and because there were limits on who would pay for these services. Parents and families were left with coping by changing the way they thought about their situation, about their child, and about themselves. This led to changes in their relationship schema and to changes in world views. Families who developed congruence across these levels of meaning seemed to be managing best.

CONCLUSION

Families are complex social units and they vary widely in their adaptive capacities. One of the challenges we face is to extend our understanding and describe the range of this variability. This is particularly important in light of mandates (e.g., PL 99-457) to provide services to families, such as the individualized family service plan (IFSP). In implementing IFSPs, it is too easy to impose one or only a few templates on family process. Particularly important is the need to have a better understanding of racial and cultural variation. The ethnocentric approach of many white, middle-class service providers attests to this need. (For an in-depth discussion of this topic, see Lynch & Hanson, 1992.)

One of the most interesting questions still facing us is why some families develop positive, adaptive beliefs and meanings and others do not. In this chapter, I have argued for the importance of the social context in this process of meaning making. We need studies of daily family process to learn how individuals and families successfully change meanings in the context of their natural support systems. Such findings would provide the basis for improved practices in working with families adapting to the presence of disability or chronic illness.

Finally, I have alluded to the importance of emotions in the adaptation process. Adaptation to chronic illness and disability clearly involves emotional, cognitive, and behavioral tasks that change over time as the development of individuals, families, and the illness proceeds (Patterson, 1988a). Meanings, as discussed in this chapter, are intricately interwoven with emotions. The relationship between these three domains needs to be understood and incorporated into interventions. In our hierarchically structured systems of delivering care and services, we are prone to "teach" what we believe to be best knowledge and practices without adequate attention to the learner's readiness. Unidentified or unmanaged emotional factors may block what we perceive and what we learn, and limit our behavioral repertoire. Balance of focus across these domains is necessary if the goal is to promote successful family adaptation to chronic illness and disability.

ABOUT THE AUTHOR

Joan M. Patterson, Ph.D.   As director of research for the Center for Children with Chronic Illness and Disability and assistant professor at the University of Minnesota, my work focuses on the study and promotion of psychological and social competence in children with chronic illness and disability and in their family members. My interest in cognitive coping began during my doctoral studies in family social science at the University of Minnesota where I collaborated in explicating a family stress theoretical model, which incorporates several levels of cognitive appraisal. I continue to learn about living a balanced and meaningful life as I am challenged with my own diabetes and as I take on the developmental task of generativity through very positive interactions with my own young adult children and in working with graduate students.

REFERENCES

Antonovsky, A. (1979). *Health, stress and coping*. San Francisco: Jossey-Bass.

Antonovsky, A. (1987). *Unraveling the mystery of health. How people manage stress and stay well*. San Francisco: Jossey-Bass.

Berger, P.L., & Luckman, T. (1966). *The social construction of reality*. New York: Doubleday.

Boss, P. (1987). Family stress. In M. Sussman & S. Steinmetz (Eds.), *Handbook of marriage and the family* (pp. 695–723). New York: Plenum.

Boss, P.G. (1988). *Family stress management*. Newbury Park, CA: Sage Publications.

Combrinck-Graham L. (1985). A developmental model for family systems. *Family Process, 24*(2), 139–150.

Dell, P.F. (1985). Understanding Bateson and Maturana: Toward a biological foundation for the social sciences. *Journal of Marital and Family Therapy, 11*, 1–20.

Fisher, L., Ransom, D., Kokes, R., Weiss, R., & Phillips, S. (1984, October). *The California Family Health Project*. Paper presented at the Family and Health Preconference Workshop of the National Council on Family Relations, San Francisco.

Goffman, E. (1974). *Frame analysis*. Cambridge, MA: Harvard University Press.

Hill, R. (1949). *Families under stress*. New York: Harper.

Hill, R. (1958). Generic features of families under stress. *Social Casework, 49*, 139–150.

Janoff-Bulman, R., & Frieze, I.H. (1983). A theoretical perspective for understanding reactions to victimization. *Journal of Social Issues, 39*, 1–17.

Kluckhohn, F.R. (1960). Variations in the basic values of family systems. In N.W. Bell & E.F. Vogel (Eds.), *A modern introduction to the family* (pp. 304–315). Glencoe, IL: Free Press.

Kobasa, S., Maddi, S., & Kahn, S. (1982). Hardiness and health: A prospective study. *Journal of Marriage and the Family, 47*(4), 811–825.

Lavee, Y., McCubbin, H., & Patterson, J. (1985). The Double ABCX Model of family stress and adaptation: An empirical test by analysis of structural equations with latent variables. *Journal of Marriage and the Family, 47*(4), 811–825.

Lazarus, R.S. (1966). *Psychological stress and the coping process*. New York: McGraw-Hill.

Lynch, E.W., & Hanson, M.J. (Eds.). (1992). *Developing cross-cultural competence: A guide for working with young children and their families*. Baltimore: Paul H. Brookes Publishing Co.

McCubbin, H.I., & Patterson, J.M. (1982). Family adaptation to crises. In H.I. McCubbin, A.E. Cauble, & J.M. Patterson (Eds.), *Family stress, coping, and social support* (pp. 26–47). Springfield, IL: Charles C Thomas.

McCubbin, H.I., & Patterson, J.M. (1983a). Family stress and adaptation to crises: A Double ABCX Model of family behavior. In D. Olson & B. Miler (Eds.), *Family studies review yearbook* (pp. 87–106). Beverly Hills, CA: Sage Publications.

McCubbin, H.I., & Patterson, J.M. (1983b). The family stress process: The Double

ABCX Model of famiy adjustment and adaptation. *Marriage and Family Review*, *6*, 7–37.

Patterson, J.M. (1988a). Chronic illness in children and the impact on families. In C. Chilman, E. Nunnally, & F. Cox (Eds.), *Chronic illness and disability* (pp. 69–107). Newbury Park, CA: Sage Publications.

Patterson, J.M. (1988b). Families experiencing stress. The Family Adjustment and Adaptation Response Model. *Family Systems Medicine*, *6*(2), 202–237.

Patterson, J.M. (1989a). A family stress model: The Family Adjustment and Adaptation Response. In C. Ramsey (Ed.), *The science of family medicine* (pp. 95–117). New York: Guilford Press.

Patterson, J.M. (1989b). Illness beliefs as a factor in patient–spouse adaptation to coronary artery disease. *Family Systems Medicine*, *7*(4), 428–442.

Patterson, J.M. (1991). A family systems perspective for working with youth with disability. *Pediatrician*, *18*, 129–141.

Patterson, J.M., & Leonard, B.J. (in press). Caregiving and children. In E. Kahana, D.E. Biegel, & M. Wykle (Eds.), *Family caregiving across the lifespan*. Newbury Park, CA: Sage Publications.

Piaget, J. (1952). *The origins of intelligence in children*. New York: International Universities Press.

Reiss, D. (1981). *The family's construction of reality*. Cambridge, MA: Harvard University.

Sargent, J., & Baker, L. (1983). Behavior and diabetes care. *Primary Care*, *10*, 583–594.

Steinglass, P. (1990, October). *Multiple family discussion groups and chronic illness*. Paper presented at Family Care-giving Across the Lifespan Conference. Case Western Reserve University, Cleveland, OH.

Taylor, S. (1983). Adjustment to threatening events: A theory of cognitive adaptation. *American Psychologist*, *38*, 624–630.

Thompson, S., & Janigian, A. (1988). Life schemes: A framework for understanding the search for meaning. *Journal of Social and Clinical Psychology*, *7*, 260–280.

Wallston, K.A., & Wallston, B.S. (1978). Development of the Multidimensional Health Locus of Control (MHLC) scales. *Health Education Monographs*, *6*(2), 160–170.

Watzlawick, P., Weakland, J., & Fisch, R. (1974). *Change: Principles of problem formation and problem resolution*. New York: Norton.

Weisz, J.R., Rothbaum, F.M., & Blackburn, T.C. (1984). Standing out and standing in. The psychology of control in America and Japan. *American Psychologist*, *39*(9), 955–969.

White, R.W. (1974). Strategies of adaptation: An attempt at systematic description. In G.V. Coelho, D. Hamburg, & J.E. Adams (Eds.), *Coping and adaptation* (pp. 17–32). New York: Basic Books.

chapter 18

Family Schema, Paradigms, and Paradigm Shifts

Components and Processes of Appraisal in Family Adaptation to Crises

Hamilton I. McCubbin, Elizabeth A. Thompson, Anne I. Thompson, and Marilyn A. McCubbin

Ted and Susan Johnson [not their real names] had anxiously awaited the birth of their first child. Susan (age 35), an active high school teacher, and Ted (age 33), an established and relatively successful new-car salesperson, knew that the child would present a major change in their lifestyle, but they had spent a lot of time during Susan's pregnancy planning for their roles as parents and for the child's care. They attended infant and child development classes together and prepared their home together; wallpaper, furniture, and stuffed animals were ready. They had postponed having a child until they had money, a home, and their careers in order; they planned and now they were ready. They felt excited and confident that they could adjust to their new role as parents. Their plans and dreams were about to become a reality and they were pleased.

The birth of their son, David, was smooth and relatively routine. Soon after delivery, they were informed of an unexpected situation that placed both parents in a state of shock. They refused to believe it when the doctor informed them that David had been born with Down syndrome. Susan's pregnancy had been seemingly normal, and she had planned so carefully to avoid having a child "too late in life," when these "risks" had a chance of occurring. This could not be happening; it was all a mistake. Double check, triple check, provide evidence; they pleaded with their doctor, expecting a different outcome with each demand. While Ted and Susan had spent many hours planning for and discussing the changes they would make for the baby, they had never discussed the possibility of having a child with special needs. As they held and looked at David, scanning for and focusing upon physical features cited by their doctor, it gradually and painfully became more clear that *David was different.*

Initially, Ted and Susan had markedly different reactions to the diagnosis. Neither Ted nor Susan had any experience with Down syndrome and, for a while, they found it difficult to discuss the situation with one another. After an initial period of sharing their anger, frustrations, reflecting upon what they could have done differently had they known, and blaming themselves and each other, they began to deal with the matters at hand with the future in mind. They both realized that their expectations and plans would need to be altered; David and his needs must be taken into account.

FAMILY APPRAISAL

The reaction of the Johnson family to the diagnosis of their child with Down syndrome can be seen as an illustration of the critical components of family appraisal and the dynamic role of appraisal in the family's processes of adaptation in crisis situations. One of the critical and still relatively understudied factors in family life that both mediates and facilitates family adaptation is the various levels of family appraisal and their relationship to family patterns of functioning under stress. The complex interplay among three levels of appraisal—the family's appraisal of the stressor, the family's paradigm or appraisal of the total crisis situation, and the family's schema or world view—has been developed only to a minimal degree in the literature on family resiliency in the face of stress (H. I. McCubbin & McCubbin, 1987, 1988; M. A. McCubbin & McCubbin, 1991, 1992; Patterson, 1988; Reiss & Oliveri, 1980). These researchers have agreed that the family's efforts to cope with the stressor and to develop the family's patterns of functioning designed to adapt to a crisis situation such as that faced by the Johnson family will shape and be shaped by the family's appraisal at the following three levels (H. I. McCubbin & McCubbin, 1987; M. A. McCubbin & McCubbin, 1991, 1992):

- Level 1: the family's definition of the stressor or crisis precipitating event and its severity (e.g., the diagnosis of having a child with Down syndrome)
- Level 2: their paradigm or appraisal of the crisis situation (e.g., the family's appraisal that takes into account the stressor, community stigma, friends' reactions, extended family reactions, social norms, husband's reaction, spouse's reaction, and their future expectations)
- Level 3: the family's schema or world view (e.g., shaped by the family's values, shared beliefs, goals, expectations, and priorities)

The dynamic interaction among these three levels of appraisal in relationship to the family's coping and patterns of functioning is the focus of this chapter. Through the use of the Johnson case study, which is developed further in the chapter, we examine the dynamic nature of family adaptation in crisis situations with a specific emphasis on a re-examination of the structure of family schema, the influential role of family paradigms, the changing nature of family paradigms, and the interactive relationship of these aspects to the family's patterns of behavior.

FAMILY ADAPTATION

In looking back to the third trimester of Susan Johnson's pregnancy, one could describe the Johnson family as being in an optimal state of *bonadaptation*. That is, the anticipated crisis-producing event of having a child was defined as a wonderful event. The family's paradigm or view of the anticipated stressful situation was equally affirming and positive, with an appropriate emphasis upon a shared sense of congruency between how they were functioning as a couple together, making shared decisions, and sharing activities around child-bearing and anticipated childrearing. There was also a sense of fit between the family (couple plus developing fetus) and the community of relatives and friends who were also affirming. The family's world view was shaped by its own identity, which developed over the prior 7 years of marriage preceded by 2 years of courtship (living together), and was characterized by family values underscoring openness, sharing, careers, and respect, with goals and priorities emphasizing economic stability, career development, and a future with children. As depicted in Figure 1, the Johnson family experienced a shared sense of congruity between their family's schema, the family's paradigm around children, and the family's established patterns of functioning that supported this sense of harmony.

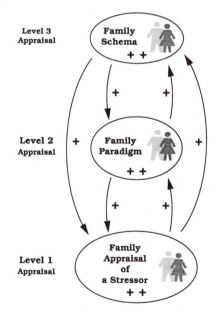

Figure 1.   The Resiliency Model and three levels of appraisal. (+ indicates congruency.) (© Copyright 1992 by H. McCubbin.)

Two indices of this positive and optimal level of adaptation may be noted. At one level, the family has cultivated a climate of congruency (reflected in the "+" symbols in Figure 1) among the three levels of appraisal, and congruency between the three levels and the family's established patterns of functioning. Additionally, the family has cultivated a climate characterized by a sense of coherence and order in their lives with a shared sense of confidence, predictability, and trust (Antonovsky, 1979, 1987).

For Susan, David's being a child with special needs only meant that he was special. As far as she could see, his needs would be that of any child even though his development would be slower and he would look "different." As she projected into the future, the difficult issue of David being "retarded" was something to be reckoned with in the years ahead; for now, David needed them. David needed them as parents. Her world view that she would be a parent and a good one remained unchanged. She was now a parent, she had always wanted to be one, and now she needed to act as one. Raising a child, she argued to herself, was going to be a challenge; David's situation was going to be just a little more challenging. He was her child, and she couldn't help feeling happy when she held him. Sure, he was different from the other babies in the nursery, but she had heard of the great affection and sweetness of children with Down syndrome, and she felt confident that he could be an active member of their family. She devoured all the information nurses and other medical staff offered. She learned and sought new information about Down syndrome and its consequences with intensity and commitment; Susan was committed to raising David as best she could. She also felt assured that Ted would join her with equal enthusiasm.

For Ted, David's "condition" was completely unacceptable. He felt angry that his child was going to be "retarded," and when he went to visit at the hospital, he felt embarrassed that he was David's father. How would David's "condition" and "appearance" affect Ted's public image, which for salespersons was no small matter. People would gossip about him; sales would drop and the family's financial future might be in jeopardy. Having David as a son was a threat to his world view. It meant that as a parent he was flawed, and raising a child with special needs was totally out of his realm of thinking. This could not be happening to him. He had seen a young man with Down syndrome working at the local fast-food restaurant, and although he seemed like a hard worker, always smiling, Ted also remembered seeing a group of teen-agers making fun of this young man. He resented even the thought of his child's being looked at and ridiculed. He was angry over the change in events that threatened his world view and future plans, and this situation made him resent David. While Susan was still in the hospital, Ted began investigating private "placements" for children with mental retardation. In his mind, there were other options. "We must look at this situation objectively," he argued to himself and to Susan. There were professionals, he believed, who were better qualified than he and Susan to care for someone like David. Because this was a "medical problem" it should be treated as such and thus David deserved the "best professional care possible."

After Ted and Susan had recovered from the initial trauma and they brought David home, they realized they had many problems to face and decisions to make.

It became clearer, however, that Susan and Ted saw the presenting "problems" needing "solving" differently. Ted remained inflexible and steadfast. He believed in and was committed to convincing Susan that they could still have a relationship with David even if he were cared for by "other more qualified persons." Ted felt strongly that they should not be forced to abandon their personal and wonderful dreams for the future, which included having another child. "Think about David's needs, not yours," Ted argued, realizing that he was hurting Susan with these confrontations. These hurtful remarks, Ted rationalized, were necessary to bring Susan to her senses and to shock her into thinking more rationally.

But Susan rejected the idea of having David "cared for by professionals." Susan had spoken with her parents and close friends. While cautious in offering advice, they were encouraging of Susan's belief that parenting didn't stop because they had a child with special needs. Susan saw the future differently than Ted; it was one filled with more joy and hope. In fact, even with the delays in physical, social, and intellectual development ahead, a predictable life course for a child with Down syndrome, Susan felt a sense of congruity between her values, dreams, and priorities and the challenges that lay ahead.

FAMILY CONGRUENCE AND COHERENCE

In the face of an unexpected family crisis-producing event—the birth of their son with special needs—the Johnson's family situation was disrupted. Instead of continued stability in functioning, the family's appraisal of the situation became incongruent (see Figure 2), with both husband and wife developing conflictual definitions of the stressor (i.e., unfortunate versus catastrophic) and conflictual family paradigms (i.e., child's basic needs for continued parenting versus a medical problem demanding professional care), with the total crisis situation and the family's appraisal creating conflicts with the family's schema (i.e., maintaining their careers, fitting in the community, raising "normal" children with the goal of independent functioning of all members, and so on). Understandably, the family's ability to achieve a satisfactory level of adaptation will depend upon its ability to re-establish changes at all levels of appraisal as well as in its patterns of functioning—to achieve, once again, a high level of congruency and coherence.

FAMILY PARADIGM SHIFTS

The concept of shared family schema may be traced to the general literature on the psychology of schemata. Drawing from this literature (Bem, 1981; Fong & Marcus, 1982; Taylor & Crocker, 1981) and adapting definitions to fit the context of the family system, a family schema may be defined as a generalized structure of shared values, beliefs, goals, expectations, and priorities, shaped and adopted by the family unit, thus formulating a generalized informational structure against and through which information and experiences are com-

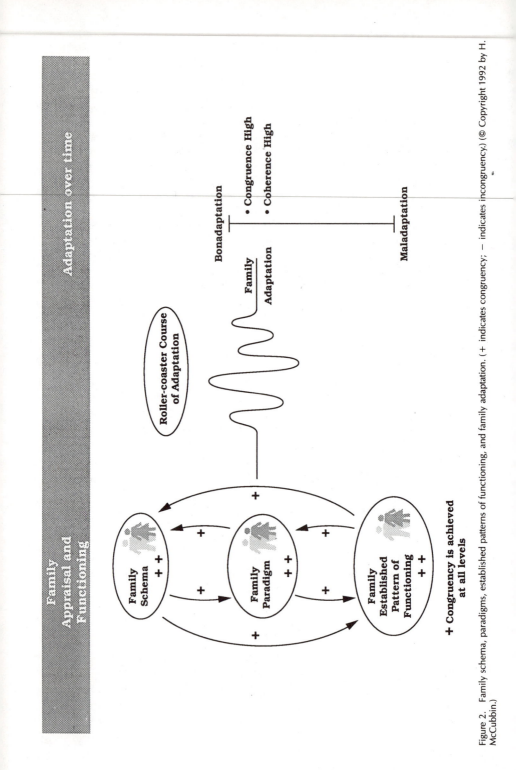

Figure 2.   Family schema, paradigms, established patterns of functioning, and family adaptation. (+ indicates congruency; − indicates incongruency.) (© Copyright 1992 by H. McCubbin.)

pared, sifted, and processed. A family schema develops over time and evolves into an encapsulation of experience that serves as a framework used to evaluate incoming stimuli and experiences (Martin & Halverson, 1981; Segal, 1988). Although changes in the family's schema are possible, the ability of the family schema to accept, compare, and process relevant information, adding those experiences to the family's schema, while simultaneously rejecting family information irrelevant or contradictory to the schema, leads to a self-imposed stability and rigidity of the family's world view (H. I. McCubbin & McCubbin, 1989; M. A. McCubbin & McCubbin, 1991, 1992). Not only is a family's schema highly resistant to change, but it plays a major and highly influential role in shaping the family's appraisal of a stressor, shaping the family's paradigm for problem solving, and the development of the family's effective coping strategies and newly instituted patterns of functioning needed to facilitate family adaptation in crisis situations.

The concept of family paradigms in the Resiliency Model of Adjustment and Adaptation (M. A. McCubbin & McCubbin, 1991, 1992) can be defined in terms of Kuhn's (1970) landmark work on the paradigmatic structure of science in his book *The Structure of Scientific Revolutions*. A paradigm, as defined by Kuhn (p. 19) is a model of shared or agreed-upon patterns of beliefs and expectations that allows for "further articulation and specification under new or more stringent conditions" of a given discipline. Generalizing from this definition to the family system, a paradigm may be viewed as a model of shared beliefs and expectations shaped and adopted by the family unit to guide the family's development of patterns of functioning around specific domains or dimensions (e.g., work and family, communication, spiritual/religious orientation, active/recreation orientation, childrearing) of family life. These patterns of functioning, also shaped over time and depicted in Figures 1 and 2, in turn, serve to support the family's paradigms.

Once a paradigm is shaped and adopted by the family system, family patterns will then be guided, if not governed, by that paradigm or successive paradigms. Kuhn's (1970) assertion of the influential role of paradigms for science may be paraphrased to apply to the importance of paradigms in family functioning: Once a paradigm is shaped, adopted, and used to interpret phenomena and to guide family behavior, there is no such thing as family functioning in the absence of any paradigm. Concomitantly, for a family unit to reject a paradigm that has served to shape a domain of family life without simultaneously substituting another is to reject the nature of family functioning itself.

The development of family paradigms within the family system may be viewed as a seemingly undetectable integration of the schemata and paradigms of its individual members—particularly its adult members—over time. Once shaped, adopted, and employed to shape family behavior, the paradigm would be maintained and upheld as long as it is successful for the family unit. As is true for the nature of paradigms in the scientific community, the paradigm is not likely to be doubted or questioned until the family faces a crisis or a series of crisis situations that places the paradigm in question. Alternative paradigms are then introduced and tested by the family to determine their acceptability, congruency with the family's schema, and efficacy in shaping family patterns that would be helpful in achieving a satisfactory level of family adaptation in the face of the crisis. This process of testing, rejecting, and substituting family paradigms may be referred to as a paradigm shift.

Like the paradigms in science, the accumulation of anomalies or crisis situations may call the current family paradigm into question and create a paradigmatic crisis and thus stage the possibility of a paradigm shift. By generalizing from Kuhn (1970), a crisis may be viewed as a reaction to the emergence of problem-solving failures under the accepted family paradigm. It is during this family crisis situation that other paradigms arise in contrast to the accepted paradigm. The new family paradigm that challenges the original paradigm must be tested in two fundamental ways: 1) for its success in solving the key problems presented, and 2) by withstanding a comparison to the merits of the original paradigm that may have served the family well. The emergence of new or novel paradigms do not automatically demand the rejection of the family's original paradigm. Although the family may begin to lose faith and then consider alternatives, they do not renounce the paradigm that has led them into a crisis and that may have flaws in achieving family adaptation. When a competing paradigm, which may coexist and operate alongside an existing family paradigm over time, proves more successful than the original, a paradigm shift evolves. This, in turn, requires or is accompanied by a redefinition of rules, family norms, and newly instituted patterns of family functioning.

This view of family paradigms, as based on an adaptation of Kuhn's (1970) definitions, appears to differ from Reiss's (1981) concept of paradigm on several levels. Whereas we concur with Reiss on his assertion that paradigms are manifested in the family's organizational patterns of daily living, his concept of family paradigm appears to be global, bordering on a world view, and not focused upon specific domains and dimensions of family life as argued here and in the scientific application of the concept. Reiss defined paradigms as "framing assumptions specifying—with great generality—certain fundamental properties of the perceptual world, properties which are given, are not subject to dispute, and cannot be either verified or disproved with experience, analysis or discussion" (p. 174). It seems reasonable to infer that while family paradigms must have some rigidity and stability in order to guide the family's patterns of functioning, in our view, paradigms are not immutable; rather they are best viewed as dynamic, resistant but changeable.

COURSE OF ADAPTATION

In the family system, it is commonly noted that crises lead to the replacement of established patterns of functioning with newly instituted patterns created to cope with and adapt to the crisis situation. These changes and their efficacy in facilitating adaptation may also cause the family unit to change its paradigms to achieve a greater sense of congruity and coherence. By revisiting the Johnson family and Susan and Ted's efforts to adapt to the situation, we can begin to shed light on the complex processes of family adaptation involving both paradigm shifts and changes in the family's patterns of functioning.

> With David at home and Susan taking a leave from her job, the transition to parenthood seemed to go smoothly. David's care was solely in Susan's hands, with Ted remaining aloof—as if in waiting to see if the demands of David's home care would wear Susan down and thus legitimize his predictions that professional care was necessary. Ted's distancing from his wife and child was reinforced by marital conflicts and arguments. "You don't love me. David is far more important to you than our marriage," Ted complained. Ted wanted life to be like it was before David was born. Susan saw Ted's requests as demands on her and as a rejection of David and his needs. Ted questioned her "smothering" of David. Susan felt hurt by his remarks; clearly she and Ted defined and responded differently to the situation. She wanted to invest in this parent–child relationship. Ted wanted to avoid any commitment, expecting it all to end soon. He thought, "Susan will come to her senses." Their marriage, and intimacy between them, deteriorated.

The Johnson family's roller-coaster course of adaptation was predictable in light of the incongruities in the family's three levels of appraisal and the differences in appraisal between adult family members. By using a " + " symbol to reflect congruency and a " − " symbol to reflect incongruency, we can begin to portray the nature of paradigmatic conflict and the influential role of paradigmatic conflict in helping families to give meaning to a crisis situation, a vital process underlying the roller-coaster course of family adaptation (see Figure 3). We can also begin to see the dynamic nature of family paradigms in conflict and the complementary emergence of new patterns of functioning (i.e., increased confrontations, blaming, pointing out faults), which serve to test as well as support one family paradigm over another.

To establish periods of relative peace resembling harmony and adaptation, other family patterns are introduced and adopted, such as reducing periods of intimacy and reducing communication to avoid "triggering an incident." In these situations, the paradigms coexist in the family and remain in conflict. With such family patterns in place to keep "peace in the family," the Johnson family is able to achieve what may be called *pseudoadaptation*—what some families call "purgatory" along the continuum of adaptation. Because of the family's highly vulnerable condition, particularly to the possible impact of another stressor, they remain in a state of constant tension—even though, to the outside world, things appear to be moving along smoothly. With David at home, and given the basic congruency between "mother's paradigm" to provide basic care and the family system's shared schema "to parent and love your children," which in turn renders legitimacy to Susan's family paradigm, the family moves forward with "parenting" as the dominant family paradigm. In

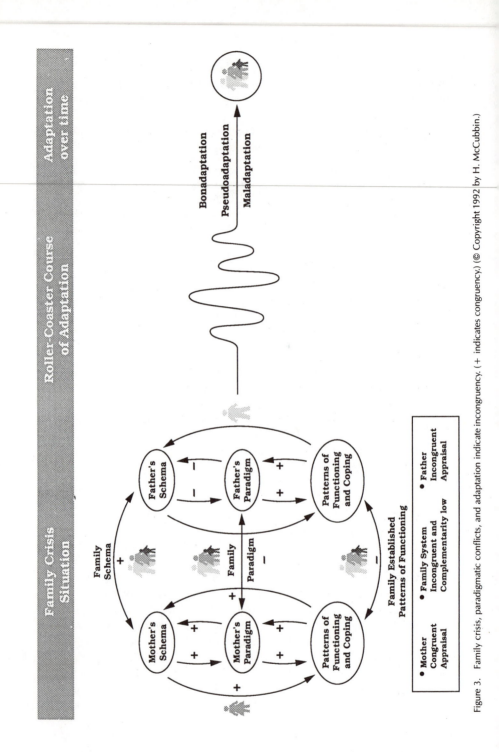

Figure 3.   Family crisis, paradigmatic conflicts, and adaptation indicate incongruency. (+ indicates congruency.) (© Copyright 1992 by H. McCubbin.)

contrast, while sharing the family's schema and thus affirming the importance of their parenting responsibility and roles, Ted has chosen to introduce and impose a competing family paradigm that calls for separating David from the family. Ted's appraisal of the situation reveals the incongruities in the family system. These are exacerbated by patterns of behaviors that challenge, if not undermine, the family's stability and contribute to a deterioration in the family's sense of coherence. This situation may be depicted in a diagram (Figure 3) emphasizing the incongruities in appraisal and functioning and their role in shaping the family system's rather bumpy and severe roller-coaster course of adaptation.

Simple as this case study may be in depicting the prominent levels of family appraisal—schema and paradigms—in facilitating family adaptation, we need also to become acutely aware of the conflictual nature of family paradigms as they serve a vital but situational function of promoting congruity in a constantly changing family milieu. Adaptations, we come to appreciate, are not achieved with a miracle cure, by a family adaptation "pill" prescribed by a family physician, but rather through a dynamic and often intense struggle among competing family paradigms and between paradigms and family patterns of functioning. The roller-coaster course of adaptation is made difficult by the very nature of family systems that strive to achieve congruency among all levels of appraisal; congruency in paradigms among family members; congruency between the family's schema, paradigms, and the patterns of behavior families adopt to adapt to the situation; and a complementarity among coping strategies taken by family members.

FAMILY CRISES

Family crises, much like Kuhn's (1970) paradigmatic crises, oftentimes set the stage for paradigm shifts, a situation in which a family paradigm "wins out." That is, it proves to be more successful in solving the key problems presented and achieves a level of congruity with the family's schema that serves as a necessary, but not sufficient, condition for achieving a state of bonadaptation.

> Ted found that with their shared, although challenged family schema, and faced with his basic love for Susan and his growing attachment to David, the family's fundamental paradigm underscoring commitment to family and child prevailed. Without fanfare and public apologies, Ted delved into full-time parenting with conviction and enthusiasm, much as he had done in other areas of his life. Susan complemented this obvious, although unannounced change with encouragement, love, and support. Given the solid foundation of their family schemata, it came as no surprise to both Ted and Susan that the paradigm's shift seemed relatively uneventful and occurred seemingly without "notice." This change or shift, however, was noted by others. Friends who were acutely aware of Ted's frustration and public pronouncements of the "nonacceptability" of David's being home had kept their distance, not wanting to be embroiled in private matters. With this obvious shift in

family appraisal and the accompanying newly instituted patterns of functioning—which included shared child-care tasks, Ted's spending more time at home, and open display of couple intimacy—friends and relatives responded with affirmation. There emerged a growing sense of "fitting in" to the community, which eased the family's effort to adapt to the situation.

Family bonadaptation is not an absolute point on the continuum of all possible outcomes following a family crisis. Obviously, families continue to struggle with both normative and nonnormative life changes and events that rock the family boat often when it is least expected. The Johnson family was no different as it struggled over the next year of continuous vigilance over David and adjusting to the normal ups and downs of both family life and parenting. As we revisit the Johnson family, we have the opportunity to observe the surprising "side effects" of family coping, the outcome that pushes the family back into a crisis, all precipitated by a seemingly harmless shift in the family paradigm.

> Things were going well for everyone. Ted became a central part of daily routines and his attachment to and love for David increased with each day. David's development, except for expected delays, was "normal." Susan, often missing her teaching and her role as a professional, found herself becoming an "activist" for the needs of children with Down syndrome. Because she was so good as a public speaker, she easily became a spokesperson for other families of children with special needs. She became chairperson for this committee and that, and traveled here and there to represent these families. The community counted on her and Susan enjoyed this role. It made her feel good and she could see the value of her work. She was also helpful in shaping policy and public opinion, paving the way for David's future. A more caring and sensitive country, better programs, and more assistance for families could not help but be good for David. As far as Susan was concerned, the "public's" demand for her time was a natural extension of her role to support David. Incongruity? Not from Susan's perspective.
>
> At first, Susan's activities were accepted and applauded. As time passed, however, Susan became overcommitted. Late nights, fatigue, frustration, and tension in the marriage signaled the emergence of newly instituted patterns of functioning, a new family paradigm of extensive outside commitments with resulting incongruities in the family. The Johnsons once again found themselves in a family crisis. Ted and Susan knew why this had happened, but they were at a loss as to how to change things for the better.
>
> The crisis-producing event was Susan's change in family roles. She had been committed to David's care. Now, she was seldom home. Ted and Susan were sharing tasks; today, Ted feels he cannot count on Susan "to be there." David's well-being is now served by Susan's belief in new state and federal policies for all children with special needs. Susan's time away from Ted and David can no longer be rationalized as being in their best "long-term" interest. The family is overstretched and vulnerable.

The course of family adaptation for the Johnsons and other families who will face these rather commonplace crises appears to be relatively predictable.

When confronted with the imbalances created by Susan's commitment to addressing the needs of all children with special needs, oftentimes at the expense of the Johnson family and even David, this situation is accompanied by a subtle but discernible shift in the family paradigm. This appraisal is intended to legitimize Susan's behaviors. Phrases Susan used to explain her commitments such as "we must adopt a long-term view" or "better programs and policies will make things better for David when he grows up" reveal the emergence of a new paradigm, a rival to the current paradigm that places David first among choices.

FAMILY COPING

In the relatively recent literature on family adaptation (see Antonovsky, 1987; Figley & McCubbin, 1983; H. I. McCubbin & Figley, 1983; H. I. McCubbin & McCubbin, 1987; H. I. McCubbin & Thompson, 1991; M. A. McCubbin & McCubbin, 1991; Olson et al., 1983) a great deal of emphasis has been placed upon the critical role of family coping in shaping the course of family adaptations. From the literature, a repertoire of coping strategies emerged, which include reframing, spiritual beliefs, social support, passive appraisal, family integration, and seeking community services, to name a few (H. I. McCubbin & Thompson, 1989; Olson et al., 1983). Seldom do we touch upon the iatrogenic (adverse) side effects of efficacious coping efforts that may serve an individual family member's well-being, but ultimately may prove to be problematic or even catastrophic for the family system.

In the Johnson family, we see the affirming but conflictual nature of Susan's coping. Created and executed on behalf of the family and David, the accompanying demands on Susan's time, emotions, and commitments ultimately had adverse side effects. They took their toll in disturbing the family's functioning and unity in spite of the good intentions and the efficacy of the coping strategies chosen. Unfortunately, because families do not, as a matter of routine, anticipate the side effects of their coping strategies, their taking notice of and confronting the incongruities created by new patterns of functioning is an even more remote possibility—that is, until conflicts, expressions of discontent, and a new family crisis situation is created or emerges that calls the family's current paradigms and level of functioning into question.

FAMILY INTERVENTION

The search for understanding of the overt and covert processes families create, develop, adopt, reject, change, and maintain represents an emerging emphasis upon the normative and resilient aspects of family life so often ignored or set aside for a family dysfunction and family pathology-oriented view of the family under stress. Among professionals studying and working with families under stress and focusing upon the family's struggle to find a meaning and the most

effective combinations of coping, there is a tendency to classify and characterize, if not judge, the family system in terms of its dysfunctional properties
rather than its strengths and capabilities. The Resiliency Model of Family Adjustment and Adaptation (M. A. McCubbin & McCubbin, 1991, 1992) and its
predecessors, the Family Adjustment and Adaptation Response (FAAR) Model
(H. I. McCubbin & Patterson, 1983; Patterson, 1988) and the Typology Model
of Adjustment and Adaptation (H. I. McCubbin & McCubbin, 1987, 1989),
which have evolved and have been used to guide our research on family behavior in response to crisis situations, have emphasized those family properties and
processes that shape and maximize the possibility of a successful adaptation.
Built on past research and theory building, and drawing from the rich and insightful work of Antonovsky's (1979; 1987; see also chap. 8, this volume) emphasis on salutogenesis and coherence, these family-oriented frameworks have
underscored the importance of determining what it is about family systems that
allows them to endure and develop as a unit in the face of adversity. Family
systems, as these conceptual frameworks emphasized, have properties, capabilities, and processes that serve them well in promoting family adaptation as a
natural part of its functioning.

In the context of this body of research, family schemata and paradigms
emerge as critical components of this natural process. The family's efforts to
achieve greater congruency and coherence in the context of shifting or changing paradigms also emerge as the family's natural process of healing itself. It is
also true that families do develop and cultivate rather dysfunctional paradigms
such as the independence-stifling forms of intimacy referred to as enmeshment.
Recognizing that adversity can bring about dysfunction, particularly in highly
vulnerable families with a history of dysfunctional paradigms and patterns of
behavior, we have strategically underscored the vital importance of understanding those healing and self-sustaining properties and processes of family life that
are often overlooked in the professional's effort to understand families under
stress. We have much to gain as researchers and practitioners by underscoring
the resiliency in families, and in so doing strengthen and broaden our repertoire
of interventions in support of these families under stress. Health care professionals, for example, play a crucial role in shaping the paradigms families and
parents develop in response to the birth of a child with special needs. Health
care professionals are often available to families at the acute phase of a crisis
situation—namely, when a diagnosis is presented and immediately following
the impact of the information on the family unit. Through the information and
education they provide about the diagnosis and its consequences, health care
professionals may determine to a major degree whether parents view the stressor
as a catastrophe or a challenge. The educational function of health care professionals to provide information cannot be overlooked as a critical intervention, a
therapeutic intervention, if you will, when conceptualized in the framework of
resiliency. Not only do paradigms, paradigm shifts, congruency, and coherence
become viable targets for both prevention and treatment, but these properties of

family life push both professionals and families to examine more thoroughly how and why families can care for themselves. Through an emphasis on resiliency and its components, namely schemata and paradigms, families may come to understand more fully what is involved in achieving a satisfactory level of adaptation. They may also come to understand why family tensions may linger if not heighten, even in the face of positive and successful coping efforts by individual family members.

CONCLUSION

In arguing for the importance of family schemata, paradigms, and paradigm shifts, we have introduced a host of challenges for family scholars. We are hard pressed to define with greater precision and measure with reliability and validity these important dimensions of family life. While we have conducted such developmental work with families of various ethnic backgrounds (H. I. McCubbin, McCubbin, & Thompson, 1992; H. I. McCubbin & Thompson, 1992), affirming that ethnicity plays a critical role in shaping family schemata and paradigms, we continue to be challenged by a demand for greater scientific rigor if we are to move this line of scientific inquiry forward.

This emphasis on resiliency and the role of paradigms and paradigm shifts in adaptation raises other important issues about the dynamics of normal family functioning. Clearly, this chapter has underscored the normative nature of stress, coping, and adaptation as predictable if not necessary aspects of human and family development over time. It seems reasonable to argue that paradigm conflicts and paradigm shifts are also normative but that the success of family adaptation depends upon, to some degree, other factors that mediate and facilitate changes in a family's paradigm. It is highly probable that other critical factors such as hope (Snyder, chap. 20, this volume; Snyder et al., 1991), problem-solving communication (M. A. McCubbin, McCubbin, & Thompson, 1988), and coherence (Antonovsky, chap. 8, this volume; Antonovsky & Sourani, 1988) play important mediating roles in sustaining family stability while members negotiate, test, and shift conflicting family paradigms. How families negotiate among paradigms and achieve congruence among levels of appraisal remains unanswered—in spite of the fact that families agree and family scholars affirm that these processes do occur, most often with positive outcomes.

ABOUT THE AUTHORS

Hamilton I. McCubbin   My research emphasis is on ethnic families, resiliency, and the dynamics of family processes in adapting to stressful life events.

Elizabeth A. Thompson   My research emphasis is on ethnic families, particularly Hispanic, Costa Rican, and Native American families.

Anne I. Thompson My interests focus on work and family issues, the impact of economic stress on families, and families with children with disabilities.

Marilyn A. McCubbin My interests focus on families who have children with chronic health conditions. I am currently principal investigator on a 5-year grant from the National Center for Nursing Research for longitudinal studies on families who have children with chronic health problems.

REFERENCES

Antonovsky, A. (1979). *Health, stress and coping*. San Francisco: Jossey-Bass.
Antonovsky, A. (1987). *Unraveling the mystery of health: How people manage stress and stay well*. San Francisco: Jossey-Bass.
Antonovsky, A., & Sourani, T. (1988). Family sense of coherence and family adaptation. *Journal of Marriage and the Family, 50*, 79–92.
Bem, S. L. (1981). Gender schema theory: A cognitive account of sex typing. *Psychological Review, 88*(4), 354–364.
Figley, C., & McCubbin, H.I. (Eds.). (1983). *Stress and the family, coping with catastrophes* (Vol. 2). New York: Brunner/Mazel.
Fong, G.T., & Marcus, H. (1982). Self schemas and judgments about others. *Social Cognition, 2*, 191–204.
Kuhn, T.S. (1970). *The structure of scientific revolutions* (2nd ed.). Chicago: University of Chicago Press.
Martin, C.L., & Halverson, C.F. (1981). A schematic processing model of sex typing and stereotyping in children. *Child Development, 52*, 1119–1134.
McCubbin, H.I., & Figley, C. (Eds.). (1983). *Stress and the family, coping with normative transitions* (Vol. 1). New York: Brunner/Mazel.
McCubbin, H.I., & McCubbin, M.A. (1987). Family stress theory and assessment: The T-Double ABCX Model of Family Adjustment and Adaptation. In H. I. McCubbin & A. Thompson (Eds.), *Family assessment for research and practice* (pp. 3–32). Madison: University of Wisconsin–Madison.
McCubbin, H.I., & McCubbin, M.A. (1988). Typologies of resilient families: Emerging roles of social class and ethnicity. *Family Relations, 37*, 247–254.
McCubbin, H.I., & McCubbin, M.A. (1989). Theoretical orientations to family stress and coping. In C.R. Figley (Ed.), *Treating stress in families* (pp. 3–43). New York: Brunner/Mazel.
McCubbin, H.I., McCubbin, M.A., & Thompson, A.I. (1992). Resiliency in families: The role of family schema and appraisal in family adaptation to crises. In T. Brubaker (Ed.), *Families in transition*. Beverly Hills: Sage Publications.
McCubbin, H.I., & Patterson, J. (1983). The family stress process: The Double ABCX Model of Adjustment and Adaptation. In H. McCubbin, M. Sussman, & J. Patterson (Eds.), *Advances and developments in family stress theory and research*. (pp. 7–37). New York: Haworth Press.
McCubbin, H.I., & Thompson, A.I. (1989). *Balancing work and family life on Wall Street: Stockbrokers and families coping with economic instability*. Edina, MN: Burgess International Group.
McCubbin, H.I., & Thompson, A.I. (Eds.). (1991). *Family Assessment Inventories for Research and Practice (FAIRP)* (2nd ed.). Madison: University of Wisconsin–Madison.

McCubbin, H.I., & Thompson, A.I. (1992). Resiliency in families: An East-West perspective. In J. Fischer (Ed.), *East-West connections in social work practice: Tradition and change* (pp. 103–130). Honolulu: University of Hawaii.

McCubbin, M.A., & McCubbin, H.I. (1991). Family stress theory and assessment, the Resiliency Model of Family Stress, Adjustment and Adaptation. In H.I. McCubbin & A.I. Thompson (Eds.), *Family Assessment Inventories for Research and Practice (FAIRP)* (pp. 3–32). Madison: University of Wisconsin–Madison.

McCubbin, M.A., & McCubbin, H.I. (1992). Family coping with health crises: The Resiliency Model of Family Stress, Adjustment and Adaptation. In C. Danielson, B. Hamel-Bissell, & P. Winstead-Fry (Eds.), *Families, health and illness*. New York: C.V. Mosby.

McCubbin, M.A., McCubbin, H.I., & Thompson, A.I. (1988). *Family Problem-Solving Communication Index* (Family Stress, Coping and Health Project). Madison: University of Wisconsin–Madison.

Olson, D., McCubbin, H.I., Barnes, H., Larsen, A., Muxem, A., & Wilson, M. (1983). *Families—What makes them work*. Beverly Hills: Sage Publications.

Patterson, J.M. (1988). Families experiencing stress: I. The Family Adjustment and Adaptation Response Model; II. Applying the FAAR Model to health-related issues for intervention and research. *Family Systems Medicine, 6*(2), 202–237.

Reiss, D. (1981). *The family's construction of reality*. Cambridge, MA: Harvard University Press.

Reiss, D., & Oliveri, M.E. (1980). Family paradigm and family coping: A proposal for linking the family's intrinsic adaptive capacities to its responses to stress. *Family Relations, 29*, 431–444.

Segal, Z. (1988). Appraisal of the self-schema construct in cognitive models of depression. *Psychological Bulletin, 103*(2), 147–162.

Snyder, C.R., Harris, C., Anderson, J.R., Holleran, S.A., Irving, L.M., Sigmon, S.T., Yoshinobu, L., Gibb, J., Langelle, C., & Harney, P. (1991). The will and the ways: Development and variation of an individual differences measure of hope. *Journal of Personality and Social Psychology, 60*, 570–585.

Taylor, S.E., & Crocker, J. (1981). Schematic bases of social information processing. In E.T. Higgins, C.P. Herman, & M.P. Zanna (Eds.), *The Ontario Symposium on Personality and Social Psychology* (Vol. 1, pp. 89–134). Hillsdale, NJ: Lawrence Erlbaum Associates.

chapter 19

Boundary Ambiguity
A Block to Cognitive Coping

Pauline Boss

The *salutogenic* perspective implies discovering and learning how best to use one's own resources to meet challenges (see Antonovsky, chap. 8, this volume). I translate this to mean a search for what makes families competent and resilient even when faced with uncertainty. As a family process researcher, I have tried to identify how families remain strong in spite of *ambiguous loss*— in this case, not knowing clearly the etiology and outcome of the disability of a loved one.

My work with families who cope with such uncertainty is threefold: research (identifying the problem), theory development (explaining *why* it's happening), and interventions (lowering its impact on the caregiving family). Elsewhere, I have written about the advantages of this multifaceted approach for easing family stress (Boss, 1987, 1988). My position is that we cannot build valid family stress theories and do meaningful research without first talking with and listening to stressed families themselves. We must also listen to professionals from other disciplines who work with these families. My research-theory-intervention approach is, therefore, based on a cooperative model with the goal of breaking down separate turfs, not only to inform one another, but to work together as a team. The common goal is to make life better for all challenged families, especially where there is a member with a chronic disability.

I define family stress as pressure, an upset in the steady state of the family—and, importantly, not necessarily negative (Boss, 1987, 1988). While crisis (immobilization) is to be avoided, stress (pressure) is viewed as inevitable and manageable. Highly stressed families are studied because there is something to be learned from the ones who are able to cope as well as from those who fall into crisis and become immobilized. The approach is primarily preventive (focusing on health and prevention of crisis) rather than medical (focusing on disease and treatment after crisis). The guiding research question is: Why are some families able to cope when others cannot, even when the burden is equal? The following assumptions are the basis of this family stress research (Boss, 1988):

The research upon which this chapter is based was supported by the National Institute on Aging (Project No. 1 Pol − A606309 − 01) and the University of Minnesota Experiment Station.

- Stressor events of different types are an inevitable part of normal, everyday life for both individuals and families and are assumed to be omnipresent.
- Stressor events, though in themselves benign, may stimulate the production of stress levels that must be coped with if a crisis is to be averted. For this reason, it is valuable to study highly stressed families and individuals to determine how they adapt to and manage stress without detrimental effects.
- Coping is a process involving the cognitive, emotional, and behavioral responses of both individuals and the family as a collective. Assessment of the coping process must include all those responses from both the individuals and the family as a whole if we are to have valid information on how families manage stress.
- In this coping process, the contexts of both individual and family systems are salient. The *external context* is woven out of the family's history, culture, religion, economics, developmental stage, and constitutional state (the health of the family members). The *internal context* is based on the family's philosophy (its values, beliefs, and paradigms), its psychology (use of defense mechanisms), and its sociology (structure and function). The study of families in stress must be contextual in order to be valid.
- Inasmuch as context, internal and external, may influence the coping process, the evaluations of specific coping behaviors by both scientist and therapist must be as objective as possible. For example, we must bear in mind that even though different coping mechanisms are used in different cultures, the same end may be achieved: the emotional and physical health of the individual family members, as well as the functional interaction of the system as a whole (Boss, 1987, p. 705).
- No social rituals exist for ambiguous losses as they do for clear-cut losses, as when a family member dies. Families, therefore, must usually find their own way to manage the unclear losses without support and guidance from social rituals.
- When an event of loss cannot be changed, change is still possible in the family's *perception* of that event (Boss, 1987, 1988, 1991). Families can alter their definition of the situation.

From this work, the complexities for caregiving families become apparent—coping is a process, not a one-time event. Coping has cognitive, emotional, and behavioral components; it has individual as well as familial indicators. Whether or not a family copes is influenced by its internal perceptions of who is in and who is out of the family as well as external contexts over which the family has little control (Boss, 1988).

BOUNDARY AMBIGUITY THEORY

Precisely because of the complexity of this family coping process, I searched for a more general theoretical idea. *Boundary ambiguity* (psychological presence while there is physical absence or vice versa) began to surface (Boss, 1977, 1980a, 1980b, 1983, 1987, 1988, 1991; Boss & Greenberg, 1984). This novel idea opened new windows of understanding for family researchers, family support staff, and, most of all, for the families themselves who were experiencing something they could not change, something irretrievably lost. In the case of developmental disabilities, the irretrievable loss is having a healthy, "perfect" child.

With boundary ambiguity, we can now label the immobilization families feel. This allows them to shift their perceptions even when the illness or disability remains unchanged. Most of all, the boundary ambiguity theory provides a perspective that does not blame caregivers and families for their stress. Let me explain.

Boundary ambiguity is a phenomenon in families resulting from their not being able to clarify who is in and who is out of the family system. (See Figure 1 for examples of each category of boundary ambiguity.) The family may perceive a physically absent member as psychologically present or a physically present member as psychologically absent. In either case, the family boundary is unclear (Boss, 1991, p. 165). The system is highly stressed, caregivers become depressed, and the family becomes dysfunctional.

Previous research has indicated that boundary ambiguity resulting from psychological presence while there is physical absence of a family member causes dysfunction for the remaining spouse (Boss, 1977, 1980b). Similarly, previous research has linked the value orientation of mastery (seeing oneself as being in charge of the situation) with successful adaptation to a variety of stressful situations, including care of chronically ill family members (see Pearlin, Menaghan, Lieberman, & Mullan, 1981).

Boundary ambiguity in families develops from either of two situations. First, an event can happen to the family where facts are unavailable, diagnoses are unclear, and news fluctuates from good to bad and back again. Sometimes there is absolutely no information available to tell the family what is happening to their loved one. Families with members who have developmental disabilities may indeed find themselves unclear about the presence or absence of their loved one for these reasons.

There is also a second way that boundary ambiguity can occur in caregiving families: Even if facts and diagnoses are available and clear, the family can ignore or deny this information. There may be a cognitive decision to ignore the information or, because of the pain, the family's denial system is so powerful that it blocks cognition; the coping process therefore cannot begin.

When this phenomenon of boundary ambiguity is long term, such as with chronic illness, families cope in various ways. They may prematurely close out the ill member from the family system and act as if he or she is already gone; or, they deny the illness and act as if nothing is wrong, expecting the ill person to act "normally." I think of the wife who insisted that her husband, who had Alzheimer's disease, no longer use his tools since he couldn't be the precise

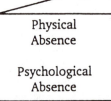

High Boundary Ambiguity

| Physical Absence Psychological Presence | Physical Presence Psychological Absence |

Example: Families with missing member(s). There is a preoccupation with thoughts about the absent member(s). The process of grieving and restructuring cannot begin since the facts surrounding the loss of the person(s) are not clear. This may also happen in divorced families since the loss is not clear-cut.

Example: Families in which a member is physically present but not emotionally available to the system. The family is intact, but a member is psychologically absent due to preoccupation with something outside the system (e.g., work, another person, chemical dependency) or due to chronic illness (e.g., Alzheimer's disease, in a coma, chemical dependence, schizophrenia).

Low Boundary Ambiguity

| Physical Absence Psychological Absence | Physical Presence Psychological Presence |

Example: Families in which a member is both gone and grieved, may still be thought of and missed, but there is no longer a preoccupation with the loss. The system has restructured without that person and goes on.

Example: Families in which a member is both physically and psychologically inside the system, such as in a marriage where the spouses are constantly together, physically and psychologically.

Figure 1. High and low boundary ambiguity. (From Boss, P.G., Caron, W., Horbal, J., & Mortimer, J. [1990]. Predictors of depression in caregivers of demential patients: Boundary ambiguity and mastery. *Family Process, 29,* 247; reprinted by permission.)

carpenter he once was. A grandson finally redefined the situation, realizing that Grandpa might want to "play" with hammer and nails and some wooden blocks just as he used to do when he was little. But Grandma rigidly persisted. In her perception, if her husband couldn't be what he used to be, he couldn't be anything.

CONTEXT OF CHANGE AND COPING

Changing perceptions to fit the objective physical reality of a family member's status and what family roles and tasks he or she can perform is indeed stressful. It is often easier for caregiving families to deny rather than to accept change. In the long term, however, denial is dysfunctional—but we must recognize that the family's culture, beliefs, and values influence what information is acceptable for them to take in and how it is construed. In more mastery-oriented cultures, such as the United States, it appears that there is less tolerance for uncertainty (see Boss, 1988). Nevertheless, I have seen families in Minnesota where even dementia appears not to be stressful; where people "flow with the tide"; where family members remain flexible and adaptable and even find some humor in how childlike Grandpa has become. I am always amazed when I see this resilience. There is something to learn from such families.

In my observation of stressed families, even those with differing values and beliefs, the problem-solving strategies that they use always have a cognitive component. People make choices either to fight and resist a situation or to give in to it—even in dangerous environments and when they are seemingly powerless. For example, many caregivers fight back and challenge the authority of medical specialists who withhold information from them—or they may enter dangerous territory when they travel across forbidden boundaries. Over time, most families may in fact both fight and give in. I wrote the following to sum up this point about active versus passive coping:

When a family is faced with a problem, its beliefs and values determine its action (or lack of it) in the coping process. Indeed, a barrier to the coping process could then be a highly fatalistic value orientation because it implies passivity rather than action; the family would do nothing about the cause of the event on the grounds that the options for change are controlled by forces outside the family. Individuals might discuss options for changing the event or their perception of it, but they would reject any option intuitively. Such a family's conclusion would be, "We just accept what comes"; "We've never been very successful before in coping with problems so why try now"; or "We are losers anyhow, so why fight it." Antonovsky (1979) referred to individuals who saw the world as unmanageable and unpredictable as low in coherence and therefore less able to cope with stress. The same may be true for the family.

The major point that must be kept in mind is that, given the suggestions in the coping literature that active coping strategies are more effective than passive strategies, it is logical to assume that families with value orientations of mastery cope with stress more functionally than do those with an orientation toward fatalism (in the sense of Schicksal[1]). There is need for caution about this assumption. The issue of active versus passive coping is more complex than saying one is functional and the other is dysfunctional. Effectiveness, for example, is influenced by larger cultural and contextual variables. (Boss, 1987, pp. 715–716)

BOUNDARY AMBIGUITY RESEARCH: NEW DIRECTIONS

While family researchers focused in the past on the variable of burden in caregiving research, the hypothesis of a direct link between how ill the family member is and how much burden the caregiver reports has not found support. Some of us, therefore, have looked for other correlates (Boss, Caron, Horbal, & Mortimer, 1990; Poulshock & Deimling, 1984; Zarit & Anthony, 1986).

Influences on Caregiver Assessment of Burden

My colleagues and I (Boss et al., 1990) set out to discover what influences the caregivers' assessment of burden. If not the severity of illness, then what? What is this cognitive shift that takes place in a caregiver's perception that helps her or him to overcome the burden? This called for process variables. Boundary ambiguity was one example.

We tested the impact of two variables, boundary ambiguity and mastery, in attempting to predict the level of depression in caregivers. The sample was based on 70 caregivers and families of persons with Alzheimer's disease. Seventy-five percent of caregivers were women. Stepwise regression and path analytic techniques were used to compare the effects of variables related to the degree of illness and of those related to caregiver perception.

Both boundary ambiguity and mastery were significantly related to the caregiver's level of depression, whereas severity of the family member's dementia was not (Boss et al., 1990). That is, it was the caregiver's perception of high boundary ambiguity and her or his subsequent lack of mastery, more than the illness itself, that predicted the caregiver's depression (see Figure 2). The caregiver's boundary ambiguity score (perceiving a mate as psychologically absent while still physically present) predicted a low mastery score; the caregiver's low mastery score in turn predicted high depression. This new research direction may also hold promise for research on families where there is a developmental disability since family processes of coping may have some similarities.

Thus far, my colleagues and I have found that boundary ambiguity serves as a mediating variable linking family member functioning and caregiver's sense of mastery over what is happening in spite of his or her burden (Boss et al., 1990; Caron, 1991; Garwick, 1991). Mastery, in turn, is more directly re-

---

[1]The word *Schicksal* (unlike other definitions of fatalism) does not carry with it the implication of predestination; it simply means "this is the way life is." Thus, while I use the English word fatalism, I give it the German meaning.

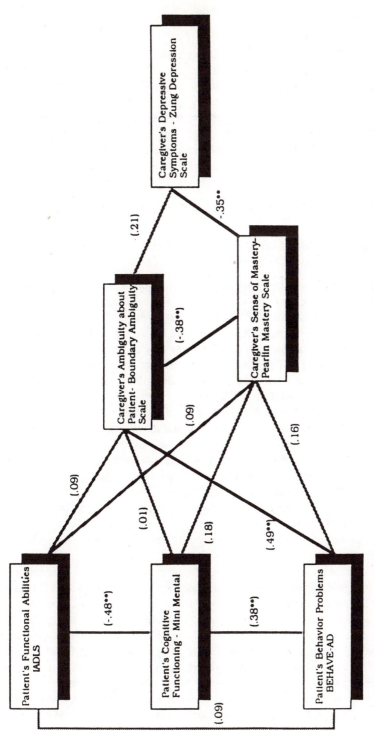

Figure 2. Path coefficients. (*p<.05, **p<.01; overall R² = .26, p = .002.) (From Boss, P.G., Caron, W., Horbal, J., & Mortimer, J. [1990]. Predictors of depression in caregivers of demential patients: Boundary ambiguity and mastery. *Family Process, 29,* 251; reprinted by permission.)

lated to the degree of the caregiver's depression. We now have a theoretical basis for designing and testing an intervention. Our tentative strategy is to: 1) help caregivers and families clarify as much as they can about the family member's role and presence in the family system so the family can reorganize their celebrations, decision-making rules, and task-performing roles in a new way even as the illness progresses; and 2) empower and support caregivers' beliefs in their own efficacy so they can have an impact, even in a situation they cannot really fix. The results of a pretest using this strategy are now being analyzed.

New Strategies for Research with Families and Disabilities

Applying the theory of boundary ambiguity specifically to families of children with disabilities, health professionals as well as researchers may form more valid questions to guide their work:

1.   While family members have taken the child into the boundary of their family system, have they also accepted the child's disability? That is, do they accept the child even though he or she no longer fits their perception of what they originally wanted their child to be like? Or, do they have the even more confusing situation in their family where they may be perceiving their child as she or he really is, but their mate does not? Is there increasingly more conflict over who this child is, what he or she can or cannot do, how much care he or she requires, and what the future will bring?

2.   Are mothers of children with disabilities more often than fathers carrying the burden of caregiving (and expected to do so by the health professionals) but also blamed or "pathologized" by the medical community for being "enmeshed" or "overinvolved" with their children? Mothers traditionally have given care to children with disabilities more than have fathers. As one mother of a child with a severe disability said, "Fathers more often jump ship when the going gets tough." This example indicates that the mother and the child are inside the family boundary while the father is outside, perhaps staying longer at work or getting more involved in community activities. The mother no longer sees him as her helpmate.

Using the boundary ambiguity theory, we can investigate whether mothers of children with disabilities are double bound by being expected to do the caregiving and, at the same time, blamed for being too involved inside the system. Such binds for mothers of children with disabilities need to be recognized by health care professionals and researchers as extremely stress producing and more stress producing than the burden of caregiving is in itself. Research is needed for professionals who work with children with disabilities to make sure they are supporting primary caregivers—usually mothers—rather than adding to their stress. Research and clinical terms such as *enmeshment, overprotecting, hovering,* and *engulfing* are mother-blaming terms and should be eliminated. Using a more systemic model, one example being boundary ambiguity, we may see that the behavior of these mothers should be supported rather than pathologized. A child with a severe disability needs a hovering parent! The more valid issue to investigate is what we can do so the primary caregiver doesn't always have to be the mother.

3. Are parents prepared for the recurring periods of loss and grieving that happen developmentally with a child with a disability? For example, Wikler (1981) wrote about life-cycle transitions when parents of children with mental retardation cannot celebrate events as they had expected. While graduations, marriages, college, and athletic contests are more and more a part of the lives of persons with disabilities, these events and transitions remain different from those of the general population. Can parents reframe (rethink) their perceptions of what their child with a disability can and cannot do? Such cognitive reframing must take place, not only when the baby is born and brought home from the hospital, but as a lifelong process. The psychoeducational approach— giving families information as well as support—would be useful for helping parents cope when a child's development does not follow the usual path.

New Strategies for Family Interventions

Chronic ambiguous losses create serious distress for caregiving families. Improving the management skills of caregivers will have two benefits: 1) the family member will be better cared for at home, and 2) the development of a "second patient" (the caregiver) will be avoided. This approach to family intervention research is new in that it is based on family stress management theory rather than on disease/treatment models. It is also a systemic model, taking the larger context into account, thus allowing for cultural and geographical diversity in how people cope with long-term stress.

Previous stress research focused primarily on events that could be improved or would eventually go away. The economic depression of the 1930s eventually righted itself; the second world war and subsequent wars eventually ended. But some families are never relieved of their stressful situation— families of persons with disabilities for example. The situation of their loss is ever present. Losses may range from severe to mild, short term to long-lasting, and normative to catastrophic, but in all cases the basic criterion is that families are unclear about the absence or presence of a family member.

The following strategies are recommended for service providers working with families stressed with ambiguous loss (Boss, 1991):

1. Label the uncertainty as a major stressor for family members since ambiguity, more than the disability, may be causing distress. Families report that labeling their uncertainty helps them to cope with it.

2. Provide a setting and structure for family members to meet and talk together so that they can hear each other's definitions of the situation and the

meaning it has for them. Once family members can tolerate differences in their viewpoints about the disability, the coping process is begun. Feelings no longer need to be kept secret. Professionals may be most helpful in providing a format by which other family members can voice less incriminating attributions for the family dilemma. This is important because blame and guilt are major blocks to coping.

3.   The psychoeducational approach should be part of the intervention. Family members need to be given as much information as possible—technical as well as psychosocial. The assumption is that families can help solve their own problems if they are cognitively aware of options for making decisions and changing behavior. In the case of disabilities, psychoeducational interventions are helpful regarding management guidelines and resources, but information is also useful for public awareness and policy changes. The psychoeducational approach for intervention remains compatible with the cognitive coping and stress model presented in this chapter. That is, in order for the family to cognitively reconstruct their perception of who is in and who is out of their family and on what basis, they need information and skills so that they can guide their own destiny even though the stressful situation remains.

4.   Provide community and social supports that enhance the family's options for caregiving and help them to find meaning in their situation. Social interaction is necessary to combat the family's tendency to remain isolated when in trouble and for our tendency as professionals to isolate them.

FUTURE DIRECTIONS FOR RESEARCH

In my own work, I will continue both basic and applied research in order to identify further what hinders as well as helps families to cope and remain resilient in spite of chronic stressors. Since I believe that effective interventions must take into account the diversity of caregiving families in order to adequately reflect processes influencing outcomes, we will in the next 5 years attempt to empirically identify these diverse coping processes by using more varied samples in our research. Large random samples may therefore be less useful than focusing on particular populations. Even within our homogeneous Minnesota sample of older families, we found diversity in coping styles and belief systems as we listened to Lutheran, Jewish, and Native American families tell their stories (Boss et al., 1990). Clearly, our future research must ask more questions about diverse families regarding how they perceive their situation and how they cope (or fail to cope) with it over time.

More generally, there are some pressing measurement issues that need attention from all researchers interested in how families cope with chronic stressors. For details, I refer the reader to Mortimer, Boss, Caron, and Horbal (1992), but here I apply our outline to focus specifically on research with families of children with disabilities:

1. *Selection Bias* Most caregiver research is done with clinical families. We are missing data from those families who are doing so well that health care providers are not hearing from them or from families at the other extreme who are so stressed that they remain isolated from all research and health care systems. Qualitative research using participant observer methods may be more effective in gaining these data.

2. *Small Sample Size* Researchers usually select samples by the particular disability (perhaps because grants are funded this way); thus, samples have remained relatively small. To gain larger samples, we might instead select them by behavioral problems of the child (e.g., acting out) or the caregiver (e.g., depression), or by identifying more general causes of family stress (e.g., boundary ambiguity).

3. *Information Bias* Gathering data from one family member, usually the mother, biases findings more than if we used a systemic approach of collecting data from father, mother, care recipient, siblings, and extended family. We developed alternatives to relying solely on caregiver data. We videotaped chronically ill family member, caregiver, and family interactions so that both behavioral problems and their immediate antecedents can be studied more objectively. We used computerized content analysis of whole family conversations about their caregiving situation to identify how they perceive their situation (Garwick, 1991). Since perception of the problem is more predictive of caregiver depression than is degree of burden, we obtained subjective as well as objective data from caregiver interactions with the care recipient. In-home videotaping proved fruitful in this regard and we will continue to perfect this methodology.

4. *Need for Longitudinal Studies* Cross-sectional studies do not get at the *process* of coping and caregiving. Furthermore, those families who do well over time may be those from whom we can gain the most useful data simply because they have learned how to remain resilient in spite of caring for a loved one with a long-term disability. While longitudinal studies are expensive and difficult to fund, they may, nevertheless, yield the most valuable information.

5. *More General Variables* Researchers and clinicians may find more useful intervention strategies if they focus less on a particular disability than on more generalized situations of boundary ambiguity. De-emphasizing the symptom-focused approach and concentrating instead on the situation of uncertainty that surrounds many stressor events opens new windows of understanding for coping as a process where perceptions shift and family interactions are continually redefined over time.

6. *More Diverse Family Studies, Not Just Caregiver Studies* The focus on the single caregiver does not reflect what is happening in real-life families with loved ones with disabilities. If we continue to interview only women, then we as researchers and clinicians are supporting the notion that only mothers and wives, daughters, and daughters-in-law can be caregivers. In most families,

there is a caregiving *system*. Researchers need to develop techniques to measure systematically who is participating and at what level. Societal assumptions that only women can answer questions about caregiving do not hold up with most of the families in our Alzheimer's disease research nor could these assumptions be maintained with families who differ culturally and ethnically even within our state. Research designs must incorporate diversity in assumptions of caregiving, family roles, and family structure.

7. *More Systemic and Valid Outcome Measures*   Caregiver burden may no longer be a fruitful variable on which to focus. More than the degree of burden, it is the *outcome* of burden that indicates trouble (Boss et al., 1990). Depression in members of the caregiving family, for example, may be a more important outcome variable than the degree of caregiver burden or degree of stress.

8. *Family (Group) Measures*   True family measures are rare. Garwick (1991) has used the caregiving family's conversation (taken from one segment of the in-home videotaped interviews) as one indicator for assessing the family's construction of their reality. This gives us a typology of caregiving families rather than an outcome variable, but it is a necessary place to begin. Researchers will need to develop new assessments and improved methodologies for outcome measures.

CONCLUSION

Antonovsky (1979) said that to cope successfully one must first believe that one understands the problem. Lazarus (1966, 1976, 1977) stated that the first step in the coping process is cognition, that is, recognizing the problem. There is little disagreement about this cognitive component as the first step in the coping process. But what happens when a family cannot get enough information to understand the problem, when the situation is uncertain, when the diagnosis and prognosis are unclear—or what happens when some or all family members deny what is happening? Indeed, a family that sees their world as clear and understandable can more readily begin the coping process. But what about a family where the situation remains chaotic, uncertain, and incomprehensible? They are stuck. The coping process cannot begin because cognition is blocked.

While I have identified and operationalized boundary ambiguity as one major block to family coping, I am at the same time coming to the conclusion that a necessary coping mechanism for families, especially for those where the loss cannot be ameliorated, is to develop more tolerance for ambiguity. This may be a major indicator of resiliency. Sometimes families cannot have things the way they want. When there are disabilities, families must chart their own developmental course, find out what works and what does not, and use humor and creativity to find new ways to clarify who is inside the family and on what basis.

Indeed, families need a sense of coherence—but how do families get a sense of coherence when nothing makes sense, when they have done everything right and things still go wrong? Although the research and intervention strategies discussed in this chapter were developed specifically with families where a loved one has Alzheimer's disease, they may nevertheless stimulate a broader level of research, questioning, and thinking for what might work with families where there is a developmental disability. By linking the core idea of "sense of coherence" with an idea such as boundary ambiguity, we propose new ways of intervention for any family faced with an irretrievable loss.

ABOUT THE AUTHOR

Pauline Boss, Ph.D. My research focuses on how families manage long-term stress and ambiguous loss. My interest in chronic illness and the family was no doubt influenced by the personal experience of having lived previously with an alcoholic spouse. That experience fueled my deep curiosity about how caregivers and families overcome situations that they cannot fix. As a family process researcher and a family therapist in a major university training program, I am now able to serve as a mentor for young researchers, clinicians, and educators who will carry on such work—since ambiguity is, I believe, an inevitable part of family life.

REFERENCES

Antonovsky, A. (1979). *Health, stress and coping.* San Francisco: Jossey-Bass.

Boss, P.G. (1977). A clarification of the concept of psychological father presence in families experiencing ambiguity of boundary. *Journal of Marriage and the Family, 39,* 141–151.

Boss, P.G. (1980a). Normative family stress: Family boundary changes across the life-span. *Family Relations, 29*(4), 445–450.

Boss, P.G. (1980b). The relationship of psychological father presence, wife's personal qualities, and wife/family dysfunction in families of missing fathers. *Journal of Marriage and the Family, 42*(3), 541–549.

Boss, P.G. (1983). The marital relationship: Boundaries and ambiguities. In C. Figley & H.I. McCubbin (Eds.), *Stress and the family* (Vol. 2, pp. 26–40). New York: Brunner/Mazel.

Boss, P.G. (1987). Family stress: Perception and context. In M. Sussman & S. Steinmetz (Eds.), *Handbook on marriage and the family* (pp. 695–723). New York: Plenum.

Boss, P.G. (1988). *Family stress management.* Newbury Park, CA: Sage Publications.

Boss, P.G. (1991). Ambiguous loss. In F. Walsh & M. McGoldrick (Eds.), *Living beyond loss: Death and the family* (pp. 164–175) New York: W.W. Norton.

Boss, P.G., Caron, W., Horbal, J., & Mortimer, J. (1990). Predictors of depression in caregivers of demential patients: Boundary ambiguity and mastery. *Family Process, 29,* 245–254.

Boss, P.G., & Greenberg, J. (1984). Family boundary ambiguity: A new variable in family stress theory. *Family Process, 23,* 535–546.

Caron, W.A. (1991). *Dementia of the Alzheimer's type: The influence of caregiver and family adjustment on patient behavior.* Unpublished doctoral thesis, University of Minnesota, St. Paul.

Garwick, A.W. (1991). *Shared family perceptions of life with dementia of the Alzheimer's type.* Unpublished doctoral thesis, University of Minnesota, St. Paul.

Lazarus, R.S. (1966). *Psychological stress and the coping process.* New York: McGraw-Hill.

Lazarus, R.S. (1976). *Patterns of adjustment* (3rd ed.). New York: McGraw-Hill.

Lazarus, R.S. (1977). Cognitive and coping processes in emotion. In A. Monat & R.S. Lazarus (Eds.), *Stress and coping* (pp. 145–158). New York: Columbia University Press.

Mortimer, J.A., Boss, P.G., Caron, W., & Horbal, J. (1992). Measurement issues in caregivers research. In B.D. Lebowitz, E. Light, & G. Niederehe (Eds.), *Alzheimer's disease and family stress.* New York: Springer.

Pearlin, L.I., Menaghan, E.G., Lieberman, M.A., & Mullan, J.T. (1981). The stress process. *Journal of Health and Social Behavior, 22*(4), 337–356.

Poulshock, S., & Deimling, G.(1984). Families caring for elders in residence: Issues in the measurement of burden. *Journal of Gerontology, 39*(2), 230–239.

Wikler, L. (1981). Chronic stresses of families of mentally retarded children. *Family Relations, 30*(2), 281–288.

Zarit, S., & Anthony, C. (1986). Interventions with dementia patients and their families. In M. Gilooly, S. Zarit, & J. Birren (Eds.), *The dementias: Policy and management.* Englewood Cliffs, NJ: Prentice-Hall.

chapter 20

Hope for the Journey

C. R. Snyder

I went to 12 different schools before I finished high school. This was not because I was a troublemaker who was expelled from one school after another, but because I had a need. My need was to live with my mom and dad. My dad was a salesman, and he was transferred frequently from one major city to another. My childhood was, literally and figuratively, as the saying goes, "quite a trip." My parents and I repeatedly had to get ourselves "up" psychologically for the next move; moreover, we had to figure out how to achieve the myriad sub-goals related to setting up our new home. I can still vividly remember the importance of finding a corner space, or better yet a room, entirely to myself, where I could re-establish my turf. Next, my goals were to get some new friends, and to adapt to my new school. Through all of this *Gulliver's Travels*–like childhood, something always made the move with us. That something was hope, and my mom taught me how to keep it alive. If I were to give a title to my personal mythology, the story would be called "Hope for the Journey." In this regard, this chapter has special autobiographical significance to me. More importantly, however, I believe that the hope process forms the basis of a much larger human tale. But already I am getting ahead of myself, and as such I would like to take a large step back in time in the history of our species.

PHYLOGENIC MESSAGES FROM THE CAVE: BIRTH OF HOPE FOR OUR SPECIES

One theory about Homo sapiens is that we initially lived in caves. Imagine, for a moment, what it would be like if we could collectively move backward chronologically via some time machine and view the world the way our ancient ancestors did. Ages ago things would have looked something like those depicted in Figure 1 as we peered from our caves. This schematic has several important characteristics that I wish to highlight. First, at some point in our evolution we

This chapter is based, in part, on an invited address presented to the Southeastern Psychological Association, New Orleans, Louisiana, on March 21, 1991.

I would like to thank the following doctoral and postdoctoral students for their theoretical and empirical work that led to the ideas expressed in this chapter: John R. Anderson, Carla Dykeman, June Gibb, Pat Harney, Cheri Harris, Sharon H. Holleran, Lori M. Irving, Charyle Langelle, Joni Padur, Sandra T. Sigmon, and Lauren Yoshinobu. Gratitude is also extended to Joan Patterson for comments on the present chapter.

Figure 1. Schematic of self-representation and goal-related cognitions.

humans were able to generate cognitive representations of ourselves and the world around us. Perhaps this ability is what distinguishes our species from other animals. We also developed a linear sense of time, in which, roughly speaking, there was a past, a present, and a future. Because we lived in this temporal envelope, we thought of ourselves as persons moving across time. What made this temporal issue very salient to us, however, is that we always have been goal-directed creatures. Our earliest goals were basic, perhaps to get some food, or not to be killed and eaten by some other animal. Whatever the goals, we began to think of ourselves as moving toward the achievement of those goals, especially as our species succeeded in the grand survival game.

To the extent that we were adaptive as a species, we began to think of ourselves as having the two necessary ingredients to reach our goals. A first ingredient is the willful determination to get what we want. I call this the *agency component*. A second component is the sense of having a capability to generate the ways to get the thing or things that we want. I call this the *pathways component*. From our early history as a species, therefore, having the will and the ways to reach our goals was the essence of hope. Further, those who had such a hopeful cognitive set to achieve their goals may have had an evolutionary advantage.

ONTOGENY RECAPITULATES
PHYLOGENY: BIRTH OF HOPE FOR AN INDIVIDUAL

Biologists suggest that the physical development of the human from the embryo to the adult stage mirrors how our species evolved over time. That is to say, the individual biological maturation of each person over a period of a few years parallels an evolution that our species underwent over the ages. I suggest that the same can be said about our cognitive capabilities in general, as well as our cognitive coping strategies in particular. To the extent that we adults become effective and "adaptively" functioning in society, it is precisely because we have acquired the cognitive strategies to cope.

Consider, for a moment, the task that each of us faced as a newborn. Our earliest and most fundamental task, so to speak, was to "survive" (does this ever really change?). From the moment of biological birth, we are separated from our mother, but we nevertheless continue to remain enmeshed with her in order to obtain our nourishment and care. Rather quickly, we learn lessons about how to get the things that we want (whether this is food, a diaper changed, or the myriad other goals that we have during our first months). Around 18 months of age, however, the typical child for the first time realizes that she or he is a separate entity from the mother and the other physical entities in the environment. This process has been called "psychological birth" (Kaplan, 1978), and as a marker of this psychological birth we begin to use the personal pronoun "I." Such growth signals the same cognitive self-representation processes that I suggested earlier were necessary in the evolution of our species. Just as the cognitive self-representational skills are developing in the individual child, it also should be noted that the child becomes more adept at setting goals and trying to achieve these goals. To the degree that the child has acquired some sense of agency and pathways in relation to his or her goals, then the foundation of hope cognitions also has been laid. In the language of the hope-filled 2-year-old, the agency for one's goals is inherent in the phrase "I can . . ." and the pathways are inherent in the phrase "Do it like 'dis' . . ." Just as hope was the cognitive set that fostered the evolution of our species, it also is the very stuff by which each individual can successfully journey through a lifetime.

BIRTH OF HOPE THEORY

In 1987 I faced a paradoxically frightening year. I had been awarded a sabbatical from my regular faculty position in the psychology department at the University of Kansas. In contrast to my previous routine, I was to have this extended period of time to think and write about my own ideas. I also had "celebrated" my 42nd birthday, and was on the verge of a midlife crisis in which, roughly speaking, I was wondering "where I was going."

Components of Hope Theory

In this spreading shadowy mood, I found myself reading about people who had undergone dire circumstances, including prison camps, loss of loved ones and physical capabilities, and a number of other stressors that humans encounter. From these pages there emerged a common theme that was surprising and refreshing. Namely, against the backdrop of some of the most abysmal circumstances that one could imagine, people's thoughts were filled with goals. For example, the diaries of the Nazi prison camp inmates in World War II centered around the goal of getting out of the camps (see Bettelheim, 1960). Such goals were like brightly lit lampposts that persons used cognitively to guide them from the darkness of their plights. But, beyond the goals, there appeared to be two accompanying cognitions that people exhibited. First, there was a sense of investment and energy that the persons exhibited for their goals. While it was apparent that this sense of willfulness was attached to a given goal, it also appeared that the individual was the repository of this sense of agency. In other words, the person thought of him- or herself as being the kind of person who has a sense of successful determination in meeting his or her goals. It was not simply the case, however, that such persons had only the cognition that they had the agency to reach their goals. Rather, a second component was operative. In this regard, people thought of themselves as being able to generate viable avenues to achieve their goals. This cognitive component provided the pathways for the goal-seeking process. If one or more pathways were blocked, people continued to generate additional ones. My personal "aha" experience at this point was that the ingredients of agency and pathways formed an important cognitive package. That package is hope.

Previous and Present Definitions of Hope

Before settling on this working definition of hope, however, it is useful to see how others have defined it. The dictionary typically yielded a definition such as "a wish or desire accompanied by confident expectation of its fulfillment" (*American Heritage Dictionary*, 1982, p. 622). Interestingly, however, scholarly writers on the topic of hope have emphasized the importance of goals; moreover, these writers have shared a common definitional theme in that hope involves the overall perception that goals can be met (e.g., Cantril, 1964; Farber, 1968; Frank, 1968; Frankl, 1963; Lewin, 1938; Melges & Bowlby, 1969; Menninger, 1959; Mowrer, 1960; Stotland, 1969). I would agree that hope does reflect "an overall perception that goals can be met," but what I also would suggest is that this "overall perception" actually involves the necessary subcomponents of agency and pathways. More specifically, I would define hope as "a cognitive set that is based on a reciprocally derived sense of successful (a) agency (goal-directed determination) and (b) pathways (planning of ways to meet goals)" (Snyder, Harris, et al., 1991, p. 571). This definition is depicted in Figure 2.

Several points of elaboration may be helpful in regard to this hope model. For my purposes, I would like to make a slight alteration in the saying "Where there is a will there is a way." People who have the personal sense of agency, or will, typically should have the accompanying pathways to their goals, but sometimes they may not. If the person does not have both the agency and pathways for goals, according to my model, then the cognitive set of high hope is not operative. Put another way, neither agency nor pathways alone is sufficient to obtain the high-hope cognitive set. As such, the present definition of hope may be contrasted with the usual notion of optimism. On the one hand, an optimist may believe that "things will work out," but may be lacking the pathways cognitions that become important when the practicalities of goal-directed behaviors, may be stuck. The high-hope person, on the other hand, may generate new pathways when the original avenue to goal attainment is blocked (see the "end runs" depicted in Figure 2).

Another point worth mentioning is that the analysis of agency and pathways related to a goal reiterates constantly in the cognitive activity of the individual. As can be seen by the bidirectional arrow between the agency and pathways cognitions shown in Figure 2, the set of high hope invoives multiple

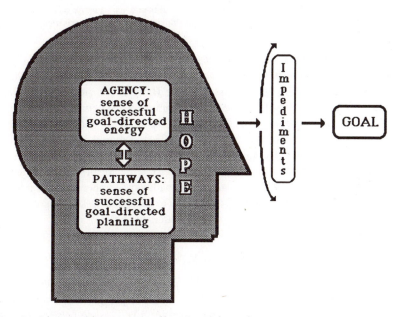

Figure 2.   Schematic of the components of hope in regard to goals.

iterations in which the elevated levels of agency-to-pathways and pathways-to-agency play off of each other.

Hope and Other Similar Constructs

The present model of hope obviously is based on the person's *cognitive* appraisals of goal-related capabilities (i.e., agency and pathways). This definition stands in contrast to older historical views that hope is one of the fundamental emotions; included in this latter group are the 13th-century theologian Thomas Aquinas (Aquinas, 1967; Arnold, 1960), Hume (1739/1888), Hartley (1749/ 1966), and Kant (1800/1978) (see also Averill, Catlin, & Chon, 1990, for a modern emotion-based analysis of hope). Although cognitive appraisals form the basis of the present model of hope, I do not mean to suggest that emotions are irrelevant to this construct. Rather, my belief is that emotions reflect the sequelae that flow out of the agency and pathways cognitive appraisals of goal-related activities. The nature of the particular emotion-related markers should be related to the level of hope. In this regard:

> the high-hope person's analysis of sufficient agency and pathways in a given goal setting should lead to the perception of relatively high probability of goal attainment, a focus on success rather than failure, a sense of challenge, and a relatively positive emotional state as goal-related activities are conceptualized and undertaken. Conversely, the low-hope person's analysis of insufficient agency and pathways in a given goal setting should lead to perceptions of relatively low probability of goal attainment, a focus on failure rather than success, a sense of ambivalence, and a relatively negative emotional state during goal-related activities. (Snyder, Harris, et al. 1991, p. 571)

Although hope shares similarities with other recent theories emphasizing cognitive/motivational states such as optimism (Scheier & Carver, 1985, 1987), generalized expectancy for success (Fibel & Hale, 1978), self-efficacy (Bandura, 1977, 1982, 1986), helplessness (Abramson, Seligman, & Teasdale, 1978; Burns & Seligman, 1991; Peterson & Bossio, 1991), and resourcefulness (Rosenbaum, 1980; Rosenbaum & Palmon, 1984), it should be noted that these latter constructs generally emphasize either the agency or the pathways components (although not necessarily labeled as such), while the present hope theory is based on an equal role for the agency and pathways components. For a fuller description of the relationship of hope theory to these other related theories, the reader is referred to Snyder, Irving, and Anderson (1991).

MEASUREMENT OF HOPE IN ADULTS

After arriving at the aforementioned definition of hope, the next step was to develop and validate an individual differences self-report scale that tapped this cognitive set. Because this process has been described in detail elsewhere (see Snyder, 1989; Snyder, Harris, et al., 1991), I provide only a brief summary here.

Selection of Items

Initially, a large number of items that reflected a sense of agency (successful determination in meeting one's goals) and pathways (the sense of being able to generate successful pathways to reach goals) were written and administered to people with instructions to rate how true each item was for each person. From this larger pool of items, four were retained as an index of the agency component, four were retained as an index of the pathways component, and the total Hope Scale score was the sum of the eight agency and pathways items (see Figure 3). Because persons can respond on a 4-point continuum to each of the eight items, total Hope Scale scores can range from a low of 8 to a high of 32.

Psychometric Properties

Statistical tests of the various psychometric properties of the Hope Scale suggested that it met or surpassed the normal standards for self-report measures. More specifically, all eight Hope Scale items intercorrelated strongly, and yet the agency and pathways subscales were easily identifiable by factor analyses (see Babyak & Snyder, 1991, for an in-depth analysis and corroboration of the agency and pathways components of the Hope Scale). Thus, the Hope Scale has internal consistency, and the factor structure identifies the agency and pathways components. In tests in which the same people retook the Hope Scale over time intervals varying from 3 to 10 weeks, the scores appeared to be temporally stable (i.e., the scale had test–retest reliability). Thus, consistent with the un-

---

Directions: Read each item carefully. Using the scale shown below, please select the number that best describes YOU and put that number in the blank provided.

1 = Definitely False   2 = Mostly False   3 = Mostly True   4 = Definitely True

   1. I can think of many ways to get out of a jam.
   2. I energetically pursue my goals.
   3. I feel tired most of the time.
   4. There are lots of ways around my problem.
   5. I am easily downed in an argument.
   6. I can think of many ways to get the things in life that are most important to me.
   7. I worry about my health.
   8. Even when others get discouraged, I know I can find a way to solve the problem.
   9. My past experiences have prepared me well for my future.
   10. I've been pretty successful in life.
   11. I usually find myself worrying about something.
   12. I meet the goals that I set for myself.

Figure 3. The Hope Scale. (The Agency subscale score is derived by summing items #2, 9, 10, and 12; the Pathways subscale score is derived by adding items #1, 4, 6, and 8. The total Hope Scale score is derived by summing the Four Agency and the four Pathways items. Items #3, 5, 7, and 11 were added as distracters so as to make the content of the scale less obvious.) (From Snyder, C.R., Harris, C., Anderson, J.R., Halleran, S.A., Irving, L.M., Sigmon, S.T., Yoshinobu, L., Gibb J., Langelle, C., & Harney P. [1991]. The will and the ways: Development and validation of an individual differences measure of hope. *Journal of Personality and Social Psychology, 60,* 585; © 1991 American Psychological Association and C.R. Snyder; reprinted by permission.)

derlying theoretical premise that hope should be a relatively enduring cognitive set, the Hope Scale scores did not change much over time.

Concurrent Validity

In an effort to find out the characteristics of high versus low hope as measured by the Hope Scale, my colleagues and I administered the scale to many different samples of people along with other self-report scales (Snyder, Harris, et al., 1991). First, we found that higher hope related to having a general sense of optimism about one's outcomes in life. Second, higher hope persons perceived that they had more control in their lives, and they reported that they were more facile at problem solving. Third, persons with higher hope were also higher in self-esteem and positive affect, and lower in reported depression and overall negative affect. Fourth, within a psychiatric inpatient sample, the persons with higher hope evidenced less pathology as measured by the Minnesota Multiphasic Personality Inventory (MMPI; Hathaway & McKinley, 1951). Fifth, when asked to give responses to stimulus words, higher hope persons elicited responses with more positive content. Sixth, higher hope persons tended to have a positive bias about the events about them, and often used humor to cope with stressful events.

Construct Validity

Turning to the actual goals that people set, we have found that higher hope persons have more goals in general in their lives, and when they are faced with a blockage to their goals, they keep engaged toward the goal by generating and trying other pathways (Snyder, Harris, et al., 1991). Thus, to twist an old saying a bit, "When the going gets tough, the hopeful keep going." Higher hope people are successful in attaining the higher goals that they set for themselves, while the lower hope persons are successful at attaining their goals that are set at an easier level. Interestingly, the higher hope persons' success in attaining their higher goals is not explicable in terms of their having superior cognitive/intellectual aptitudes. In other words, the beneficial effects of the hopeful cognitive set in regard to goal behaviors are *not* due to the higher hope persons' being intellectually brighter.

Appraisal Processes Related to Hope Scale

In studies where we asked persons to set goals in their lives, we have found that the higher hope persons perceive their goals in terms of challenges to be met; moreover, higher hope persons see their goals as being arenas for success, and they appear to have positive emotional states as they undertake their goals (Snyder, Harris, et al., 1991). The lower hope persons, however, perceive their own goals with considerable ambivalence, are rather fearful of failing, and display negative feelings. Obviously, there are qualitatively different sequelae to the higher versus the lower hopeful cognitive sets.

Coping Processes Related to Hope Scale

Lastly, it should be noted that the higher relative to the lower hope persons report that they have more coping strategies in their armamentaria, and prospective studies have shown that the higher hope persons report a more satisfactory psychological adjustment over time (Snyder, Harris, et al., 1991). The ability of Hope Scale scores to predict subsequent psychological adjustment has been very robust, and it remains even when the effects of other psychological variables are removed statistically. For example, after the predictive effects of positive affect, negative affect, positive life stress, negative life stress, optimism, and locus of control (whether one perceives the reinforcements to be within or outside one's control) are eliminated statistically, Hope Scale scores still significantly augment the prediction of mental health symptoms (Snyder, Harris, et al., 1991). The notion of hope as measured by the Hope Scale, therefore, promises to be one very useful approach to measuring the cognitive coping process. My belief is that one of the major reasons for this is that goal-directed behavior is important in a wide range of human activities, with coping being one prime example. In other words, cognitive coping often involves cognitive strategies that the person employs in order to obtain important life goals, whether the pursuit of such goals is done under facilitating or debilitating circumstances.

MEASUREMENT OF HOPE IN CHILDREN

Kid Hope Scale and Kiddy Hope Scale

The Hope Scale was developed and validated with adult populations of persons 18 through 70 years of age. My colleagues (Carla Dykeman-Berkich, Michael Rapoff, and Leanne Ware) and I are presently in the process of developing and validating two additional measures of hope for younger age groups than was the case for the Hope Scale. In particular, we are developing a Kid Hope Scale, which is a self-report index for children ages 8 through 16. The same agency and pathways components will be tapped as was the case for the adult Hope Scale, but the language is simplified so that it is understandable for the younger group. Additionally, we are in the process of developing a Kiddy Hope Scale for children ages 4 through 9. This Kiddy Hope Scale is based on the same two agency and pathways components, but instead of responding to a paper-and-pencil self-report scale, the child is read a series of short stories about two children. After hearing the stories for one pair of children, the child is asked to point to the picture (with the name of the child in the story) that is most like him or her. A series of paired stories about two different children are read to the child, and the hope score is determined by summing the number of times that the child identifies with the child in the story who is manifesting a sense of agency or pathways for his or her goals.

Future Directions for Theory and Research with Children

With the eventual availability of these measures of hope for children, one goal would be to undertake longitudinal research in which we trace the development of hope, as well as the predictions for various life outcomes (e.g., school performance, psychological well-being, health; see Snyder, Irving, & Anderson, 1991). Furthermore, a looming question for future research involves the sources of hope for those children who exhibit high levels. For example, to what degree does the child's mother or father contribute to the child's level of hope? My hunch is that hope may be found in family or environmental contexts that would seemingly be less than positive, but as long as the child has one forceful role model, hope may be engendered. This model may be a parent, a member of the extended family (e.g., a big brother or sister, an aunt or uncle, a grandmother or grandfather), or an older friend.

Michael Rapoff, one of my colleagues at the University of Kansas Medical Center, and I are beginning a series of videotaped interviews with children who have manifested a sense of hope in the face of serious physical stressors such as cancer, cystic fibrosis, asthma, and juvenile arthritis. The lessons of these remarkable children are the same ones to which I alluded earlier in my brief review of the emergence of hope in seemingly dire human circumstances. Namely, the high-hope child often is the one who has undergone some major ongoing trauma, and yet he or she remains hopeful. With such children, it appears that one significant role model is a necessary ingredient to foster hope (recall my earlier suggestion that my mother was such a model for me). Conversely, it occasionally may be the case that the child may serve as a source of hope for the parents or healthcare professionals (see Kelly, 1991, for an excellent example, that of 14-year-old Corey Svien). In this latter regard, our eventual goal is to develop a series of case histories about these hopeful children, and to publish these in a book entitled *Faces of Hope: Lessons From the Children*. As the subtitle suggests, we have much to learn from children and their significant role models about the acquisition and maintenance of hope.

HOPES LOST AND FOUND

I have become increasingly convinced that many of the most important issues in psychology, both in terms of theoretical and practical significance, must be traced to developmental questions. This is especially the case with hope. Although I have briefly discussed some of the basic individual differences questions about children with low and high hope in the previous section of this chapter, I now focus upon the task of parents, teachers, and society as we begin to consider our role in fostering hope. Parents in general, and especially those of us who have raised or are still raising children with developmental or learning disabilities, may find that our children appear to be lacking in hope. Although my subsequent comments are perhaps the most speculative ones in this chapter,

I nevertheless make the rather bold assertion that the present hope theory may provide a useful framework for beginning to understand how hope operates in the lives of our children; more importantly, hope theory may yield suggestions for nurturing hope in our children.

I begin the present analysis by suggesting that we can conceptualize the goal-directed hope cognitions of our children in the context of the schematic depicted in Figure 4. Here, the agency and pathways components of hope are crossed with a focus of "the person" or "the environment." This approach yields a 2 × 2 matrix in which we can examine each of the four quadrants where the child may need to enhance his or her level of hope. As can be seen in Figure 4, this hypothetical child with an overall sense of low hope has few resources (a resource is signified by a + as shown in Figure 4) relative to the weaknesses (a weakness is signified by a − as shown in Figure 4) in each of the four quadrants.

A first point that emerges is that a child with low hope is *not totally devoid of resources*. In this regard, hope is only "lost" in the sense that the few resources are swamped by the weaknesses in any given quadrant. To enhance the sense of hope in children, we must do the careful analyses of whatever strengths the child already brings to each quadrant. Over time, the task is to increase the spread of goal-directed strengths in our children in one or more of the four quadrants. As can be seen in Figure 5, therefore, we help our children to build their goal-directed strengths.

Facilitating the Child's Agency/In Person

It may be helpful to examine each of the four quadrants shown in Figure 4, and to discuss the possibilities for enhancing the child's strengths. First, consider the upper left quadrant involving the child's agency as she or he describes her- or himself in particular goal-directed activities. In this sense, the agency is "in the person (child)" because it is the child's perception that is the focus of the inquiry. Agency should be fueled by the child's perception of successful goal-

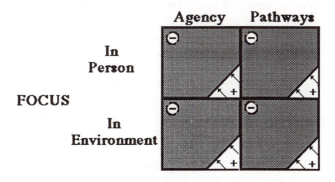

Figure 4. Schematic of focus (in person, in environment) × hope component (agency, pathways) quadrants for a child with low hope.

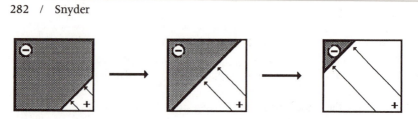

Figure 5.   Schematic of change from low to high in given hope quadrant over time.

directed determination in the past, present, and the future *in regard to a particular goal*. This latter point is worth elaborating in that it is helpful to have the
child articulate the goal that he or she is pursuing as clearly as possible. Children can understand and quickly use the terminology of goals because goals are
often very concrete. Clarifying the goal, in and of itself, is sometimes a source
of renewed determination on the part of the child. Additionally, the child may
have forgotten some past success in the very same goal arena, and the adult can
help to rekindle the sense of willfulness that was inherent in the previous success experience. Yet another approach would involve telling the child stories of
other similar children who have undertaken the same goals that the child is
considering. Naturally, the stories, whether told to or read by the child, involve
another child protagonist who has come to perceive her- or himself as being
successfully agential toward a given goal. If there are movies or videotapes
available (recall my previous discussion of the videotapes that Michael Rapoff
and I are preparing), these would be potential sources of agency for the child.
Likewise, simply having the child imagine him- or herself in the particular situation and being successful at goal attainment may enhance that child's sense of
agency.

Facilitating the Child's Pathways/In Person

Moving to the quadrant in the upper right portion of the matrix in Figure 4, the
focus is on the child's perceived sense of being able to generate successful pathways for his or her particular goals. The approaches outlined in the previous
paragraph can be applied here, but with an emphasis on having the child remember how he or she has generated successful pathways in the past. Or,
through stories, the child can be given examples of other children who have
produced pathways to their goals; moreover, imagery can be employed to enhance the child's self-perceptions of pathways capabilities. The point of these
lessons is to have children come to view themselves as being more capable of
finding ways to get what they want. Merely clarifying the goals may enable the
child to realize that she or he has more capabilities at producing pathways than
previously thought.

    With both the perceived agency and pathways "in the person (child)," the
low-hope child may tend to get swamped by perceived weaknesses in regard to
goal attainment, and it is therefore necessary to build new self-perceptions. In

doing this, it is important that the child and the parent (or teacher, psychologist, or helper) realize that it takes some time to make such changes, and as such everyone inolved should be prepared for slow progress.

Facilitating the Child's Agency/In Environment

Many psychologists have tended to look for the solutions for changes in people as residing solely in the person's perception. This is the basis for the agency and pathways quadrants shown in the top row of Figure 4 and discussed in the previous paragraphs. I certainly agree that to understand and change hope we must deal with the cognitive sets that people (in this case, little people) have about their goals, but I believe that a full analysis of hope demands that we also look at the environmental underpinnings of agency and pathways (the bottom two quadrants of Figure 4). In regard to the lower left quadrant, the child's agency that may be related to environmental factors, I would suggest that it may be useful to set up some system for rewarding the child's agential cognitions. Or, working with the home context, or with teachers and schools, we can build in successes that will be translated to the child's self-perceptions.

Facilitating the Child's Pathways/In Environment

For the lower right quadrant of Figure 4 involving the pathways related to the environment, we can teach the child to break down a long-term goal into short-term subgoals. (Persons with high Hope Scale scores suggest that they do this routinely as they pursue their goals [Snyder, Harris, et al., 1991].) Another skill that may be taught pertains to problem-solving training. Skill acquisition training in a particular arena should enable the child to derive a sense of agency and pathways from environmental sources (e.g., teachers, teaching machines), and these gains should translate to the child's perceptions about him- or herself.

Spill-Over Effect

Although I have treated the four quadrants separately, it should be the case that gains in one arena should spill over into the other quadrants. A child who begins to have agential self-cognitions, for example, may soon find that his or her pathways cognitions also are growing. Conversely, the child with burgeoning pathways cognitions may find the agency cognitions also are coming to life.

Learning To Regoal

Beyond the previously discussed approaches for facilitating the growth of hope in each of the four quadrants, there are two other strategies for obtaining higher hope that can be deduced from the clues produced by persons scoring high on the Hope Scale. If one is really stuck, it may be the better part of valor to disengage temporarily (or perhaps permanently) from the original unobtainable goal and regoal. Regoaling appears to be a very freeing and energizing process, and as such this may be a skill we should impart to our children.

The regoaling process also is important for the parents of a child. In this regard, parents of children with physical or developmental disabilities often must change the nature of an original goal. For example, if the child cannot walk, he or she can gain mobility through the use of a wheelchair; the child who cannot talk can learn to communicate through sign language.

Learning To Laugh

Another characteristic of high-hope people is that they appear to be capable of laughing at both themselves and their circumstances. I am reminded here of a conclusion that a recent therapy client and I reached: If you don't laugh at yourself, you have missed the biggest joke of all. As parents and helpers, not only should we teach our children the regoaling and humor strategies, but we should learn and use them ourselves.

Final Comments on Fostering Hope in Children

I do not mean to suggest that the process described in this section for promulgating hope in our children are either easy or fast. It is empowering, however, for the entire family to know that there are things that can be done to make the hope of the child and the family grow. Children are extremely sensitive to the verbal and nonverbal messages that we send, and this is especially the case when it comes to hope. To know that hope is rarely totally lost and that it can be found and nurtured are important lessons for the grownups as well as the children.

HOPE JOURNEY IN PERSPECTIVE

The fundamental premise upon which I have built hope theory is that we human beings, from the youngest to the oldest, are goal-directed creatures. As I think about goals at the larger societal level, I have three requests to make of all of us. First, it strikes me that there are not enough acceptable goals that are highly rewarded. The big goals appear to involve money making, physical appearance, intellectual achievement, and athletic accomplishments. Why not add caring for others, protecting the environment, and other more altruistic goals? Second, there are not enough *reachable* goals for the majority of our people. The skills and education necessary to obtain the few select goals are increasing with the advances of technology. Third, whether it is based on gender, ethnicity, or physical or psychological status, the discriminatory limiting of the number of persons who have access to the valued and obtainable goals in our society is counterproductive. The majority, and not the minority, of children should be allowed to "play the hope game" as I have outlined it in this chapter. Indeed, if the majority of our children cannot "play the hope game," a tremendous talent pool will be wasted. None of these three trends, if they are indeed operative, are conducive to allowing anything but a select, homogeneous group of our children to succeed in the future. If anything, it seems as if a smaller and smaller proportion of people have access to the major rewards in our society. To keep hope alive, we therefore must make certain that our society allows a wider segment of our citizens to have access to a more diverse and obtainable set of goals.

In closing, I suggest that the journey metaphor is a powerful one for the endless lessons of coping that we pursue in a lifetime. It is not just by chance that two of the most widely read psychology books over the last 20 years— Robert Pirsig's (1974/1975) *Zen and the Art of Motorcycle Maintenance* and M. Scott Peck's (1978) *The Road Less Traveled*—are built upon journey metaphors. We are collectively on a journey from the past to the future. As such, if we are to continue our journey from the apes to truly civilized people, hope will help us to reach our destination.

ABOUT THE AUTHOR

C. R. Snyder, Ph.D. As director of the doctoral and postdoctoral clinical psychology programs at the University of Kansas, much of my time is spent in coordinating the educational efforts of faculty and graduate students. Additionally, I oversee the research activities of undergraduate, graduate, and postdoctoral students who work with me on the measurement and intervention issues related to my theory of hope. I am very interested in the diversity in children and adults, and see this as an asset that we need to cultivate, rather than squelch.

REFERENCES

Abramson, L.V., Seligman, M.E.P., & Teasdale, J.D. (1978). Learned helplessness in humans: Critique and reformulation. *Journal of Abnormal Psychology, 87,* 49–74.
American Heritage Dictionary (2nd college ed.). (1982). Boston: Houghton Mifflin.
Aquinas, T. (1967). *Summa theologiae: Vol. 19. The emotions.* New York: McGraw-Hill.
Arnold, B. (1960). *Emotion and personality.* New York: Columbia University Press.
Averill, J.R., Catlin, G., & Chon, K.K. (1990). *Rules of hope.* New York: Springer-Verlag.
Babyak, M., & Snyder, C.R. (1991). *The Hope Scale: An analysis of the underlying structure.* Unpublished manuscript, University of Kansas, Lawrence.
Bandura, A. (1977). Self-efficacy: Toward a unifying theory of behavior. *Psychological Review, 84,* 191–215.
Bandura, A. (1982). Self-efficacy mechanism in human agency. *American Psychologist, 37,* 122–147.
Bandura, A. (1986). *Social foundations of thought and action: A social cognitive theory.* Englewood Cliffs, NJ: Prentice-Hall.
Bettelheim, B. (1960). *The informed heart.* Glencoe, IL: Free Press.
Burns, M.O., & Seligman, M.E.P. (1991). Explanatory style, helplessness, and depression. In C.R. Snyder & D.R. Forsyth (Eds.), *Handbook of social and clinical psychology: The health perspective* (pp. 267–284). Elmsford, NY: Pergamon Press.
Cantril, H. (1964). The human design. *Journal of Individual Psychology, 20,* 129–136.
Farber, M.L. (1968). *Theory of suicide.* New York: Funk & Wagnall's.

Fibel, B., & Hale, W.D. (1978). The Generalized Expectancy for Success Scale—A new measure. *Journal of Consulting and Clinical Psychology, 46,* 924–931.

Frank, J.D. (1968). The role of hope in psychotherapy. *Journal of Psychiatry, 5,* 383–395.

Frankl, V. (1963). *Man's search for meaning.* New York: Washington Square Press.

Hartley, D. (1966). *Observations on man.* Gainesville, FL: Scholars Facsimiles & Reprints. (Original work published 1749)

Hathaway, S.R., & McKinely, M.C. (1951). *The Minnesota Multiphasic Personality Inventory (MMPI) manual.* New York: Psychological Corporation.

Hume, D. (1888). *Treatise of human nature. Book II* (L.A. Selby-Bigge, Ed.). Oxford: Clarendon Press. (Original work published 1739)

Kant, I. (1978). *Anthropology from a pragmatic point of view* (V.L. Dowdell, Trans.). Carbondale: Southern Illinois University Press. (Original work published 1800)

Kaplan, L.J. (1978). *Oneness and separateness: From infant to individual.* New York: Simon & Schuster.

Kelly, M. (1991, Summer). Bearing the burdens: A young cancer patient shares his wisdom about life, friendship, and healing. *Health Sciences,* pp. 15–17.

Lewin, K. (1938). The conceptual representation and measurement of psychological forces. *Contributions to Psychological Theory, 1,* 1–36.

Melges, R., & Bowlby, J. (1969). Types of hopelessness in psychopathological processes. *Archives of General Psychiatry, 20,* 690–699.

Menninger, K. (1959). The academic lecture on hope. *American Journal of Psychiatry, 116,* 481–491.

Mowrer, O.H. (1960). *Learning theory and behavior.* New York: John Wiley & Sons.

Peck, M.S. (1978). *The road less traveled: A new psychology of love, traditional values and spiritual growth.* New York: Simon & Schuster.

Peterson, C., & Bossio, L.M. (1991). *Health and optimism.* New York: Free Press.

Pirsig, R.M. (1975). *Zen and the art of motorcycle maintenance.* New York: Bantam Books. (Original work published by William Morrow, 1974)

Rosenbaum, M. (1980). A schedule for assessing self-control behaviors: Preliminary findings. *Behavior Therapy, 11,* 109–121.

Rosenbaum, M., & Palmon, N. (1984). Helplessness and resourcefulness in coping with epilepsy. *Journal of Consulting and Clinical Psychology, 52,* 244–253.

Scheier, M.F., & Carver, C.S. (1985). Optimism, coping, and health: Assessment and implications of generalized outcome expectancies. *Health Psychology, 4,* 219–247.

Scheier, M.F., & Carver, C.S. (1987). Dispositional optimism and physical well-being: The influence of generalized outcome expectancies. *Journal of Personality, 55,* 169–247.

Snyder, C.R. (1989). Reality negotiation: From excuses to hope and beyond. *Journal of Social and Clinical Psychology, 8,* 130–157.

Snyder, C.R., Harris, C., Anderson, J.R., Holleran, S.A., Irving, L.M., Sigmon, S.T., Yoshinobu, L., Gibb, J., Langelle, C., & Harney, P. (1991). The will and the ways: Development and validation of an individual differences measure of hope. *Journal of Personality and Social Psychology, 60,* 570–585.

Snyder, C.R., Irving, L.M., & Anderson, J.R. (1991). Hope and health. In C.R. Snyder & D.R. Forsyth (Eds.), *Handbook of social and clinical psychology: The health perspective* (pp. 285–305). Elmsford, NY: Pergamon Press.

Stotland, E. (1969). *The psychology of hope.* San Francisco: Jossey-Bass.

THE PARTICIPATORY PROCESS IN ACTION

Throughout the conference, small group meetings were held to discuss issues related to research on cognitive coping and families who have a member with a disability. Each small group meeting had members of all groups represented at the conference—families, service providers, and researchers/theorists. From the notes of these meetings, information was compiled and synthesized for the two chapters in this section.

The next chapter, 21, by Joan Patterson, Shirley Behr, and Martha Blue-Banning, is based on discussions that focused on issues surrounding the research process, such as the ethics of research, the dissemination of results to all interested parties, methods for obtaining diverse samples, ways to measure the concepts involved in research on families and cognitive coping, and the nature and intent of research questions. A synthesis of these discussions and a summary of the perspectives offered by the different participants are presented in this chapter.

Chapter 22, by Douglas Murphy and Janet Marquis, focuses directly on research questions. That is, what questions related to cognitive coping and to the needs of families who have a member with a disability are most important for researchers and theorists to address *now*? The lists of questions in this chapter reflect the issues that are of concern to families and service providers as well as researchers and theorists. The topics for research that emerged from the small group discussions ranged from very concrete and practical issues to quite abstract and theoretical issues. The chapter organizes these topics under three main themes: 1) need for clarification of definitions and concepts, 2) need for research on the various factors of individual coping style, and 3) need for research in the area of family coping. The agenda discussed in this chapter is presented as a "starting point" for what is hoped will be a dynamic, ongoing process of research in cognitive coping.

chapter 21

Putting Participatory Research into Action
Conference Dialogue Between Family Members, Providers, and Researchers

Joan M. Patterson, Shirley K. Behr,
and Martha J. Blue-Banning

As stated in the Introduction, one of the guiding principles of the conference from which this book evolved was to enable representatives from each of the stakeholding constituencies—theorists, researchers, service providers, and family members—to talk with each other about cognitive coping in a way that would advance their work and would make a difference in the lives of families who have a member with a developmental disability. In essence, the conference itself was a prime example of participatory research at work. The dialogue that ensued was provocative and rich and there was a kind of synergy that emerged from the diverse viewpoints represented. Critical issues to be considered in future work emerged from this dialogue in the general sessions and in small group discussions. The small groups were organized to include representatives of each of the constituencies. In these groups, the next steps for cognitive coping research were discussed, with a particular focus on problems and solutions related to methodology, sampling, and dissemination.

The purpose of this chapter is to provide some evidence for participatory research in action by, first, synthesizing these group discussions and highlighting the important issues that emerged. Second, "perspectives to consider," offered by participants for addressing these issues, are summarized so that they may be used as guidelines for future work by theorists, researchers, service providers, and families. The primary issues discussed were: 1) ethics in conducting research, 2) paying attention to diversity, 3) the nature and intent of research questions, 4) measurement of research variables, and 5) dissemination to multiple audiences.

ETHICS IN CONDUCTING RESEARCH

What happens to and for individuals who take part in research studies? While informed consent is a prerequisite for doing research in any institution, there often is variability regarding how much research participants are told about the study: its purpose, what they will be asked to do, how the information will be used, what risks and benefits there are to them, and so on. High standards and best practices for managing informed consent need to be explored and implemented, especially for those who are more vulnerable (i.e., children and those with severe disabilities). Researchers need to acknowledge that participating in a research study is a kind of intervention in itself because being asked and answering questions can change behaviors; participants need to be aware of this. Strategies should be designed to make participation in research studies a worthwhile and meaningful effort for everyone involved.

Since most researchers aggregate the data obtained from the participants and report about groups, there is often no effort to interpret findings that are meaningful to individual family members who have participated. Sometimes expensive assessments (that ordinarily would have to be paid for by the family) have been done as part of the research protocol; yet there is no provision for, or informed consent procedures preclude, providing individual feedback to the participant. In some cases, the participant may have no other opportunity for this assessment.

Researchers need to examine their obligations to individuals or families who have multiple needs, some of which may not be addressed by the research study. Similarly, researchers must be sensitized to the reality that the measures or procedures used may result in the identification of persons at serious risk and in need of interventions; procedures should be developed for providing participants with needed information, services, or protection.

When intervention studies are undertaken, the potential loss of benefits to a participant who is randomly assigned to a control group needs to be evaluated. The point at which it becomes imperative to suspend a study because the intervention is "known" to have benefits is the critical issue here and often more difficult to determine with psychosocial interventions. Researchers should consider the possibility of research designs that do not require the use of control groups.

Perspectives to consider include:

1. If a study participant wants to participate in an intervention sooner than it is scheduled (or when it is not scheduled), he or she should be allowed to drop out and be reclassified as a nonparticipant in the study.
2. Providing reimbursement to participants for their time and effort can help them feel vested in the research and perceive that their time is valued.
3. If participants indicate that they have needs beyond the research effort, they should be offered information about local, state, and/or national resources and services.

4. Researchers need to consider informed consent procedures carefully to make sure that participants really understand what is being asked of them and what the possible risks and benefits are. They also need to understand that services to them will, in no way, be jeopardized by their willingness to participate or not.
5. Findings obtained from research studies should be shared with participants in sensitive, respectful, and meaningful ways. Participants should not be patronized and have information withheld to protect them.

PAYING ATTENTION TO DIVERSITY

Designing quality research requires that researchers know and understand the culture, ethnicity, socioeconomic status (SES), religious beliefs, and values of the persons they study. They need to find ways to access information about the general characteristics of study participants from different backgrounds without risking generalizations or stereotyping. There is a fine line between having a sensitive awareness of differences and stereotyping groups of individuals.

Research samples should be inclusive and representative of the populations being studied. Obtaining samples that are truly representative is difficult; often the sample is determined simply by expediency. Threats to external validity too often are ignored or minimized at a time when research knowledge is critically needed for policy formation, for training professionals, and for program development and implementation. There needs to be a willingness to work through layers of bureaucracy to get access to and recruit population-based samples, even though this is costly in terms of time and money. Funding sources need to take this into account in setting expectations and awarding funds.

The same families that are underrepresented in the wider service delivery system are often the same ones not represented in research studies. Researchers and service providers, who are primarily from the middle and upper class, are often naive concerning the barriers that deter participation both in research studies and in services. Studies about barriers to accessing and using the full range of services need to be undertaken. Similarly, studies about barriers to participation in research projects need to be done. It is not sufficient to say that these professional systems comprise educated persons who relate poorly to those of a different race or social class.

Persons representing these underserved and understudied groups need to be included in all phases of planning and carrying out both research and service. Many argue that this is a "Catch-22" because there are so few persons of minority cultures or lower SES trained to do research or provide service. However, this is the same argument that long prevailed in excluding persons with disabilities from participation in the research process and program planning and service delivery. Inclusion of the full range of diverse constituencies must come first because they have experiential competence; joining the ranks of professionally trained providers and researchers (should that be desired) will follow. The inclusion of persons of color on research teams and service delivery teams should be a high priority.

Many conference participants emphasized the need to focus on salutogenesis versus pathogenesis when studying persons with disabilities. However, there is not unanimity across all groups on what is a salutogenic, healthy, functional, competent outcome. For example, in mainstream American culture, autonomy, independence, and self-sufficiency for all persons, including those with disabilities (e.g., the phrase "independent living" is widely used), is valued; however, some cultural groups value and prefer group solidarity over independence. In this example, judging dependence as an undesirable outcome may be in direct conflict with the preference of a cultural group. (For an in-depth look at this topic, see Lynch & Hanson, 1992.)

Many of the instruments used in research projects have been developed and tested using predominantly white, middle-class populations. The reliability and validity of these instruments have not been demonstrated for persons from different cultural and socioeconomic backgrounds. The same question (or response choices) may mean different things to different respondents, particularly those of different cultures or lifestyles or with different beliefs and values. More grounded approaches are needed to develop instruments that are reliable and valid for persons from diverse backgrounds.

Similarly, many instruments have been developed for persons without disabilities and have no known reliability and validity for persons who have disabilities. Group comparisons or comparisons to norms can lead to invalid results and to the creation of or perpetuation of stereotypes and biases.

Perspectives to consider include:

1. In all of our work, we need to cultivate positive attitudes and show greater sensitivity and respect for other ways of thinking, feeling, and being—especially for persons who are different from ourselves.
2. Research methods that allow for greater understanding of persons who differ from the mainstream of middle-class white America should be employed, for example, qualitative, anthropological methods.
3. Research teams and service delivery teams should include persons who represent the groups being studied.
4. Researchers should take care not to confound differences due to race and ethnicity with differences due to socioeconomic status.
5. Care should be taken to develop and use research instruments that have tested reliability and validity for the population being studied, especially for racial and ethnic minorities and persons with disabilities.
6. Studies should be undertaken of barriers to participation by diverse groups in research studies and in programs and services.

7. In recruiting study participants, every effort should be made to obtain an inclusive and representative sample. Funding agencies should be encouraged to provide the financial support needed to do this kind of work.

NATURE AND INTENT OF RESEARCH QUESTIONS

Who decides what research questions are worth asking? All too often, a researcher may unwittingly ask a question in a way that shapes the answer she or he will find. For example, if a researcher asks about the prevalence of negative outcomes (e.g., depression in caregivers or behavior problems in children with disabilities) and uses instruments that measure negative outcomes, he or she is bound to find a certain amount of this. In contrast, if a salutogenic perspective is taken (see Antonovksy, chap. 8, this volume), and the question asked is "Why do so many people do so well in the face of the many chronic challenges associated with disability?" competence and resilience will be found in research participants. In other words, careful attention needs to be given to the nature of the research question, why an answer to it is desired in the first place, and what outcomes are being examined.

For example, on the one hand, there are some service providers who seem to be primarily interested in documenting the presence of pathology in persons with disabilities and their family members. Pathology suggests a need for treatment and hence the need for persons to provide these services. Families, on the other hand, usually want to know how well they are doing and what resources and behaviors will help them to succeed.

With regard to outcomes such as depression or pain or sadness, there was considerable discussion among conference participants about how different constituencies view this and whether, in fact, it is a measure of pathology or should even be construed as totally undesirable. There is evidence that persons living with chronic conditions often carry along a certain amount of sadness and pain, even when they are functioning effectively (Breslau & Davis, 1986). If a good outcome is defined as the absence of suffering, it would be possible to miss how well a family or person with a disability is actually coping and managing. In other cultures more oppressed than our own, Antonovsky (a conference participant) noted, pain and happiness are more openly acknowledged to coexist. Families living with disability report this too. Hence, only focusing on pain and believing that a good outcome is when it is absent or gone may overlook all that is healthy and functional about such a person or family. While this is a controversial issue in that no one advocates that we should be oblivious to the suffering of families, the issue of the meaning of sadness in the lives of persons coping with chronic challenges warrants more consideration and study.

The source of funding is another factor that often influences the research questions asked and the studies done. Given the competition for scarce resources and the pressure within research institutions to obtain research grants and publish papers, investigators often study what they know will get funded and what they can publish. For many, there is a question as to whether some studies really add to the body of knowledge that will improve the system of providing services to persons with disabilities and their families and training professionals to do so. To guard against this tendency, it is important that all of the stakeholding constituencies participate in the process of helping funding agencies set the research agenda and establish priorities.

Policymakers often are interested in different research questions, particularly ones that have social and financial implications. Policymakers are most concerned about policies that can reduce public costs, that make families more self-sufficient, and that reduce the need for public programs and services. In addition, policymakers often place greater emphasis on short-term outcomes in an effort to retain personal credibility with the constituencies that elect them. This makes it harder to demonstrate the efficacy of systemic intervention, as well as preventive interventions, for which it often takes longer to realize the true benefit or even the true cost savings.

Perspectives to consider include:

1. In formulating research questions, researchers should ask persons with disabilities and family members what they want to know, should listen to them, and should incorporate their concerns in the research questions.
2. Similarly, researchers should ask service providers as well as policymakers what they need to know to do their work more effectively and ask them to state research questions.
3. All of the stakeholders involved with research should be cognizant of and clear about their individual values and biases that may be influencing the research activity.
4. More research questions should be focused on the healthy end of the continuum—on why persons succeed. Measures that assess variability in health and competence should be developed and used. It is important to remember that competence is not just the absence of pathology, but is the opposite end of the continuum and has its own normal distribution. Perhaps it is only one standard deviation on the low end of competence that overlaps with one standard deviation on the high end of pathology.

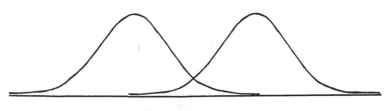

range of pathology   range of competence

5. Care should be taken not to pathologize persons who show patterns of functioning that differ from the researchers' values. Rather, it is important to examine consensus among any given cultural group about what is a desirable outcome and to understand desirable outcomes from the point of view of those being studied.

6. More emphasis should be placed on long-term as well as short-term outcomes. The quick fix may not have long-lasting effects. More longitudinal studies and long-term follow-up studies are needed to determine the long-term outcomes of an experience or an intervention; funding for such studies should be encouraged.

MEASUREMENT OF RESEARCH VARIABLES

In any interdisciplinary group of researchers, theorists, service providers, and families, there is a lack of clarity in definitions of variables and constructs, to say nothing of a lack of consensus. For example, the word *coping* can have different meanings. Janet Vohs, a parent and conference participant (see chap. 4, this volume), expressed concern that coping can have a pejorative connotation, suggesting that persons or families who cope are overburdened with life in a way that sets them apart from others who presumably don't have to cope. Even in this book, which focuses on one particular type of coping—cognitive coping—the authors have used different definitions. We must be sensitive to the different meanings and connotations conveyed in the language of our concepts so we don't create barriers to effective collaborative work. Even if we agree on which word to use, it is unlikely that there will be total consensus on a theoretical definition, to say nothing of an operational definition. However, it is still possible to collaborate with each other and learn from each other if care is taken to start from a theoretical base, provide conceptual definitions of constructs, and clearly state what the operational measures are. Staying well grounded in theory (letting it inform definitions and letting findings shape and test theory) will also enhance science, since ultimately it is only theory that is generalizable.

For the many researchers attempting to measure both family constructs and individual constructs, it is important to keep the distinctions between these two units of analysis clear. Some constructs can only occur at the individual level, such as thinking, although they are mistakenly applied to the family unit at times. Ransom (1986) has suggested that there are at least three levels of family measurement: 1) a family member reports a subjective opinion about the family unit, such as "we are close"; 2) individual family member self-reports are compared to obtain a consensus or a discrepancy score; and 3) an outside observer rates the family unit on some property. We need to be cautious when much of the literature uses the term *family,* when data are derived from mothers and/or fathers only.

There are, however, true family-level or group measures, such as degree of consensus about beliefs. Also, there are certain structural outcome measures of the group, such as divorce or the person with a disability living at home, that often are of interest to policymakers.

There is a need to incorporate more than quantitative measures in research designs. This is particularly true when phenomenological constructs such as "meanings," beliefs, definitions, and cognitions are being studied. Qualitative methods need to be used, along with quantitative ones. Funding agencies, as well as academic institutions, should be encouraged to support such studies. It is often qualitative information that can be translated into useful and effective information for persons with disabilities and their families.

There is concern that one-shot, cross-sectional measurement, or even annual measurement in a longitudinal study may be inadequate to capture the richness of family process as it unfolds over time. Particularly when adaptation is being studied, there is a need for many more data points in a short span of time to capture the daily processes that contribute to adaptation. (See Tennen, Suls, & Affleck, 1991, for a discussion of issues related to daily experience research.)

Perspectives to consider include:

1. Researchers are encouraged to provide clear conceptual definitions of the constructs in their studies. Ideally, these definitions will be derived from theory.
2. A reliable and valid operational definition of the construct should follow from the conceptual definition.
3. Family-level constructs should be differentiated from individual-level constructs and they, too, should have clear conceptual and operational definitions.
4. Qualitative methods should be encouraged to complement quantitative studies.
5. More micro-analytic studies of daily process are needed to capture day-to-day fluctuations of living with and adapting to chronic conditions.

DISSEMINATION TO MULTIPLE AUDIENCES

The age-old question of "If a tree falls in the forest and no one is present, is there sound?" is an appropriate analogy to the issue of dissemination. If knowledge learned from research does not reach people who can benefit from it, is it knowledge? Conference participants struggled with the reality that there are many constituencies who can benefit from what is learned by doing research—but, too often, some of them do not have ready or practical access to this information. Who is responsible for dissemination? To which audiences? Using what strategies?

While there is ready consensus that there are multiple audiences—researchers, service providers, policymakers, and persons with disabilities and their family members—it is the researcher audience that seems to have benefited most from dissemination efforts. Researchers publish in journals read by other researchers because these are the only publications that are genuinely valued among most of their academic peers and the rewards in academia (e.g., tenure) flow from this. "Publish or perish" has long been the motto for academicians and most resent it. However, researchers should be encouraged to write more for popular audiences. We should work for institutional change that will allow this to be valued and supported, and encourage tenured faculty to lead the way in these efforts.

The audience that conference participants thought to be neglected most in dissemination efforts is consumers: persons with disabilities and their family members. Ironically, it is they who stand to benefit most from research results (assuming that meaningful research questions are addressed). The primary barriers keeping research findings from consumers appear to be: 1) the language in which researchers write, which is often full of jargon; and 2) the vehicles in which they publish, which are primarily journals. In addition to journal publication, which is necessary for dissemination to the scientific community, research findings need to be written in a style useful to consumer audiences and need to be disseminated in popularized media sources readily accessible to most consumers. Newspapers, magazines, self-help books, television and radio programs, videotapes, and audiotapes are examples of media sources that should be tapped to include more information about supporting people with disabilities.

While some researchers are capable of writing in a popularized style, and do so, others are not. In the latter case, ways to link researchers (or at least their findings) to popular media writers should be explored.

Several ideas were offered for how research findings could be disseminated more effectively to consumer audiences.

Perspectives to consider include:

1. Contact should be made with the public relations office or the research technology transfer office of the universities or institutions where the research is done. They often are interested and anxious to get this information out because it also benefits the institution.
2. For research and training centers, whose mission includes dissemination (as well as research), and for other centers doing multiple research studies, staff should be hired who can effectively translate research findings into language and formats more accessible to consumers and who also have the skills to find consumer markets where it can be distributed effectively.
3. Parent centers, parent-to-parent networks, and other organizations serving persons with disabilities should be primary targets for distributing re-

search findings. Through their newsletters, conferences, and other mechanisms, they maintain contact with multiple audiences.

4. Publications already targeted for persons with disabilities and their families, such as *Exceptional Parent*, should be contacted and encouraged to publish research findings.

5. A kind of *"Reader's Digest"* approach to summarizing research findings would be an excellent publication for several audiences that do not have time to read the journals: policymakers, service providers, and family members.

6. Disseminating information using newer technology such as teleconferencing, computerized bulletin boards or electronic mail, and toll-free telephone numbers to resource information centers should be explored. This may require translating research findings into smaller bits of information.

In any dissemination effort, caution has to be taken not to overinterpret or overgeneralize research findings. When working with popular media, this is a particular challenge because they tend to report in a more sensational style to capture attention. Another caveat researchers should keep in mind when translating research results for multiple audiences is not to be patronizing by "talking down" to the nonresearcher.

Finally, it is important to keep in mind that responsibility for dissemination rests with all the constituencies involved. Families and service providers need to be proactive in stating what they need and how it might best be received. Researchers need to be creative and responsive to these requests. Again, this brings us back to the importance of participatory research. When all of the constituencies are involved in the research process, the likelihood of planning for and following through with multiple dissemination strategies is enhanced.

CONCLUSION

Despite the differing perspectives that often emerged in the conference dialogue, most participants agreed that the tension it sometimes produced ultimately enhances the research process. Researchers and theorists were challenged to make their questions/concepts more relevant and their methods more sensitive; service providers were challenged to incorporate research findings into best practices and to be more accountable for their interventions; and families were challenged to be more assertive with both groups of professionals and to raise the questions that need to be answered. Together we can make our work more sensitive, honest, relevant, and effective.

ABOUT THE AUTHORS

Joan M. Patterson, Ph.D., Shirley K. Behr, Ph.D., and Martha J. Blue-Banning, M.Ed. The three of us participated in the cognitive coping conference, each bringing our personal and professional experience in the field of disabilities. Martha is the parent of a 15-year-old son with Down syndrome, and is a doctoral student at the University of Kansas, majoring in family studies and disability. Shirley has been a primary caregiver of a family member with a disability. Joan has been challenged with her own chronic illness for the past 13 years. Professionally, each of us is involved in research, training, and service delivery with persons with disabilities and their families so they can successfully manage the challenges they face and have the opportunity to realize the lives they want for themselves. At the conference, we experienced firsthand the value of dialogue and collaboration among parents, service providers, and researchers who share a commitment to improving the lives of persons with disabilities. This chapter represents our effort to capture some of the spirit and content of this dialogue.

REFERENCES

Breslau, N., & Davis, G.C. (1986). Chronic stress and major depression. *Archives of General Psychiatry, 43,* 309–314.

Lynch, E.W., & Hanson, M.J. (Eds.). (1992). *Developing cross-cultural competence: A guide for working with young children and their families.* Baltimore: Paul H. Brookes Publishing Co.

Ransom, D.C. (1986). Research on the family in health, illness and care—State of the art. *Family Systems Medicine, 4,* 329–336.

Tennen, H., Suls, J., & Affleck, G. (Eds.). (1991). Personality and daily experience [Special issue]. *Journal of Personality, 53*(3).

chapter 22

A Research Agenda

Douglas L. Murphy and Janet G. Marquis

Conference discussions concerning research needs in the field of cognitive coping and families with a member who has a disability centered on three themes: 1) the need for precise definitions and clarification of relevant concepts regarding coping, generally, and cognitive coping, specifically; 2) the need for studies into the determinants of individual coping and coping style; and 3) the need for research that takes a broad view of family coping (i.e., research that looks at both how individuals cope as members of a family and how the family as an entity itself copes). In addition, conference discussions dealt with obstacles and difficulties in conducting research in the area of cognitive coping and families. The research agenda presented in this chapter is organized in accordance with these themes.

CONCEPTUAL–DEFINITIONAL ISSUES

One of the obstacles to progress in research on cognitive coping in individuals and in families is the lack of commonly used definitions for such key concepts as: adaptation, adjustment, coping, coping processes, and cognitive coping. Almost 20 years ago, Grinker (1974), a participant in a multidisciplinary conference on coping and adaptation, noted the difficulties presented by the interchangeable use of such terms as adaptation, coping, mastery, and defense. Others at the same conference (Lazarus, Averill, & Opton, 1974; White, 1974) echoed these concerns and offered definitional and classificational schemes in attempts to clarify the issue.

Judging from the diversity in definitions of and assumptions about coping, generally, and cognitive coping, specifically, reflected in the chapters in this volume, it is obvious that efforts must still be directed toward common understandings and definitions of key concepts. It is not necessary to delineate a single definition for cognitive coping. However, without a relatively few definitions tied to models for understanding, discussion among researchers and theorists, practitioners and clinicians, and families and individuals centers on commonplace definitions, themselves often not explicit.

Essentially, two broad areas of concern were discussed in regard to definition of key concepts. First, researchers must provide straightforward definitions of primary concepts. An obvious requirement of such definitions is that they say what a concept *is*. Given the common use of *coping* terms in everyday conversation, it is also necessary for definitions to explain what the concept *is not*. On the one hand, the term *coping* is used by most individuals to denote a person's attempts to deal with extremely negative circumstances. On the other hand, social psychologists sometimes conceptualize coping as one's responses to positive or negative events that require the individual to change. A good definition, then, would specify that coping occurs not only in response to negative, threatening events and situations, but also in response to pleasant, beneficial circumstances.

Second, definitions must be made more meaningful by placing them in a conceptual framework. This strategy serves to distinguish between similar concepts and provides a means of understanding interrelationships. For example, White (1974) attempted to clarify coping by identifying it as a subclass of adaptation. Lazarus et al. (1974) created a classification system for various kinds of coping that clarifies the distinction between, for instance, modes of expression in coping and specific coping responses.

The following questions, raised during small group discussions, reflect these basic concerns and others:

- How can cognitive coping be defined best (i.e., as a process, set of strategies, goal-directed cognitions)?
- Can typologies or styles of cognitive coping be defined? Is it meaningful to speak of cognitive coping styles for individuals and families?
- Can a taxonomy of coping, consisting of behavioral, emotional, cognitive, and other kinds of coping, be devised?
- Is there a cognitive coping "process"? If so, what methods should be used to study it?
- How should the outcomes of cognitive coping be incorporated into conceptual definitions? What outcomes should be considered? How can they be measured?
- How can other constructs (e.g., denial or rationalization) be redefined in terms of cognitive coping?

DETERMINANTS AND INFLUENCES ON INDIVIDUAL COPING

In the study of individual coping, questions center around two basic issues: 1) differences in coping styles, strategies, and effectiveness between individuals and 2) origins and development of coping styles and strategies.

Individual Differences

What determines or influences whether one person will cope differently than another? This question is not one of mere scientific interest; it has real implications for those who deal with individuals in troublesome circumstances and for the individuals themselves. From a pragmatic perspective, answers to the question can lead to changes and opportunities in our communities, institutions, service systems, and homes that will enable individuals to maximize the effectiveness of their coping efforts.

Much research has examined differences in coping between adult males and females in American culture, and some patterns seem consistent. For example, males tend to use behavioral coping strategies and females tend to use emotional strategies. However, differences between males and females in their use of cognitive coping strategies has been largely unexplored. Much of the early work on which cognitive adaptation theory was based focused on women who were coping with such traumas as breast cancer and rape. Will further research uncover distinctive cognitive coping styles for males and females?

Beyond gender, other factors might be related to individual differences in coping. Some raise questions about the influence of the community and its definition of disability on an individual's and family's coping. Others might ask whether there are personality factors, such as optimism and pessimism, that are related to particular cognitive coping strategies and outcomes. Questions related to the issue of individual differences include:

- Do males and females define effective coping in different ways? What influences might different definitions of coping have on preferred cognitive strategies?
- Do males and females typically appraise events differently and, therefore, cope with them differently?
- How do differences in cognitive coping between males and females change with age? Do they become more or less pronounced?
- How do cognitive coping styles and strategies differ among cultural groups?
- Are some cognitive coping strategies more effective for some individuals than for others? If so, what factors (e.g., availability of social support, family or cultural expectations, personality factors, cognitive abilities in general) appear to be related to their differential effectiveness? What interactions between circumstances and these factors might account for differences in coping effectiveness?

Origins and Development of Coping Styles and Strategies

Another major issue in the study of individual coping is that of the origins and development of cognitive coping styles and strategies. Of course, a beginning point for speculation and study is the perennial "nature versus nurture" debate. Understanding the origins of coping styles and strategies has important implications for how it is studied, for determining which correlates and factors are selected for investigation, and for planning potential support interventions for individuals who cope with difficult events in their lives.

If one assumes the nature perspective, relevant questions may be:

- To what extent are tendencies for using cognitive coping strategies, as well as the actual strategies themselves, inborn (i.e., unlearned)?
- To what extent do individuals display stable coping styles (i.e., reliable sets of cognitive coping strategies that are engaged in relatively predictable circumstances)? Can cognitive coping styles be attributed to inborn tendencies?
- Does cognitive coping develop naturally over the individual's life span in a predictable sequence? If so, what indicators or stages can be used to describe the progression in development?

If the nurture perspective is accepted, other questions are relevant. For example, it is important to discover how environmental conditions influence the individual's use of cognitive coping strategies, or how individuals learn a repertoire of strategies (e.g., by social learning principles or even direct instruction).

- What environments facilitate or inhibit the use or effectiveness of cognitive coping? What are the characteristics of those environments?
- How can characteristics of supportive environments be incorporated into service systems for individuals with disabilities and their families?
- What effects do interpersonal relations and interactions have on the development, use, and effectiveness of cognitive coping strategies? What are the characteristics of interpersonal relations and interactions that either enhance or inhibit cognitive coping strategies?
- How can characteristics of supportive interpersonal relations be incorporated into the training of those who work with individuals with disabilities and their families? How can the effects of such training be evaluated?
- To what extent can cognitive coping strategies be taught, either directly or incidentally? If the strategies can be taught, which methods (e.g., direct instruction, peer support groups, peer coaching) are most effective?
- Is there a stage for readiness that must be attained before teaching or learning can be effective?
- Are there critical, personal experiences that result in readiness for learning of cognitive coping strategies? If so, what are the characteristics of those experiences?
- Do particular kinds of circumstances activate particular kinds of cognitive coping strategies? For example, are events that occur in social contexts or have social consequences for the individual more likely to be associated with the use of social comparison strategies than events that are largely intrapersonal?

FAMILY ISSUES

Research issues involving families may be discussed in several broad categories. One primary issue is the distinction between the family as a system or an organism with its established patterns of functioning and the family as a collection of individuals, each with his or her own way of functioning. Another issue is the lack of knowledge about family needs with respect to coping, and a third issue is the need for theory from which research questions may be generated.

Family as a System

Many researchers view the family as a system or an organism; the members are differentiated, but they are also merged such that the whole is greater than the sum of the parts. In a family, a shared history, traditions, rituals, and rules (both implicit and explicit) govern the interactions among family members. Strong emotional ties also bind the family and influence interactions. The entrance into the family of a member with a disability usually causes the family to renegotiate the rules and rituals while still attempting to maintain the stability and integrity of the family. Thus "family coping" may be viewed as the restructuring, compromising, assimilating, and adapting of family goals and functioning that occurs in the family as a whole system rather than that which occurs in individuals. From this point of view, some relevant research questions are:

- Is there a family "mind" or schema or gestalt? If so, how can it be studied, identified, or measured?
- Does a family have a "coping style" that is distinct from that of its individual members? If so, what kinds of different coping styles do different families have? How can family coping styles be identified and measured?
- What are the implications for service delivery of different coping styles?
- What are appropriate outcome measures for family coping?
- What is the relation between family problem-solving skills and coping?
- How does the culture with which the family identifies have an influence on the family coping style? How can the influence be measured or determined? What implications does the family's cultural identity have for service delivery with respect to coping?

Family as a Collection of Individuals

Some research issues focus on the individual as a member of a family. All of the previous issues relating to individual coping are relevant, but in addition the researcher also considers the family context within which the individual functions. Thus, the family role of each individual must be considered as well as the complexity and the emotional nature of relationships with other family members. Some research questions are:

- How does individual coping influence family coping, and how does family coping influence the individual? Is what is effective for the individual also effective for the family? Are there patterns of coping for each that are useful? not useful?
- How does the role the individual plays within the family influence the family's coping? How does the role influence the individual's coping?

- What is the effect on family coping and the network of family relationships when an individual member decides that the family rules no longer function effectively for him or her? How is family coping affected as individual members mature and change their own individual coping styles?
- How does the emotional nature of family relationships influence individual coping? What is the relationship between emotional state and behaviors within the family?

Lack of Knowledge About Family Needs

While some issues in cognitive coping have received much attention in the research community, other issues have received very little. For example, much of the research to date has focused on the mother in the family; very little research has dealt with the coping of other family members such as fathers, siblings, or grandparents (see Meyer, chap. 6, this volume). Another area where lack of knowledge is a concern is in knowing what family members and service providers need and in knowing or having a methodology to determine these needs. Some research questions related to these issues are:

- What do we know about cognitive coping of family members other than mothers? Do fathers have different concepts of what coping is? Are the fathers' concepts of what coping is related to their perceptions of gender roles? of family roles? What do we know about the coping of siblings and grandparents of the member with the disability? How are the coping skills of siblings or grandparents affected by their family relationship to the person with the disability?
- What do families perceive their needs to be with respect to coping? What are satisfactory methods for determining these needs?
- What do service providers perceive their needs to be regarding service delivery to families, in their efforts to assist family coping? How can these needs be determined? What do we know about models for formal service delivery to families and the relationship of these models to family coping? Would models other than the currently predominant hierarchical model (the model based on the premise that the professional provider knows what is best) be satisfactory in providing service to families?

Need for Theory and Conceptual Clarification

Theoretical models serve as one of the best guides to research in any field. From theories, research questions may be generated and instruments developed to measure the constructs embedded in the theory. In the fields of cognitive coping and family studies, research is often not guided by theory. Consequently, much of the current research lacks the interconnectedness and coherence that is a result of being related to theory; the research tends to be more descriptive and exploratory in nature, using many different concepts and variables. Also, the concepts related to families and coping are often vague, having different meanings in different research studies. Some research questions related to these issues are:

- What are some appropriate theoretical models for studying family coping? What constructs are involved in the theoretical models? Are there reliable and valid measures of these constructs?
- What is meant by a "family"? Who is in the family? Who is not in the family? What are the implications for family coping studies of varying definitions of family?

DIFFICULTIES FOR RESEARCH IN FAMILIES AND COPING

Any discussion of specific issues in research involving families and coping must be placed in the context of an understanding of the general difficulties involved in such research. The lack of appropriate instruments has been mentioned previously. Related to this issue is the widespread use of self-reports and the difficulty of trying to verify that what people *say* they do is what they *really* do. Another issue in research is the conflict between the requirements of university research (having articles published regularly in research journals) and the needs of the field (having results that address real needs disseminated quickly in nonacademic jargon-free language). The length of time from initial grant application to final publication of results is often 10 years, and sometimes results are never published in ways that reach service providers or families. In addition, the federal funding agencies often want manuals that present step-by-step interventions, but because families are so different, such manuals are not useful for many families. Thus, a successful program of research in the area of cognitive coping needs to address not only the important research questions, but also the important methodological funding, service, and dissemination issues.

CONCLUSION

The questions presented in this chapter are primary: that is, they are the key questions that need to be answered to build a body of knowledge from which more specific questions can be asked and about which hypotheses can be tested, and to determine clear implications for application. The research agenda represented here is unique for two main reasons. First, it is the product of collaboration among groups of parents of children with disabilities, service providers, researchers, and theorists—all of whom have a stake in the outcomes of research on cognitive coping. Second, it is based on the work of persons from an array of professional disciplines—social psychology, family sociology, clinical psychology, disability services, disability research, and others.

The agenda is useful because it makes distinctions among key concepts: 1) coping, in general, and cognitive coping, specifically; 2) inborn versus learned origins of cognitive coping; 3) coping as a process and coping as outcome-directed cognition and behavior; and 4) individual coping and family coping. This agenda should be recognized as a starting point, and not a set of limitations, for further research.

Activating such an ambitious research agenda as this will require the concerted efforts of individuals with disabilities, their families, service providers, and researchers in many disciplines. Models for participatory research of the required breadth are rare, and developing new models will not be easy. However, we believe that it is only through collaborative research endeavors that we can answer expeditiously the questions raised here and those that will be raised in the future. Further, we believe that a continuing participatory process is the most effective way for our answers to have a positive impact on the lives of individuals with disabilities and their families.

ABOUT THE AUTHORS

Douglas L. Murphy, Ph.D.   As assistant director for research at the Beach Center on Families and Disability, I have ample opportunity to work with other researchers at the center and elsewhere. I find it stimulating to work with those who are charting new territory in the search for ways to enhance the lives of persons with disabilities, their families, and those who provide services for them. For several years my research interests have centered around cognitive psychology, including social cognition and cognitive adaptation. One of the challenges of this work has been to consider how new knowledge in this area can be used to benefit families of individuals with disabilities.

Janet G. Marquis, Ph.D.   For many years I have been interested in research questions, research design, and the philosophy of science: the questions of what is to be investigated and how to investigate it. As a research statistician for the Institute of Life Span Studies at the University of Kansas, I serve as a statistical design consultant and data analyst to the Beach Center on Families and Disability, helping with research design and measurement issues. I also teach a course on research and design at the University of Kansas.

REFERENCES

Grinker, R.R., Sr. (1974). Foreword. In G.V. Coelho, D.A. Hamburg, & J.E. Adams (Eds.), *Coping and adaptation* (pp. xi–xiii). New York: Basic Books.

Lazarus, R.S., Averill, J.R., & Opton, E.M. (1974). The psychology of coping: Issues of research and assessment. In G.V. Coelho, D.A. Hamburg, & J.E. Adams (Eds.), *Coping and adaptation* (pp. 249–315). New York: Basic Books.

White, R.W. (1974). Strategies of adaptation: An attempt at systematic description. In G.V. Coelho, D.A. Hamburg, & J.E. Adams (Eds.), *Coping and adaptation* (pp. 47–68). New York: Basic Books.

INDEX

ABCX model, 152, 224
cognitive coping as strategy versus
    goal and, 160–161
Academics, *see* Education
Acceptance, as coping strategy, among
    older mothers of adults with
    retardation, 177
Active coping, passive coping versus,
    261–262
Active involvement, self-efficacy coping
    and, caregiver well-being and,
    195–205
Adaptation
    appraisal components and processes
        in, 239–253
    to developmental phases and
        transitions, 200–203
    role of family meanings in, 221–237
    see also Family adaptation; Family
        meanings
    stress and, milestones in theory of,
        223–225
    see also Cognitive adaptation to
        adversity; Cognitive coping
Adaptational outcomes, stress process
    and, 126
Adjustment
    process of, new ways of under-
        standing, 103–104
    relationship to cognitive coping of, in
        adoptive and birth families,
        190–191
Adolescence, family concerns about, 27
Adoptive families
    birth families compared with, 187–191
    functioning of, when rearing children
        with developmental disabilities,
        184–187
    longitudinal follow-up of, 185
    positive outcomes for, 184–185
Adults
    with disabilities, professional

standards for, versus standards
    for children, 39–40
hope measurement in, 276–279
with retardation, coping strategies
    among older mothers of, 173–180
Adversity, cognitive adaptation to, *see*
    Cognitive adaptation to adversity
Affect, self-control and, relation
    between, 214
Age, of mothers, *see* Older mothers
Age phases, different
    caregiver self-efficacy, involvement,
        and well-being differences and,
        202–203
    major stressors at, 200–202
Ambiguous loss, 257
    see also Boundary ambiguity
Americans with Disabilities Act of 1990,
    63
Anxiety, defense mechanisms and,
    illusions versus, 130
Appraisals
    processes of, Hope Scale and, 278
    in stress process, 124
    illusions and, 126–127
    see also Family appraisal
Assumptions
    about children's feelings, 57–58, 60
    about situations, 60
    violation of, medically fragile infants
        and, 136–137
Attention, to child with disability,
    avoiding excessive attention, 25

BDI, *see* Beck Depression Inventory
Beck Depression Inventory (BDI),
    adoptive versus birth families
    and, 189
Behavior, cognitions and, emotions and,
    235–236
Behavioral interventions, 211

Newborn intensive care unit (NICU),
parents of infants in, cognitive
adaptation of, 135–147
NICU, *see* Newborn intensive care unit
Nonnormative events, impact of, life-
span developmental perspective
and, 173–180
Normative events, 173

Older mothers, coping strategies of,
173–180
acceptance, 177
future research directions on, 179–180
planning, 178–179
positive reinterpretation and growth,
177–178
prevalence of, 176–177
religion, 178
research questions about, 174–175
Optimism
in family, 23
unrealistic, 129
see also Illusions; Positive illusions
see also Hope *entries*
Oregon Research Institute (ORI),
research program of, 207–218
see also Cognitive interventions, for
parents
ORI, *see* Oregon Research Institute
Outcome measures, 268
Overlooked family members, 81–92
specific programs for, 82–84
lessons learned from, 84–88
need for increase in, 88–90
need for programs targeting other
members, 90–91
research needs and, 90
Overprotection, individual differences in
cognitive adaptation and,
168–169

Paradigms
defined, 245
see also Family paradigms
Parent(s)
cognitive interventions for, 207–218
see also Cognitive interventions
as equals in partnership, 106
of medically fragile infants, cognitive

adaptation to adversity and,
135–147
perceptions of, about lack of real
understanding, 213–214
see also Family *entries*; Fathers;
Mothers
Parent-directed family resource center
(PDFRC), PHP as model for,
102–103
Parent–professional collaboration,
fostering of, PHP and, 103
Parent-to-parent contacts, enhancement
of, 104–105
Parent-to-Parent programs, 90
Parent Training and Information Centers
(PTIs), 101
Parent training programs, future
expansion of, PHP and, 105
Parents Helping Parents (PHP), 95–108
case example of, 96–101
current efforts of, 101–104
future directions for, 104–107
Part H, *see* Infant and Toddler Program
of Individuals with Disabilities
Education Act
Participatory research, 1–13, 287
in action, 289–298
agenda for, 301–308
conceptual–definitional issues in,
301–302
difficulties in, 307
family issues in, 304–307
individual coping and, 302–304
cognitive coping and, 1–4
conference on cognitive coping and,
10–13
defined, 4–5
dissemination of knowledge from, to
multiple audiences, 296–298
diversity and, 291–293
ethics in, 290–291
move toward, concerns influencing,
5–8
questions in, nature and intent of,
293–295
variables in, measurement of,
295–296
see also Family research; Research
Partnership, parents as equals in, 106
Passive coping, active coping versus,
261–262

Terminology
   issues involving, in research agenda,
      301–302
   problems with, salutogenesis and,
      112–115
Theorists, *see* Researchers
Transitions, developmental phases and,
   adaptations to, 200–203
Typology Model of Adjustment and
   Adaptation, 252

Uncertainty, boundary ambiguity and,
   265
Understanding, lack of, parents'
   perceptions of, 213–214

Valuation, selective, 128
Variables

generality of, 267
measurement of, 295–296

Well-being
   assessment of, in older mothers of
      adults with retardation, *see* Older
      mothers
   caregiver
      age-phase differences in, 202–203
      in families of persons with mental
         retardation, 195–205
      influence of coping on, 197–199
      stress and, relationships between
         perceptions and, 155–157
World view
   family meanings and, 232–233
   disability and, 234–235
   see also Family schema
   family perspectives and, 58–59,
      61–62
   individual differences in cognitive
      adaptation and, 167–168